PRAIRIE WARSHIPS

PRAIRIE WARSHIPS

River Navigation
in the Northwest Rebellion

GORDON E. TOLTON

Heritage
House

VANCOUVER • VICTORIA • CALGARY

Heritage House Publishing Company Ltd.
#108 – 17665 66A Avenue
Surrey, BC V3S 2A7
www.heritagehouse.ca

Heritage House Publishing Company Ltd.
PO Box 468
Custer, WA, 98240-0468

Library and Archives Canada Cataloguing in Publication
Tolton, Gordon E. (Gordon Errett), 1963–
Prairie warships: river navigation in the Northwest Rebellion/Gordon E. Tolton.

Includes bibliographical references and index.
ISBN 978-1-894974-30-1

1. Riel Rebellion, 1885—Riverine operations. 2. Riverine operations—
Prairie Provinces—History. I. Title.
FC3215   971.05'4   C2007-901082-2

Library of Congress Control Number: 2006940149

Edited by Joe Wilderson
Proofread by Marial Shea
Cover design by Frances Hunter

Printed in Canada

Heritage House acknowledges the financial support for its publishing program
from the Government of Canada through the Book Publishing Industry Development
Program (BPIDP), Canada Council for the Arts, and the province of British Columbia
through the British Columbia Arts Council and the Book Publishing Tax Credit.

The Canada Council | Le Conseil des Arts
for the Arts | du Canada

BRITISH COLUMBIA
ARTS COUNCIL
Supported by the Province of British Columbia

For Pierre Berton,
who, though I never met him, showed
me how to write history,

and

for Richard Shockley,
who, I knew well, always knew
I could write history.

Across that Great Divide,
around that fire, there must be some
great discussions.

Acknowledgments

I thank the following people for their excellent assistance: Susan Krooyman of the Glenbow Archives in Calgary; Scott Stephen, Hudson's Bay Archives, Winnipeg; Claudette Gessner, Library Assistant, Special Collections, University of Saskatchewan Archives, Saskatoon; the staff of the Saskatchewan Historic Sites service; and the staffs of the Lethbridge Public Library and the Coaldale Centennial Library. Ultimately I have always been able to count on the resources of my friends in the Lethbridge Historical Society, the Fort Whoop-Up Interpretive Centre and the Galt Museum & Archives in Lethbridge, in particular, archivist Greg Ellis, who reviewed the earliest complete version of the manuscript. Colin Paul of Saskatoon, guiding spirit of the Midland Historical Volunteers, read the original draft as well, which is fitting since the Midlanders' story figures so prominently in the book. John Motherwell, a steamboat enthusiast from Victoria, BC, offered some information on the Todd family, even after the book was completed.

I single out in particular three close friends:

- The late, great Richard Shockley, who always cheered me on and encouraged my work, and I know he still does in that better place.

- Doran Degenstein, outfitter extraordinaire, who got my nose out of a book and me onto a horse to see history from the perspective of reality.

- Lori Porter, a co-worker and voracious reader who knows a good story when she sees it, and knows how to hearten one to do their best.

Lastly, I would be unfair not to mention my biggest fans, and probably my only ones: my wife, Rose, and my daughter, Robyn, who put up with any number of the absences, blank stares, tantrums, interferences and problems that crop up from living with someone who fancies himself a writer. I feel their love and support in everything I do.

List of Abbreviations Used

AFF	Alberta Field Force
CPR	Canadian Pacific Railway
DLS	Dominion Land Surveyors
HBC	Hudson's Bay Company
HG&C	Hill, Griggs & Co.
MISL	Merchants' International Steamboat Line
NWC&NC	North West Coal & Navigation Company
NWFF	North West Field Force
NWMP	North West Mounted Police
NWNC	North West Navigation Company
RRTC	Red River Transportation Company
ST&TC	Saskatchewan Transportation & Trading Co.
W&WTC	Winnipeg & Western Transportation Company
YTC	Yellowstone Transportation Company

Contents

Prologue

Shot across the Bow

It happened on the Saskatchewan, whose lazily rolling waters flow from the faraway Rockies, through the pine lands and plains of the Canadian Northwest and empty into murky Lake Winnipeg, from which they are carried to Hudson Bay, and for all I know mingle with those of the Arctic and Atlantic oceans. And it came about through that almost incomprehensible perversity or foolhardiness or obliging disposition which impels one to help a fellow out of a hole and causes a certain class of happy-go-lucky people to rush in where white-winged spirits would not attempt to fly, let alone tread.[1]

The golden words of George Henry Ham, a frontier journalist who climbed aboard a steamboat to provide a first-hand account of an attack on a village of insurgents. But before Ham could lick his pencil, he had to pick up a rifle to fend off the defenders of Batoche. Such were the ironies that arose in the strange days of 1885, a year of revolution, counter-assault and the demise of a culture. A year of endings amid an age of beginnings: virtually, if the pun could be forgiven, a watershed year.

The young Canadian nation was ablaze with the news of civil revolt on the upper reaches of the South Saskatchewan River. The revolutionary Louis Riel had succeeded in galvanizing a few hundred Métis and Cree guerillas into an armed uprising against the government. The swift-moving locomotives of the barely completed, already nearly bankrupt Canadian Pacific Railway made possible a quick, punitive strike against the rebels by Canadian militias. The service of the hundreds of freighters and teamsters hauling myriad supplies and provisions was an integral part of the war effort.

Ultimately all military campaigns are won or lost based on their commanders' transportation and communication networks. Ballistics are as nothing without logistics. Often overlooked in histories of the North West Rebellion is the hastily assembled fleet of sternwheelers and barges which their private owners put at the disposal of the federal government. This inland fleet carried supplies, medical relief and troops to the scenes of battle. In one incredible moment in time, a motley collection of soldiers and riverboat roustabouts even heralded the beginning of the climax of the Rebellion, the battle of Batoche's Landing.

To anyone unfamiliar with the story, it may seem absurd right from the start. Naval campaigns on the prairies? Admirals of Alberta? Sailors in Saskatchewan? Gunboat diplomacy in the arid Palliser Triangle? Even the notion of any kind of maritime conveyance on western Canada's thin inland ribbons of often shallow water seems far-fetched. The reality is that the Saskatchewan is no Missouri, still less a Mississippi, Nile or Mekong. Navigable transport on the Oldman and the North and South Branches of the Saskatchewan was a barely feasible notion in the 19th century. In today's age of air, rail and highway transportation, it's not even discussed.

But before railways were built, the only available conveyance from A to B involved some form of relationship with one or more four-legged trail buddies, and the only alternative was nautical. The idea harkens back to the 1600s, when Indian traders paddled furs downriver to the European newcomers camped on the Arctic Ocean at Hudson's Bay. Before a century passed, the Hudson's Bay Company (and its French and American competitors) had traced the water routes inland and given rise to new settlements and an enormous trade empire. As time passed, the fur economy increased demand for supplies, and the adventurous boat brigades gave way to new technology.

Born in the United States, baptized on the Mississippi and Ohio rivers, and brought to maturity on the Missouri, the steam-powered paddlewheeler literally chugged its way into western Canada, by way of the Red River, in the 1860s. By 1873, the Hudson's Bay Company had begun to invest in sternwheelers, using steamers to supply their inland fur posts at Fort Carlton, Fort Pitt and Edmonton. Other competitors too were getting in on the action. By 1883, steamboats were bringing the West into the industrial age, hauling coal down the Oldman River from the mines of Lethbridge, paradoxically to fuel the engines of their own doom. As abruptly as the sternwheelers had appeared on the scene, another technology, the Iron Horse, arrived to slay the future of river navigation.

Then, as the ice was breaking up in the spring of 1885, as if to bring dignity to a lingering economic demise, a call to glory was signalled from a nondescript back-woods clearing. On March 26, 1885, a party of Métis settlers, feeling threatened by encroaching government control and inspired by the fiery rhetoric of Louis Riel, clashed with a brigade of Mounted Police and armed volunteers at Duck Lake. Soon, a wholesale native uprising threatened to stain the peaceful waters of the Saskatchewan with blood.

Duck Lake was a shot heard 'cross the nation, and fanciful imaginations freshly recalled the battles of the Sioux wars on the U.S. plains. As the violence spread, the Canadian government mobilized a three-pronged response. From the outset, the expedition commander could not possibly have looked at his war map without being inspired by the reality that his intended target, the village of Batoche, was situated on the South Saskatchewan River. Seven sternwheelers sat idle in winter port, their owners rubbing their hands in glee at the prospect of new, war-fuelled transport revenues. With the Canadian government in full agreement, a steamboat navy was born.

Besides the steamers, the war saw other water-borne action as well. At various times, canoes, York boats and flat-bottomed scows had brief moments of renown. A small troop of Mounties floated away from a siege in a leaky scow, only too glad to have made their escape. A doctor, having missed his ship, happily chose to paddle a canoe to the front. An entire column of infantry sailed down the North Saskatchewan in a flotilla fortified with homemade armour. Even the ferries of the prairies played a role. Western Canada's eccentric little skirmish had a bizarre ending, too, as the last casualty of the war resulted from a fight over a rowboat.

Odd as it may seem, this is the story of an actual prairie naval campaign. It's not the battle of the North Atlantic nor the South Pacific. It's not Trafalgar nor the Battle of Lake Erie. It's not even the Campaign of Vicksburg. There's not a lot of glory, battle honours or captains going down with their ships. One writer referred to it as "a comedy of errors." But who says comedy can't be interesting as history? Journalist George Ham put the whole river campaign succinctly in context when humbly talking about his experience as a sitting duck aboard the *Northcote*: "Just another incident, which, while it does not amount to much, was all-important to me at that critical moment."[2]

This is a tale of an era before trucks, trains and planes, when merchant boats endeavoured to supply the sparse settlements of the far-flung West. It's the story of the brief era when the landlocked towns of Edmonton, Lethbridge, Medicine Hat, Saskatoon and Prince Albert—even Swift Current to a degree—were port towns. Today we flit down highways and across river spans in the time it takes to blink an eye. We may think about the prairie rivers only on lazy Sunday afternoons with fishing lines in the water or strolling along the banks for an appreciation of nature as respite from a stressful world.

Anyone today living along the Oldman River, classically called the Belly, must laugh at the thought of trying to float anything bigger than a fibreglass canoe, never mind steamboats, on a watercourse more accurately described by the wry old prairie adage as "too thick to drink, too thin to plow!"

Today, few give the rivers much thought as they flush their waste into the sewer. Perhaps we should think about the day when a sarcastic river captain, frustrated by low water and constantly running aground, growled out to a settler with a drinking bucket: "Hey, you! Put that water back!"[3]

CHAPTER ONE

Days of Rivers, Age of Steam

The waterland empire

From a large bay on the Arctic coast of North America, a British company held court, waiting for the beaver peltry they desired, which would be floated downriver by Cree middlemen, the aboriginal traders who ventured far into the country to collect its bounty. What actually lay upriver the men of the Hudson's Bay Company (HBC) cared not, confident in the knowledge that they held a monopoly over all the land draining into Hudson's Bay.

Officially, the corporate holding was known as Rupert's Land, but in an age when North America was treated as a mere bump on a log on the way to China, the HBC would not know for nearly a century that an inheritance as huge as all of Europe had been granted them. There were people who could have told these newcomers the extent of their real estate. But no one asked the indigenous peoples who lived off the very land the HBC came to exploit, much as nobody bothered to inform them they were now considered British subjects. And no one asked if the name of their river, Kisiskatchewani Sipi, could be mangled and abbreviated to another name: the Saskatchewan.

By the mid-1700s, rival forces of trade goaded the HBC to act. Competitors—the La Vérendryes, various independents and the North West Co.—infiltrated the Company's fiefdom and made inroads of their own into native fur country. Eventually the HBC woke up and sent explorers inland to look over their territory. From the inland sea, the river Saskatchewan stretched erratically backward, separating into smaller, feeder tributaries, all the way back to the shining mountains first noticed by white eyes in the person of Anthony Henday.

In time, voyageurs and tripmen representing both the HBC and the company's enemies found their way inland on the courses of the Saskatchewan. They paddled the currents, portaged around the rapids, blazed trails and bivouacked with the Cree and Chipewyan. In camp, the voyageurs satisfied their recreational needs with music and

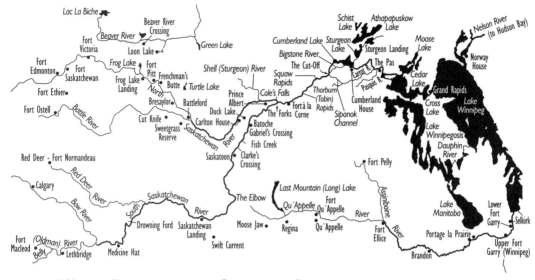

WATER ROUTES OF THE CANADIAN PRAIRIES

GORD TOLTON

drink. And when the fiddles and the rum could warm their hearts no longer, they sought to warm their bedrolls with members of the fairer sex among their trading contacts. Over the course of a century, the progeny of these unions between Native inhabitants and pedlars of French, Scots and Irish origin produced a new culture of mixed faith, language and blood. The waters of the Saskatchewan gave life to a new people borne of the rivers, those known as the half-breeds, les Bois Brulés, or their prouder name as a society, the Métis.

The course of the big river

From the mountains, the river winds 2,070 miles, dropping 600 feet in elevation. The North and South Branches sprawl across the map, with an erratic family tree of countless creeks, coulees and smaller rivers involuntarily marrying into the clan. About 30 miles east of the city of Prince Albert, the North and South Branches converge their already impressive separate streams into a single colossus. The route to its relief is circuitous through the muck-encrusted northern forests, strained by trees that lie drowned by their own life stream. Forests "stand, bearded with moss, dead and grim, until they decay and fall into the swamp, making an inextricable tangle of stumps and stems, all but impassable."[1] Emptying into creeks that dare call themselves rivers, the northlands break their nine months of frozen stillness to accumulate enough of a stream to offer to the mighty Saskatchewan.

After draining hundreds of miles of mountains, foothills, prairies, parkland and forest, the big river squeezes around the trees and oozes into a gentle, shapeless lake. Finally, the expanse concentrates into a channel of cascades that shatters the nerves of iron-willed rivermen in the passage called the Grand Rapids, a cavernous limestone canyon where the Saskatchewan drops 75 feet in only two miles of travel.

For the voyageur returning back upstream, the first port of call is The Pas (pro-nounced "Paw"), on the south bank of the big river, where worlds collide. In the land of the Swampy Cree, The Pas boasted a mission of the Church of England. This was the world of the Reverend Henry Budd, wholly Cree, fully ordained Anglican minister, preaching the gospel to his own people.

At Cedar Lake, the accumulated silt solidifies. This is where a bit of the old High-lands first arrived as Thomas Corey plodded his canoes through hostile territory to build a post. Braced with "Spirituous Liquors" as well as tobacco and guns, Corey's men secured an inroad that brought even more Scots and English, Irish and French.

In 1774, as New England colonists were getting their reviled tea-tax bills, two HBC luminaries, Matthew Cocking and Samuel Hearne, established Cumberland House. It was the first of their posts by the Saskatchewan River, on a lake they named after the post, from whence an oarsman could swing north, follow the Sturgeon to the Churchill River, and eventually head off into the sub-Arctic barrens.

At the Forks near Prince Albert, the La Vérendryes were the first Europeans to see not just one, but two arrows they hoped would point to their fabled Western Sea. But though the two branches have the same source, they are like the proverbial road less travelled: their streams pass through very different landscapes, the North through roll-ing, dark-soiled parkland, the South traversing the Great Plains. The trading compa-nies realized that one road should take them to beaver country, the other to the land of the buffalo. The beaver being their optimum goal, the voyageurs and traders pointed their boats into the North Branch.

When Europeans first paddled the North Saskatchewan, they arrived in a frame of cedar with a birch bark covering. The canoe was built for diverse waters: large lakes or fast or shallow rivers. Since portaging (carrying the canoe overland around dangerous rapids) was a reality, craft had to be light enough to tote overland, yet sturdy enough to survive the river. The canoe was a native notion, one that Europeans did not care to embrace. But common sense prevailed, and hardy, singing voyageurs eventually found the North Branch.[2] As loads became heavier and trips more numerous, navigators were forced to invent methods more conducive to freight. Crude "bumboats" were little more than a flat raft of bound-up willow poles, covered with a lining of moose skins. But as trade moved further inland, ever larger forms of river craft had to be constructed, and the York boat was born.

Named for the depot of York Factory, these heavy, flat-bottomed, banana-shaped boats, 24 to 28 feet long, 4 feet wide and 18 inches deep, could ship five to eight tons of furs and merchandise tucked safely within their gunwales. The boats were powered by six to nine strong oarsmen, assisted by a single, Viking-style mainsail to catch the prevailing winds whenever possible, a welcome innovation when crossing lakes. The disadvantage was the craft's great weight: a York had to be dragged with ropes on skids over a portage. Just the same, the dozens of boats that made up the York brigades supplied posts along the North Saskatchewan for a century.

When the frigid winter of the Canadian Rockies finally relents, the ice breaks up and the river deposits huge chunks 20 feet high on the banks, as if the river were a furry animal shedding its winter coat. At first, a huge freshet raises the water level, and then the river drops as the sunlight of April and May musters the strength to turn the layers of snow gathered on the eastern slopes into the liquid of life. Helped along by the occasional warm rain or a snow-eating chinook wind from the Pacific, the Rockies bleed their meltwater into the various tributaries. The result is a race of churned-up foam bound for the Grand Rapids, carrying ice, silt, deadfall and anything else unfortunate enough to be in the way.

From the Columbia Icefields, the North Branch gathers the Clearwater and the Brazeau near the Bay post of Rocky Mountain House. By the time it reaches Edmonton, the North Branch is a river worthy of what would become the capital of Alberta. In fact, the city owes its existence to the river; it's where the HBC sought to centralize its operations in the interior to consolidate its northern, mountain and prairie trade. John Rowand, the czar of the trade, built an imposing three-storey log mansion as the centrepiece of Fort Edmonton to impress the Indians and establish the HBC as an inland empire. Here was both the destination and the departure of the great York boat brigades.

Past Edmonton, the North Branch meets other installations of the HBC, as if the corporation owned the river. In many ways, it did, having shaken off the upstart North West Co. by simply buying it out. Other sentinels stand guard: the police post, Fort Saskatchewan; Fort Victoria, home to the Methodist McDougalls; those twin monuments to competition, Fort George and Buckingham House; the tragic Frog Lake Landing; the indefensible Fort Pitt; Battleford, once the capital of the North-West; and Fort Carlton, where the North Branch meets the other great highway of the West, the Carlton Trail, and where the despotic Lawrence Clarke ran an immaculate post where "the offices and stores were neat, and over each door was painted in French and English the names of the store and office, together with the class of goods in the buildings."[3]

Before meeting its southern twin at the Forks, the North Branch files past Prince Albert, where the prairie meets the deep forests. But the navigator must tangle with Cole's Falls. With 14 short rapids in 13 miles, and a sharp change in elevation, tight bends strewn with jagged boulders, and a canyon that narrows by half in low water,[4] river challenges mariners to pass through with their craft intact.

nuth Branch starts in a series of fits and starts. Near what is now the tourist ff, the Bow River is formed from pristine alpine lakes. Coursing down ils, it enters what is now the prosperous city of Calgary, where it takes a southeasterly course, past timeless, wide-open, bar-nce mighty indigenous confederacy. It was at Blackfoot and eloquent Siksika chief Crowfoot met a plethora of e and government representatives as the negotiations for

Near the little village of Grassy Lake, the South Branch of the Saskatchewan is formed by the Bow River and a stream that derives its name from Napi, a timeless mythical trickster and the creative spirit of countless Pikani campfire tales. Today the river is known as the Oldman for its entire course from the Gap in the Livingstone Range of the Rockies until its marriage with the Bow. But in an earlier, saner time, the Oldman only held that appellation until the point on the prairie where it met with the Belly. The Bloods called the Belly the Mokowan, "the Bend," in reference to the huge boomerang loop the river makes near Fort Whoop-up, and somehow "bend" became "belly." But then, as always happens with encroaching societies, changes were made. Sik-oko-toks—the place of the black rocks—became Coalbanks, and eventually

Voyageurs, traders and their families "At The Portage." H.A. OGDEN, IN *PICTURESQUE CANADA*

Lethbridge, named for a businessman that never visited there. And since the name "Belly" was considered too barbaric for gentle folk, an act of legislation shortened one river and lengthened another, and today the Oldman River just keeps on rolling along.

The newly formed South Branch meets a railway bridge at a town whose name seems to come from some Indian legend—Medicine Hat—but was really named by a railway official, William Cornelius Van Horne, who wished to convey just that image. A great bridge had to be built across the South Branch, and Van Horne desired that a great city would follow. Frontier folk knew better than to defy Van Horne, and built such a burg.

Past Medicine Hat, the South Branch passes one of the HBC's few posts on the southern plains, Chesterfield House, operated at the Bull's Forehead, where the Red Deer River makes a late entry, passing out of the dinosaur-encrusted Badlands.

The South Branch meanders through nearly desert conditions, agricultural lands where hearts have been broken by dust and patched back together time and again with binder twine and barbed wire as farmers and ranchers continually fight climate. At Saskatchewan Landing, an unlikely prairie port was formed, as the railway, the river and the Battleford Trail conspired to make a wide spot in the road called Swift Current into a modern city. At the Elbow, where "the river that turns" makes a right-angle bend, politicians decided to tame the erratic stream with a massive dam. The nearby Moose Woods, a virtual oasis of wildlands, was entreatied to a refugee band of Minnesota Sioux that refused to return home to face a vengeful U.S. Army. White Cap and his people became loyal to Queen Victoria but would later be dragged by Métis into rebellion.

Voyageurs and tripmen of the fur trade poling a York boat. GLENBOW ARCHIVES NA 1598-

The South Branch meets its last great city, Saskatoon, named for the abundance of succulent summer fruit that line the riverbanks up and down its entire length. The town was founded by a band of temperance colonists to form a refuge from demon drink. A hopeless task indeed, as though one could survive a Saskatchewan winter without a bracer.

Past Saskatoon, the river meanders into parkland: lush, fertile, dark soil that attracted Métis and eastern Canadian settlers alike. In May of 1885, a newspaper correspondent aboard a steamboat built for war was lulled by the lush surroundings. "There was a remarkable similarity in the surroundings for many a mile, so much that one portion was confusingly like another—but it was a winsome scene whose restfulness and calm were accentuated by the jarring, discordant events of previous days. In these northern latitudes, Nature is unusually lavish with her gifts and here she had created a picturesque domain that was remindful of well-kept ancestral estates in the Old Country. It was nature in her simple beauty—unadorned except with that adornment which the hand of the Master alone can give. It was the summer dreamland—a scenic poem—a fragment of incomparable Kentish landscape in a glorious Canadian setting."[5]

At a certain point the South Saskatchewan bends west for nearly a mile, then north for a mile and a half before bearing east by northeast. These abrupt contortions create a rectangle characterized by a widely contoured, gentle coulee. The bench on the east drops only 40 feet over more than a mile, a subtle slope that made the reach a natural crossing for the Métis cart caravans freighting on the Carlton Trail.

During the wars between the HBC and the North West Co., there settled on the benchlands one Jean-Baptiste Letendre, jovially known to friends and family alike by a certain nickname that would one day become famous. His son, Louis, inherited the moniker and so did his grandson, Xavier. In 1872, with Métis refugees from the

Red River as well as white settlers from the East moving into the area to farm, Xavier Letendre set himself out to capitalize on the trade. He built a store and a ferry on the Carlton Trail crossing, granting his family alias to a community that became a service centre for the area's farmers and hunters. But in 1885 the sleepy little village that bore Xavier Letendre's family nickname gained an unwanted notoriety. The place was called Batoche.

The age of steam in trade

If the 20th century was the age of oil, the 19th was the age of steam. Ships, locomotives, mills and factories, even farms, measured progress in pounds per square inch. The steam engine literally drove the wheels of the Industrial Revolution, in North America as well as Britain, and helped transform the United States from an upstart backwater republic into a world power by the early 20th century. By virtue of proximity, the loose-knit British colonies that would become Canada were permitted to come along for the ride.

Steam power was at work on the Mississippi River by 1812, when the first sternwheeler began to ply the broad, brown stream. Steamboats appeared on the Missouri in 1819. In the age of carts, floating to one's destination was always preferable to bouncing overland behind four-footed beasts of burden. A great load to be freighted any great distance went by river, and waterways dictated where settlements would arise. The cities of the U.S. Midwest grew with the steamers: New Orleans and St. Louis; Cairo, Illinois; the twin cities of St. Paul and Minneapolis; up the Missouri to Kansas City, Omaha, Sioux City, Yankton, Bismarck; and the gateway to the far western Canadian prairies, Fort Benton. Before railways, the steamer was the mass transit to the West. But the paddlewheelers always played bridesmaid to the more lucrative locomotive. To survive, steamboat interests had to struggle to keep pace with the railway building frenzy across the continent, always plying ahead into waters not yet crossed by twin steel tracks.

In the latter half of the 1850s, two expeditions, one British, one Canadian, ventured into the West to assess the feasibility of adapting the West to agriculture. The forces of expansion were eyeing up the HBC duchy, and the British sent the flamboyant John Palliser, who immortalized himself and his journey by assessing the prairie as "desert." The lower-key Canadian effort sent forth the naturalist Henry Youle Hind. Among Hind's assessments was the eventual end of fur-trade control over the territory, and the prediction that transportation would be affected by the style of riverboats seen in the U.S. It would take some decades for Hind's forecast to evolve, but it would bring another breed of mythmaker to the prairies: the steamboat pilot.

U.S. folk tales tell of the mythic Mississippi River captains and pilots, and steamboating was a uniquely American import. Much of the machinery, building materials and technical expertise for the floating venture came from the experience of the U.S.

navigation industry when veterans of the Ohio, Mississippi and Missouri Rivers voyaged north in search of employment, adventure and new streams to conquer.

But the Saskatchewan had to wait its turn to hear a steam whistle. The Red River was first, and the push to get the steamer into the North came from the Mississippi River town of St. Paul, Minnesota, to the Red River Colony. Métis freighters had trampled a well-worn oxcart rut across the prairie, hauling freight north from the U.S. port as the HBC looked on in horror. Until the 1850s, the Red River of the North, that wide, often flooding stream flowing from the wilderness of Minnesota past the settlement of Fort Garry, had yet to be churned by machine-driven paddles, but one hapless pilot was going to try.

John Davis of Rock Island, Illinois, had begun learning his craft in 1848 on the Ohio and the Mississippi. Steamboat pilots were a wandering lot, and new activity brought Davis to St. Paul in 1859. The eager St. Paul Chamber of Commerce offered a cash reward to the first adventurer who could put a paddlewheel on the Red and crack the HBC monopoly on commerce across the border. His eyes on the prize, Davis put his own money into a freighter named, well, the *Freighter*. But whatever Davis may have lacked in imagination for ship christening, he more than made up for in daring. In the spring of 1859, he took on a load of St. Paul cargo bound for the Red River. Problem was that St. Paul, on the Mississippi, does not directly connect with the Red. Davis had to defy nature and gravity, and use spring flooding to virtually drive his boat overland!

Spring flooding offered a narrow window at best. From St. Paul, the *Freighter* sailed up the Minnesota River as far as its source, Lake Traverse, and through to its headwaters, Big Stone Lake. Scant miles past Big Stone lay the outlet Davis hoped to take to the Red River. His goal within reach, he pushed his crew and boat past Big Stone's shores, through the flooded sloughs toward a date with destiny. But the *Freighter* grounded and grunted and finally capitulated in the sand 10 miles from the lake, practically on dry land. Their attempt to connect Hudson's Bay with the Gulf of Mexico ignobly defeated, Davis and his crew returned to St. Paul in a canoe, leaving the *Freighter*, trapped in the quagmire, to the tender mercies of the Minnesota elements and the local vandals.[6]

Later that same year, however, the Red River Valley did get penetrated, and St. Paul's spoils got claimed. Captain Anson Northrup whipped a team of oxen to drag an old boat called the *North Star* over the dryland divide to the Red. Successfully plunged into a new river, Northrup's none-too-modestly renamed vessel, the *Anson Northrup*, proudly sailed across the border on June 10, 1859, yanking the Red River at last into the age of steam.

Northrup's triumph proved to be short lived. The HBC was terrorized by the thought of open trade, and quietly urged a pair of agent brothers, J.C. and H.C. Burbank, to purchase Northrup's boat and dub it the *Pioneer*. The Burbanks also pried the skeleton of Davis's *Freighter* out of the muck, salvaging its components for the new *International*. But by that time, much of the manpower and expertise required for

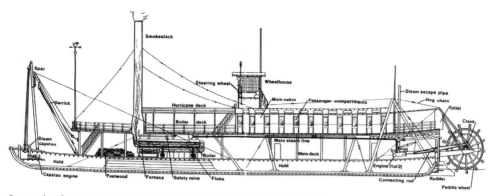

Sternwheeler cutaway. COURTESY SASKATCHEWAN ENVIRONMENT &
RESOURCE MANAGEMENT, PARKS & FACILITIES BRANCH

steamboat operation was being drained away by the U.S. Civil War as General Ulysses
S. Grant's riverboat campaign on the Mississippi raged into the western heart of the
Confederacy. Soon, Minnesota was drawn into a civil war all its own when the Santee
Sioux rose up in arms against settlers. For the duration of these conflicts and beyond,
navigation on the Red was suspended, as the U.S. fought itself. Ironically, it would take
another outbreak of internecine violence, this time Canadian, to bring the steamboat
industry back to the Red River.

In July 1870, the *International* churned north again, into a changed land. For one
thing, the remote colony was now a part of the fledgling nation called Canada. But the
handover was fraught with trouble, as residents resisted the transition, taking armed
occupation of the colony, countered by a British–Canadian force sent from Ontario
to take control. The *International* brought a spy, Captain William Butler, gathering
information for the advancing expedition. The army took control and the rebels were
scattered to the wind as the province of Manitoba and the North West Territories
entered Confederation.

The age of steam proclaimed the birth of Western Canada, and had come to stay.
Soon the whistles would be heard on the Saskatchewan. The spy, William Butler,
pushed forth to Fort Edmonton and became an explorer, advocating the creation of
a police force for law and order, and later calling for a military expedition up the Nile
River in Egypt. The leader of the Red River revolt would return time and again as a
thorn in the side of the government of Canada. His name was Louis Riel, and 15 years
hence, further west on the wide open prairie, rebel, government, police and sternwheel
riverboat would all meet again. To quote a soldier of 1885: "Through this mighty space
coursed a great river that gave it a distinctive character and had so much to do with
the military movements."[7]

The means of steam

The sternwheeler was not designed to cut through a stream so much as to glide across
the surface of it. Really, it's just a raft with a motor, a creature of function for slow

but shallow navigation. Its design required an oversized paddlewheel that dipped only a few inches into the water to send the craft's wedge-shaped bow sliding over obstructions, "so built that when the river is low and the sand bars come out for air, the first mate can tap a keg of beer and run four miles on the suds."[8]

Builders preferred to use lightweight poplar or pine for the hulls. The decks, floor timbers, bulkheads and superstructures were usually of sturdier oak, from the forests of Minnesota. But simple availability dictated the actual material used. Density and weight were the chief concerns, because any boat with a draft deeper than 24 inches was of little value.

The engines were powerful but crude, and fantastically hazardous. They were sinfully wasteful too, but riverbanks were abundant with cheap fuel, and the boilers burned cordwood like there was no tomorrow. In the dangerous, erratic world of steamboating, there often were no tomorrows. All the sternwheeler had to be was big enough to carry mass freight, just powerful enough to overcome the downstream current, and simple enough to be manned and maintained by unskilled labour.

Engineering a boat required a mindset as rough-hewn as the frontier itself. The western sternwheeler was hard to love, and few rivermen saw their craft as a sleek feminine vessel as their saltwater counterparts did. Few referred to "it" as "she" or "her."

The upper works of these flat-hulled monoliths was an awkward, tumble-down, multi-layered wedding-cake assembly of decks. The first deck atop the hull was the main deck, open-sided to provide easy access for cargo and natural airflow cooling for the firebox, boilers, steam lines and engines. The noisy main deck also provided limited cabin space for deckhands or steerage-rate passengers. The second level, the boiler deck, was an enclosed cabin with private staterooms—occasionally having a ballroom, lending it the alternative name of saloon deck. On top, the open-aired promenade, or hurricane deck sat the centrepiece of the cake, the wheelhouse, from where the pilot ruled all below.

Situated for maximum visibility, the wheelhouse gave the helmsman a panoramic view of his domain: the riverboat and the reach of river he was expected to navigate. The captain, the master, the helmsman, the wheelsman, the pilot—all these are synonyms for the undisputed czar of the steamboat. He was a skilled artisan, forced by virtue of his responsibility to take a personal stake in his vessel. Working for straight wages, he could make $150 a month, but often there was a profit-sharing arrangement or even partial ownership of the boat itself.

The pilot had to be fuel conscious, to know when to order more steam and when to simply ride the current. He had to know how to "read a river": how water looked in contact with obstructions; how swirls, ripples and colouration of the water can indicate the river's depth. He had few maps, and no map could ever help to locate the ever-shifting channel. He dealt with blazing heat, thunderstorms, monsoon rains, high winds and tornadoes, all witnessed from his sitting-duck station atop the boat.

He played dodgeball with outcroppings, dead trees, hills, bends, sandbars, rocks, rapids, passing wildlife and the relentless current itself. A good pilot had the nerve of a rattlesnake, the heart of a gambler and the split-second judgment of a bird in flight.

A skilled helmsman could tell when a river was getting shallow just by the vibration of the deck planks beneath his feet as the boat itself reacted to the changing current and volume of the water. In time, a pilot's skills became intuition, his wizardry creating a reputation that preceded him whenever a new route opened.

For all his nerve and skill, however, the pilot still depended on the watchman, and when the helmsman couldn't determine the depth of a channel by his own unorthodox means, a tap of a signal bell would send a roustabout with a long pole astride the bow or onto the accompanying barges to take soundings of the water level, calling out the depths in feet as he measured them.

Running aground was not a special occasion, but a way of life. Sternwheelers were just too awkward to forestall the inevitable beaching. It was just easier to accept the groundings and "walk" the boat back into the stream. Steamboats carried their own bizarre self-towing system, a sort of Rube Goldberg mechanical affair consisting of stiff wooden poles and a winched cable. In the dormant position, the poles, called "spars" or "grasshopper legs," towered from a derrick at the bow of the boat, an ever-present reminder of the need to avoid shallow water. Whenever the boat did run aground, the spars would be lowered into the mud. A tough wire cable ran from the spars to the derrick and back to a winch called the "capstan." The capstan was driven by a small auxiliary steam engine often called the "nigger" engine, a term revealing the fact that steamboat crews were far from politically correct. When the capstan tightened, the spars would rise erect, lifting the boat and vaulting it forward in a crutch-like motion, gradually limping toward deeper pools. The process of this self-propelled tow job fascinated Victorian travellers, who marvelled at the poling and winching technique and coined all manner of fanciful names for it: warping, grasshoppering, mud-skipping.

The sparring process was assisted by the boat's main means of propulsion, the paddlewheel, which would churn sand and shallow water all the while to help the vessel gain precious inches back to a decent depth. The paddlewheel was a simple, open cylinder, 18 feet in diameter and 24 feet wide (on average), with radial wooden slats reinforced with iron strapping. Two steam engines and a pair of scissor-like timbers called Pitman arms rotated the paddle wheel 20 times a minute to exceed 10 miles per hour. In low water, the wheel could slow to 14 rpm.

Riverboat builders came from a multitude of trades. There were carpenters, boatwrights, millwrights, blacksmiths, tinsmiths, steamfitters, machinists and all manners of backwoods artisans. Supervising were the captains, acting as the owners' agents. Techniques were aggressive and reckless, but always with an eye to practicality.

Nothing gave the steamboat its romance like its signalling devices. Its whistle, powered by a bypass of steam, raised a foreboding shriek through the wilds. More flamboyant rivermen acquired three- and five-toned whistles, and pilots delighted in creating a distinctive pitch. The bell was another instrument prized for its melody. One captain, in his hunger for better resonance, even melted 500 of his own silver dollars into the molten cast of his bell.

The development of engines and boilers also illustrated the nature of steamboating. The objectives were speed and power, but the technology had to be able to be maintained by reckless and uneducated attendants. In the mechanic and smith shops of places like Pittsburgh, St. Louis, Cincinnati, La Crosse (Wisconsin), Dubuque (Iowa), and Minneapolis, machinists hammered out engines while setting a pace for an industry and making up the rules as they went along. In the early 1800s mechanic Oliver Evans perfected the advance that made the western steamboat possible. He created a high-pressure, high-output engine that was 95 per cent lighter in weight. Further tinkering resulted in mounting the engine on its side, redistributing the weight and mitigating the pounding impact of the cylinders on the boat's structure.

Steam for the engines came from the boilers, usually two or four wrought-iron cylinders mounted in parallel at the bow of the boat, where their fireboxes could catch the breeze of forward motion for more efficient combustion. Once the water got up to boiling temperature, the steam was conducted to the engines at the stern by a copper pipe nearly as long as the boat itself. Exhaust was vented through twin iron chimneys, also called stacks or funnels, that towered dozens of feet tall to prevent hot cinders from falling back on deck. The height of the stacks was also a function of the process, controlling the updraft to maintain boiler pressure.

Pressure was always a problem. An order from the wheelhouse for more speed meant more steam and more firing. But pressure rose fast and unexpectedly, and if not controlled, a head of steam could blow a boiler, endangering the boat and all aboard, with less than 30 seconds notice. Multiple boilers meant multiple problems, as water levels had to be equalized between them and the water supply lines—quite a chore if the boat were listing from having been loaded improperly. The boilers had to make use of river water pumped in through unfiltered suction lines. Impurities created any number of problems. Silt and sand were constantly sucked into the tanks, resulting in the boilers having to be extinguished, shovelled out and refired, a time-consuming process. Often, particulates crept right into the engines and scored the pistons and cylinder walls.

Engineers on steamboats usually carried their position in name only. Many were green youths attracted by good wages. Alcohol and steam made a bad mixture, but the danger, intolerable heat and constant noise kept an engineer's hand never far from a jug. Such indiscretions were usually forgiven if a man could do his own blacksmithing and perform required miracles such as holding down the bypass on a scalding-hot safety valve while praying that valve, boiler and all didn't blow him to steamboat Valhalla.

Deckhands, variously known as "roosters" or "roustabouts," were essentially common labourers. Their wages were low, about $15 a month plus board. These workers usually came from the lower end of the economic scale—immigrants, former slaves, itinerant farm labourers or cash-strapped farmers—and from many origins: Americans, Irish, Scots, French, white, black, Métis, and even from among the natives along the river.

O-ge-mas-es, or "Little Clerk," the *nom de plume* of Reginald Beatty, an HBC trader who took up craft as a writer, said that "American captains and mates . . . were hired exclusively, but our own natives took to piloting and some of them became experts; the crews were all Indians chiefly drawn from The Pas and Grand Rapids, but a few Plains Indians from above Prince Albert occasionally engaged for a trip or two."[9]

Anybody who could splice a rope, man a pole, shunt freight, chop wood and dig coal could apply, regardless of creed. As long as he could endure blistering heat, deafening noise, eternal dampness, constant insults and racial slurs, and didn't mind isolation, boredom, storms, mosquitoes, blackflies, leeches or wading neck deep in icy waters. Is it any wonder that "rooster" became synonymous with "drunk." Deckhands were treated as expendable by those in higher stations, though an experienced rooster could always work his way up if he was patient enough to eventually make watchman, mate, fireman or higher. Many a captain and pilot learned his craft toting heavy freight on the main deck. L.R. Goderidge, on the *North West* in 1897, downplayed his role as he excused the low wages: "Half the time we were sleeping. We had a snap as far as work goes on the boat."[10]

Deckhands had no sleeping berths. Usually they napped on open decks amid the cargo, as they were never considered off duty. They were on call 24 hours a day to cut wood, run spar lines, dig cofferdams, tug barges in freezing water, or a hundred other jobs. They had to be strong as oxen to hoist bales, barrels, cordwood, lumber, crates and carcasses, and as sure-footed as mules to pack those same dead weights across narrow, springy, slippery gangplanks. Red River captain Gilbert Hackland taunted his men with "If you don't work, you don't eat!"[11] and often made good his threat. Food was prepared by on-board cooks, but deckhands had to wait until paying passengers and officers had dined first, and usually had to be content with leftovers.

Roosters also had to put up with their boss, the mate, who handled the job with varying degrees of brutality, threats and profanity. One incident witnessed by Reginald

(Top) The port engines on a sternwheeler. The large intake pipes conveyed steam from the boilers at the bow of the ship. SCHWINDEN LIBRARY, FT. BENTON, MONTANA

(Bottom) The flywheel and pumps that filled the boilers with river water. SCHWINDEN LIBRARY, FT. BENTON, MONTANA

Beatty at Grand Rapids Landing in 1877 illustrates that the frontier stew that comprised a steamboat crew was not always the most congenial. Beatty, a clerk, was about his business of shipping and receiving merchandise in the dockside warehouse when he noticed trouble brewing on deck. "A big fat Yankee mate ... was standing on the deck at the gangway singing a rough chantee song to the Indians passing him heavily loaded, from one to two hundred pounds a man being the general load."[12] As the loading continued, the besotted bully would launch a swift kick into the rear-end of the labourers and bellow, "Come along, come along, you sons of——, come a-running." Beatty noticed one Cree from the Fort Pitt region, a decorated buffalo hunter, who seemed to be less than amused with the American's antics. The clerk was most concerned about the hunter's showy scalping knife, and the dark eyes that flashed with rage whenever the mate would raise his voice and his boot. Beatty thought a warning was in order, and thought to remind the Yank that he was not on the Mississippi cotton docks now and that any one of his barbed remarks could conceivably be his last.

Beatty made his way up the gangplank, and in his words, "tapped Mr. Mate on the shoulder and warned him this was not a crew of southern niggers, but red Indians and dangerous men to monkey with." The mate showed his gratitude by venting his spleen: "'You attend to the freight checking' and he would hustle the—and so on." Suit yourself, Beatty shrugged, and went back to his warehouse.

Before long, the Fort Pitt hunter, with a heavy load on his shoulder, felt the American's boot once more on his posterior. In a heartbeat, the load was on the deck and the American was on his back with the hunter's knee on his chest and the scalp knife at his throat. Beatty and others rushed up to pull the Indian off the Yankee. The enraged Cree was in a mad fury, yelling that "he had never been insulted before and that only death could wipe out the stain." Despite the blood on the knife, the American survived the scrape. "Never was a man so changed. The Yankee would not work after that, certain his scalp to be at risk. Eventually the reformed blusterer left the Landing, gradually the Yankee mates were done away with and our steady Scotchmen replaced them."

But deckhands could keep the mate in line in other ways as well. Since no quarter was asked, none was given, and a hand could walk off the job at any time. If they knew they had a bargaining position, such as a labour shortage, or the boat was desperate enough, they would organize a strike for better wages, food or whisky. Bad food, abuse, machinery noise, bugs and non-stop drudgery made the life of a rooster intolerable, and drunkenness and fights were often the result. Other positions on the boat had more prestige, but were no less burdensome.

An American steamboat mate learns a little lesson in Canadian Cree civility. *THE BEAVER*, APRIL 1922

A carpenter was also on crew, often the boatwright who built the vessel in the first place. His job was to keep the decks in shape, build barges, and be prepared at a moment's notice to plug a hole punched through the hull by a boulder or a gravel bar, often having to cut his own lumber from trees or deadfall. Whenever the steamer had to put in to shore for firewood, the carpenter commanded the "woodhawks": work parties that would collect, cut and load timber from the river flats. Often the crew would luck out and find that some local resident, a professional woodhawk, had already cut a pile of cordwood and left it by the shore for the steamer to pick up. Whenever such a fortunate pile was spotted, the captain would leave a purse of money or a bag of gold on a rock as payment to the cutter. The code of the West usually meant the money would still be there when the woodhawk returned. Woodhawking had dangers as well, though, and many a cutter was attacked or killed by bandits or unfriendly natives.

The fireman was charged with keeping the firebox full of wood, or coal if available. Working with the engineer, he had to be attentive and steady if the boilers were to maintain working pressure, and be able to pick up the pace if the pilot ordered more steam. Though this was hot, dangerous and exhausting labour, a fireman could endure four shifts, then after four hours rest, be back at it again. Fortunately, boats would drop anchor at night, giving the fireman some badly needed sack time.

The clerk, also known as the purser or the supercargo, was the boat's business manager, keeping track of all matters pertaining to the cargo: loading and unloading, quantities, values and freight rates charged. He also kept the crew records, the payroll, the ship's log, the passenger register, mail, maps and any other required paperwork. The clerk's position usually meant he was the most literate person aboard and the man charged with making a boat pay its way.

One would think a steamboat crew had enough to do on Western rivers. But as the West expanded, change brought the possibility of conflict, which only made the prospect of being a riverman that much more interesting.

The age of steam and war

In 1861, the steaming cauldron of war was fired to full boil in the U.S. as the War between the States raged between North and South. One of the first strategies of the War was a naval blockade that would control the rivers that geographically split the nation, the Mississippi and its little brother the Missouri. From New Orleans to Minnesota, whoever controlled those big rivers would control the conduct of the war in the West and could use the river to ferry troops and supplies and, most importantly, deny use of the river to the enemy. From his base at the port of Cairo, Illinois, a rumpled, still obscure general named Ulysses Simpson Grant ordered that the campaign would take place not only with the armies at his command, but with a war fleet that would be constructed to regain control of the Union river routes.

A motley assemblage of federal ironclads and civilian steamboats, a virtual "western navy," was put together by an independent riverman, James B. Eads, who was commissioned to produce a fleet capable of sailing into certain death. The vessels had to meet what for that time was a considerable engineering challenge: to be armoured with protective plating and be capable of carrying huge, heavy cannons and still be able to navigate in less than 10 feet of water. The resulting ironclads, with their cumbersome accoutrements, were slow and clumsy but nonetheless effective. Grant's gunboats took Fort Henry, Tennessee, on February 6, 1862, and "U.S." Grant became known as "Unconditional Surrender" Grant, obscure no longer, as the Confederates lost their dominance in Kentucky and western Tennessee. Now with access to the Tennessee river, Grant sailed right into the heart of enemy territory when he moved the fleet and his army upriver to Pittsburg Landing. An attempt to crush his position turned into victory for Grant at the bloody battle of Shiloh in April 1862, but not before steamboats arrived with 25,000 fresh reinforcements.

Later that same month, Captain David Farragut wrested the mouth of the Mississippi River away from Confederate forces, and the Union held control of New Orleans and southern Louisiana for the rest of the war. By early June, the Union held the northern approach as well, as far south as Memphis. By April 1863, Grant and the fleet of Admiral David Porter had neutralized the Confederate port of Vicksburg, Mississippi, "the Gibraltar of the West," opening the river to make resupply of Union forces much easier than by land. Grant's siege of the city began in late May, by land and with artillery barrages from gunboats on the Mississippi. Vicksburg finally surrendered on July 4, 1863, giving the Union control of the Mississippi River and splitting the Confederacy in two. Of course, the most intense battles of the Civil War were fought and determined in the East. But the Union gained immensely by controlling the river, driving a wedge into the heart of the Confederacy that would never be removed.

To control the waterway was to control the war, and "Unconditional Surrender" Grant joined the ranks of Alexander and Napoleon as a military genius, paving the way for his eventual election to the presidency in 1868. His tactics at Fort Henry and Fort Donelson, Shiloh and Vicksburg became case studies for students of warfare. Could one of these armchair observers have been an officer named Frederick Middleton? For it would come to pass in 1885 that a British general, appointed to an outpost of Empire, would be charged with the conduct of a bitter frontier campaign. Would a military commander again see the rivers of the region as an ally, and waterborne transport as a weapon of war? In the year of rebellion, as Ulysses S. Grant lay on his deathbed, in pain from throat cancer, the tactic that made him a U.S. folk hero was revived by that British general in the Canadian West, on a river that a British company had tried to own for 200 years.

CHAPTER TWO

Hudson's Bay Workhorses

The Red River regime

In 1869, the HBC handed over the land it controlled under its corporate charter to the new nation of Canada. Freed from administering a vast frontier holding, the company directors turned their attention to the business of business. The time had come to improve the archaic transportation network between Winnipeg and the company's distant outposts. The Northern Pacific Railway had reached the Red River on U.S. territory, at Moorhead, Minnesota. HBC goods could be easily freighted from eastern Canada to Moorhead, then steamed down the Red into Manitoba. But U.S. goods, too, could arrive by that route. The HBC's classic tactic of bullying and buying out the competition wasn't going to work this time. State-of-the-art technology had been thrust before their noses, and it forced them into progressive thinking. If you can't beat 'em, join 'em.

Steamboat rivalry was intense on the Red River, in the race to dominate commerce in the new Manitoba. Farm goods and new immigrants were transforming the region into an agricultural heartland. The HBC was shut out of the business when a U.S. customs law clamped down on the river trade by requiring all export and import goods passing through U.S. territory to be bonded. The HBC's only steamer, the *International*, was stalled, having failed to fulfill the bonding requirements. But in the shadows, the wily James Jerome Hill was only too willing to hold the HBC at his mercy.

Hill was a Canadian who became America's greatest railroader, and it was not for nothing that he was called "the Empire Builder." Ruthless in business, he could always see, with his one good eye, a way to make a dollar toil in his favour. With the bond law to his advantage, he formed Hill, Griggs & Co., and in 1871 launched a new steamer. His *Selkirk* was the only game in town and Hill gouged the HBC and others with inflated freight rates. It would take a businessman just as wily to put up a fight in order to shear the gilded edge from Hill's pockets.

Donald Smith, destined to be an unscrupulous legend in Canadian business and politics, was Chief Commissioner of the HBC at the time and held sway over commercial policies of his company. Smith struck a pact with Norman W. Kittson, a St. Paul merchant who doubled as the HBC's official agent in Minnesota, and had the *International* transferred on paper to Kittson's private concern. By the end of the 1871 season, there was fair market competition on the Red for the first time, as the *Selkirk* and the *International* raced from port to port.

Smith, the future Lord Strathcona, was more than just a company and government servant. He was a weaver of webs, a master of corporate intrigue. By the time he finished drafting a plan for Red River transportation, one would think he would have made a blood enemy of J.J. Hill. But Hill came out very well, and accepted Smith as an opponent worthy of partnership. In 1872, Norman Kittson organized a variety of small shippers into the Red River Transportation Co. (RRTC), one component of which was Hill, Griggs & Co. But the deal was not a buyout of HG&C. Actually it was a merger, a consortium of interests, formed by Kittson and Hill, but also from personal capital supplied by none other than Donald Smith! Once more the HBC had finagled a monopoly, and used its enemies to do it.

The RRTC was poised to gain complete control as Kittson bought out competing boats such as the *Dakota*, the *Cheyenne* and the *Alpha*. The RRTC now ruled the Red, hiking freight rates to what the traffic would bear and beyond. In 1874 the indignant businessmen of Winnipeg and St. Paul organized the Merchants' International Steamboat Line (MISL) to break the Hill-Kittson-HBC headlock. A rate war would ensue as the MISL prepared to launch the *Minnesota* and the *Manitoba*.

In the winter of 1874/75, the MISL had commissioned James Douglas of Moorhead to construct the *Manitoba*. Douglas tailored the boat to the river: 165 feet long, with a beam of 31 feet. When launched, it displaced 4 feet of water, a perilously deep draft for western rivers but not too deep for the Red. Douglas ordered the *Manitoba*'s twin horizontal, non-condensing engines from the North Star Iron Works of Minneapolis, and together they formed a power plant that produced 29.2 hp. On completion, the ship weighed 195 tons.[1]

The *Manitoba*'s first season was fraught with excitement and peril. Races between RRTC and MISL boats were frequent, and encouraged, and the proliferation of steamer traffic on the Red attracted some of the best steamboat pilots. Two pilots, Jerry Webber and John Segers, would meet fatefully and recklessly one dark night south of Winnipeg in 1875, and their introduction would be less than cordial.

Webber had become an authentic folk hero at the beginning of the U.S. Civil War, when, in April 1861, on a commission from Union General William Tecumseh Sherman, his sternwheeler, the *Fanny Harris*, moved a heavy cannon downriver from Fort Ridgely, Minnesota, to Fort Snelling, careening and bouncing off the banks on the twisting reaches of a Minnesota river in full flood.

John Scribner Segers, born in Bangor, Maine, in 1834, had immigrated to Henderson, Minnesota, in 1853. Having done little else than work on riverboats, and having been part of the landmark 1859 *Anson Northrup* crew, Segers had a right to be at the helm of the *International* that night, and as we'll see later, he would have a lifetime of further adventures ahead.

On the fateful night of June 4, 1875, Jerry Webber's *Manitoba* delivered a load to the docks at Winnipeg and headed back upstream toward Moorhead. Nine miles south, Webber rounded a bend to find Segers's *International* directly in his path. Segers, following the river law that the boat headed downstream always has first choice of passing lane, sounded his whistle to pass on the port side. With the approaching vessels just 150 feet from each other, Webber stubbornly whistled for his own right to the starboard lane. Both boats were intent on taking their half of the right-of-way, straight down the middle.

Quickly Segers reversed engines and signalled again for port, as it was now impossible for him to swing the boat to starboard. With the current relentlessly pushing, the *International* struck the *Manitoba* broadside, rending a 10-foot hole in Webber's hull and decks. In less than a minute, the brand-new *Manitoba* was under water.

Webber and Segers both cried foul to their respective owners, both intransigent in their blame of each other. Undaunted, the MISL owners had the *Manitoba* raised and repaired. But the next year, on April 26, 1876, to be exact, the *Manitoba* was seized for debt and sold by the receiver to the rival. For $9,446 the Red River Transportation Co. took possession of the resurrected steamer and operated it for the next three seasons. Before the rivalry ended, Norman Kittson had absorbed all MISL ships and cornered the market again. But bigger and better things were on the way to divert his partners' attention.

Eventually, as capitalists will do, the owners of the RRTC shifted their interest from river freighting to a new enterprise: railroading. On October 8, 1877, the *Selkirk*, as if to signal its own doom, delivered the *Countess of Dufferin*, the CPR's first locomotive in the West. Steel tracks reached Manitoba from the south in 1878, built by the St. Paul & Manitoba Railroad, which was financed by the transport triumvirate of Hill, Kittson and Smith. In 1881, Hill and Smith joined in yet another syndicate to build the continent's most difficult railway, the Canadian Pacific, with the full support of the Canadian federal government. Transportation in the West would no longer be subject to the vagaries and intricacies of the Red River steamer companies. But as rails were crossing the Red, sternwheelers were pushing on to the next great frontier: the Saskatchewan.

Changing the course of history from a London boardroom

The first to recognize the potential of the steamboat delivery system was the HBC's governor, Sir Stafford Henry Northcote, later the Earl of Iddesleigh. In the HBC hierarchy, Northcote was essentially what today would be called the chief executive officer, a guiding force for the company and a reliable servant of its shareholders. In the summer of 1871, Northcote told the annual General Court Meeting of shareholders that their system of shipping goods to York Factory from England via the Arctic Ocean was antiquated and uncompetitive. The surrender of the company's lands to the new government of Canada had meant the end of the company's monopoly in the North West Territories, and competition for trade into the prairies from Minnesota and Montana was intensifying as U.S. interests augmented their supply chains with river freighting. To assess the situation, business consultant Cyril Graham was contracted to tour the North American operations of the HBC with the objective of streamlining the fur trade, updating the company's relationship with its employees, and recommending new competitive strategies.[2]

The irony wasn't lost on Northcote, as he noted that the crucial HBC depots of Cumberland, Carlton, Fort Pitt and Edmonton were located on rivers still serviced by York boats. But U.S. steamers were already established at Fort Garry, and the West's economy was turning from barter to agrarian. The HBC's policy of discouraging settlement would change abruptly to one of fostering the growth of communities. Such development would increase merchandise sales and substantially increase the value of the still vast real-estate holdings left over from the Canadian land surrender. In addition, there was the Far North and the problem of access to the rich pelts of the sub-Arctic, which had yet to be tapped seriously.

With the backing of Cyril Graham's report, Governor Northcote made the recommendations that would drag the HBC kicking and screaming into the new commercial reality. Though the fur trade was still profitable and far from dying, a new means of supplying inland posts would have to be found. Previously the company had relied on the service of hundreds of Métis and native freighters to transport goods across the prairies in York boats and in creaky Red River carts. But as competition encroached across the border, the costs of this native transportation increased, cutting into already slim profit margins.

The HBC was also finding the cart brigades unreliable in light of work stoppages during the Red River Rebellion. So Governor Northcote recommended a major shift in thinking: the implementation of steamboats on the inland river and lake systems of Manitoba and the North West. With the promise of a new railway to British Columbia, Northcote saw the advantage of a steamboat system not only to maintain dominance in the fur trade, but also with an eye to establishing a merchandising empire to feed new agricultural development in areas not previously serviced by the HBC.

London moneymen, concerned about the expense, did not share the governor's vision, and the General Court Meeting turned into a shouting match before a vote could take place. But one shareholder took the floor to put the plan into perspective: "Gentlemen, this company has not been very celebrated for doing things in a hurry. It is really much like Rip Van Winkle waking up in the year 1871 and finding out that steam engines and steam boats will be of advantage to the trade."[3]

After much grumbling, Northcote's proposals were accepted by the shareholders and a blueprint for the future of the HBC was approved. With restructuring in place the company announced that two steamers would be purchased: a lake steamer and a river sternwheeler. The lake steamer would sail between Selkirk and the mouth of the Saskatchewan at Grand Rapids, by way of Lake Winnipeg. A secondary notion to sail the laker on the smaller bodies of Lake Manitoba and Lake Winnipegosis was scrapped, as it would have required the construction of three canals to connect the Assiniboine River with the lakes.

The only impediment preventing a steamer from passing directly from lake to river was the cavernous portage known as Grand Rapids, the final gateway where the Saskatchewan gives way to Lake Winnipeg. The canyon's cataracts were too much for a steamer to ascend or descend without being pounded into kindling. It was decided to treat the river's mouth as an inland port and build giant warehouses at both ends of the rapids. Expending another $20,000 the HBC constructed a 3½-mile-long shortline railway, with flatcars that could carry up to four tons of freight. With no locomotive available, the train was pulled upstream by a team of mules. On the downgrade, the train was allowed to freewheel, held back only by a brakeman. Some interesting crashes into the warehouse occurred while operators were learning to use those brakes.

The lake and river system also meant two fleets for service, both requiring different sciences. A sternwheeler was little good on a lake, due to tidal action that often kept the wheel out of the water. With that in mind, a single-funnelled, screw-driven steamer was designed and built at Lower Fort Garry by Captain D.W. Hewitt during the winter of 1871/72. Donald Smith oversaw construction. The schemer behind the Red River cartel was an early advocate of the HBC's switch from oars to steam, and was likely influential in the Cyrus Graham report as an expert on trade and transportation.

On May 7, 1872, Mary Flett smashed a bottle of wine over the bow of the laker christened the SS *Chief Commissioner,* in honour of Donald Smith.[4] The *Chief*'s maiden voyage was not as felicitous, however, as an attempt was made to reach the calmer waters of Lake Manitoba by way of the Dauphin River. The vessel promptly bottomed out in shallow water. But by the time the ice was out in 1873, the *Chief Commissioner* was firmly afloat in the choppy, deep waters of Lake Winnipeg. The screw steamer's first cargo was bound for Grand Rapids, where the *Chief* delivered a deckload of raw, Minnesota-milled lumber for building a brand new sternwheeler for service on the Saskatchewan.

Construction seemed cursed from the start. Builder D.W. Hewitt was under pressure from the HBC to get the vessel into the water in time to supply the trading posts for fall. The new steamer was to be 142 feet in length, powered by two horizontal engines imported from C.J. Dymont of Cincinnati. But the engines and machinery hadn't been properly tested and the lumber of the hull had yet to cure when the HBC hastily ordered the new flagship into service without so much as a name. On August 2, 1872, Captain François "Frank" Aymond, in defiance of tradition and fate, sailed the vessel out of Grand Rapids despite the bad luck that an unchristened ship could bring. Sure enough, three days and 13 miles from embarkation, the vessel was cast onto a rocky shoal at the Demi-Charge Rapids, destroying the hull.

HBC employees salvaged damp cargo from the wreck and freighted the recovered goods to Fort Defiance. Two hundred kegs of sugar and hardware were lost, as were numerous bolts of cloth. Native women fished the cloth out of the river and unfurled the textiles on the nearby foliage, dubbing the shoal "Calico Island." Some of the sugar was saved through boiling and evaporation. The nameless wreck eventually limped back to the Roche Rouge Rapids, and was left to rot as an expensive memorial.

Sir Stafford somberly reported the £9,000 loss of the SS *Whatsitsname*[5] to another dour London shareholders meeting.[6] Though distressed by the loss of their debut riverboat, the HBC directors were undaunted and remained faithful to their 1871 mandate. Systems still had to be modernized and plans were undertaken to design and build a bigger, better riverboat—a flagship that would announce to the west that the HBC was still a force to be reckoned with. As one chief trader bragged, "the old Company was in the forefront of development and progress."[7]

Shriek in the wilderness: the Northcote

The Hudson's Bay Company had a naval tradition dating back to 1668, what with the windjammer *Nonsuch*, the Pacific coastal steamer the *Beaver*, and a plethora of unnamed rivercraft. A new legend was about to join the annals of the company. In the summer of 1874, Captain J. Reeves, a Dakota boat builder from Grand Forks, gathered a load of heavy oak from Georgetown, Minnesota, and the best shipwrights he could find in St. Paul, and shipped the lot to Grand Rapids. His objective: to build a 150-foot sternwheeler, 28½ feet wide, with a hull 4½ feet deep. Among his carpenters was Roderick Smith, a massive Scot from the Isle of Lewis, who'd been cobbling together HBC rivercraft for six years. Smith was a Paul Bunyan prototype, as thick and rugged as the oak trees he hewed and shaped: "A big, brawny, brown-whiskered chap with a pair of shoulders wide enough for a couple ordinary men, he looked like the voyageur, the woodsman and the trapper all in one."[8]

The boilers for the new steamer were shiny new, imported from Cincinnati, and shipped north in sections. "As these were the days before the rat-a-tat-tat of the pneumatic riveter, the boilers were riveted by hand to the song of the Saskatchewan mosquito."[9] The engines installed were the same Dymont units recycled from Frank Aymond's wreck, "a type long since obsolete"[10] yet capable of generating 40 horsepower after being cleaned up and rebuilt. The new flagship weighed 291 tons, but could carry more than 150 tons more. Fully loaded, the new boat drew 3½ feet of water, which was problematic.[11] Built for a total cost of $53,000, the vessel was launched on August 1, 1874. Rectifying the blunder of the Aymond wreck, the craft was grandly christened the SS *Northcote* in honour of the HBC governor. But Sir Stafford had to accept the homage as a past participant: he'd stepped down as HBC governor earlier that year.

Two weeks after launch, the *Northcote* sailed for its first port of call, The Pas, 140 miles upriver, under the command of Frank Aymond, whom company officials had by now forgiven for his 1872 crash. When the *Northcote* arrived on August 26, the Cree Anglican missionary Reverend Henry Budd was there. As he wrote in his journal: "The long expected steamer North-Cote came puffing up in sight. They blew the whistle so loud they made the cattle rear up their heels, and took to full gallop with their tails up in the air in full speed to the woods. But, not only the cattle but the people of all ages and sexes were no less excited at the sight of the boat, the first boat of the kind to be seen by them all their life; in fact the first steam boat going in this river since the Creation."[12]

Twelve days out of Grand Rapids, the *Northcote* made port at Fort Carlton. Dropping off cargo destined for the Athabasca, the *Northcote* returned without incident to Grand Rapids. Neither the *Chief Commissioner* nor the *Colville* had made it to Grand Rapids to resupply, so the *Northcote* was put into winter dockage. As the HBC busied itself with building huge warehouses to accommodate the business now expected in the new age, the steamer was collecting accolades such as this: "Some years ago the press was accustomed to enlarge on the prospect of navigation ... on the Red ... through Lake Winnipeg and the North Saskatchewan to Fort Edmonton at the foot of the Rocky Mountains ... The steamboat just launched on the Saskatchewan is the forerunner of a great fleet of steam craft which is hereafter to navigate this long line of waterways."[13]

Aymond was at the helm again on July 22, 1875, when the *Northcote*, laden with 130 tons of freight from Winnipeg, sounded her whistle at Fort Edmonton after an 18-day journey from Grand Rapids. By comparison, the journey back to the lakehead was accomplished in a breakneck three days. Having seen Edmonton thus connected with the world, pundits romanced the *Northcote* and called on "our brilliant government" to "expend a little money on the improvement of the Saskatchewan navigation." If a public work were undertaken to dredge the channel of its boulders, the project "would confer a benefit on the country"[14] by making the Saskatchewan a more navigable waterway.

The *Northcote* wasn't the only fledgling western institution to debut that season. In the fall of '74, the newly minted Royal North West Mounted Police limped their way into Fort Edmonton after a harrowing march from Manitoba. By the time the *Northcote* met the Mounties, Police Inspector William D. Jarvis had been authorized to build a major post on the North Branch, and Factor William Hardisty hoped it would be built beside his HBC post. But with an eye to the engineering demands of a rumoured railway, Jarvis sited the post 20 miles downstream from Edmonton instead, where the cliffs were more gentle. As Jarvis built Fort Saskatchewan, he used the *Northcote* to transport construction supplies.

The ship's whistle was a signal of progress to traders, trappers and settlers huddled around the fur fort. No longer just a forlorn outpost, Edmonton was a destination of choice for modern transportation, now only 33 days from communication with the world. They had steamboats, they had police, soon perhaps a railway. For 10 incredible summers between 1874 and 1883, the *Northcote* was as much a fixture on the North Branch as the old fur forts that lined its shore, and the boat accompanied incredible change, with the establishment of towns like Fort Saskatchewan, Battleford and Prince Albert.

The navigation season was short, usually late May to September, a highly fluid schedule that depended on the weather, snowpack accumulation and how long the spring and summer melt could sustain river levels. The *Northcote*'s first two seasons saw Frank Aymond in command, with Joseph Favell as pilot, though Aymond's tenure proved problematic. In 1875, valuable time was lost waiting for the lakers to deliver freight from Winnipeg. Twice in 1876, the *Northcote* was unable to ascend Cole's Falls. Favell and the ship's engineer filed grievances to their employers about Aymond. His Swampy Cree deckhands were surly, and the hands walked off the boat, refusing to discharge freight and load firewood. The strike required the help of Reginald "O-ge-mas-es" Beatty, the Grand Rapids HBC clerk, to quell.[15] At the end of the '76 season Aymond was fired, and he retired to a Dakota farm.

The 1877 season saw more promise when J.J. Hill's old partner James Griggs took charge. That year, the *Northcote* ran a record six round-trip voyages up and down the North Branch. A sister ship was launched, the Scottish-built, iron hulled *Lily*, christened at Grand Rapids by Lord Dufferin, Canada's Governor General. The HBC's river enterprise now had the official stamp of Empire from the Queen. The formerly minor consideration of passenger traffic took prominence, as the *Northcote* was altered to accommodate 50 passengers. River travel was coming into its own. One passenger got free fare on July 30, 1880, when the wife of missionary Charles Reader gave birth to a baby boy, who received the only name that seemed natural: Northcote Reader.

In 1878, the *Northcote* suffered damage while running the boulder-strewn Cole's Falls. Even after repairs, the flagship lost crucial time aiding the *Lily*'s own navigation of the falls. In 1879, the terms of Treaty Six brought increased business delivering cargo, livestock, farm equipment and agents and instructors to new Indian agencies along the river. Goods were delivered for $6.25 per hundredweight, seriously undercutting the $8.50–$14 rate charged by Métis cartsmen for goods delivered from Winnipeg. Passage from Grand Rapids to Edmonton ran as high as $70 per person.

The HBC used its new position as transport mogul to have its land commissioner lobby the federal government for capital improvements to the river: building dams, deepening channels, dredging boulders and so on. If the feds would do this, it was promised, the HBC would put more and bigger boats on the river. But Ottawa took no action and the shipyards lay silent save for the refitting of the *Northcote* and *Lily* with new machinery and accoutrements. The boats also received new masters: the *Lily* got the Métis pilot John "Josie" Smith, while the *Northcote* received a legend we have seen before, Jerry Webber.

Steamboat captains followed the evolving frontier, and when the cantankerous Jerry Webber found his way to the pilothouse of the *Northcote* in 1881, the Saskatchewan River was introduced to the artful profanity that Webber had such acknowledged mastery of. Captain Jerry could fly into a fit of rage at the slightest provocation, slamming his broad-brimmed hat to the deck and pouncing on it with both feet while streaming a flurry of epithets and enough blasphemies to shame the devil. Fortunately, he either held his tongue or at least stayed out of earshot on the occasion of the *Northcote*'s welcoming aboard its most prestigious passengers ever. The new Governor General the Marquis of Lorne and his consort, Princess Louise, daughter of Queen Victoria, were touring the North West Territories with their extensive entourage and had met the flagship of the Saskatchewan at Fort Carlton.

On August 26, 1881, the only royal reception ever held on a Saskatchewan steamboat was in the close quarters of the *Northcote*'s saloon, at dockside in Prince Albert. The vice-regal party transferred to the *Lily* to go upriver, but the Marquis was impressed enough to describe the mechanical sparring operations in his memoirs, and noted "much shouting, rocking of the boat and convulsive effort."[16] More vital to Jerry Webber than royal visits, however, was this reassuring passage in the *Saskatchewan Herald*: "Shippers will be glad to know that not a single piece of private freight remains at Grand Rapids,"[17] a testament to the skipper's skill and management. With professionals like Webber, the HBC could easily justify expansion.

The evolving empire

Navigation on the Saskatchewan depended on a good Lake Winnipeg fleet to maintain profitability and keep Grand Rapids full of freight. As river service was implemented, the HBC needed to improve its lake fleet. Without a keel, the *Chief Commissioner* had extreme difficulty navigating the choppy waters of the lake, so in 1875, Captain J. Reeves, the builder of the *Northcote*, was called upon to build a one-deck laker to be called the *Colville*. The *Chief*'s hull was made into a floating warehouse and its engines were cannibalized for the *Colville*.

As the buffalo ground of Manitoba gradually gave way to the farmer's plough, demand increased for the transportation of goods further into the plains. Destiny was having its way with the prairies, and a creaky, primitive infrastructure strained to keep up with change. To a Westerner, Sir John A. Macdonald's tall promise of a transcontinental railway seemed like a typographical error in an election pamphlet, or maybe another of Sir John's gin-inspired witticisms. The prime minister's railway negotiations fell into a quagmire of bribery and scandal that destroyed his government in 1873, leaving the country beyond Manitoba served by little more than rafts and ox carts. Only the HBC's sternwheelers offered progress.

Opportunity was waiting for the right entrepreneur, as fresh consortiums formed to conquer new rivers. As Kittson, Smith and Hill prepared to abandon rivers for rails, a less flamboyant but hopefully more responsible sextet of merchants, lawyers and bankers pooled $50,000 to form the Winnipeg & Western Transportation Co. (W&WTC). In the spring of 1879, the new syndicate bought the leftover boats *Cheyenne*, *Alpha*, *Minnesota* and *Manitoba* from Kittson to compete on the Saskatchewan River system.

When the W&WTC assumed the *Manitoba*, they became the ship's third owner in as many years. But there were broader plans for the boat than merely the Red. In 1880, the *Manitoba* began steaming up the Assiniboine River, to advance agricultural activity by connecting fertile wheat country with the trade centre of Winnipeg. To perform this service, management ordered the decks extended by 40 feet, giving the *Manitoba* a massive 205-foot deck.

The *Minnesota* was transferred to British registry, rechristened the *City of Winnipeg*, and refitted as a showy liner with the finest of interior ornamentation. It was to be the first of the Red River ships to relocate to the Saskatchewan. The W&WTC would compete head to head with the HBC fleet, offering settlers a fresh shipping alternative.

In September 1881, the *City* was to be towed across Lake Winnipeg to Grand Rapids and "warped" up the canyon to the Saskatchewan. Veteran pilot William Robinson, of the rival North West Navigation Co., was contracted for the tow job. Robinson was at the wheel of his laker, the *Princess*, with James Sheets, a veteran U.S. captain new to Manitoba steering the *City of Winnipeg*. A series of storms arose and the *City*'s sides were battered and torn apart by the waves. With the sternwheeler being progressively dashed to bits, pilot Robinson had to make a decision and cut it loose from the *Princess,* so as not to endanger both ships. The *City of Winnipeg*, its boilers unlit and engines inert, was left to the mercy of the elements, its hog chains snapping and timbers ripping into splinters. The elements had no mercy, as the *City*, adrift and useless, ultimately was dashed on the rocks of the lake shore. Its beleaguered captain had tried to ride out the storm like Pecos Bill aboard a tornado: "Captain Sheets was the last to leave the craft of which he had proven himself so excellent and popular a commander."[18] The *City* was an expensive experience for the W&WTC, but at least it attracted one of the toughest and most competent shipmasters in the West.

James Sheets had been on the decks of riverboats since 1844. Having come to the Red as first mate on the *Manitoba* in 1876, he soon was in the wheelhouse. His black-bearded presence attracted attention, and his barrel-throated manner commanded respect and trust. Sheets was a dictator who could bellow the most colourful of expletives at the crew when they deserved it, and the next minute conspire with the hands in practical jokes played on the ship's musicians. "Certainly no mutiny by either passengers or crew dare raise its head while he commanded the ship. The Captain was a past master in the art of using 'language,' his speech being terse, epigrammatic and picturesque to a degree. In fact, the passengers often remarked that that 'language' ran the boat."[19] Sheets could also turn the parlance around and belt out the sweetest of melodies in the ship's saloon, in duets with John Segers, capturing the attentions of the ladies and the hearts of little girls. A baritone to boot, Jim Sheets piloted a mean helm.

Competition would become keen on the Assiniboine River as well. The North West Navigation Company (NWNC) was a homegrown interest of two dynamic locals, Peter McArthur and William Robinson.

McArthur was an ambitious, pious young Scot who had come to the Red in 1869, armed with an apprenticeship as a cabinetmaker and a homestead certificate for Portage la Prairie. But McArthur was welcomed only by a jail cell, as an unwilling guest of Louis Riel's provisional government. Three years later, he built the *Prince Rupert* to haul timber on the Brokenhead River. The *Manitoba Free Press* had expressed the hope that "some enterprising citizen will test the navigation of the Assiniboine to Fort Ellice through that region with a steamer built for the purpose,"[20] and McArthur eventually fulfilled that hope. In 1879, he launched the *Marquette*, with the reckless but proficient Jerry Webber at the helm. The new boat reached Fort Ellice, establishing McArthur as a shipper to reckon with.

McArthur's partner, William Robinson, was a cool, careful lake mariner, master of the *Princess*. Born in Quebec and based in Selkirk, he would eventually become the king of Lake Winnipeg shipping. Unlike most river pilots, Robinson was highly educated, a calculating businessman who had left a promising career in railway construction to bring his business acumen to the rivers and lakes of the West, and learn to run a boat. He'd navigated flatboats and log booms to supply lumber mills, and in 1878 built the eponymous tug *William Robinson* for that purpose.

Robinson's and McArthur's new enterprise, the North West Navigation Co., had powerful alliances that guaranteed smooth cooperation with the W&WTC. The NWNC chartered to run ships on the Red, Assiniboine and Saskatchewan systems as well as on the big lakes, Winnipeg, Winnipegosis and Manitoba. One of their investors was C.J. Brydges, land commissioner of the HBC, who was adept at using the subtle, intrusive tactics of old Donald Smith. Under the new partnership, Robinson built the *Princess*, a glamorous sidewheel lake steamer with 26 staterooms, to pull a 132-foot scow, the largest oak barge ever built to that time.

The *City of Winnipeg* fiasco had been a blow to all shippers, but Peter McArthur soldiered on, constructing a pair of ships that were the envy of the West. His *North West*, completed in 1881, set a new standard for sternwheelers, with a 200-foot main deck, a 33-foot beam, and a pilothouse that towered 20 feet above the water. With an unheard-of budget of $27,000, McArthur had contracted boat builder John Irish of Moorhead to construct the vessel and fit it with two horizontal, non-condensing, double-level engines from the Pioneer Iron Works of LaCrosse, Wisconsin. The engines boasted enormous 16-inch cylinders that pulled a five-foot stroke to propel the sternwheel, powered by two solid steel boilers that had 10 flues each to equally distribute the steam.

When completed, the *North West* displaced 305 tons empty. It boasted 80 berths, indicating that the ship was intended for passenger service as well as freight. The prairies were sparsely populated, and the steamboat services sought to enhance immigration along their routes. To enhance the *North West*'s image, a $5,000 grand piano and two honeymoon suites were installed. In 1882, McArthur sold the *North West* to his company, the NWNC, which in turn sold it to a partner company, the W&WTC, in 1884. The old web was being spun again.

The year 1882 proved a busy season for McArthur as he supervised the construction of an even grander vessel. The W&WTC commissioned a "Mr. Gregory" to lay a keel at the foot of Bannatyne Street in Winnipeg and construct a gargantuan double-deck sternwheeler, the largest yet built on the prairies. Gregory built the hull of white oak, setting its length at 201 feet, with a beam of 33½ feet and an unheard of draft of 5.3 feet. When completed she was a regal-looking beast, and was given a regal name to match. The *Marquis* was symbolic of the Governor General of the day, a reminder of the recent vice-regal tour by the Marquis of Lorne and his entourage on the *Northcote*. The steamer companies were only too willing to capitalize on such a regal stamp of approval.

On July 25, 1882, the *Marquis*, towed by the *Princess*, arrived at Grand Rapids to have its machinery installed. The new ship would not want for power. The owners had ordered the customary two horizontal engines, but these were state-of-the-art, high-pressure units from the Iowa Iron Works at Dubuque.[21] The cylinder bore was 19 inches, with a piston stroke of 6 feet. Three boilers produced 135 pounds of steam pressure per square inch. When the engines were fired, they yielded an unheard-of 84 horsepower, nearly triple that of the *Manitoba*. The new ship would need that kind of power, though, for it displaced 475 tons empty and was registered for 754 tons loaded, yet could attain a speed of 16 miles per hour. When James Sheets nudged the new *Marquis* up to the docks of Prince Albert, it was greeted with immense jubilation.

In 1882, an agreement was struck between the W&WTC (with a minority of shares held by the HBC) and the NWNC that would establish the customary river monopoly. A third, more shadowy organization, the Saskatchewan Transportation & Trading Co., its ownership unclear, piqued the HBC's interest. In fact, the ST&TC may have been an HBC construct, a feint to enable the old company to pounce upon the interlocking directorships of shipping firms. The ST&TC vanished as fast as it appeared, without a ripple.

Amid this haze of corporate intrigue, a heavy infusion of capital and promised business from the HBC, the W&WTC emerged as the victor in the stampede to install boats on rivers. As an added carrot and stick to the consolidation, the HBC paper-sold their two established boats, the *Northcote* and the *Lily*, to the W&WTC. Purchasing the lake steamer *Princess* from William Robinson through their new subsidiary, the HBC reestablished their foothold in the trade and transportation network in western

Canada. The wily old fur trade lords had created a cartel, appearing to retreat while actually advancing.

The corporate restructuring endowed Peter McArthur with a prestigious position as the W&WTC's Inland Navigator, the commodore of the fleet. But the new commodore was a strict teetotaler whose Presbyterian ethic dictated the banishment of alcoholic substances from the fleet's cargoes. McArthur's edict was short lived, however, as the W&WTC decided they needed the revenue from booze transportation more than they needed the piety of Peter McArthur. In more modern times, McArthur would have had quite the legal case against his employer: the North West Territories was under a liquor prohibition, and freighting the stuff to Edmonton technically constituted smuggling. But in that era, McArthur had no ground to stand on. He was fired, banished from his own creation, without so much as a canoe to command. The disgraced commodore's last act was to order the transfer of three sternwheelers across Lake Winnipeg and through Grand Rapids into the Saskatchewan River in 1882.

Separately and together the W&WTC and the NWNC formed a serious shipping concern: the W&WTC on the river, the NWNC on the lake, each fleet enhancing the other's mission. Besides the flagship *Northcote*, the W&WTC assembled three Red River boats, and set them up for service and adventure in the channels of the Saskatchewan. In their new basin, the *Marquis*, the *North West* and the *Manitoba* could conceivably travel to within sight of the Rocky Mountains. With the *Northcote* and the *Lily*, they were now a fleet of five. And why not? The *Northcote* had been going to Edmonton for a number of years.

The North West Territories was bursting with business once the transcontinental rails had finally been laid. Sir Stafford Northcote's dream had come true: his feverish vision had dragged his already two-century-old company hemming and hawing into the age of steam.

CHAPTER THREE

The Belly River Coal Fleet

Coal in the coulees

The Belly River had a limited heritage of water craft. The horse-bound Blackfoot Confederacy saw little need for such conveyances outside of bullboats: small frames covered with stretched buffalo hide used mainly for ferrying deep river crossings. Voyageurs and York boat brigades never penetrated Blackfoot territory, as the HBC preferred the tribes to freight their buffalo robes north to Rocky Mountain House or Edmonton of their own accord. But even so, the fabled warrior hunter bands knew of the awesome, steam-belching fireboat.

The Blackfoot, Blood and Peigan first saw the contraptions in the 1850s when sternwheelers first plied the upper Missouri River. The native buffalo robe trade created an inland port 2,285 miles from its eventual outlet in the Gulf of Mexico. Fort Benton was the impetus for the beginnings of competitive trade in what is now southern Alberta and Saskatchewan. From St. Louis, Americans shipped goods to service native trade, gold rush towns and the rest of the trappings of Manifest Destiny. The infamous whisky traders used Fort Benton as their southern staging point, and used various independent posts along the tributaries of the South Saskatchewan as the northern gathering points for shipping buffalo hides back south on the Whoop-up Trail. Those whisky traders were more than their name implies. The Montanans were unassociated free merchants whose competitive forays economically damaged the HBC and aroused the monopoly's powerful allies to act.

This resulted in the arrival of the North West Mounted Police to the Oldman River in October of 1874, to put the free trade out of business. But with the implementation of Treaty Seven three years later, steamer traffic on the Missouri increased exponentially. New towns and a cattle industry around the NWMP forts of Macleod, Calgary and Walsh created an impetus for business that was unheard of in the region. The freighting of supplies for the police and the goods required for honouring the treaty saved Fort Benton from economic ruin and made millionaires out of T.C. Power, I.G.

Baker and the Conrad Brothers, the merchants who arranged the supply lines and dominated the business. The Benton trade encouraged new homesteads and ranching leases in the Canadian territories. With the arrival of the Canadian Pacific Railway as an alternative mode of transport, steamboat activity to Benton diminished. But for one enterprising Big Muddy captain there would be new shores to pilot.

That story began in 1874 when a former U.S. hide trader named Nicholas Sheran turned to the Belly (now called the Oldman) for opportunity after the bottom dropped out of the market for Indian buffalo hides. With previous experience as a sailor on an Alaskan whaler, and knowing that a nearby crossing would become important to the NWMP and that settlement would follow, Sheran built two flat-bottomed scows and established a toll ferry. The service proved popular with the police and the many teamsters freighting supplies from Fort Benton to the force's new post of Fort Macleod.

On lazy days when business was slow, Sheran would take his wagon downstream a few miles and pick out coal from an outcropping he'd discovered a few years earlier. He sold a few tons to the trading post at Whoop-up and to the NWMP at Macleod, and even shipped a few wagonloads to Fort Benton, over 200 miles away. The Bloods knew of the coal, but rarely burned it in their lodges for fear of asphyxiation by carbon monoxide. Their name for the seams in Blackfoot was sik-oko-toks, "place of the black rocks," a location renamed by the Americans as Coalbanks.

Nick Sheran's businesses thrived. In order to tend both operations, Sheran moved his ferry closer to the mine, and built a house on a knoll beside the works. It didn't take long before his little mine attracted the attention of Sir Alexander Tilloch Galt, a prominent old-guard politician, a Father of Confederation and Canada's first Minister of Finance. Galt was a keen financier, a man always in the mood for a ready investment. But he knew little of the West and had never even visited. Sir Alexander's interest in a remote little hillside mine was piqued by a first-hand account by a reliable source on the scene: his own son, Elliott Torrance Galt.

In the fall of 1879, the younger Galt was riding the circuit as the government's assistant Indian commissioner, a job he probably would never have obtained had it not been for the name of his father. Though competent enough, he was not content with a safe patronage appointment and longed for some venture to give him a chance to make his own mark. When Elliott encountered Sheran and his diggings, he was suitably impressed with the richness of the coal seams. Under instructions from the elder Galt, Elliott returned a year later to take samples from the mine for analysis.

The assay proved the coal to be a volatile bituminous variety high in carbon, greatly coveted for steam generation and for making coke, the tempering fuel used in manufacturing steel. Though more of a genteel type than his son, the old politician Sir Alexander Galt knew steel rails would soon come to the West, and that locomotives ate coal. The coming transcontinental railway had considerable government input, and Galt, a close confidant of the prime minister, had the ear of those in high places. His influence in Ottawa and London could pave many rough spots for the venture.

Elliott Torrance Galt, the local representative for Eastern Canadian and British capital, parlayed knowledge of a far-flung coal mine into a business syndicate based on mining, agriculture and transportation. GALT MUSEUM & ARCHIVES P19737727000-G

Sir Alexander Tilloch Galt, a Father of Confederation, Canada's first Minister of Finance, and High Commissioner to London. Galt left public service to conduct interests in Western Canada that included mining, shipping, railways and land speculation. Galt appealed to his friends in government for his languishing steamboats to be used for military service in 1885. GALT MUSEUM & ARCHIVES P19740056000

Other coal deposits were researched, but Coalbanks was the selected site. A mine across the river from Sheran's was to be the base of a larger scheme. But Nick Sheran, whose cottage industry had stirred London drawing rooms, wouldn't get to enjoy the rewards, nor would he be around to lend his experience as a seasoned mariner to the new navigational experiments. After assisting an NWMP patrol across the upper Belly River, his ferry boat overturned and the very river he loved so much claimed Nicholas Sheran's life.

The syndicate

As Canada's High Commissioner to London, Sir Alexander Galt was the most powerful Canadian in Britain. That prestigious appointment connected Galt with the most influential of elite London capitalists, those with bankbooks of the size necessary for establishing the first large-scale mining venture on the prairies. Galt canvassed the posh, stuffy parlours and drawing rooms of Victorian-era London and pulled together £50,000 sterling to capitalize the North Western Coal & Navigation Co. (no relation to the North West Navigation Co. on Lake Winnipeg). The company's name expressed its mission: to exploit the coal deposits and navigate the river to freight the product.

The investors were from the cream of British society: a board of "Williams," including bookseller and controversial Lord of the Admiralty William H. Smith; publisher William Lethbridge, whose name would grace the city that would rise above the coulees of the original mine site; and an eager young U.S. expatriate with a mouthful for a name, William Ashmead Bartlett Burdett-Coutts. But "young William's" name will forever be associated with the wealthy noblewoman from whom he had received his title by marriage. Though it is Bartlett's name on the investor list, in all likelihood the actual capital probably came from his wife, the Baroness Burdett-Coutts, England's wealthiest woman and the greatest philanthropist of her times.

Angela Georgina Burdett-Coutts had been born into luxury in 1814, the daughter of Sir Francis Burdett and Sophia Coutts, heiress to the Coutts Bank family fortune. But a bizarre soap opera of relationships would occur before Angela could receive her legacy. First, a December-June marriage between her father and actress Harriet Mellon scandalized London society when the death of Sir Francis left Mellon in charge of the family fortune. Harriet remarried a younger nobleman, but the Burdett-Coutts estate was eventually left to Angela's disposal.

Thus it was that, in 1837, the 23-year-old Angela came into an annual income of £400,000. She refused to be an idle dilettante, however, and immediately began putting her fortune to charitable work, trying to right the Dickensian social wrongs of the day. Countless schools, churches and housing projects benefited from her personal crusade against the misery of the downtrodden. Angela's largesse was not confined to England, either. Many forgotten corners of the Empire could count on her help, even unpopular causes such as a foundation for displaced aborigines in Australia and a relief fund for refugees from the Russo-Turkish war of 1877–78.

Eventually Angela's benevolence was acknowledged by her personal friend Queen Victoria. In 1871, at the age of 57, the lady was created the Baroness Burdett-Coutts, the first woman in the Empire to receive a peerage in her own right. But in 1883, as seemed a family tradition, Angela scandalized London society. At the age of 69, she wed her personal secretary, the 29-year-old American William Ashmead Bartlett. The Yank took her name, and on the Baroness's behalf, invested in the NWC&NC.

The Baroness Angela Burdett-Coutts, the British philanthropist who also invested in the far-flung Canadian frontier. In return, a steamboat was named for her. GALT MUSEUM & ARCHIVES P19770258000

The Baroness never did set foot on Canadian soil or see the coal mines she'd financed or the city that resulted from them. She never rode on the railways her money paid for or saw the two Alberta communities, Burdett and Coutts, christened in her honour. Yet her title and her benevolence play a role in the story of steamships and rebellion.

Philanthropy and dynamic personalities aside, the coal mines were first and foremost a business, and the syndicate in faraway England expected dividends. The market selected for the Belly River coal was the fuel-hungry, finally advancing Canadian Pacific Railway. After many years of false starts, corruption scandals and extensive political infighting, the railway had begun its trek to the Pacific, the first railway designed to stitch together a new, still loosely bound Canadian nation. The dream of Sir John A. Macdonald was the reality of a barony of capitalists, among them Donald Smith. Unable to keep his fingers out of all the prairie pies, Smith invested in the Galt company too.

A contract was hammered out with the CPR to supply 20,000 tons of coal per year, and on October 13, 1882, shovels and picks attacked a seam of coal in the side of a coulee on the eastern bank of the Belly River.[1] A settlement called Coalbanks grew around the mine in the river bottom lands, a ramshackle collection of shacks and company buildings that hardly appeared on the maps of the era.

The hamlet, tucked into the cottonwoods by the banks of the Belly, was touted by boosters as "another Pittsburgh." With the railway creeping across the prairies, the yield and quality of the coal here were of national significance. But to be of any value, the coal had to get to the railhead, and the closest point on the CPR survey was over 100 miles away. The tracks were sited to reach the South Saskatchewan River at a spot where the valley widened sufficiently to enable a gradual descent to a low-level crossing. There, where the embryo of another prairie town, Medicine Hat, would emerge, a strategic bridge would carry the railway across the river on its way to Calgary and the Rockies. The townsite was chosen by CPR general manager William Cornelius Van Horne for its abundant water supply and relative proximity to the valuable mineral at Coalbanks.

But Coalbanks and Medicine Hat had but one connecting artery: the Belly River and its big brother, the South Saskatchewan. Enter the "navigation" aspect of the Galt family syndicate. In imitation of the W&WTC's plans to use Medicine Hat as an inland port, the Belly River coal fleet was created.

Crews building the bridge and laying the tracks made Medicine Hat a rough-and-tumble boomtown. Publicity surrounding the arrival of the tracks and launch of a river flotilla touted Medicine Hat as a transportation hub, a Canadian rival to Fort Benton. In a fit of boosterism, townsmen petitioned the CPR to install a swinging span in its railway bridge across the South Saskatchewan, to allow steamboats with tall smokestacks to pass. Hope sprang eternal for a region entering the age of steam.

Getting the coal to market

Theorizing that mountain-fed streamflows in the spring and early summer might make a channel deep enough to float a craft of substantial size, Elliott Galt's engineers developed plans to build a fleet of sternwheelers to float the coal to market. They consulted the best technical advice available in the port of Fort Benton, and in the spring of 1883 Galt lured that consultant from his Missouri River habitat to build his first boat, on location, right on the Belly.

Josephus Todd was described by one historian as "an old British salt who had sailed the seven seas."[2] But the rivers and the era Todd sailed are deeply steeped in Americana: the Ohio, Mississippi and Missouri, land of Huckleberry Finn and Big Mike Fink, in an age that mythologized rivermen like today's pop stars. Probably the son of Wellsville, Ohio, steamer captain John Todd, Josephus partnered with the German-born Nicholas Buesen on river craft in Columbiana County, Ohio.[3] His reputation led to working on civilian boats in service to General Ulysses S. Grant in his

Civil War campaign on the Mississippi. With the opening of the post-war West, Todd pointed his bow into the setting sun, and in the 1872 and 1873 seasons he skippered for the steamboat king, Sanford Coulson.

Coulson had founded the Missouri River Transportation Co. in 1872. Based in Yankton, an important riverport in the Dakota Territory, the company was better known as the Coulson Packet Line. The firm had many partners and shareholders, mostly Pennsylvania bankers but also seasoned rivermen like Buessen and Todd, who held partial ownership in several Coulson steamers for 11 years.[4]

Another acquaintance of Todd's was Grant Marsh, who gained national prominence for having piloted the *Far West* up the Yellowstone and Little Bighorn rivers in 1876 to evacuate the wounded from the infamous "Custer's last stand."

Relationships with legends like Buessen and Marsh were enough for any résumé, and if Todd is ignored in the pantheon of legendary Missouri River captains, it likely is only because of his "lost" years on foreign, Canadian waters.

The late 1870s and early '80s found Joe Todd most often at the wheel of the *Rosebud*, "not remiss in using strong language if crew members proved slow."[5] Besides the ordinary hazards, Todd proved adept at the grisly task of navigating past "islands made in the river by the carcasses of hundreds and hundreds of buffalo often drowned in their attempts to swim the river. This mass of dead buffalo would collect silt and branches and gravel, forming huge mounds that were most difficult to avoid. In time

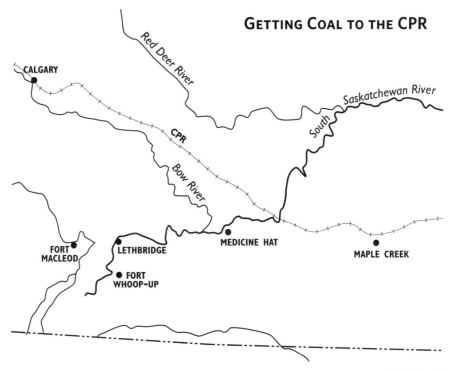

GETTING COAL TO THE CPR

GORD TOLTON

this would form a permanent island that stood quite a height in the river waterway."[6] A river pilot never knew what nature might throw at him.

When the Galts decided to navigate the Belly, Fort Benton was the best place to look for good, solid river savvy. The Coulson line had been run out of business by heightened competition, so Josephus Todd was available for hire, right off "the Bismarck to Benton run,"[7] but first he would have to construct the entire fleet from the water up.

Shortly after New Year's Day 1883, the "old salt" was appointed chief navigational officer, commissioned to supervise construction of the first ship. Josephus and other "skilled shipbuilders were brought from Yankton and Pittsburgh,"[8] including his brothers, Nelson and Wesley, and Josephus's two sons, William and John, and shipwrights Abe Whistler and Bill Hughes. The Todd crew shared a 12- by 16-foot shack, where they cooked and slept in minus 35 degree weather as they plotted and planned their boat. "One half lay in bed while the other half ate, as there was not room for them all on the floor at once."[9] As mine superintendent William Stafford and his miners scratched black diamonds from the coulees, Elliott Galt gave Todd free rein on construction of the boat.

For raw materials, Josephus and Nelson journeyed upriver into the Porcupine Hills, where the Galts had purchased a 50-square-mile timber limit. A sawmill, built in 1882 to cut shoring timbers for the mine, provided wood for the steamer and barge. "This Captain Todd seems to have been quite a fellow, and he certainly got things done."[10] Under the river captain's domineering eye, hillside cutting crews were instructed in the science of cutting jack pines for the steamer's hull. "If porcupines could talk up in the quiet Hills what grumbling must have gone among them as their hitherto uncontested territory was disturbed by the shouting Captain Todd with his mill, his bull teams, his shredding saws, and his workmen."[11] As the timber was cut, mule and bull teams freighted the lumber out of the hills to the north bank of the Oldman, near Fort Macleod.

There the Todds assembled a series of huge, flat-bottomed scows that would convey timbers to the Coalbanks where the new steamer was to be built. "Twelve barges in all were also built, six of those being 40 × 60, the six others being 30 × 40 feet. The larger barges had a carrying capacity of 100 tons each, the lesser ones that of 60 tons each."[12]

The *Macleod Gazette* eagerly documented their town's short career as a boatyard, wishfully promoting itself as a future port. "The boat being built by Capt. Todd's party on the other side of the river is making good progress. We expect a steamer to come to Macleod sometime this summer."[13] On March 26, the first of the barges was sent downstream and it arrived uneventfully. But the next one "ran on a sand bar about five miles down and considerable difficulty was experienced in getting her off."[14] It was a harbinger of things to come. On April 24, the *Gazette* reported that the barges only got as far as the junction of the Belly and the Oldman, where the heavy lumber was unloaded from the cumbersome barges and nailed together into rafts to float itself downstream.

Lumber and barges continued downriver from Fort Macleod all that spring, and the town's boosters were forecasting the arrival of a boat they would never see. "It is stated by old river men that steamboats can come to Macleod for three months of the year. Some work needs to be done on the river, particularly from Kipp down, and it is hoped that the government will make an appropriation for the purpose."[15] No such funding would ever materialize, but that didn't stop the dreamers: "These barges experience no difficulty in getting down to the Coalbanks and we shall expect to see a steamer come up just as easily."[16] A nice fantasy, but there was little motivation for the Galts to send the steamers further upriver. Fort Macleod would never be an inland port.

As Nelson Todd divided his time between the Macleod boatyard and the Porcupine sawmill, Josephus returned to the riverbank near the Coalbanks mine, to set up another boatyard and lay out a flat-bottomed subframe on the gravelly shore. Soon a genuine Missouri-style river steamboat took shape on the flats, 173 feet long (or 175, depending on the source)[17] and 30 feet wide. Any materials not available onsite or from Fort Benton came by bull team from wherever the CPR's track then ended.

Construction attracted attention even from an officer of the British Royal Navy. Warrant Officer Peter Wellington wrote for a description of the boat from his young nephew, Brit Stephens, who lived in the coulee near the site. After relating the dimensions, the boy quite accurately described the steamers habitat: "The river they have here is very narrow and crooked, and the current runs at the rate of six miles per hour. The river is full of boulders and sand bars, and the art of navigation is looking on the water and telling which is the deepest water, I have been told it takes considerable practice to learn to navigate these rivers. There are only about three months in the year when the river is navigable. Pilots on boat get £30 per month."[18]

The first of the fleet was christened the *Baroness*, in honour of Angela Burdett-Coutts, free-wheeling patroness of the company.

River operations commence

As the barges that brought the lumber to Coalbanks were fitted to carry coal, a wharf was built and a short line track laid from the mine to the river to facilitate the loading of the barges. The CPR was demanding the Galt coal, to replace the expensive Pennsylvania carbon it was importing, and Galt's venture had to recover from the initial start-up costs. With his investors nipping at his heels, Sir Alexander demanded that Coalbanks coal be delivered, steamship or no steamship, so from May through July, fleets of unpowered barges loaded with bitumen were rafted downriver. Mounted policeman Tom Clarke viewed, with curiosity and optimism, a typical journey on the unpowered, coal-laden scows: "The barges were loaded and, one after the other, were sent adrift and borne by the current to their destination. A crew of four men accompanied each barge. To keep her in the centre of the stream, four large sweeps were necessary, two at the bow and two others at the stern, each being controlled by a single arm, no difficulty being experienced avoiding shoals and other obstructions met with here and there on the journey."[19]

Clarke makes the operation sound easy, but the hundred-ton scows often ran aground. The same diarist records the travails of a rafting barge hung up on an unforgiving boulder causing a two-day delay and no small amount of effort. "Finally a heavy hawser (cable) was put entirely round her, a block and tackle was rigged up and taken ashore and secured to a cottonwood tree. A powerful team of mules was attached and pulled and tugged for a long time in vain. After hours of strenuous labour, the men working up to their waists in the ice-cold water, an extra heavy side-wise heave wrenched the vessel from the obstruction and she floated clear …"[20]

The process was costly for the workers, though the company was not unsympathetic to the men's ordeal in the chilly river. "Benumbed with their long submersion in the stream, the men climbed aboard, all feeling having left their lower extremities. Each man was then handed a quart bottle of liquor, the gift of Alexander Galt, the only condition attached to the gift being that only after the refloating of the barge could the liquor be used. Five men accepted the … liquor, drinking it down as if it were water and feeling no after effects so chilled were they, but the sixth man could not be persuaded to accept it and his share went to two of the others."

Even so, pneumonia did claim one of the labourers: "The temperate man contracted fever followed by pneumonia as a result of the exposure he had under gone and died shortly after his arrival at the Hat. He was the first man to be buried in the town's newly laid out cemetery. The liquor might have spared his life. Who knows?"[21]

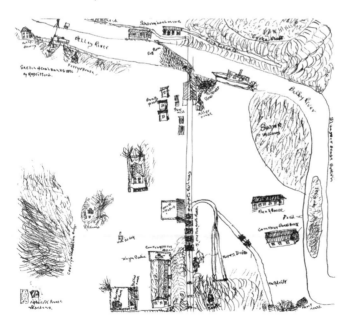

Sketch of the Lethbridge/Coalbanks mine and shipyards on the Belly River flats, drawn by R.H. Stafford, son of the mine superintendent. GALT MUSEUM & ARCHIVES P196405060001

On June 25, 1883, Captain Todd launched the *Baroness* into the Belly River for the hull's shakedown run. She arrived on July 2, just in time for Medicine Hat's first-ever Dominion Day celebration.[22] The first steamboat either city would ever see arrived to receive her machinery. But the celebration was marred when an early evening windstorm threatened the clapboard village. Gale force winds left most of the buildings in town shaken but unhurt. The same could not be said for the barges. Elliott Galt and Josephus Todd were quick to instruct their crews to tie the *Baroness* and most of the barges hard and fast to the shore. But the rivermen could not secure two of the scows, which were heavily laden with newly arrived coal. The barges were swept over and their costly cargo went to the bottom of the South Saskatchewan. Newspapers reported, "their loss cannot be less than four or five thousand dollars,"[23] a fortune in 1883, particularly for a fledgling operation that was yet to see any revenue.

Shrugging off that ordeal, the crew set to with hammers, bars, wrenches and winches to install the *Baroness*'s power plants and construct the crucial sternwheel. A CPR freight delivered a pair of 49-horsepower high pressure horizontal steam engines manufactured by Rees & Sons in Pittsburgh. Each of the twin cylinders was 15 inches in diameter and had a power stroke of five feet. Installation of the engines, boilers and giant smokestacks took a month. The only initial fault Todd could find was that the pump feeding the boilers was too small to keep up with the water required. But the syndicate had deep pockets, and a new pump was ordered.

A serious flaw in the *Baroness*'s construction was discovered when "it was found that the six-inch copper pipe conducting steam to the engine was six inches too long."[24] Scarcely believing he could have made such an error, Captain Todd carefully measured the ship from bow to stern. He was astounded to discover the hull did not measure 175 feet as he'd believed. The *Baroness* measured exactly 174 feet 6 inches, short by exactly the extra length of the steam-conductor!

Such a problem should seem trivial to machinists. Cut off the offending length and weld it up. The closest thing to a hacksaw was obtained and the tube was cut. But there was still the matter of reinstalling the flange to make the connection steam-tight. The proper precision tool capable of reattaching the tube was not something to be found in the average 1883 blacksmith kit. But in the same great Western tradition dictating that a rock can be used for a hammer, a solution was found. The engineer took to "babbiting," or welding the tube's joint with babbit metal, a soft, white alloy of tin, copper and antimony. The lack of proper tools showed when the steam valve was opened, and when the boilers attained a pressure of 200 psi, the minute pinholes in the welded joint hissed and screamed.

For Captain Todd, the timing couldn't have been worse. Standing on the boat was none other than his boss, Sir Alexander Galt himself, come west for the inaugural maiden voyage of his flagship. And standing beside the pompous magnate was the crafty, white-bearded tycoon Donald Smith, in Medicine Hat to inspect railway progress and congratulate Sir Alexander on his endeavour.

Some canny technician among the deckhands stepped forward and offered a solution. Unfortunately, Tom Clarke named neither the hand nor the miracle used to rectify the malfunction. "It fell to the lot of an ingenious member of the ship's company to handle the situation and he made a splendid job of it, being warmly congratulated by both Alexander Galt and Donald Smith, who showed their appreciation by liberally rewarding him. In addition to this, he won a good-sized bet by successfully carrying out the task assigned him."[25] Whatever it was the hand did, it was to the relief of all—the embarrassed Galt, the perplexed Todd and of course the steam-conduction line itself.

On August 6, 1883, Todd prepared for a grand maiden voyage, to the fork of the Belly and the Bow. With boilers and engines fully functioning, the *Baroness* weighed 202 tons, yet drew only 18 inches of water. Boarding the newly dedicated vessel were Galt, Smith and a bevy of corporate secretaries and executives. Constable Tom Clarke was along for the ride, noting the presence of "125 tons of farm machinery . . . which was unloaded on the river bottom at the end of the run. Who the machinery was for or where it went from there we never knew." Historian John Higinbotham, however, knew that "the implements were unloaded and forwarded overland by bull team to Macleod."[26] Camping overnight at the "Grand Forks," the steamer returned to Medicine Hat with its cargo of dignitaries.

A day later the *Baroness* made her steam-powered return to Coalbanks, with barges in tow. But the big problem for the rest of the 1883 navigation season was going to be that temperamental river with the seasonal mood swings. Though drawing only 18 inches, the vessel fully loaded grossed 320 tons and nearly hit bottom. The river fell rapidly after cresting on June 20, and the *Baroness*, unable to travel loaded in the channel, was resigned to just bumping the barges on the return trip downstream. Tom Clarke described the trip: "They [the barges] were gathered about the parent vessel in a peculiar fashion. Two were placed tandem in front of the stern, the other four, two on each side followed, and occupying less than one-half of the forward end of the vessel. Thus they were pushed instead of being towed as is the usual custom."[27]

The *Minnow* and the *Baroness* docked at Medicine Hat, their coal barges off the bow. The CPR bridge yielded to the fleet by including a hinged span that could be swung open to allow the tall smokestacks to pass through. GALT MUSEUM & ARCHIVES P19770217000-GP

Despite the implementation of the *Baroness,* less than 200 tons were delivered in 1883, due to low water and the short time the *Baroness* could safely float on the river's 18 inches of water. But the Galts were undaunted and persuaded their shareholders that the fate of the plan rested in building an additional freighter and purchasing another. Construction began at Medicine Hat in the fall of 1883.

The new steamer was to be named *Alberta*, after Princess Louise Caroline Alberta. The christening was more than just a gesture. The Princess and the Marquis of Lorne were recent visitors, the first such royalty to touch the plains. A poem written by the bardish Governor General bequeathed her name to the Territorial District and ultimately the province. As Lorne was coming to the end of his term, the Galts commemorated the Lornes' return to England by recalling the viceregal's lines: "By thy dear name to be hereafter known. Alberta shall it be!"[28]

And *Alberta* it was. The new steamer was scaled down, 100 feet long by 20 feet wide. The difference in size between the *Alberta* and *Baroness* was influenced by the use of imported building materials, as opposed to the domestic lumber used in the first boat. The Porcupine Hills jackpine, while a serviceable and efficient milling wood, was soft and tended to wear fast. The *Alberta* would be built from sturdier Minnesota oak shipped on the CPR. Unlike the *Baroness*'s flat bottom, the *Alberta* was constructed with an actual keel, which allowed six inches less draft.

Again Rees & Sons of Pittsburgh were contracted to build the engines, similar to the sister ship's, with a combined rating of 30 horsepower. Wesley Todd was to pilot the new ship, and assisted in construction. When the *Alberta* was ready to sail, on April 15, 1884, it weighed 86 tons and had a gross capacity of 150 tons. Relative to its reduced size, the *Alberta* was more powerful and more manoeuvrable, and "the *Baroness* was never as successful as the *Alberta* in navigating these uncertain rivers."[29]

The NWC&NC also realized a need for a tugboat to assist the two large steamers in navigating the shoals in the Belly and the South Saskatchewan. Such a craft was found at the boatyards of Rat Portage (present-day Kenora, Ontario), and was quickly snapped up by the Galts. A mere 73 feet long by 10 feet wide, the *Minnow*, as the tiny sternwheeler was dubbed, was loaded aboard a flatcar and shipped to Medicine Hat.

Though the *Minnow*'s engines yielded a paltry six horsepower, photos show the power plant was nearly as large as the 16-ton boat itself, a dynamo relative to the hull's diminutive size. The vessel was launched four days after the *Alberta*, piloted by Nelson Todd. The gentle-born Galt family may have held the wallet, but the water-bred Todd clan controlled their navy.

When the new armada arrived at Coalbanks in the spring for loading, few were as curious as the nearby Blood Indians. Seeing the "fire canoes" on their home river aroused no small amount of interest, and the bands "expressed a desire to see the wonderful sight and permission was given them to leave the reserve for that purpose. Their arrival created no little excitement amongst the workmen; many of them had never seen an Indian. The motley bunch was first observed making its way down the steep slopes west of the Sheran mine and appeared endless in number." The sight of an Indian camp so near their settlement alarmed the workers of Coalbanks, their attitudes reinforced by the lurid tales of their grandfathers. "The natives pitched their tents further up the stream, contenting themselves for the while at a safe distance. Their timidity wore off in a day or two, and by degrees they began to show up around the mine, becoming considerable of a nuisance, as they diverted the attention of the workmen, obstructing the work that was being gone on with."[30]

With 17 barges, the fleet prepared for the first full-fledged season of coal transport. The *Baroness* and the *Alberta* could each transport 500 tons between their cargo space onboard and the barges that were pushed, pulled or lashed alongside. The *Minnow* was employed mostly for tugging, but also to assist in warping off shoals or relieving loads when necessary. Presumably the *Minnow* would also tow a barge of its own.

But the 1884 season revealed how horrifyingly flawed the whole scheme truly was. The trips were too slow and the river level was unreliable. The necessary high water did not arrive until May 24. Sir Alexander Galt fussed and fumed that for all his vaunted power, his money could not fight the river: "In 1884 I waited at Medicine Hat for water till after the twenty-fourth of May, and by the twenty-eighth of June our boats and barges were tied up for the season."[31] The river crested by June 8, and had completely receded by the summer solstice. The entire shipping season had lasted only 33 days. While a loaded steamer could make the distance from the mine to Medicine Hat in eight hours, the return trip could take as long as five days in fighting the upstream current, burning huge amounts of scarce firewood and coal, its own cargo. When the river ran low, the silt and gravel deposits threatened the fleet's progress, "sticking now and again on sand bars and having multifarious adventures on the way."[32]

One writer states that "the boats required more coal to get back to Lethbridge from Medicine Hat than they hauled from Lethbridge in the first place,"[33] a humorous exaggeration, yet illustrative of the inefficiencies of the steamboat experiment. Deckhand D.J. Whitney Sr. remembered that "we were continually running out of fuel for our boilers, and as there were seams of coal along the riverbanks we dug out coal and packed it in sacks down to the boat."[34] For the most part, despite the luxury of coal, steam crews had to resort to good old-fashioned woodhawking. "I can recall on one occasion … that we stopped and sawed down two or three big cottonwood trees. They were dead trees, dry and hard and made excellent fuel, which we found superior to the soft surface coal."[35]

The steamer network of the upper reaches was deemed even more inefficient than its cousins on the main branches. In the 1884 navigation season, the NWC&NC steamers and their 25 barges made 17 trips between Coalbanks and Medicine Hat, the *Baroness* accomplishing nine runs, the *Alberta* eight. Less than 4,000 tons were delivered on a contract that called for 20,000. Competition was looming for a fuel contract the network seemed incapable of fulfilling. The answer was clear: to feed a railway the Galts would have to build a railway. In light of the company's need to fulfill their

(Left) At the South Saskatchewan waterfront of Medicine Hat, Captain Todd's workmen put the steamer *Alberta* into shape in the spring of 1884. GALT MUSEUM & ARCHIVES P197381500000-GP.

(Right) The *Minnow*, its machinery, sternwheel and pilot house yet to be installed, is launched into the South Saskatchewan at Medicine Hat, 1884. GALT MUSEUM & ARCHIVES P19760238103

contract, and expand to take in new orders, the NWC&NC announced plans in January of 1885 to build a narrow-gauge track from Coalbanks to the CPR railhead at Dunmore. Work was begun early in the spring, and construction continued throughout 1885.

The Galt line would eventually make its shareholders wealthy through further endeavours in coal, railways and land development. The town surrounding the Coalbanks mine would move to the top of the coulee and be incorporated as Lethbridge. But the technology that had for two years inspired the Belly River fleet totally doomed their very existence.

The boats remained tied up for the rest of the summer of 1884, their crews laid off. In the fall, the idle Galt fleet was joined by the *Northcote*, all of them beached on the bank of the South Saskatchewan at Medicine Hat. Ironically the *Northcote's* masters were also seeking an alliance with the CPR to keep their own fleet viable, but the low waters of the 1884 season were as disastrous for the Winnipeg & Western as for the NWC&NC. The W&WTC offered the *Northcote* to the Galt family, but were politely refused; Sir Alexander and Elliott Galt had had enough of navigation. The boats had already outlived their usefulness, and steamboat days on the South Saskatchewan River were at an end, doomed as an experimental footnote to history.

The fleet's last days as coal freighters were captured in an 1884 visit by Montreal photographer William Notman Jr. On a whirlwind tour to capture the vistas of the frontier, Notman produced a spectacular portrait of the *Baroness* and the *Minnow* tied up near the CPR bridge. The photograph is stunning in its clarity, and in it, intentionally or not, Notman succinctly summarized a key moment in industrial history: the river boats face to face with the railway that killed them.

But as the winter of 1884 became the spring of 1885, war drums far downstream summoned the steamers into service. Before the ice went out, the battle of Duck Lake gave the coal fleet a new role to play, and Galt's steamers prepared for war.

CHAPTER FOUR

A Tale of Two River Revolts

Triumph to tribulation: the disastrous navigation season of 1884

When the Winnipeg & Western and the Galts embarked on their steamboat adventure, they expected the government to share their vision. Improvements were needed on the rivers to remove hazards such as boulders that could chew up hulls like kindling, rapids that took days to ascend, and shallow channels that stopped ships dead in the water. The HBC's land commissioner, C.J. Brydges, nagged the government about its responsibility to upgrade conditions in the West to foster commerce, especially HBC commerce. Though Sir John A.'s people promised capital to dredge the main channels, remove stones and construct small dams, the river really needed more improvements to be friendlier to shipping. Reports were written and money was promised, but little practical work was done. Steamboat operators were on their own against the river.

Those operators included some of the most capable captains of the river networks of the U.S. and Canada. Steamboating was an adventure, and pilots and masters tended to be of a breed that psychologically needs to live on the edge. Mere steady employment wasn't enough; they had to challenge new rivers, and be challenged. Folks like Pennsylvania-born Aaron Raymond Russell, who followed the waterways west until he hit the Red in 1871 as a mate and later a captain. When the Saskatchewan beckoned, Russell took command of the *Manitoba*, a ship nearly as old as the *Northcote*, which the cantankerous Jerry Webber still ruled.

In 1882, Webber made the run from Grand Rapids to Edmonton in a record 14 days, with 75 passengers and 51 tons of cargo, whipping the *Northcote* up the hazardous Coles Falls in a day and half, normally a four-day chore. Not to be outdone, James Sheets took the throne of the *North West* on July 12, 1882, taking great sentimental interest in the huge boat after landing 180 tons of freight at Edmonton in 15 days. He would've beat Webber's record had the crew not lost 72 hours rebuilding the paddle wheels. Sheets's skill was proved on his second trip, when the current proved too strong and threatened to suck the ship down the Grand Rapids, which would surely have been fatal to boat and occupants. As the Reverend Abraham Crowley watched and waited to meet his Maker, Jim Sheets fought the river and "kept cool & self-possessed, ordering the anchor to be ready as soon as the wheel was free, [and] plied the steamer in great force, brought the vessel round & stemmed the current right nobly."[1] With such leadership, newspapers started calling the *North West* the "greyhound of the Saskatchewan."

In the 1883 season the river retaliated, and the news wasn't good for the captains, the companies or the towns that depended on the riverboats. Near Cumberland Lake, ice jams blocked the river, carving a new course that left a wild maze. Fifty miles of riverbed dried up, as the channel diverged into several new pathways and offshoots from the lake, at one point even drifting into the smaller Sturgeon River. Now the river did not so much run as ooze, into a series of marshes. The challenge to pilots was shallower, hazardous waters. A new course to Cumberland House had to be blazed, a trip through hell called "the Cutoff."

Finding the path wasted time and risked the boats. Jerry Webber barely nursed the *Northcote* through. Finally, Aaron Russell on the *Manitoba* mapped a decent channel through the Sturgeon River. But the season was complicated by a cool summer that released little meltwater from the mountain snowpack. Levels dropped and the boats had to finish the season early. Mountains of cargo were left at Cumberland House and Grand Rapids while Prince Albert fell short of provisions. Land freighters from Fort Victoria and Edmonton made up the shortfalls, but townsmen dependent on the river trade lost all confidence in the steamers.

Also that year, the *Northcote* hit a rock, forcing it into drydock at Fort Pitt for repairs. The loss of the flagship sounded the need for the river to have a deeper channel dredged if such time-wasting calamities were to be avoided in future. The Department of Public Works reacted, and Russell's *Manitoba* delivered a crew and materials to build

Bows of the Hudson's Bay Company's steamer *Northcote*, showing gear for lifting her off shoals. Sydney Hall, August 26, 1881. LIBRARY & ARCHIVES CANADA C-012961

two "snag scows," specialized boats designed to excavate the channel and remove rocks. One snag worked the North Saskatchewan from Edmonton to Prince Albert, scooping and blasting the river, removing boulders as large as 10,000 pounds. The other scow worked downstream from Prince Albert on the dangerous Cole's Falls. But the crews' equipment was too fragile to cut a channel into the hard gravel, and in many cases the scow could not even reach the boulders in the rapids. In all, over $23,000 was spent on the operation in 1883 and 1884, but the effort was wasteful and half-hearted, as the snags never had the resources or equipment to make much difference.

The irony was that the cash dedicated for river improvements was but a ripple compared to the waves of subsidies granted to the railway. The best the W&WTC could hope to do was to scrutinize their concerns more intently. But the retirement of its general manager, Captain Holcombe, and the firing of Peter McArthur left a vacuum of leadership. The company's prime shareholder, the HBC, insisted on an overseer to streamline the fleet, so on the advice of Holcombe a man was resurrected from the past.

John B. Davis was the luckless captain who'd foundered the *Freighter* in 1859 trying to find the Red River. He was now "an experienced officer of some thirty-five years in the transport business."[2] The 1870s found him contracting for war duty on the Missouri. The hostilities between natives and the U.S. Army that caused the spectacular demise of Custer in 1876 were proving to be a boon to Missouri River steamship companies. The Sioux, Cheyenne and Nez Perce tribes were being hunted relentlessly. Although General Nelson Miles built Fort Keogh on the Yellowstone, U.S. commanders required more options for moving military goods. They chose to use the steamboat fleets readily at hand. On March 15, 1877, no fewer than 20 different interests gathered in St. Paul to file tenders for the lucrative government contract.

The leading bidders were relatively old hands on the Missouri, but William Davidson of St. Paul, and his Keokuk Northern Packet Line, was an outsider from the Mississippi fold. To assist with the bid, Davidson hired a representative, John Davis, who was just as green on the Missouri as himself. Offering to ferry the goods for 14¢ per 100 pounds on the main branch, and 57½¢ for the more problematic Yellowstone, Davis's penny-splitting tender was the low bid,[3] and was rewarded by the grant of the 1877 military contract for the Department of Dakota.[4] Davidson established the Yellowstone Transportation Co. (YTC) in Bismarck to ship nearly 8,000 tons of cargo. But the contract was a disaster. Captain Davis's towed barges grounded in the low waters of the Upper Missouri and Yellowstone;[5] his crews knew nothing about mountain rivers; and one ship, the *Osceola,* was smashed by a tornado.[6] Defaulting on the contract, the YTC lost the 1878 tender and went bankrupt. Davis lost his job, and his whereabouts remained unknown for some years afterward. Surfacing in Winnipeg in 1884, he was named superintendent of the W&WTC Saskatchewan fleet. Now in charge of a line even more tempestuous than the YTC, Davis proved to have the same bad luck as before, and his new command was troubled as he braved another new river.

A boom was on at Prince Albert, with new lumber and flour mills giving hope for the town to become a riverport of great economic importance. With the arrival of the railway to the South Saskatchewan, thought turned to supplying Prince Albert from Medicine Hat. That brought the launch of the Scottish-built *Lily*, the first test of the navigability of the South Branch.

On July 18, 1883, the HBC "sold" the *Lily* to the W&WTC for $25,000, though the sale was actually only a transfer, since signing over the *Lily* gave the HBC controlling interest in the shipping concern. The ink wasn't even dry on the deal when newspaper ads were already touting the *Lily* to "run between Prince Albert and Medicine Hat during the season of navigation."[7] John Davis was aboard in his new job, and the salty John Segers, hired away from the Red River, was at the helm when the *Lily* left Prince Albert to ascend the South Branch. At Saskatoon, the temperance colony cheered the *Lily*'s arrival, and settlers scrambled to snap up real estate, anticipating that the town would become a northern St. Louis. But the din died down the further upriver the *Lily* crawled.

Past Saskatchewan Landing, the poles and winches came out as water became scarcer and sandbars more numerous. Scant miles from Medicine Hat, the boat lost one of its four rudders, and a barge was abandoned. These were small complications compared to what happened on the return trip. On August 28, loaded with 50 tons of bacon for Prince Albert stores, the *Lily* embarked on a river that had dropped six inches during the month-long demurrage. Davis and Segers were optimistic they could reach Prince Albert, but 40 miles downstream, confidence turned to horror when a submerged boulder ripped an eight-foot gash into the starboard side.

In minutes, the *Lily* sank in what rivermen and locals call the Drowning Ford. As hands and passengers abandoned ship, the vessel settled into a meagre three feet of water. No lives were lost and the bacon was saved, but the wreck's location in a

A rare photo of the *Lily* (mistaken as the *Alberta*) at the Medicine Hat waterfront, identifiable by its single funnel and unique caged sternwheel. ARCHIVES OF MANITOBA/ROSS BEST COLLECTION N13049

valley with steep banks made recovery impossible. Some machinery was salvaged, but the rest of the ship was abandoned, its registry returned and cancelled later that year. Another John Davis gamble gone bust. Undaunted, the W&WTC announced they would "continue to use the South Branch"[8] the following season and the flagship *Northcote* was brought in to do the job intended for the lost *Lily*.

But the 1884 season proved even more dreadful economically, as the new railway the navigators hoped to ally with cut into the freight work. Confidence in the steamboat network evaporated with the summer freshets. The misfortunes of 1883 had made shippers leery of river delivery, and tonnages plummeted. The river itself denied the start of season, as low water in the swamps of the Cut-Off isolated Grand Rapids from the main stream. For some weeks, the *North West* had to travel with half loads, while the *Marquis* beached in the Cut-Off.

The lack of freight forced Davis to cancel all trips to Edmonton but one. The *Edmonton Bulletin* wisecracked that bacon landed in 1884 had left Winnipeg in 1881. When Aaron Russell's *Manitoba* delivered a single load of lumber and shingles to Prince Albert, that was the sum total of his entire season.

At the beginning of the 1884 season, a jack of all trades named Donald G. MacIvor, who had "been in the army in Scotland for twelve years,"[9] joined the *Northcote* crew at Prince Albert, signing on as fireman. On the ship's first upriver trip that year, the crew was hired to install a cable for the Batoche ferry: "seven strands of seven wires in each strand,"[10] modernizing the pole-driven scow that previously had served the Carlton Trail crossing. Ferryman Alex Fisher was ecstatic, and the *Northcote* crew sailed on to Medicine Hat, oblivious that the cable would ever be turned back on them, or that deckhands and ferrymen could one day become enemies.

Another ferryman watched the steamboat experiment with some irritation. Gabriel Dumont was a living legend on the prairies, veteran captain of the Métis buffalo hunts and a man who could truly be said to be the soul of the prairie. Activity on the carting trails had created the need for a ferry, and in 1872 Dumont took a homestead and established a crossing on the summer trail from Humboldt. His boat was a crude, flat-bottomed scow, 23 feet long by 12 feet wide, propelled with oars and kept on course with a long rope stretched across the 200-yard reach. One traveller described the crossing this way: "Our animals were unhitched, the carriage and cart put in the centre of the boat, the mules on one side, the horses on the other. Gabriel gave some instructions by signs and some doubtful French. The mules were very obstinate and troublesome to put on board … Each of our party undertook to row with an unyielding oar, first keeping along the shore and working upstream; fortunately, the wind was favourable, which counteracted the force of the rapid current."[11]

Dumont's fares were moderate, 25¢ per single wagon, 20¢ for horse and rider, 10¢ for livestock and single passengers, and 2¢ per hundredweight of freight. These tolls may sound trivial to us, but in the currency of the day they provided a good living for the old hunter, supplemented by revenue from his store and poolroom nearby. It was a good location, as the wide river reach had an average depth of 8 to 15 feet. By 1884, Gabriel Dumont was a wealthy man in frontier terms, highly respected as a leader of men, and a generous soul who denied a helping hand to no one.

In the face of the steamboat travails of 1884, the floundering town of Saskatoon, at another ferry crossing, gave rise to another navigational experiment. The Temperance Colonization Society had founded the community as a proving ground for their utopian ideals. But the village needed lumber and raw materials to build their paradise on the South Saskatchewan. Such goods could be purchased at Prince Albert mills or brought in by rail from Moose Jaw, but colonists winced at the thought of hauling such volume by team to their new home. So in spite of the problems faced by more experienced enterprises, the temperance colony weighed their options and decided to float their lumber in.

With most prairie sailors up to their knees in river sand, petition was made to a ship's captain to take on the commission. E. Shelton Andrews was no frontier salt, but a career Atlantic seaman from St. Andrews by the Sea, New Brunswick. He had worked on ocean-going vessels from the time he could stand on a deck, and had earned his papers at a naval academy in Belfast, Ireland. But time had stricken him with arthritis, and he was forced to seek a drier climate. When Andrews received word of a piloting job in a temperance town on the far prairies, he must have figured you just couldn't get much drier than that. To the pioneers along the South Branch, Andrews, with his full beard and heavy overcoat, looked every inch a sea captain, and for all they knew, a river captain.

Andrews accepted $100 a month plus expenses, but first had to select his ship. In the spring of 1884, he visited Selkirk, Manitoba, shipbuilding centre of the West, where he purchased the diminutive *May Queen*, and had it hauled by rail to Medicine Hat. Despite its small size, the *Queen* drew five feet of water by the time a barge full of lumber was tied on. Embarking on May 7, 1884, Andrews soon learned he was not in the Maritimes anymore, as he navigated the sandbars, rocks and shifting streambeds. At least there were no icebergs. Andrews reached Saskatoon two weeks later, with no confidence he could make a return trip against the current. But that was okay with E. Shelton. The tranquility of the prairie agreed with the captain; he dropped anchor in Saskatoon, filed a homestead and never left.

The *Northcote*'s first season on the South Branch didn't start until July 15, held back at Prince Albert not by low water but in anticipation of a possible sale to the Galts. Finally, after being accidentally sunk and refloated in port, the *Northcote*, under John Segers's command, reached Medicine Hat in 17 painful days, including stringing the ferry cable at Batoche. Its season was over before it began. With nothing else to do, Segers pulled the *Northcote* ashore at Medicine Hat and grounded it alongside the hapless coal fleet. Medicine Hat's waterfront was becoming known for its beached whales. Donald MacIvor was laid off but soon found work "when I became known in town [and] engaged as a blacksmith"[12] in the nearby Saskatchewan Coal Mine.

Sir Stafford Northcote's dream was a nightmare for Saskatchewan sailors, especially after the accountants got through auditing the ravages of 1884. The W&WTC, at their high point, could realize a $125,000 profit[13] in a season's first haul, supplying northern fur posts. But railway competition plunged freight rates to a rockbottom $2.50 per hundred pounds; by comparison, the *North West* shipped 500 tons to Edmonton, for a gross of around $24,000 and no mention of profit. The shortage of ship space and the vagaries of the river often meant some freight had to be unloaded at downstream depots and reloaded later to reach its destination. This double handling of cargo was costly to the balance sheet. Margins were down overall for the HBC, and the resignation of its second chief commissioner, James Grahame, had been requested

Joseph Wrigley, new-style businessman hired to head the archaic Hudson's Bay Company as trade commissioner, which made him responsible for the Saskatchewan River steam fleet.
ARCHIVES OF MANITOBA

the previous year. Both Grahame and his predecessor, Donald Smith, had worked their way up through the company ranks virtually from the fur-trading counters, but self-interest and personal business dabblings had made them liabilities in such a crucial position. The HBC board decided a stricter, more businesslike manner of thinking was required in Winnipeg, so they did the unthinkable: they hired outside the company.

Joseph Wrigley had been introduced to the HBC Board of Governors by a personal connection of family friends. He was a Yorkshireman, 25 years old when the HBC noticed him as president of the Huddersfield Chamber of Commerce, at the centre of England's wool and textile industry. The Wrigleys were an established name in the Huddersfield milling district, and Joseph entered the business himself after graduating from Rugby College. He and his brother Norman had not been in the family mill long when the death of their father left them the business. When sales of Wrigley products declined, the brothers detached their emotions and sold the company. Freed from the rag trade, Wrigley took the chair of the chamber, promoting Huddersfield products on missions to Russia and France.[14]

The HBC was impressed with Wrigley's credentials, his willingness to adapt to alien climates, and his youthful enthusiasm to learn a business undergoing such radical change. Accenting that the HBC was evolving, its foreign head of operations was to be not so much a territorial czar as previous "in-country" potentates had been, but a representative charged with turning immediate profits. The word "chief" was dropped from the title and Joseph Wrigley was appointed the company's Canadian "trade commissioner" on June 8, 1884. Wrigley moved his family to Winnipeg in August, arriving just in time to wade into the mess of the navigation season and the growing political unrest on the Saskatchewan River.

HBC's control of the W&WTC made Wrigley the president of the navigation company as well. Early in his tenure, he decided that a fleet without freight hardly needed a $4,000-per-year commodore. And so it was that on November 26, 1884, John Davis's position was abolished and he was once again unemployed, a victim of the feast-or-famine nature of his career. Davis had been fired before, lack of tenure being part and parcel of the trade, and so he bided his time in Winnipeg, where by spring he could find some kind of vessel to skipper.

In Davis's stead, captain James Sheets became superintendent of the line, pulling double duty in addition to being captain of the *North West*. His first duties were in Prince Albert: to modify the boats and resecure the *North West*'s sagging hog chains, and adapt all of the ships to accommodate a more cumbersome payload. With milled construction lumber for growing villages the most profitable shipping commodity, Sheets took a saw to the *Marquis*'s lavish cabins, cutting them down to allow more cargo space on an open deck. Financial corners had to be cut as well, and Wrigley decided that only the *North West* would operate in 1885. The *Marquis* would be fired up only if there was any work for it, while the *Northcote* and the *Manitoba* could rot in drydock for all he cared.

Supplying goods for settlements and northern posts was profitable only when the boats remained the only game in town. The steamers had only a short time to capitalize on their position before the trains put them out of business altogether. After the 1884 navigation season, the writing was already on the wall. Token public works expenditures for channel improvement were meaningless, and the government had little interest in the river. Attention was on other modes of transportation, with funds and subsidies in the pockets of the railways. Farther west, the Galts similarly saw slim prospects, and reinvested their transportation budget into rails.

With maybe only one meagre season foreseeable, the steamers put in to winter port. The *North West* was pulled up onto the bank near Prince Albert, while the *Manitoba* and the *Marquis* put in to the mouth of the Sturgeon (Shell) River, a tributary just west of town. The ships began their long winter's sleep, tended at the Sturgeon by a single watchman in a ramshackle cabin on shore, where Captain Julian Dougall began a lonely vigil.

If not for a violent trick of fate, 1884 would have seen the swan song of the sternwheelers. But the logs of the 1884 shipping season would not note the dénouement of 1885. Likely the captains and crews had heard of the discontent among the Métis and among the Cree and Stoney around Battleford. But did they know that four riders from Batoche had travelled to the St. Peter's Mission in northern Montana to seek the aid of the schoolteacher there? The teacher returned with them to the old North West, and Louis Riel's subsequent activities would draw the wrath of the Canadian government. Would Julian Dougall understand that his solitary winter's nap would foreshadow a war as Riel laid his plans for revolt? Dougall's colleagues held no hope for any navigation season at all in 1885. They sought work elsewhere, and found it half a world away.

Prelude on the Nile

Charles George "Chinese" Gordon was a true adventurer of the Victorian era, a British Army general who exemplified military professionalism with distinguished service in India, Egypt and the Crimea. He had gained his nickname during an expedition to China in 1860 to help capture Beijing, and he later won victories as commander of imperial Chinese forces in the Taiping Rebellion. As a fighting officer of the first order, he was respected by politician and soldier alike, ready to serve his Queen anytime, anywhere. Among his colleagues were career army commanders like Garnet Wolseley, William Butler, Frederick Middleton and Thomas Strange. Among his close friends was the Baroness Angela Burdett-Coutts.

In 1873, the Khedive of Egypt installed Gordon as governor of Egyptian-controlled Sudan. The interests of Britain were to support the Khedive's occupation, and four years later, he was named Governor General of the Sudan. He served from 1877 to 1880, before returning to England, but returned in 1884, again at the service of the Khedive, whose holdings were at stake. A fundamentalist revolt against Egypt's rule was raging and the city of Khartoum was threatened by troops led by Muslim leader Muhammad Ahmed, better known as the Mahdi.

In 1883, with patriotism and religious fervour his weapons, the Mahdi had begun his quest to send the Egyptians packing. The situation was mostly a lost cause and few had any heart to sacrifice British blood for parched sand on behalf of the Khedive. So Gordon's mission was to let the Mahdi have Sudan, tidy up affairs in Khartoum and withdraw British and Egyptian officials and soldiers. But somehow Gordon changed his mission, and tried to repel the Mahdi with his tiny garrison. The enraged Mahdi discarded political niceties, and any respect for Gordon. Weeks after Gordon's arrival in early 1884, the Mahdist army overran and occupied Khartoum, cutting off retreat, leaving the general and staff as virtual hostages.

The British public was outraged, and exerted pressure on the government of Prime Minister William Gladstone to rescue Gordon. Little matter that the general may have ignited his own fire, or that his actions were nearly mercenary. Right or wrong, Gordon was a beloved native son, and his captivity was not to be tolerated. Among those sounding the alarm was the Baroness Burdett-Coutts, who spent days lobbying Gladstone and waging a war of words in the pages of the *London Times* to motivate the government. At Burdett-Coutts's own expense, a volunteer movement was struck to raise a force, even employing daring couriers to covertly deliver words of encouragement to the besieged general. Besides the morale, Baroness Angela anteed up £200,000 as ransom to the Mahdi.

After much dithering, Gladstone ordered a relief expedition, naming General Garnet Wolseley to command. Wolseley, like Gordon, had seen the world on the British Army's ticket. But where Gordon's name had been made in Asian and African theatres, Wolseley had earned his stripes in North America. After a period as an observer for the Confederate Army in the U.S. Civil War, Gilbert & Sullivan's "very model of a modern major general" had led an expedition from Ontario to the troubled Red River colony, on the cusp of its admittance to Canada as Manitoba. His nemesis at that time was a young Louis Riel. Reaching the Red in 1870, over all-Canadian ground, had been a trial requiring the construction of several boats to convey his contingent and supplies.

The Red River Expedition showed Wolseley the native-born stamina of the Canadian boatman. And 14 years later, as he mapped his Sudan strategy, Wolseley noted the blistering desert between the Red Sea and Khartoum, and concluded that the mission would need a marine expedition up the Nile River. But instead of the Royal Navy, Wolseley recalled that spring of 1870, when Canadian boatmen had effected his transfer from the Great Lakes, and made his decision: Britain needed voyageurs.

Wolseley ordered the construction of 800 boats, and commissioned Yarrow & Co. in Clyde, Scotland, to supply two iron-hulled sternwheelers. Remembering the skillful Canadian volunteers, Wolseley asked the Colonial Office to provide 400 Canadian boatmen, calling them "voyageurs."

When the latter request reached the government of Canada, it was referred as a colonial matter to the Governor General, who dropped it on the desk of his military secretary, Gilbert Elliott, a.k.a. Lord Melgund. Melgund must have scratched his head in disbelief when he read the word "voyageurs." The Colonial Office might as well have asked for knights in armour or Caribbean pirates. The Canadian voyageur, the canoeman of the Great Lakes and Saskatchewan fur trade, was a long-ago legend, and very few were still alive. But Wolseley revelled in the term, and of course what he really meant was the men he remembered from 1870, the Métis sons and grandsons of those original voyageurs, who still knew how to handle a boat. Melgund was able to find 400-odd labourers among the Métis on the Red, Mohawks from the St. Lawrence, Ottawa River lumbermen and Great Lakes sailors. A home-grown water-borne regiment was assembled, a quarter-century before Canada would form its first official navy.

Having found his boatmen, Melgund turned to a related matter. Wolseley's plan called for steam power to push the heavy freight barges and boats up the Nile. But the British military knew nothing about sternwheelers or navigating a river plagued with rapids, which the English called "cataracts." "Can you obtain eight good men thoroughly accustomed to working and steering stern wheel Steamers in Rapids for service on the Nile?" read the letter from the War Office.

Such expertise did exist, and four wheelsmen from the lumber boats of the Ottawa were commissioned. But from the far-flung western frontier, the name of William Robinson came to the desk of Melgund. With winter coming, the Saskatchewan River fleets were stilled and perhaps Robinson could make some suggestions. He responded, and soon Western river captains reported for duty: Jerry Webber, John Segers, Aaron Russell and Robinson himself, "employed to take the charge of the boats and attempt the hazardous undertaking,"[15] with "the honor of making the first successful experiments in passing the cataracts."

The captains left Winnipeg on October 8, 1884, and on arrival for briefing in Ottawa, were brought up to speed on their mission: "to take charge of two steel steamers constructed with the view of navigating the Nile, their use being to transport spies, troops, and supplies from Alexandria to the front of the seat of war, or more properly to form a link in the chain connecting General Lennox with Generals Wolseley and Gordon."[16] In the heart of Canadian bureaucracy, the captains went through the silly formality of writing official examinations to qualify as mariners. But eager for employment, they wrote the tests and passed. On October 15, with frock coats, string ties and broad-brimmed hats, they posed for an Ottawa photographer, a fortunate event, since it produced for historians the only extant image of Segers, Russell and Webber.

Registries in hand, the quartet left for New York City to board the *Republic* for Liverpool, transferring to the *Magdalla* bound for Alexandria, Egypt. Calling at the island of Malta, the knights of the steamers toured the catacombs to visit the remains of the fabled Knights of Malta. On November 11, the tourists reached Alexandria, where Russell said "the gardens bloom all winter, the temperature getting as high as 90 in the shade, while at night I have seen it as low as 45."[17] Cairo, Alexandria and Egypt in general impressed the backwoods captains and took their breath away, especially in sense of the temperature: "The climate of Egypt in the winter season is the most delightful in the world,"[18] recognizing that at least they were missing a Winnipeg winter.

The Western steamboat pilots bound for North Africa sit for a photo while in Ottawa. This is the only known image of most of the captains. Standing: William Robinson Seated left to right: Aaron Russell, John Segers, Jerry Webber. LIBRARY & ARCHIVES CANADA C-00287

Cairo reminded them of St. Louis, with its wide streets and open markets. But, as born rivermen, they saved their greatest testimonies for the Nile itself, and like all rivermen, they knew that mysteries lurked beneath the placid surface: "majestic in its breadth and great sweep, and the water is pure and beautiful, although it needs to be filtered before being drank."[19]

But the pilots were not there for the sights. As Robinson put it: "I did not come here to eat and sleep, but I came to run a Steamboat."[20] Soon they were called to the docks to meet their vessel, the *Water Lily*, one of the two metal-hulled steamboats they would be piloting. Segers in particular must have felt a pang of nostalgia or perhaps a stroke of regret upon seeing the *Water Lily*: the iron-hulled craft built by Yarrow & Co. in Scotland was the sister ship of the *Lily*, which he'd piloted and sunk in the Drowning Ford the year before. If he did have trepidations, though, none were noted. The *Water Lily* was still in pieces, and William Robinson supervised its assembly. With construction and testing complete, the mercenary mariners took control of their new charge. Robinson was appointed captain, Aaron Russell took the crew in hand as first mate, while Jerry Webber and John Segers initially shared the helm as pilots. The *Water Lily* proceeded, towing the barges up the Nile through the Egyptian desert to the village of Wadi Halfa.

That thousand miles went uneventfully but swiftly, and much time was made up by Robinson's insistence on running at night, a practice uncustomary on the Nile. "We were told that ours was the fastest trip that was ever made with a Steamer while encumbered with a tow."[21] Once upriver, the *Water Lily* was employed towing barges between Assouan and Wadi Halfa, the staging point where the boat became a relay craft "carrying mail between Assouan and Wady Halfa, the first and second cataracts, a distance of 225 miles," keeping the lines of supply and communication open.

Robinson's command was challenged by military interference when a British captain "a nice gentleman but [one who] knew no more about running a steamer than I would know about making a watch"[22] insisted on taking charge. Robinson, realizing that he was on the Army bill, bit his tongue and let the officer have his head. Finally the Brit concluded that he was out of his element, admitting Robinson's "calculations were always correct and that it was a pity [he] should be burdened by men who did not understand River Navigation."[23] Subsequently the Canadian was tendered full command of the *Water Lily*.

But the team of pilots was broken up and a second boat employed. Initially, Will Robinson was to take charge of the *Lotus*, but his unnamed foil, the British captain, wouldn't have it. Under regulations, there had to be a naval officer in charge of the *Lotus*. But the officer's denial was not a slight, but a compliment: "he [the Navy man] did not want any [one else] in charge over me." They were making an impression, these western Canada rivermen.

In Robinson's place, Segers and Russell were transferred to the *Lotus*. Robinson wished them well and prayed that "the Naval Lieutenant will only have sense enough to allow them to use their own judgment."[24] The *Lotus* was another iron-hulled Yarrow Co. ship, intended "to run above the Sennah cataract. We took her in charge and completed our first trip on Jan. 1 [1885]. We took the steamer to Dongola, a point above what is known as the Fourth cataract, the distance being 250 miles."[25] On the New Year's cruise, Russell was the pilot, with Segers in charge of the crew as mate.

En route, the *Lotus* navigated seven of the cataracts, which Russell described as "very dangerous and peculiar. For some distance the water of the Nile rushes through broken ridges of granite and rock. The ridges are of every conceivable formation, and the water foams into eddies and sweeps through one succession of whirlpools after another, the current being fearfully strong and swift. As may be imagined the task of taking a sternwheeler through these treacherous eddies was not an easy one, but we made it successfully."[26]

To overcome the peril, the *Water Lily* and the *Lotus* relayed between the cataracts, saving the risk of damage on the jagged rocks, and allowing efficient delivery of supplies and troops between Alexandria and Sudan. The technique was similar to the HBC system at Grand Rapids, as depots were set up all along the great length of the Nile.

The second cataract, at Tangour Wasby, was the most difficult to ascend, and five days were spent climbing 14 miles of tough eddies. When a boulder punctured the iron hull, the pilots could have been forgiven a comparison to Cole's Falls on the North Saskatchewan. Even anchoring became a problem, when the river tugged at the *Lotus*'s anchor cables until they became uncoiled. Powerless to resist, the crew could only brace themselves for a wild ride as the Nile's current spun the boat around and sent it downstream and in danger of being swamped in the cataracts. Fortuitously, one of the cables at the stern dragged on the bottom and caught a rock. The snag allowed the pilot to right the boat, preventing its destruction.

On another cataract, the captain ordered soldiers to become beavers by jumping into the water to dam the channel with loose rock to raise the water level and allow the *Water Lily* to ascend. William Robinson said "the upper reaches of the Nile were the worst on which he had ever had experience as a pilot in his four decades."

To this day, in Selkirk, Manitoba, a hometown legend persists about Robinson's time with the Nile voyageurs. A group of Canadians had gathered in camp on the riverbank one evening, it is said, when suddenly the silence was broken by the whistling of a steamboat. Watching the masterly manner of the captain steering, Colonel Kennedy of the Red River Settlement said, "I wonder who it can be?"

Suddenly another Manitoban half-screamed, "It's Capt. Bill Robinson of Winnipeg!"

"My field-glasses," requested the officer calmly. "I thank you … Yes. Yes, it is."

"Give him a cheer, boys!" shouted Bill Galliher. And the cheer was taken up by other men up the river till the garrison 40 miles away stood at arms expecting Lord Wolseley or General Buller.

"Say, 'oo was that big bug wot just passed?" asked a cockney soldier.

"Who! Why that was Captain Bill Robinson of Winnipeg, Manitoba. He can steer a sternwheeler up the side of a mountain in the dew!"[27]

But the folk tale of the Canadian pilots' adventure on the Nile had a dismal and sobering end. Hearing the rumour of the steamer's approach, the soldier says: "'e'll come … but 'e'll be too late."[28]

And indeed Robinson, his pilots, the voyageurs and the entire expedition to rescue "Chinese" Gordon would prove to be, as the headlines would sputter, "TOO LATE!"[29] The *Lotus* reached Dongola on January 26. But by then word had come down the Nile and spread like wildfire to the outside world: General Gordon had held Khartoum for 317 days, but while the Nile voyageurs were struggling with the river, the Mahdist siege overran the city, and Gordon and his entourage were slaughtered before a British relief party could come within sight.

For fear of its own annihilation, the river column was recalled and ordered to retreat downriver. Three of the steamer pilots from western Canada were to be discharged. Jerry Webber chose to stay to help the column back to Alexandria. It would be another 13 years before the British would return. Khartoum was a disaster of epic proportions for England. Those devoted to an Empire the sun never sets upon could not bear the death of its hero. The public clamoured for the head of Prime Minister Gladstone as they built the requisite memorials and statues to Charles Gordon. The Baroness Burdett-Coutts was devastated. She considered Gordon her last hero. She had no heart for those who sought funds from her for a shrine, but instead directed patronage toward "those who carried on Gordon's work in equatorial Africa."[30] Her memorial was to a living Gordon, not a slain one.

Lost in the public grief were the efforts of the Canadian voyageurs and the western wheelsmen. But Webber, Robinson, Russell and Segers had overpowered a legendary river. The expedition as a whole may have been a failure, but the ascent of the Nile was instructive to the British. As the pilots booked passage home, the British government expressed a desire "to [purchase] and [employ] a dozen stern-wheel steamers and now that the experiment of taking them above the rapids has been accomplished, you may hope for fruitful results. We accomplished our mission in good shape, and we left our boats feeling all right. Gen. Grenfell is in charge of the Nile troops, and he was delighted when we got Her Majesty's Ship the *Lotus*, through successfully."[31]

Canadian voyageurs on the Nile. A steamboat is seen in the left corner background.

Robinson was more sardonic in assessing the *Water Lily* and *Lotus*: "I think the English made a mistake when they supposed that Canadians could do good work with any kind of a boat. They lost sight of the fact that it requires a practical River man to build a suitable River boat and although they appear to be well pleased with some of the Canadians, they would have been surprised at the results if they had allowed us to superintend the construction of their sternwheel boats. The English understand deep water boats to perfection but they only waste money when they attempt to build a stern-wheel boat for a shallow River."[32]

Jerry Webber bid his comrades a fond farewell. They were begged by the Brits to stay on, "but when we insisted on leaving they purchased first class passages over."[33]

Robinson, Segers and Russell spent a month getting back to the New World, and the grateful British picked up all expenses for the Canadians as they passed time in ports at Cairo, Turin, Paris, Liverpool and London before sailing for New York. The captains were well paid for their services, $300 per month, twice what they made on the Saskatchewan and equal to the wages of the HBC commodore, John Davis.

The volunteering of four civilian steamer captains for a dangerous foreign military journey says something for the character of the pilots. They were all Americans, except Robinson, and had no loyalty to the British Empire. None was exactly a spring chicken, either. John Segers was pushing 50; Aaron Russell, 55. Will Robinson was about the same age, judging by the Ottawa portrait, and Jerry Webber was a 62-year-old legend in an era when few people, especially stressed-out rivermen, aged particularly well. But there it was: the adventure, a lark, a chance to ride a new river. The U.S. War between the States hadn't bothered them and the prospect of dying by an Arab sword daunted them not a bit. It seems only fitting that these men were there. The Nile service fit their "have helm, will travel" character. The wages were only a bonus, as were the two service medals the captains were granted, by Queen Victoria and by the Khedive of Egypt.

But soon they would have to start thinking about their regular jobs, or whether there was to be a shipping season at all. The globetrotters took the train from New York to Minnesota and north to Winnipeg on April 8, 1885. But instead of a homecoming, they found the countryside in high anxiety. The placid, unprofitable Saskatchewan they'd left behind was heating up as the ice went out. As on the Nile, another revolutionary was stirring up the waters with religious zeal and the threat of rebellion. This prophet had been heard from before, in 1870. In describing the realm of the Mahdi, Aaron Russell remarked that "the sentiment of the great mass of the people is against the British. At first a good many of the people were not disposed to join in the movement, but they were compelled to obey."[34] The same, it could be argued, might be said of the Métis and Indian allies of Louis Riel.

Almost at once the captains' skills, and their boats, would be tested to aid another British colony against some of its inhabitants. Again the captains were sent off to military service and the potential of battle. Defeat would be tasted for the second time in only a few months. The first locale, Khartoum, had been exotic and remote; the second sounded placid, even humorous, and was also remote. Yet it raised hairs on the back of every Canadian: Duck Lake.

The Duck Lake debacle: a village goes to war

For a decade, the settlers of Prince Albert, Carlton, Battleford and Edmonton were ecstatic that the *Northcote* would end their isolated existence. But the native and mixed-bloods also could not help but see the changes. Directly, the steamers began cutting into their trade. The Métis supplemented their income by freight hauling in their Red River carts from Winnipeg to the outposts of the HBC. But now that same Red River provided a gateway for competition, and the forts, towns and Indian agencies no longer had to wait patiently for the ponderous ox carts. With the demise of the buffalo, the Métis had adapted to farming or ranching, but this too became problematic.

The Métis had settled along the river according to the time-honoured seigneurial system adopted from New France and brought west with the fur trade. The riverine lot allowed a homesteader frontage along the waterway—a place to water livestock and draw water for the household—plus a long, narrow, rectangular claim that reached far back into the fertile bench land above the river. But government officials imposed a new system: square-mile sections of 640 acres that could be divided into quarters. Only the legal quarter-section of 160 acres was to be accepted as a legal homestead. River frontage was to be a luxury granted by chance, with no legal regard for established Métis claims. It was as if bureaucracy were attempting to straighten the river onto a grid.

Relations between the government of Sir John A. Macdonald and the Métis living on the South Saskatchewan River deteriorated, as the Métis saw that their claims were ignored in favour of geometric squares. Others along the rivers were equally upset. The white settlers were agitated by years of bad crops, low commodity prices and the failure to build a railway to the north. Indian tribes were dissatisfied with their reserves and the lies of the agents. To organize all this discontent, a fine legal mind was needed and Louis Riel had just that. Almost immediately after Gabriel Dumont brought Riel from Montana to the Métis settlements around Batoche, communications were set up with the various Indian tribes as a means of gaining military allies. After several months, it was obvious that Riel was bound to do more than talk.

Among Joseph Wrigley's first correspondence in his new position as HBC's trade commissioner was contact with the Chief Factor of the Saskatchewan district, Lawrence Clarke, a conceited and thoroughly unlikable despot who had taken it upon himself to dabble in negotiations with the Métis himself. Responding to the agitation of Riel, Clarke had successfully badgered the NWMP with requests for a detachment at his home post, Fort Carlton. Though Wrigley bluntly advised Clarke to leave the governing to the government, the man would not let up. He continued to counter any talk of Métis home rule with threats of armed suppression and arrest. Riel's response to Clarke was open rebellion.

As the news from the North West reached Ottawa, the prime minister realized his usual policy of procrastination had only aggravated the situation. Under Riel's guidance, the Métis were stockpiling arms and recruiting allies, primarily among the prairie tribes. More immediately apprised of the situation, the North West Territories Lieutenant-Governor, Edgar Dewdney, struggled to stem the tide by issuing extra rations to reserves, and offering jobs to unemployed Métis as Indian agents, farm instructors and other public works positions. He also sought to send extra mounted policemen to bolster the small numbers stationed in the Prince Albert/Carlton area. Realizing the gravity of the situation, Commissioner Acheson Irvine led a column of 90 policemen from NWMP headquarters at Regina on March 18, 1885.

That same day proved fateful for the North West as the evening Louis Riel chose to establish the headquarters of his resistance at Batoche. In happier times, Xavier "Batoche" Letendre had become a relatively rich man from the ferry and trading post he ran at the point where the trail crossed the South Saskatchewan. The little village was a focal point for the families of Métis buffalo hunters settling down to a new life of farming. After the outcome of the Red River Rebellion of 1870, Batoche had become a destination for disaffected Métis settlers from Manitoba.

Louis Riel looking statesmanlike in the years between the rebellions. SASKATCHEWAN ARCHIVES BOARD R-B75

That night, Riel appointed the members of his council, the Exovedate (a term coined by Riel himself, derived from the Latin *ex*, "out of," and *ovis*, "sheep," and meaning "those who have left the flock") and established his provisional government, an act of open contempt for the government of Canada. His communiqué called for the surrender of Forts Carlton and Battleford, and for the NWMP commander at Carlton, Superintendent Lief Crozier to disarm. To top the action, Riel's force took several government authorities as hostage, and, to furnish his war against oppression, ordered the plunder of businesses in his town. Among those were the Kerr brothers, George and John, independent traders from Winnipeg who had previously had good working relationships with the Métis. No quarter was to be given by the provisional government, however, and the Kerr store was the scene of kidnap and looting. In John Kerr's own words:

They came to our store where they met Lash, the Indian instructor, Tomkins, the Indian interpreter, and George Ness, the magistrate at Battleford. Riel said nothing, but seized their horses and took the men prisoners. Then he marched into the store, and ordered my brother to deliver up the guns and ammunition. My brother asked what was the cause of this action, and Riel told him that the time was come, and that it would be better for a man if he was good. He told George to give all his men what they wanted, and charge it "high" to him [Riel]. George said if he had to do it he would. Riel said he had to do it. The Half-breeds were then handed over six English double-barrel guns and some rifles and revolvers, and ammunition. They also got a quantity of store goods.[35]

After relieving the Kerr brothers of their livestock, horses, saddlery, wagons and harness, fruit and vegetables, grain, and anything that could be forced into the barrel of a gun, Riel and his men crossed the river to the firm of Walters & Baker, and took Walters the storekeeper into custody. While the raiders were busy across the river, the Kerrs realized their lives would soon be in danger when "a friendly half-breed came down on horseback and told them to get out if they were desirous of continuing to enjoy the happiness of this world." With a trusted friend a couple of miles upstream, the Kerrs slipped away from Batoche and spent the first night in relative safety. Resuming flight the next day, the Kerrs were discovered by an Exovedate scout, but they shook him with a concocted story about being out to visit a different friend, where they would spend a few days. The scout allowed them to pass, but rode straight to Batoche, no doubt to report his sighting of the Kerrs.

The brothers took to the bush, and on March 24 arrived at the house of Joe Vandal, who harboured them for a couple of days. As independent traders, the Kerrs were officially enemies of Riel's army, but as merchants, they still had confidants among the Métis. Soon, however, the scout was at Vandal's door with six determined confederates, bent on capture of the brothers. The Kerrs were definitely on a hit list.

They scoured the house, but John and George were well concealed elsewhere on the farm. The unsuccessful posse returned to Batoche, and the Kerrs remained in hiding for two days to allow time for the intelligence that they'd slipped away to be reported. Then they escaped for real, and for several days followed the riverbank upstream, avoiding rebel scouts and Whitecap's Sioux. At Clarke's Crossing, the brothers were well past Métis lines, and decided to turn the tables and engage their own scout. At tremendous personal risk, mail carrier Frank Clark was to ride north to spy on Batoche, and rendezvous with the Kerrs at Saskatoon with any intelligence he could gather of a possible attack on the river town of 50 houses and 75 people.

By the time the Kerrs caught up with Clark, he'd completed his mission but had been unable to discover anything about a siege of Saskatoon. But he could inform the brothers that Riel's Exovedate had tried them in absentia for crimes against the Métis state, payback for their warnings to the countryside. John and George did not stick around Saskatoon to add a period on their death sentence. They took to the Moose Jaw Trail, and John didn't stop until he reached Winnipeg, where he could wait out the war at the home of another brother, and tell a local paper his tale. George, though, was of a different stripe. His path took him to Swift Current and Saskatchewan Landing, and his eventual return to Batoche, aboard the *Northcote*. And there would be war, for just as the Kerrs were fleeing from their former home toward Saskatoon, the first shots were being fired, erupting in tragic first blood.

The NWMP under Supt. Lief Crozier mobilized to stem the raids on stores and trading posts, but met only defeat near Duck Lake, forcing a retreat to Fort Carlton.
L.M. MULVANEY, *THE NORTH-WEST REBELLION*

On March 24, NWMP Commissioner Irvine reached Prince Albert with his 90-man Regina contingent. Two days later, he marched his troop to Fort Carlton to add his strength to that of Superintendent Crozier. Upon arrival at the fort, Irvine was astonished to learn that his trip was for naught, as he became the first commander to learn first-hand of the disaster at Duck Lake.

Thursday, March 26, 1885, dawned on the HBC's ancient stockade at Fort Carlton. The spring equinox was only a few days past, but instead of renewal and revival, the rites of the new season brought discontent and vengefulness. Inside the post the Irish-born commander of the Mounted Police's D Division furled his brow at the news: one of his patrols had been turned back from their mission to commandeer supplies at the trading post of Hillyard Mitchell in the town of Stobart, soon better known as Duck Lake. Crozier wasn't surprised to hear that the post had been captured already, by a loose militia of Riel-inspired Métis hunters and farmers commanded by Gabriel Dumont.

The action was an open defiance of the authority of the NWMP, one Crozier had expected and prepared for, or so he thought. Dumont's challenge had to be countered if respect for the force was to be maintained. In less than an hour, still stinging from a charge of cowardice laid by the arrogant factor, Lawrence Clarke, Crozier led a column of 52 policemen, and a corps of 43 settlers from nearby Prince Albert sworn in as special constables, up the hill out of Carlton toward the scene of the incident. At a clearing on the Beardy reserve between Fort Carlton and the town, the troops were faced with the prospect of an ambush by the Métis force. Crozier halted the column, and with his interpreter, "Gentleman" Joe McKay, rode toward the Métis leaders under a truce flag. He was met by Gabriel Dumont's brother, Isidore. Somehow a nearly blind Cree elder named Assiyiwin wandered into the discussion. What followed was a series of events that to this day remain confused and contradictory. Apparently Assiyiwin reached for, or did not know he was grasping for, Interpreter McKay's cocked rifle. McKay's carbine discharged, whether accidentally or intentionally no one will ever know, but Assiyiwin slumped from his horse, a Winchester bullet in his belly as an answer to the grabbing gesture.

The resultant melee at Duck Lake was literally a massacre for Crozier's troops. A dozen of the column were dead, with 11 wounded. The duel had been met and reacted to. The defiant Métis were prevented from pursuing Crozier by the grace of a cross-wielding Riel, who had observed the fight as five of his own people became casualties. When Crozier's column limped into Carlton, they were met by Irvine and a fresh set of volunteer recruits from Prince Albert.

Among the new arrivals in Irvine's group was Archie Ballantine, a sometime lumberjack and summertime steamboat rooster. After walking behind the police team and sleighs of Colonel Irvine for nine hours, Ballantine found Fort Carlton "in a turmoil, the wounded calling out with pain. I helped to dress [the wounds of] some of them, and then I was called to the horse barn, where I found many wounded horses, their skins being rent in several places. We stitched them as well as we could."[36] After adding "medic" and "veterinarian" to his résumé, Archie was posted as a sentry at the top of the hill above the fort.

NWMP Commissioner Acheson Irvine personally led a column from headquarters in Regina to back up Crozier. But he arrived a day late and was forced to evacuate Fort Carlton and dig in at Prince Albert. L.M. MULVANEY, *THE NORTH-WEST REBELLION*

From Archie's vantage point it was easy to determine that the old outpost of the Hudson's Bay regime could hardly hold out as a fortress, offensively or defensively. It was only built as a general store. Its stockade walls were designed not so much for fending off attack as for preventing livestock from wandering off, and thus provided a false sense of security for its occupants. Carlton was situated in a horseshoe, a few hundred yards back from the North Saskatchewan River to facilitate water-borne transport. It was in full view from the top of a three-sided hill too vast to be defended much more than symbolically by the Mounties and volunteers in occupation. A sniper with a good rifle could sit in thick brush on the coulee banks and easily pick off people within the stockaded walls. Food and ammunition wouldn't last long under siege, and resources were already being consumed by the wounded.

A basic tenet of military strategy dictates that high ground determines the victor, and Fort Carlton was definitely low ground. Khartoum was much in memory of Irvine and Crozier, and neither of them had any desire to become a prairie Gordon. Fending off Louis Riel and his forces was not an option here. In abandoning Carlton, the most damage Irvine could inflict on the Métis was to deny them the provisions the fort contained. The order was given to commandeer everything in the post that could not be nailed down, and load it all into the few wagons and sleighs available.

Obviously the entire contents of the fort could not be hauled away. As Mounties, volunteers and traders scurried about to empty the fort, Ballantine broke into the granary and began to shovel oats into sacks. Sleighs full of the valuable fodder were sledded across the frozen river and hidden in the bushes on the north side. Anything that could not be carried was ordered destroyed or made useless to the rebels. Tons of bacon were packed out from the meat house—"that old rattlesnake bacon which was yellow as gold with age."[37] Not even the milled grain was spared. Two hundred bags of flour were carried out and poured over the bacon. And then the entire mountain of foodstuffs was deliberately poisoned by pouring five heavy barrels of coal oil over the pile. Holes were cut in the river ice, and provisions that couldn't be taken away were thrown into the open water to keep them from being used by Dumont's people.

In the morning, the combined column packed up its dead and wounded and slipped out of the fort. Somewhere along the line someone knocked over a lit kerosene lantern into some straw in the barn. Before long the whole fort was ablaze. At three o'clock in the morning, under cover of darkness and smoke, Irvine led the hasty retreat to the safety of Prince Albert. The move took 12 hours, all the while pushing and pulling the transport wagons through heavy snow, jettisoning cargo and avoiding rebel scouts. That retreat would dog Irvine for the rest of his career, stopping just short of labelling the NWMP as cowards. Still, there was little else to be done, as Irvine's discretion became the better part of valour. Carlton was useless, communications non-existent, Prince Albert vulnerable, and there were three steamboats docked near town that could provide service to the armies that would surely be called west.

As March became April, farms and settlements in the vicinity of Batoche became ghost towns, as Riel ordered local Métis to concentrate camp around the proclaimed capitol. At Duck Lake, buildings were razed, and perceived enemies were imprisoned and taken to Batoche. When the jailers and their charges arrived on April 3, they found the ice in the South Saskatchewan breaking up and the water running on the side. The captured were put into boats and taken across the icy channel to the east side, where "[they were] placed in Baptiste Boyer's house, being guarded by numerous sentries, who were ordered to fire on anyone attempting to escape without calling on him to halt."[38] Batoche was now virtually a state unto itself, and Riel would brook no interference from around the countryside.

The little mission of St. Laurent was no exception, as the Sisters of the Faithful Companions of Jesus order, educators of many of the Métis children, were left with only three girls in their charge, the daughters of the Batoche ferryman Alexander Fisher. The nuns still had communication with the outside, and after hearing the news of the massacre at Frog Lake, they were implored by Mother Superior Louise Collings to join her at Prince Albert. The escape was fraught with bad weather, deceptive guides and faulty wagons, conspiring to force the nuns back to St. Laurent, where they too came under Riel's law.

On the morning of April 17, Father Vital Fourmond begged the Sisters to accept Riel's offers of safe passage to the capitol. The nuns were like everyone else, under the impression of rumours of pillaging Indians. In effect, Fourmond was asking them to become prisoners of Riel. With little alternative for their own safety, the Sisters gave in, walking the six miles to the Batoche ferry, hoping they would at least be permitted to live at St. Antoine's mission. "Our three little girls had come with us from

St. Laurent. Their father (Alex Fisher), employed in the boat service at the Crossing, had beseeched us to keep them with us. As it was judged too late for us to make the crossing, that good man offered us his home, or rather his cabin for the night."[39] The Sisters had just put Fisher's daughters to bed when Louis Riel himself knocked at the door. He'd crossed the river to reassure the nuns and politely offer his apologies for their predicament. "He showed great respect and exquisite politeness towards us. He told us that he understood perfectly our misgivings about our present position and that he felt the greatest sympathy for us."[40]

On April 18, Fisher took the nuns and his daughters aboard his ferry, along with a few rebel sentries and a regularly scheduled load of provisions from Duck Lake. "The men had taken the horses and wagons on board. Besides the five of us, a half dozen Métis, a few Indians with feathers in their hair took their places in the boat. The weather, as well as our feelings, were melancholy. It was cold. Snow falling in huge flakes covered us like a shroud."[41] The Faithful Companions of Jesus experienced the spring blizzard unaware that the same weather was hampering those on the way to Batoche with rifles, cannon and machine guns.

Even getting off the ferry proved a hazard for the Sisters, as they hiked up their habits to clamber over great blocks of spring breakup ice littering the Batoche shore. "The hill that we had to climb on leaving the boat was so steep and so encumbered with blocks of ice that the horses had a great deal of difficulty to reach the top. As for us who followed on foot we had more than one fall." Once their arduous climb was over, the Sisters were ordered to be taken to Xavier Letendre's palatial house, "the nicest home in the place," now occupied by the headquarters of Riel and his Rebellion.

After their icy sojourn up the bank, Riel wanted the nuns placed in three rooms in the Letendre house. The Mother Superior was having none of it. "Could we not withdraw to another house where we would have a peaceful corner? … Mr. Riel answered that he understood our wishes perfectly, that we would be quite safe at St. Antoine, and that he would be delighted to see us there." On April 19, relieved to be out of the rebel camp, the Sisters climbed the hill to the Catholic mission some distance from the village to attend Sunday Mass, and never returned. They took up residence in the cramped rectory of St. Antoine de Padoue, to remain prisoners in their own House of the Lord for nearly a month until the whistle of a steamboat signalled the beginning of unimaginable tragedy.

CHAPTER FIVE

Middleton's Navy

And now for business

Before Duck Lake erupted, the prime minister felt military action in the North West Territories could not be avoided. In response, he assembled his military advisers, specifically the Minister of Defence and Militia, Adolphe Caron, and the Commander of the Canadian military, the British Major General Frederick Dobson Middleton.

Middleton may not have fit the image of a Custeresque prairie Indian fighter, but neither was he inexperienced. A stocky, 59-year-old Englishman, Fred Middleton was distinguished by his ruddy complexion and a bushy white, walrus-like moustache. A

General Frederick Middleton, commander of the North West Field Force. PROVINCIAL ARCHIVES OF ALBERTA B-2026

hard-boiled veteran of foreign campaigns such as against Maori tribesmen in New Zealand and in India's Sepoy Mutiny, he had twice been recommended for the Victoria Cross but never won the honour. Serving in garrison in Quebec, he had married Eugénie Doucet, a French-Canadian from Montreal, then returned to England for a stint as commandant of Sandhurst Royal Military Academy. In July 1884, Middleton took command of the Canadian militia, hoping to ease into peaceful retirement. But again rebellion interrupted his repose. With the territory on the verge of war, Middleton travelled to Winnipeg to mobilize the few militia forces in Manitoba, taking command of Canada's first military campaign as a nation.

Word of the wilderness melee at Duck Lake sent the country into a frenzy. Though only dispatch riders and a thin telegraph wire connected the prairies to the outside world, details of the defeat were on the desk of Minister Caron in Ottawa the next morning.

The first dispatches were little more than rumours, but telegrams received from Commissioner Irvine at Prince Albert urged that any relief force be at least 1,500 strong. That advice was taken, and before the war was over, some 7,000 troops would be mobilized. Unwilling to wait in Winnipeg, Middleton rode the CPR to Troy[1] to await further news and orders. Troy's railway station became Middleton's war room, where he could communicate with officers, obtain intelligence, organize supply lines and assemble the regiments as they arrived.

In looking at the map, Middleton realized the rivers would be the key to his success. Supplies, troops and ordnance could be moved to Swift Current by rail and then shipped downriver, saving the cost of the hundreds of wagons and teamsters that would be required for shipping overland. In the U.S. Civil War, massive transport needs had been met by using civilian steamers, effectively enabling General Grant to gain ground on the war's western fronts at a time when his eastern counterparts were still stalemated. Even crucial hospital and medical needs had a precedent in Captain Grant Marsh's steamboat mission of mercy to recover the wounded from the battle of Little Big Horn. With an eye to the need for medics, Middleton, in his first flurry of telegrams, ordered surgeon Campbell Mellis Douglas to "reach him by the Saskatchewan." Nobody could guess how literally Douglas would interpret that order.

With a legion of military, economic and practical assets at hand, Middleton had carte blanche to arrange his military strategy. Assembling a riverboat flotilla seemed pragmatic. In Montreal, a powerful financier and former government official agreed with the general, for he just happened to have three dormant steamboats.

In Medicine Hat, a fleet at the ready

The outbreak of hostilities resounded in the study of the former High Commissioner to London, now a prosperous Montreal entrepreneur. Sir Alexander Galt saw an opportunity to employ his impotent, unprofitable coal boats, and rubbed his hands with glee at the prospect of war revenue.

Adolphe Caron, Minister of Militia and Defence at the time of the North West Rebellion. Caron was charged with the entire conduct of the military campaign, including the commissioning of the civilian vessels used on the Saskatchewan rivers. LIBRARY & ARCHIVES CANADA PA-026665

At Medicine Hat, where Galt's ships *Alberta*, *Baroness* and *Minnow* were mouldering in winter port, the town's hopes of becoming a centre of navigation had been dashed by the railway. Why depend on the volatile river when one has a dependable, all-season connection to the rest of the country? The CPR trestle, which spanned the river at a right angle, formed an almost psychological barrier to riverboat progress. Still, the railway had hedged its bets and installed a swinging span that would enable steamboats to pass unimpeded even at high water—a major concession, which recognized that river freighting may yet have potential.

Suddenly the idle fleet, deprived of economic significance, acquired military significance. In the midst of mobilization of the militia, Swift Current and Medicine Hat became staging areas for the Canadian prairies' only naval campaign.

The most significant of the sternwheelers laid up along the waterfront was the *Northcote*. The same chance of fate that heartened Galt was shared by the HBC, albeit more guardedly, in true company tradition, by the fastidious Joseph Wrigley. Though Wrigley's concerns were businesslike (he refused to advance supplies until given authority by the government[2]), he knew that HBC interests lay in tidying up this unpleasantness as swiftly as possible. Despite a chance to profiteer from military contracts, his long-term plans were to secure revenue from agricultural settlement in the North West. A war zone would not be hospitable to prospective investment.

Minister Caron saw fit to use Wrigley and the HBC as the primary supplier to the government forces soon to pass through Winnipeg en route to the conflict. The telegraph systems of the CPR and the government allowed Wrigley to direct supply operations at the HBC's posts throughout the West. As de facto chair of the W&WTC, Joseph Wrigley was also responsible for the fleet of ships: the *North West* at Prince Albert, the *Marquis* and *Manitoba* in the Sturgeon River and the *Northcote* at Medicine Hat. Together with Galt's vessels, that made a fleet of seven sternwheelers whose paddles would turn once more to breathe new life into the flagging navigation business. If only they could get out of port.

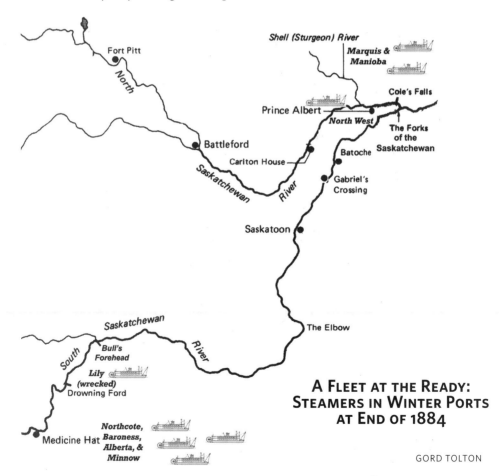

**A FLEET AT THE READY:
STEAMERS IN WINTER PORTS
AT END OF 1884**

GORD TOLTON

78

That pesky ice

A series of telegrams relate the three-way negotiations among Sir Alexander Galt, Joseph Wrigley and Defence Minister Adolphe Caron over engaging the fleet for military service. The notes reveal the caginess of the executives not to underestimate the capabilities of their vessels nor to allow natural conditions to influence the decision for the Army to use the boats. While Galt the politician was eager to sign his money-losing boats onto the government dole, Wrigley the businessman was more guarded with his company's property.

From his Montreal office, Galt must have imagined he could see the South Saskatchewan River, as he proudly declared Medicine Hat to be free from any winter ice that might stall the launch of his fleet. Though no longer officially in politics, Galt knew that a whisper from him would be heard loud and clear in the ear of Sir John A. Macdonald. He wired the prime minister to say: "River at Medicine Hat clear of ice. Have two steamboats and numerous barges there at your service. By bringing crews from Winnipeg, could be ready quickly saving overland transportation troops."[3] Galt craftily played on the government's desire to see the campaign concluded quickly.

Sir Alexander's suggestion soon found its way to Caron's office, where the possibility of river transport had also been suggested by Donald Smith, whose wily tentacles touched the HBC and by default the W&WTC. Caron wired Wrigley asking him to get the ball rolling at his end. "Mr. Smith informs me Saskatchewan River open—and Steamer laying at Medicine Hat—Have her ready to convey troops if required."[4] Wrigley's reply, however, put paid to the brash suppositions of Galt and Smith: "Just received telegram Saskatchewan River is not likely to open for week or ten days."[5]

While awaiting further details on ice conditions, a more immediate concern reached the prime minister, relating the extreme paranoia at Medicine Hat: "Rumours

Panoramic sketch of Medicine Hat and the *Northcote*, 1885, from the magazine *The Riel Rebellion of 1885*, Witness Publishing Co., Montreal. GLENBOW ARCHIVES NA-58-6

of place being attacked by Indians no arms to defend ourselves; can you furnish two hundred immediately and ammunition; actions of Indians here warrant rumours; men enrolled under my command reply immediate."[6] The response was immediate: "Send forthwith two hundred stands and ammunitions to Medicine Hat."[7]

Wrigley and Caron kept the wires singing between Winnipeg and Ottawa, as the commissioner tried to get to the bottom of the ice situation on the South Saskatchewan, all the while urging Caron to keep the riverboat option open. "Steamer at Medicine Hat can be launched on Thursday [April 2]—can take troops or provisions. Is at your service, await reply—Have telegraphed this to General."[8]

Sir John A. Macdonald, prime minister of Canada in 1885. LIBRARY & ARCHIVES CANADA C005332

Caron accented further dangers perceived from the reports he received. "Reported attack of Indians on Battleford—Send Steamer, yours or one of Galt's small ones, to Swift Current to cross troops—with reliable crew."[9] With this telegram, and his next wire to Wrigley, Caron asserted that riverboats were definitely to be used. He didn't care whose boats, just so long as something got launched and soon: "I am informed river not open. Is this correct? Of course, we should avail ourselves of river to save long land transport. Let me know what can be done."[10]

Now that Caron was advocating riverboats, Wrigley got caught in his and Galt's mild deceptions, and had to admit he just didn't know the ice situation. But he stood by his April 2 launch date: "Received information this morning that boat could be launched at Medicine Hat next Thursday. Uncertain whether ice would permit getting downriver to Clarke's crossing to Carlton district—will make every possible enquiry and report."[11]

The next day, March 31, Wrigley was finally able to disclose some reliable intelligence to the minister, provided by Captain James Sheets in Medicine Hat preparing the *Northcote*: "Ice prevents boats going down South Saskatchewan [a]t present best means of crossing River at Swift Current are on spot. When available our boat under experienced Captain prepared to launch first moment possible."[12] Later in the day, Wrigley's news was improving, though over-optimistic: "Have just heard officially that water is unusually low in South Saskatchewan, ice gone out. River fordable now but further uncertain as it is rising, boats useless at present will report moment possible."[13] Caron replied his gratitude for Wrigley's finally getting the story straight: "Thanks for information about River and for measures you have taken so far."[14]

With the tacit approval of the minister as contract, Wrigley formally offered the fleet's services to the Middleton campaign: "All our boats at your disposal and no doubt Galt's also. Have wired Capt. Sheets to place himself at your service. From information received impossible to use boats at present; understand ferry is now at Swift Current, if insufficient another can be built in two or three days. Could send men and lumber immediately. Steamers would take according to water two to four days from Medicine hat to Swift Current, boats or barges five to ten days. Steamer from Swift Current to Clarke's Crossing three days."[15]

Alexander Galt was unwilling to have his vessels left out of the fray, and sent a long-winded wire to Caron. His crocodile tears fairly staining the paper, Galt repeated the offer made to the prime minister, and in true political fashion wove in a shameless plug for another son, Jack Galt, and his Winnipeg mercantile business: "My dear Caron:—This affair in the North West is very sad but I am glad to see the energetic steps you are taking to put it down. I telegraphed and wrote Sir John on Saturday—putting our flotilla of steamboats and barges at Med. Hat at his disposal. We could, with exertion, have them ready at Swift Current Creek—in a week, and take your whole force down the River to Prince Albert in four days. Besides, the boats would be of great service, if the affair is prolonged, as giving you a floating movable base of operations. As you will want large supplies of canned goods groceries &c. from Winnipeg, I wish you would bear in mind that my son Jack is in business there and has the largest assortment, wholesale of articles of this kind. His firm is G.T. & J. Galt and you may depend on all they undertake to do. They must have customers in the Prince Albert district. Pray do this for me."[16]

So with Wrigley and Galt enthusiastically onside, Caron could advise Middleton to begin his arrangements knowing a flotilla of ships would enhance the mobility of the brigade. "All the Hudson Bay boats and the Galt boats will be at the disposal of troops … at Medicine Hat in three days or four. They will be at your disposal for conveyance of troops—steamers and boats."[17] Middleton's navy was born.

Is Battleford burning?

His parliamentary office converted to a war room, Minister Caron commanded operations like a general himself. But as a political official in a department prone to patronage, he also had to react to a host of armchair strategists eager for an instant of glory. Still, some useful advice came from a retired Indian Agent whose previous locale was at the centre of the tension. J. Walmer Clarke, "anxious to do anything I can for … success," was a former British officer recently returned from a government tenure at Fort Carlton, administering the terms of Treaty Six. Retired in Toronto, Clarke offered, as one "only actuated by a desire for the welfare of the expedition," his advice from both martial and prairie expertise. The concept of river transport was familiar to Clarke, and much of his cable reflects that knowledge:

> I understand that the 580 men from Toronto leave tomorrow night, as they have to march or drive part of the distance on the C.P.R. I think it will be the 5th of April before they are able to leave Qu'appelle for the overland march. My calculation is that it will take them eleven or twelve days more to reach the South

Branch. Now, at this season, if the weather is mild the roads will be very bad and the creeks full of water. There are places that even in July and August are so deep that the water comes in to the waggon box, and which in Spring (if the spring there has set in) would be difficult to get over at all. I therefore believe it would be a wise precaution to take at least two flat bottomed boats such as lumber men use. It would only require one extra sleigh or two at the utmost, a coil of inch rope would also be useful. Pitch and oakum with a set of caulking tools and three small beams and sufficient 2 in. plank to make a small raft 10 x 12 could go in the same two sleighs. In this way should any swollen creeks be met with or any places where the ice was rotten the ammunition could be brought over dry, It would also enable the men to get over; the horses could swim, It might also happen that when the expedition arrived at the South Branch, they would find that there was not a boat to be had, as they all belong to the half-breeds.

Should the insurrection continue I believe it would be advisable to consider the plan of taking a portion of the troops down by river. There is I am sure one small steamer near Medicine Hat, perhaps two. The South Saskatchewan will open probably about the 11th April, the water will be high and I think there will be no difficulty in running down in three or four days; however the opinion of the river men could easily be ascertained on this point. The boats could be carried over the wheel and so as to protect the machinery in fact with little trouble the whole boat could be made bullet proof. It might be necessary in any case to send a boat as an auxiliary, because if the insurgents should have secured or destroyed the only two ferries on the South Branch it would be simply impossible for a force to get across. I believe myself that if the season is a usual one that the troops could get down by boat, that is, as many as could be taken that way as early as by land. The steamer also could carry a small gun—and she ought to take down some kind of barge that could be used as a ferry.

If, unhappily the trouble should spread to the Indians, which, however, I do not anticipate, there are steamers at Prince Albert that could be prepared as gun boats for the North Branch.[18]

In a nutshell of qualified opinion, Clarke had summarized, possibly even inspired, the riverborne operations Middleton would use.

On April 1, Middleton received wires from James Rae, the Indian Agent at Battleford: nervous, panicky reports of Poundmaker's band leaving their reserve, supposedly in revolt. Rae was terrified of Poundmaker, and of Indians in general, but any report had to be taken seriously. At such an early stage, there was little Middleton could do, given he had no army. Even if he had, most rivers and creeks were ice-filled and impassable. "We are fully aware of the necessity of sending help but are powerless. The men at the different ferries have just informed us that the river is perfectly unpassable also the steamer cannot move yet."[19]

Middleton's news only got worse, as he spoke of the only force capable of reaching Battleford:

> Herchmer's party could not pass the River at Swift Current and he is now at Medicine Hat waiting to start in the steamer. I will try again tomorrow and will myself start to Battleford, the instant the river is reported nearly fit to cross without waiting for Otter's troops—Depend on my doing what is possible at all hazards—everything is against us, the weather being unusual—it is snowing hard and roads are getting in a fearful state. Riel has chosen his time most judiciously.[20]

NWMP Superintendent William Macauley Herchmer was a burly, bearded bear of a Mountie, just 40 years old and a veteran of prairie service in the Dominion Militia and the police. Ordered to reinforce Battleford, he formed what he called his "flying column." He gathered 50 of the best police troops, complete with mounts, and arranged a swift CPR express to move them. Herchmer's command bounced back and forth on the rails, from Calgary to Medicine Hat to Swift Current to Troy, back to Regina, only to pick up orders to return to Swift Current and thence gallop north to bolster the Fort Battleford garrison.

But the river had other plans. Besides being a barrier to navigation and overland travel, spring ice floes raised other problems as well. At Troy, Robert McManus, a British Army veteran and proprietor of the Royal Hotel, made the first of several reports on the conduct of the campaign, entitled "An Old Soldier's View." In his column to the *Toronto Daily Mail*, McManus asserted that a critical point was that "the ice in the South Saskatchewan may break up at any moment. This will enable Riel to hold all the crossings. The river at the narrowest crossing is 80 yards in width, and the freshets that follow the ice shoves will, of course, vastly increase the difficulty of fording it."[21]

Superintendent William Macauley Herchmer, commander of the NWMP's "Flying Column" along the South Saskatchewan: troops and mounts ready to travel to hot spots by horse, rail or steamer. The column eventually travelled to Battleford.
GLENBOW ARCHIVES NA-1036-1

About the ice hazard, Herchmer was the first to agree with McManus. Riel had no need to post even one sentry to hold the troops on the far side; the ice did the job for him. A quick canter out to Saskatchewan Landing and Herchmer saw his mission dashed. "I found that the river at Saskatchewan was impassable, the ice having given way on each side, leaving a ridge in the centre, over which it was impossible to convey the horses or waggons."[22] To attempt it was certain death, and there would be more glorious ways to get onto the Roll of Honour. It was as though the rebellion and the river were symbolically allied to prevent the forces from moving very far from the railway.

Paddles to the water

With little else to do, Herchmer returned to Swift Current to contact Middleton and await fresh orders. Concern for Medicine Hat gave Colonel Billy a new mission. Stories of Indian activity in the area had to be taken seriously for a town so strategic. Nearby were the Cypress Hills, refuge to Métis and Indian alike, and its gateway to the Montana border. The bridge was the lifeline to the struggling CPR and its link to Calgary and British Columbia. A second railway to the town was being built from Coalbanks. And of course there were the steamboats, their crews struggling to roust them from their winter's sleep.

Whether those natives were Cree or Blackfoot depends on the source. The prairies were rife with rumour, unconfirmed perceptions and a proverbial bogeyman behind every tree. A separate study could probably be made of the various unsubstantiated stories abounding in those turbulent days. Still, Medicine Hat's populace was troubled, as the loyalties of any tribe remained undefined in the aftermath of Duck Lake. Someone thought they saw a Cree warrior hanging around the beached and unattended *Northcote*. War fever even brought out tales that "two half-breed spies are suspected to be in town picking up information for Riel."[23] So much hearsay for such a little town, but with little communication, perception becomes reality, gossip becomes fact.

Only the home guard and a few Mounties were left to the security of the steamboats. A cavalry would be formed at Fort Macleod to relieve the town, but as of April 1, the Rocky Mountain Rangers had not yet been recruited. A well-placed fire on the dry timbers could destroy the boats, so Caron advised Middleton to take protective measures: "Mr. Galt has placed his steamers and barges at disposal of Department. They will be ready to leave Medicine Hat about middle of next week and can carry about One hundred and Fifty tons of freight—saving Land transport between Swift Current, Saskatchewan. I think it would be advisable to send a detachment of armed men from Medicine Hat to protect the steamers and barges."[24]

Middleton dispatched Herchmer to Medicine Hat on March 31. Herchmer hastily loaded his horses and men onto the express and travelled west to take charge and meet the purported threat. But if there were any saboteurs threatening the flotilla, they were invisible.

With the fleet engaged and in place, fuel had to be found. Though there were supplies of coal on the prairies, they could not be utilized at that juncture. Coal from Galt's mines, though of prime quality, could not be shipped from Coalbanks, as the steamers were still unable to make the journey upriver through the ice and low water. Galt's railway was barely started, and bull teams couldn't possibly haul the volumes needed. Why the coals seams at Medicine Hat's Saskatchewan Mine were not exploited for this use is unclear. It may have been a matter of contract exclusivity. Whatever the reason, Caron referred the matter to the CPR's general manager, the ham-fisted William Cornelius Van Horne: "I would like you to send one hundred and fifty tons of coal for Galt's boats to Medicine Hat and same quantity to Swift Current."[25]

The CPR had ample supplies of its own coal, imported from Pennsylvania. But Van Horne, ever mindful of logistics, warned against stockpiling coal at Swift Current that would have to be freighted to Saskatchewan Landing, an extremely expensive undertaking. "We will send all coal required but Galt's boats should take it from Medicine Hat as it would have to be hauled by team fifteen or twenty miles from Swift Current to River. He has plenty barges and can take down full supply. Answer quick. If this not satisfactory, presume Pittsburg coal the strongest [coal] to be [available] will be wanted."[26]

Out of his element, Caron left the fuel matter to Van Horne to arrange with Alexander Galt: "I will do what you consider to be sufficient—better see him."[27] Van Horne met with Galt and agreed to ship the required coal to Medicine Hat and move it by barge to Saskatchewan Landing. "Have discussed coal matter with Galt and we agree that it will be much better take the whole three hundred tons coal from Medicine Hat, teaming General Middleton's freight across from Rush Lake or Swift Current. It will be much easier to team and load the freight than the coal."[28] The minister concurred: "All right about Coal—Matter discussed with Galt"[29] and soon Pennsylvania carbon was arranged to be delivered.

On April 2, still awaiting his troops, Middleton prepared to leave Troy for Fort Qu'Appelle to arrange to cross the Qu'Appelle River: "I propose leaving to-morrow for Fort Qu'appelle and shall wait one day for the troops expected here on Saturday & then push on and hope to find the River open at Ferry—must build bridge."[30] Middleton was undecided about whether to relieve Battleford or Prince Albert, but he knew his progress would be at the mercy of the river: "Shall move on tomorrow to the Fort and then on to Clarke's Crossing where I hope to arrive next Tuesday and find the [river] open. I shall cross there and make for Battleford or Prince Albert as the case may be."

Getting the steamboats into the water was the key to the near future, and Middleton hoped something would improve by the time he reached Clarke's Crossing. "Shall leave orders for troops coming up to follow, and make arrangements for them up to Clarke's Crossing, shall still be in telegraphic communication with you. Address letter and telegrams to Troy. Hope to get steamer at work in a few days, which will help and cheapen transport. If the river opens sooner I may still send a force to cross at Swift Current, as I am anxious to get between the rebels and Montana, for which they will make."[31]

The North West Territorial Lieutenant-Governor, Edgar Dewdney, was excited that securing Clarke's ferry would be advantageous to the relief of Battleford and open the options. "I saw [Middleton] yesterday and recommended him strongly, to make Clarke's Crossing his centre and thus secure a crossing with having wire ferry, and be able to utilize the River between Swift Current and the Crossing ... large quantity of supplies

The South Saskatchewan River waterfront at Medicine Hat about a month after the departure of the *Northcote* and the NWC&NC fleet. MEDICINE HAT ESPLANADE ARCHIVES PC 152.3

now held at Humboldt could be freighted by Clarks Crossing to Battleford, or used by troops. There are other advantages by his taking this course, such as securing undisturbed telegraphic communication with South and Battleford—Can attack East or West."[32]

Organization for the Galt steamers fell to Elliott Galt, Sir Alexander's son and partner, more conservative and less given to theatrics than his father. Elliott left Montreal for Medicine Hat to personally oversee the relaunch of the fleet. "Have made all arrangements for steamers and barges to leave Medicine Hat for Swift Current on Wednesday or Thursday of next week."[33] To better facilitate communications for the river campaign, a temporary telegraph line was built from the CPR station at Rush Lake to the river.[34]

Finally on Sunday, April 5, an excited message came from Richard J. Molloy, the Dominion telegrapher at Clarke's Crossing. Molloy had been a reporter in Prince Edward Island prior to his job at Clarke's Crossing, and his telegraphic messages from the lonely little station became grist for the mill for newspapers across Canada and the world. The news that parties from Medicine Hat to Qu'Appelle to Winnipeg to Ottawa to Montreal had been waiting for, was just now signalled: "Ice just started to run—all clear in 12 hours."[35]

As the telegraph hummed with word of a clear waterway, a correspondent was able to tell eastern papers of the progress of readying the steamers: "Everything is brisk here owing to the preparations for sending a column down the Saskatchewan to Clarke's Crossing."[36] Newly returned from Egypt, the veteran pilot John Segers was sped back to the West on a special express. The night of Sunday, April 5, he returned to find the most activity the Saskatchewan River had known in five years. With the assistance of Herchmer's Mounties, Segers and James Sheets were able to perform all the work required to get the *Northcote*'s paddles into open water. Herchmer had intentions to ship his troop of Mounties and horses to Saskatchewan Landing on the *Northcote*, and was eager to get going. Even his tiny NWMP column was a part of Middleton's marine

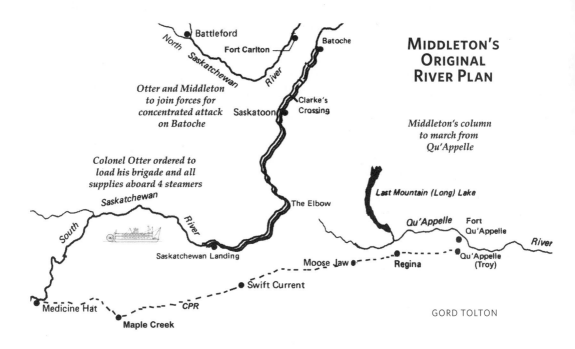

MIDDLETON'S ORIGINAL RIVER PLAN

Otter and Middleton to join forces for concentrated attack on Batoche

Middleton's column to march from Qu'Appelle

Colonel Otter ordered to load his brigade and all supplies aboard 4 steamers

GORD TOLTON

plan to sail with Colonel Otter to Clarke's Crossing. But when the telegraph clattered news of a pending raid at Swift Current, Herchmer switched paddlewheels for steel wheels and bid farewell to Medicine Hat before the steamer could sail. The volunteer home guard was left on its own, but fortunately the train had delivered the guns and ammunition they'd requested.

Some sources say fellow Nile pilot Aaron Russell was on site, but that is hard to verify. Russell may have assisted but not actually boarded. Sheets and Segers, however, had a full crew to sail from Medicine Hat. The chief clerk for the voyages on the *Northcote* that season was Walter R. Talbot—"Rennie" to his friends—an American known as "a gentleman of a poetical turn of mind"[37] whose entertaining diaries informed newspaper readers about the steamship's exploits. The fireman from the previous season, Donald MacIvor, worried about his brother in Prince Albert, dropped his blacksmith's hammer and eagerly climbed aboard to his station at the boilers. The smell of battle stirred the Scottish soldier's soul: "I thought it would be fun for me to join the victorious band."[38]

As the *Northcote* crew prepared their craft, Elliott Galt was still busy hiring labour.[39] Chief among the crews was the jinxed steamer pilot John B. Davis, who wired that he'd gathered together a crew of veteran boatmen and was ready to take them west. Davis was more than ready to take command of a ship again, willing to Master the wheelhouse of the *Baroness*.

To speed the crews up, the Galts pulled strings with Caron and Van Horne to obtain a special express train from Winnipeg to Medicine Hat.[40] The night of April 7, Sir Alexander relayed that "Elliott telegraphs to-night with crews everything complete; boats will leave Medicine Hat Friday, shall see Dewdney en route, hope to have eight barges."[41] The evening of April 8, a train ground into the station at Medicine Hat and the doors swung open to reveal Elliott Galt, John Davis and some 70 men, ready to get the trio of ships ready to sail as soon as possible.

A correspondent in Medicine Hat reported to the *Toronto Daily Mail* that "the water in the South Saskatchewan is very low at Medicine Hat, and the general opinion is that it would be difficult until the spring freshets come to navigate it at the forks of the Red Deer. There is only a depth of 22 inches at Medicine Hat."[42] If 22 inches was the best the river could offer, the *Northcote* crew prepared to deal with that. At 9 a.m. on Thursday, April 9, with two barges in tow, Sheets and Segers weighed anchor and got their vessel pointed downstream.

With the steamers launching, Middleton was finally able to give Minister Caron a rough outline of how he intended to mesh the boats with Colonel Otter's column: "Difficult to give exactly [*sic*] plan, owing to uncertainty of date of troops arriving, and state of River and course of events. At present intend pushing on this force as fast as possible to Clarke's Crossing, then to move according to circumstances. About four hundred under Otter moving up by Steamer from Swift Current, if river open to meet us. Herchmer patrolling North bank of Saskatchewan from Swift Current, perhaps to move north as we move on. As soon as Riel's force disperse, Prince Albert and Battleford relieved; shall wait further directions from you."[43]

With a strategy in place, Middleton informed Caron that he would "proceed to Clarke's Crossing by forced marches when I expect to find the river open" and make that a base. There he would rendezvous with Otter, who would ride the rails to Swift Current and sail downstream on the *Northcote, Baroness, Alberta* and *Minnow*. From Clarke's, they would "expect to meet the rebels near there" and engage Riel's forces at will, and from there ride the boats to the relief of Prince Albert and Battleford. "By that time Swift Current will have become my base for supplies and the river my line of communications."[44] Now the general had a unified force that had only to set sail in order to subjugate their enemy.

Only two obstacles could change Middleton's plan: the rebels and the river. And back at Medicine Hat, the South Saskatchewan was already conspiring. With the late arrival of the Galt crews, John Davis and Josephus Todd were not able to get the *Baroness, Alberta* and *Minnow* into sailing readiness until the afternoon of Friday, April 10, a mere day after the *Northcote* left port.[45] But as the *Northcote* rode the crest in the wake of the ice floes, the water level plunged, literally overnight, as the first ship seemed to have taken the 22 inches of water with them. The *Toronto Daily Mail*'s correspondent thought the Galt fleet would "sail tomorrow for Swift Current, which point it is expected they will make in 68 hours."[46] But for Davis and Todd, the "68-hour" voyage to its next port would draw out to an agonizing 25 days.

The delay was fatal to Middleton's plans for Otter. The *Northcote* got away in good time, but the Galt steamers missed the floodtide that guaranteed success. The interval probably changed the course of history, to the chagrin of Middleton's naval tactics.

CHAPTER SIX

The Horse Marines

Escape from Fort Pitt

The writings of Charles Dickens screamed the need for social justice, fed by his own impoverished youth and the abject deprivation of Victorian England. Dickens would've had sympathy for the Plains Cree of Big Bear and the drastic changes in their lifestyle. But it's probably fortunate he never lived to see the position his luckless son occupied in that tale. While Charles Dickens will always be a genius of literature, Francis Dickens will forever be the clumsy, ineffectual Mountie that fumbles his way into Indian wars, surrenders forts without a shot and rides a leaky scow down the North Saskatchewan River, alive by the charity of a tragic leader who takes the blame for a plethora of deaths and hostage takings.

It all started, oddly enough, on April 1, 1885, white culture's April Fool's Day, adopted by the Cree as Big Lie Day. Folks from the town of Frog Lake played the usual good-natured pranks, and the neighbours from the newly minted Frog Lake Indian reserve joined in on the fun. But frivolity turned to fear a day later, as the local "fools" took on separate roles of victim and tormentor.

"Mistahimaskwa" was born near what is now Jackfish Lake. To the Canadian government, he was the thorn in the side known as Big Bear. To his band, Big Bear was a leader keenly skeptical of the motives of the police and the government. Unlike many of his colleagues, he just plain didn't trust the newcomers, and history probably justifies his fears. But the times dictated that his questioning should brand him a "troublemaker" in the eyes of administrators only too willing to proffer a pen to a "friendly" leader's hand. The situation was always touchy, for Big Bear was no minor chief. At the height of his station, he held sway over 500 lodges. At his whim, the camp would pack up and move where he thought wise, be it the Cypress Hills or the Missouri River in Montana. After several false starts and much privation, Big Bear grudgingly signed Treaty Six, but refused to accept his reserve, putting the legality of the agreement in question. One area looked promising, with prairie parkland

The Cree chief Mistahi-maskwa, or Big Bear as he was known to the general public. LIBRARY & ARCHIVES CANADA C 001873K

and forests providing ample game, where the North Saskatchewan flowed past Fort Pitt, a principal trading post. Big Bear had dealt at Pitt for years, and the HBC was one of the few white institutions he was comfortable with. When he was ready to settle with the government, 25 mounted policemen were deployed to the region, commanded by the less than dynamic Inspector Francis Dickens.

In the winter of 1884/85, Big Bear eventually chose a reserve near the village of Frog Lake. It was a new town, created as a headquarters for the two Woods Cree reserves around its namesake lake. The addition of Big Bear's band would ensure the hamlet a good future as centre of the region's Indian settlements. A water-powered grist mill, built with Cree labour, ensured a grain industry. The steamboat landing on the nearby North Saskatchewan meant a steady supply line between Edmonton and Battleford, as well as work for freighters on the 10-mile trail to the village. There were other signs of settlement: a Catholic church, several log dwellings for merchants and workers, a blacksmith shop, liveries, an NWMP post, the HBC store, and the Indian agency, manned by Thomas Trueman Quinn.

Quinn, a mixed-blood Sioux, was probably one of the worst choices ever made for an agent. Memories of the Minnesota massacres that claimed his father made him loathe all things native. His ill temper tangled with Big Bear, and he often threatened to withhold band rations to enforce his will. In October 1884, the annual treaty payment ceremonies at Frog Lake nearly led to hostilities when Quinn refused demands for fresh beef. A war dance, firing of weapons, and spoken threats ensued. Quinn finally acceded and provided a steer for the ceremony. Believing the presence of the NWMP an irritant, Quinn ordered the five Mounties posted in town to withdraw to Fort Pitt, arrogantly figuring himself capable of mediating the mess. At first the bluff worked, and townspeople postponed their evacuation to the safety of the fort. Big Bear agreed to accept treaty payments, and violence was temporarily postponed. But the tension between Big Bear and Quinn was finally tested when Louis Riel's messengers came knocking. Big Bear listened, and even travelled to Prince Albert to meet Riel, though, ever the skeptic, he remained cautious. But Riel's dispatches inspired and instigated a few unpredictable minor leaders such as Wandering Spirit. Among the propaganda was that the Exovedate provisional government even had support from the U.S. government.

By April 1, 1885, Frog Lake received news of Duck Lake and it was no rumour. The next day saw the most grisly episode of the whole conflict. Wandering Spirit and two warriors invaded the home of Thomas Quinn and jerked him out of bed. Similar incidents occurred in other homes, as weapons and horses were appropriated by the Cree. The Hudson's Bay store was entered, but trader William Cameron had been suspicious and wary enough to have had most of the stock transferred to Fort Pitt. About 10 men were ordered to Quinn's office, where Wandering Spirit loudly berated the agent. The traders were taken to the church, joining the rest of the citizenry. Big Bear became aware of the situation and rushed to the church, but by now he'd completely lost control of the warriors. The white citizens and several Métis were in the church kneeling in prayer when Wandering Spirit broke in. The citizens were ordered out of the church, into the Indian agency buildings. The horrifying details of what occurred next are better described in other sources, but suffice to say that before the night was over, Thomas Quinn was dead, shot by Wandering Spirit. Nine others were also brutally slain, despite Big Bear's protests. Not even Big Bear's own son, Imasees, could be dissuaded from partaking in the killings.[1]

Big Bear's influence did have one effect. Several Frog Lake residents, including Cameron and Theresa Gowanlock and Theresa Delaney, their husbands among the slaughtered, were spared and taken prisoner, forced to move into the Cree camps. Big Bear apologized to the women for the warriors' actions and promised the villagers protection. But Wandering Spirit and Imasees, hearts and minds full of Riel's dreams, their followers emboldened, prepared the band for a mobile war. The entire band of Plains Cree, as well as the nearby Woods Cree and some Chipewyan from Beaver River, were coerced to join. There was no turning back. All Big Bear could do was to go along and try to exert enough influence to prevent further bloodshed and harm to the hostages.

In the two weeks after the terror, the war camp spent days dancing and feasting, almost unconcerned about strategy. Finally, on April 13, a council was held to determine what was to be done about Fort Pitt and its NWMP garrison. This brought Wandering Spirit and company into the world of "Chickenstalker": Inspector Francis Dickens. The nickname for Dickens came not from some admiring Indian leader, but from his own father, in mockery of the boy's pigeon-toed walk. Dickens' career in the police had been remarkable only by his misadventures, such as when he'd nearly angered the peaceful Blackfoot to the point of war. But a shortage of officers had led to his being posted to Fort Pitt. In the wake of Frog Lake, Dickens was indecisive and impotent to do anything about the killings. He could only garrison his own position, rely on messengers for news and give protection to locals in Fort Pitt.

NWMP Inspector Francis Dickens, son of author Charles Dickens, was left the unenviable task of surrendering Fort Pitt and its civilian residents to the Cree. BRENDA BURNS, SASKATCHEWAN ARCHIVES BOARD

Among those locals was the large family of William McLean, Fort Pitt's HBC factor.

McLean had never been very impressed with Dickens, and they quarrelled often in the anxious days waiting for the band's inevitable appearance on the rise above Fort Pitt. When Dickens grew impatient and decided to send Constables Loasby and Cowan and Frog Lake refugee Henry Quinn (nephew of Thomas) to find Big Bear, McLean exploded: "I told him plainly that to send them out was simply to lessen the strength of the fort by having three men killed."[2] Another Dickens plan showed more promise: the policemen began to repair the fort's leaky, weather-worn ferry scow, noting that "large quantity ice drifted downriver."[3]

On April 14, before the scouts returned, the war party, 250 strong, showed up at the fort, held back only by Big Bear, who had just enough authority left to restrain the warriors. Big Bear called for a parley, but showing low regard for Dickens, the band council would only meet with McLean and his clerk, Henry Halpin. The Cree position was clear and so were the options. Give up the fort, or they would use the 40 gallons of kerosene liberated from the store at Frog Lake to burn everyone out. A bad position for a good commander, a disastrous one for the barely capable Dickens. Only the good graces of Big Bear could keep the body count from rising.

A guarantee of safety for the police was obtained, an act of faith inspired by one of Dickens' earlier deeds. A message from Big Bear, translated and sent over with Sergeant John Martin, told the reason why: "Tell your Captain that I remember him well, for since the Canadian government has had me to starve in this country he sometimes gave me food. I do not forget the last time I visited Pitt he gave me a good blanket."[4] Dickens's charity would have made his father proud, and that donated blanket probably saved the lives of his contingent. Big Bear instructed the police: "I want you all out without any bloodshed. We had a talk, I and my men, before we left camp at Frog Lake and thought the way we are doing now the best, that is to let you off if you would go. Try and get away before the afternoon, as the young men are all wild and hard to keep in hand."[5]

William McLean, the HBC factor at Fort Pitt, negotiated for the lives of his family and dozens of others, at the risk of a two-month captivity. CANADIAN PICTORIAL & ILLUSTRATED WAR NEWS, 1885 SOUVENIR EDITION

The parley took two precious days and negotiations were fragile enough, but then the haphazard scouts Cowan, Loasby and Quinn returned and blundered into the heart of the Cree camp. Instead of quietly approaching or detouring around the camp, the scouts stupidly decided to gallop straight through to gain the safety of the fort. Their rush was assessed as an attack and warriors took countermeasures. Quinn escaped unscratched but the two Mounties were struck down, Cowan fatally.

The skirmish exasperated William McLean. His faith in Dickens gone, the factor chose to take his chances with the raiders instead of leaving with the police. A one-hour truce was declared as McLean's wife and children and the rest of the civilians joined the prisoners in Big Bear's camp. The police had just an hour to evacuate Fort Pitt. After that, all bets would be off.

Would Dickens defend his post and go down like Gordon at Khartoum? Or charge the camp like Custer, thereby ensuring he would become at least a valiant corpse? Alas, he was no Gordon or Custer, and a guarantee of safety could not be ignored. With hostages to consider, Dickens counted on McLean's stature to keep the prisoners alive. As for the Mounties, as Corporal Ralph Sleigh put it, it was time "to retire gracefully,"[6] and Dickens could be credited with saving his command from certain death if they could survive the icy river.

As Fort Pitt is left to the Cree's disposal, Dickens and his command escape down the North Saskatchewan. *CANADIAN PICTORIAL & ILLUSTRATED WAR NEWS, 1885 SOUVENIR EDITION*

Their means of escape, the wooden scow, didn't inspire confidence. The boards had shrivelled over the winter and leaked like a basket. The weather too was uncooperative: high winds and a spring blizzard had left the river choked with large ice floes. But faced with certain death or a freezing river, the escapees' chances seemed better in the current. Loading their badly wounded comrade, Loasby, the Mounties hurriedly prepared for launch. As the deadline loomed, Dickens' sailors were still not ready to embark. At the end of the deadline, Dickens had Anglican minister Charles Quinney ask for more time. Big Bear gave them another hour. When the police finally shoved off into the chill of the current, the Cree moved in and took possession of the fort, adding the rest of Pitt's white population to the McLean family as captives.

With little light left, the river impassable in the dark, and Loasby still critical, Dickens crossed to the east bank to camp. "Not forgetting to bring colours along,"[7] Dickens posted the flag on night camp, hoping the Union Jack might offer protection in the face of Big Bear's pledge not to attack. Just getting to the other side proved hazardous: "Nearly swamped in crossing; scow leaked badly." But in the morning, no more stalling was tolerated, as the "general idea prevailed we would be attacked going downriver." The contingent departed. Dickens was cryptic, terse and non-Dickensian in his own diary entries: "Very cold weather. Travelled."[8]

The weather couldn't have been worse, "snowing and very windy," and the night camps were miserable. In the midst of dangerous ice floes, it was all the police could do to keep the craft on course and prevent some giant ice cube from landing in the boat or splitting the boards. The hasty retreat had left little time to chink or caulk the cracks between the boards, and the scow had to be bailed out continuously to keep from sinking. The runoff current was strong and the water high. Frozen spray drenched woolen tunics, leaving "several men frost-bitten. Clothing frozen on our backs."[9]

Even with the ice, wind and leaky boat, the Mounties could not put the Cree out of their minds. At night, they camped on islands with names like "Slapjack" and "Beaver," using the river as an icy moat to prevent surprises. They needn't have worried: Big Bear was as good as his word. Still the lack of tormentors made some very human troopers shudder with fear and guilt at what may have been happening to their friends back at Fort Pitt. But in fact the prisoners were being well cared for.

Mornings were early starts, usually seven o'clock, but with the "ice running strong" and "some narrow escapes in ice jams," the novice navigators learned to get in the water even sooner, as early as 4:30. This not only gave the advantage of low light in the freezing pre-dawn, but the current ran slower, making ice-dodging easier. Days were "dull and cold" with "much ice running."[10] On April 19, the exhausted crew made only five hours before putting in to Beaver Island, where Dickens was confident enough to allow a full day's camp, giving Loasby a better rest.

But leaving the danger of one band's territory, the police knew they were entering a new unpredictability. Near the objective of Battleford was the domain of several reserves with unknown allegiances. They did not know whether a fort or a town would even still be there. While glad to be out of the water, the policemen spent the day sealing cracks and "armouring" the scow. Driftwood and their few supplies were redistributed to the sides of the boat as barricades. To solidify his command, Dickens

The Fort Pitt refugees struggle to keep their hazardous craft out of the North Saskatchewan.
MONTREAL STAR, MAY 23, 1885

held a "rough looking parade"[11] as arms were cleaned, checked and put at the ready.

At noon on April 21, the escapees met NWMP interpreter "Josie Alexander and 2 policemen on south bank with dispatches for us."[12] The party were scouts sent out from Fort Battleford. The news that Battleford was safe heartened the men and they ran the entire rest of the day, stopping only for one last night camp. Even the river was getting more cooperative, to the point of low-water groundings: "River falling; stuck on sandbars." On their last night out, "all sleep aboard scow [with] two men on picket."[13]

On the morning of April 22, smelling safety, the crew got started at 5:45, and three hours later Dickens' soggy command approached the shore near Fort Battleford. The isolated citizens welcomed the Mounties ecstatically: the "garrison turned out and presented arms," as the "police band played us into fort." After an "enthusiastic greeting," the "ladies gave us [a] good dinner."[14] Dickens and company counted their blessings: they had avoided a massacre, prevented a siege, secured a measure of safety for civilians, escaped becoming hostages and survived six days in a leaky boat in brutally cold weather. Soon after their arrival, the column of Colonel William Otter marched in from Swift Current. Assuming military control, Otter turned the NWMP garrison over to Dickens' command, relieving Inspector Morris.

In his report, Dickens gave full credit to his men for the success of his voyage, and to William McLean for the safety of the Fort Pitt prisoners. In his own helplessness, he was privately humbled. No commander ever blamed him for the abandonment of Pitt or the massacre at Frog Lake—incidents beyond his control. But few gave him much credit for lives saved, either. The shame was unspoken, never officially noted but always implied. The fact that he ended his diary, his report to the commissioner, virtually with the escape, suggests a personal torment.

Corporal Ralph Sleigh, who picked up the log of the escape where Dickens left off, had only so much luck to go around. Reassigned to the Battleford contingent, he accompanied Otter to Cut Knife Hill, and in the abortive raid on Poundmaker's camp, was shot and killed. On his body was found the diary describing the Dickens party's journey, preserving his ironic experience downriver.

A "Strange" assembly

As word of tragedy and murder spread, the citizens of many towns knew they were in danger. Edmonton was no exception, and suspicion abounded of nearby Indian camps or Métis settlements. In the wee hours of March 27, 1885, the NWMP garrison at Fort Saskatchewan was rousted out by the telegraph with news of Duck Lake. Among the rudely awakened, Sergeant William Parker was ordered to ride across the river to apprise nearby Edmonton of the fight. The moonlight trot would give Parker a newfound respect for the river, jolting him alert to the importance of the waterway in the campaign to come.

I began to cross the North Saskatchewan River on the ice at Clover Bar when suddenly I broke through, the horse going down under me. For some reason unknown to me I had put my sword on, and it caught across the hole in the ice. I am sure it saved my life, for I scrambled quickly with the bridle rein in my left hand. Then the thought struck me that the horse would come up with a rush, which he did, with his head high in the air. At that moment I gave a mighty pull on the rein and he slid out on his side to the ice. Lengthening the rein to lead him well behind me, we got across the ice all right.[15]

On his arrival, Parker literally had to be chipped loose from his saddle and thawed out inside a hotel. Duly warned by their popsicle Paul Revere, Edmontonians may have felt they needed their own Lord Wolseley at Khartoum, their own Nile voyageurs who could relieve them from the danger at hand. Enter a buckskin-clad saviour from the south, who, ironically, had actually been an old friend and classmate of the Mahdist-slain Charles Gordon.

Thomas Bland Strange, artilleryman, combat engineer, artist, world traveller and rancher, left retirement from the British Army to command the Alberta Field Force.
GLENBOW ARCHIVES NA-1847-2

As a cattleman on the Military Colonization Company Ranche, bordering the Blackfoot reserve, Thomas Bland Strange, a retired servant of Empire, was aware of the risks and dangers, and knew in his own vain way that he was probably the best officer material that could be mustered in the West. He expected he would be called into action at some point, perhaps at Batoche, perhaps at his own back door against his uneasy native neighbours. But until Frog Lake, he probably never expected to become a chip in a Middleton plan to mimic Ulysses S. Grant. Initially, Strange was invited to deal with local matters. The intentions of the Blackfoot, the Bloods and the Peigan were in doubt, as Riel's emissaries had visited the southern bands, inviting them into his movement. Fear of the unknown led a worried Minister Caron to contact Thomas Strange.

Like most British officers, Strange was a willing globetrotter. In fact, he had been born into service, in India, and educated in the usual way of the officer corps, at Woolwich, where he and Charles Gordon were mischievous cadets. Never one for English high society, Strange took postings in locales as diverse as Gibraltar, Ireland and the West Indies. When the Sepoy Mutiny broke out, he returned to his birthland to fight 13 separate battles. While there, he met a fellow officer named Frederick Middleton. Unlike Middleton, Strange was a different breed of cat, more artistic and imaginative, showing more concern for the rank and file than the average officer would. He led by example, beloved by those who served under him, especially at the cap of his career, when he organized B Battery, the regiment of Canadian artillery garrisoned at Quebec. To most British officers, a posting in the cold wilds of Canada among a French-speaking populace would be sheer purgatory. But Strange, a man who vacationed by hiking the Himalayas, revelled in the job, became fluent in the language, and even learned to skate, on the frozen St. Lawrence. When Tom Strange retired, the Western Canadian prairies seemed as exotic a place as any for his sunset years.

At Strangmuir, headquarters of his 70,000-acre spread, Strange accepted command of the Military District of Alberta. Reporting to his rival, Middleton, "Jingo" Strange began to assemble his force at Calgary. Over the Canadian Pacific Railway and from the cattle trails heading into Calgary, men and supplies were marshalled by Major General Strange in anticipation of war with the Blackfoot or with other natives raiding across the 49th parallel.

Throughout April of 1885, however, Father Albert Lacombe, Lieutenant-Governor Edgar Dewdney and NWMP Superintendent John Cotton and others had become aware that the Blackfoot nations of the south had spurned Riel. Blood chief Red Crow had little regard for the traditional enemy Cree, and made his intentions known to his friend and Blackfoot counterpart, Crowfoot. The threat to the border country was mitigated, the chiefs even going so far as to offer warriors to fight the Cree. The defence of southern Alberta was left to the good offices of Major John Stewart and his hastily thrown together Rocky Mountain Rangers patrolling the open range between the Rocky Mountains and the Cypress Hills. Strange's services were needed elsewhere. The force he assembled was to march to the relief of Edmonton and possibly engage Big Bear's Cree in Saskatchewan.

The Alberta Field Force was a military hodgepodge that included militia regiments from Manitoba and Quebec, mounted policemen, British ranchers, U.S. cowboys and Métis canoemen. For the most part, it was a mounted force, designed to travel the tremendous distance from the CPR railhead at Calgary. But moving in the spring of the year, the Field Force would battle the rivers of the West, affectionately known as "the alligators," as they moved north from parched plains to lush parkland and deep into the boreal forests. Blizzards, swollen rivers, marshy bogs and the usual transport troubles forced General Strange to consider a radical flotilla of his own in pursuit of Big Bear.

The Quebec and Manitoba components were added by Middleton: the 9th Voltigeurs, the 65th Mount Royal Rifles and the 92nd Winnipeg Light Infantry. The 92nd was a patchwork of small-town rifle companies and local immigrants of every extraction. A few were returnees from the Sudan—boatmen who had been with Wolseley's Nile voyageurs—a fortunate addition, for sailors would be needed.

Law student R.G. McBeth signed up as a private in the Winnipeg unit, but through a bizarre set of circumstances found himself promoted to second lieutenant, no one more surprised than he. As a boy, McBeth had witnessed the 1870 Rebellion first-hand,

and he would write cogently of his experiences in that conflict as well as the one now brewing in 1885. McBeth told of the train ride to Calgary, when a hungover soldier was assigned to guard the door of a train car. The benumbed guard periodically dozed off, but always clumsily sprang to attention whenever the duty officer passed through. But McBeth had kind words for the pickled private: "the wild-looking soldier of that first night, once beyond the reach of liquor, became . . . the head navigator for our flat-boat flotilla on the North Saskatchewan."[16]

The three infantry units were delivered to Calgary by the CPR, but Strange had to assemble the rest of the force himself. From British Columbia he summoned an NWMP contingent—a militia of cowboys, really—assembled by Sam Steele in the course of policing the railway camps, and dubbed, without false modesty, Steele's Scouts. Another unruly band of prairie folk, under Major George Hatton, became the Alberta Mounted Rifles. An NWMP unit imported from Fort Macleod, under the command of Inspector Aylesworth Perry, came towing a nine-pounder cannon.

By April 20, Strange was ready to march to Edmonton in three stages. The trip was plagued with wet, slushy snow that soaked military woollens, canvas broadcloth, fringed buckskins and animal hides equally to the bone. Crossing hard prairie and parkland was like crossing a sponge that doesn't bounce back. As though the slog weren't enough, the course required the column to cross many icy streams in full flood.

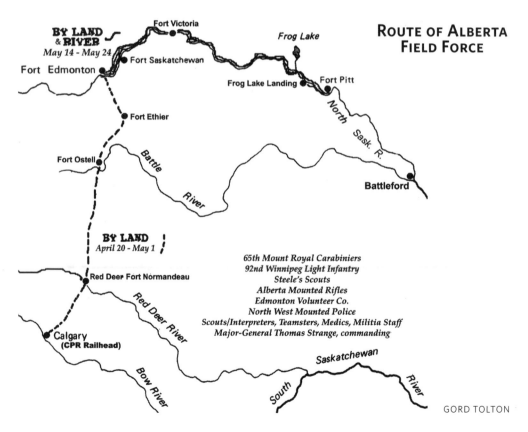

ROUTE OF ALBERTA FIELD FORCE

BY LAND & RIVER
May 14 - May 24

Fort Victoria

Frog Lake

Fort Edmonton

Fort Saskatchewan

Frog Lake Landing   Fort Pitt

Fort Ethier

North Sask. R.

Fort Ostell

Battle River

Battleford

BY LAND
April 20 - May 1

Red Deer Fort Normandeau

65th Mount Royal Carabiniers
92nd Winnipeg Light Infantry
Steele's Scouts
Alberta Mounted Rifles
Edmonton Volunteer Co.
North West Mounted Police
Scouts/Interpreters, Teamsters, Medics, Militia Staff
Major-General Thomas Strange, commanding

Red Deer River

Calgary
(CPR Railhead)

Saskatchewan

Bow River

South   River

GORD TOLTON

The first day included a trip across the Bow River. George Hamilton's ferry was not operating, because the flow was too rapid. As R.G. McBeth recounted:

About six miles out we crossed the Bow River by fording, and this was one of the first of many picturesque scenes on our route. The river was wide and swift-flowing, the water where we crossed on the stony bottom being from two to four feet deep. The loaded wagons, with four and six horses or mules driven by skilful though somewhat profane teamsters, the red-coated soldiers, the Mounted Police in scarlet and gold, and the picturesque corps of scouts, all passing through the water together, made a view worthy of being placed on canvas. Occasionally the scene would be spoiled by a mule throwing himself down in the water, but the free use of the black-snake whip, with the freer use of language not to be repeated here, overcame the obstinacy of the animal.[17]

General Strange noted the hardship that turned a simple prairie march into a boggy ordeal: "The early Spring of 1885 was most unfavourable to the advance. A few days' warm Chinook wind melted the snows, flooded the rivers and coulées, and made swamps and Sloughs of Despond … in every depression on the prairie in which the men sank to the saddle girths and waggons above the axle trees."[18] To make matters worse, prairie fires had ravaged the land, robbing the horses and oxen of even the small amount of dead grass that would otherwise be available for fodder.

Not far from the Bow, Nose Creek, though shallow, challenged the teamsters of the column, with banks wet and greasy from the mud created by frost thawing from the prairie. Then the chinook gave way to a spring blizzard, providing still other stresses. Steele's Scouts arrived at the Red Deer River completely snow-blind.

The settlement at Red Deer was a recent addition. The Cree originally called the river the "Elk," but newcomers confused elk with the red deer of Scotland, and the name stuck. In 1882, Reverend Leonard Gaetz had led a party of British and Canadian Methodists to the site, supported by the Saskatchewan Land and Homestead Co., which had purchased 205,000 acres from the Canadian government for next to nothing. Before the settlers arrived, the area had been the realm of Ad McPherson, frontiersman, wolf pelt trader and stagecoach entrepreneur. In 1884, McPherson, grumbling about civilization closing in on him, sold his claim at the crossing to Sage Bannerman.

Bannerman became the Red Deer's first ferryman, in June of 1884. Bannerman established his craft for $800, but a heavy rainfall and a torrent of debris flowing downstream tore out his cable. After a week's toil, Bannerman replaced the cable, just in time to happily ferry the more than 200 wagons that had accumulated on either side of the river. By the end of his first season, Bannerman was a local legend, marking his power on the local economy by proclaiming himself "Admiral" Bannerman. He christened his ferry the *Irish Washerwoman*, and only the Alberta winter could keep the *Washerwoman* tied up.

The citizens of Red Deer had abandoned their town for Calgary when the conflict broke out. When Strange's column of wagons reached the Red Deer on April 25, Bannerman's ferry was dormant, stalled by high water, the Red Deer evacuation and the fact that someone had deliberately cut the cable. Strange had cause to appreciate the settlers' reaction: "… Indian signal smokes showed our movements were closely watched."[19] Disappointed by the lack of a ferry, but with an assignment to fulfill, Strange ordered the brigade of teams to ford. Wagons carrying the infantrymen of the 65th Mount Royal "had to be raised on their axles by blocks of wood, the river being from three to four feet deep"[20] Once across, the Rifles fanned out in the woods to cover the cavalry baggage wagons against would-be snipers.

Teams and wagons struggling under weight and over unsure footing in about four feet of water had to contend with a current strong enough to push a deadly wall of force at a right angle to their line of travel. Bannerman's rowboat was posted downstream to catch anything that might float astray, and a few things did. "A few carts only were swept away by the strength and depth of the stream but all were subsequently recovered, though the provisions they contained were damaged." The odd misadventure was to be expected and General Strange remained heartened. "No men nor horses were drowned."[21] In fact, there proved to be an unexpected advantage to some of the dampened provisions, as only the outer inch or so of the bagged flour moistened until it caked, forming an impermeable crust against any further dampness.

Having crossed without serious incident, Strange carried on. His counterpart in the next column would not be so fortunate, and Inspector Perry learned that sleepy western rivers awaken with a vengeance. By the time Perry reached the Red Deer crossing, warm rains had caused the tributary to swell. The reach was now more than 250 yards wide, the current estimated at five miles per hour, a flow rate perilous to landlubber horses and men. What was left of Sage Bannerman's beloved *Washerwoman* lay in kindling on the bank. The only craft in sight now was the rowboat.

Waiting for the waters to recede was out of the question for Perry. Instead, he sent troops across the swollen channel in the rowboat, as others scrounged the south bank for salvageable lumber. In a couple of hours time, the remains of the *Washerwoman* were patched together and strengthened by timber-savvy soldiers. The refurbished raft was estimated to be capable of carrying six tons, and Perry ordered his cannon and gun carriage, ammunition and harnesses to be rolled aboard. The rowboat took across a 1,200-foot line cobbled together from the combined lariats and picket ropes of the cowboys. With the scow in the water and the line secure, Perry climbed on the scow with his artillerymen, and signalled for the raft to be towed into the stream.

Perry thought the operation complete as the scow approached the north bank. But then the jury-rigged ferry rope snapped and all hell broke loose. Perry felt the scow slipping back into the stream. Perry and Constable Diamond dived into the icy, rushing waters, grabbed what was left of the line and fought their way to shore. Once

The 2nd Division of the Alberta Field Force crossing the Red Deer River, 1885. The actual crossing was a little less triumphant, as Supt. A. Bowen Perry, his cannon and command were swept away in the current and nearly killed. FROM *THE FORT NORMANDEAU STORY ALBUM* JACKET

landed, Perry and Diamond secured the line to a tree, but the strong current gave the scow too much purchase and the flimsy rope broke again.

The runaway craft careened downstream to certain oblivion. For three miles the trapped policemen rode the waves without so much as a shovel to steer with, the heavy cannon only adding to their momentum. Eventually, cross-currents sent the scow crashing into the south bank. When the rafters regained their composure, they found the cannon at the base of a steep 30-foot cliff. "Up this, the gun, carriage and ammunition were hauled, with great labour, by the men of the detachment on board."[22]

Having broken their backs on that travail, the men still had to return the gun to the Crossing. Hacking through thick brush, they encountered the first of several swamps. One of the marshes they had to detour more than doubled the three-mile distance, and they had to blaze more than a mile of new trail through heavy woods.

The raft was recovered and rebuilt, and during the two days that took, the river receded enough to ensure a safer crossing. Teamsters took the wheels off their freight wagons to turn the wagon boxes into boats to carry supplies and ammunition across the Red Deer. Perry's Mounties were eventually able to install a better cable and establish a properly operable ferry.

With the arrival of the military, the Red Deer evacuees felt safe enough to return, and Lieutenant J. Bédard Normandeau of the Mount Royal Rifles posted a 20-man contingent to defend the residents of Red Deer and protect a cache of stores General Strange had left behind. Robert McLellan's year-old log hotel was commandeered, reinforced by a plank-and-log wall 10 feet tall, and dubbed "Fort Normandeau."

Lieutenant McBeth described the Red Deer crossing when the third column arrived: "We came to the Red Deer River, where, it being high-water time, we were stopped by what Adjutant [Charles] Constantine called 'a wide, swift-flowing and treacherous stream,'"[23] belying the curses and epithets of the Mounties and soldiers. McBeth was almost nonchalant: "After many futile attempts a rude ferry was constructed, upon which, under the pilotage of Sergt. Pritchard, of No. 1 Company, we all crossed in safety"[24]

A portion of the force often overlooked was the small crew of workmen known as the "pioneer corps," or "sappers," who performed advance work such as laying out picket ropes in camp or digging latrines. Lightly armed and usually working without good tools, the detail was charged with frontier engineering. General Strange had chosen his crew well: "A party of six Pioneer axemen (of the Mount Royal) and a Sergeant and three Scouts."[25] Strange praised the French-speaking units, boasting, "Most country-born Canadians are axemen; can build a house or make a toothpick with an axe. The 65th were splendid bridge-builders. They did excellent service, bridging creeks, corduroying and bushing muskegs, and in some places, cutting fresh roads through the woods."[26]

A day out of Red Deer, the Pioneers encountered the Blindman River and found what must have seemed exotic to a prairie traveller: an actual bridge. Although the bridge had been burned, the fire had failed to destroy the main structure, and it didn't take the Pioneer corps long to hack, whittle and hammer a deck onto the crude viaduct.

That obstacle passed, the sappers built corduroy roads, laying split logs side by side across boggy areas to allow wagons to pass over the muck on a pad that supports their weight. Once past the Red Deer, more corduroy was required, as the column was into parkland—rich, dark-brown soil that was perfect for farmers due to its capacity to hold moisture, but anathema to heavy freighters and marching soldiers.

One soldier thought to ease his burden by slinging his Snider rifle on the back of a wagon, against express orders. When his weapon slid off and fell into the water, the private was ordered into the icy mire without his trousers to retrieve his weapon. General Strange sat on horseback and watched the whole affair, saying nothing, considering the grunt's ordeal as penalty enough.

At the Battle River, the column encountered their first prospect of hostility. "We came upon the first bands of Indians, numerous enough and of the Cree tribe, under chiefs bearing the not very classical names of Ermine-Skin, Cayoté, and Bobtail."[27] When Strange visited Ermineskin and Bobtail, he also met with Father Constantine Scollen, the local Catholic missionary. Riel's agents had visited and the Battle River HBC post had been pillaged in response. Scollen had admonished the chiefs for the looting and talked them out of joining the fight.

That situation in hand, Strange marched on. The Cree leaders were particularly impressed when the red-coated Winnipeg Light Infantry marched through. "With bayonets fixed and rifles at the slope, with band playing and every weapon exposed to view, we marched through, while the Indians gathered in the woods by the roadside and gazed wonderingly at the spectacle." On the whole, the encounter was anti-climactic and uneventful, marked only by the establishment of a blockhouse called Fort Ostell. Further up the trail, another of Strange's "instant garrisons" was set up, Fort Ethier, on the Rivière de la Paix. Soldiers of the Mount Royal were posted to the two forts to secure the trail.

Captain Ethier told his own tale of a battle with the Battle River, over and above his traverse of "the swamps and the rivers … exposed all this time to a shot in the head."[28] Ethier's company found the river "impossible to cross as the water had risen several feet and there was no bridge." But Ethier had orders to establish a post, and in comparing the Battle to a Quebec waterway, he was not going to let some cranky Western current deter him from his duty. "We constructed a raft to carry our baggage and supplies across. The horses were swimming but the current was stronger than Hochelaga close to St. Hélène Island. The raft that we had constructed broke and one of the guides fell into the water while the other one and myself were saved from drowning, but not before taking a cold bath in these terrible conditions."[29]

The first of May brought the first of the Field Force to "the scattered little town of Edmonton, peeping through clumps of pine and poplar, the blue sky and brilliant sunshine gilding the grey old stockades of the Hudson's Bay Fort ... crowning the steep bank over the broad swift sweep of the Saskatchewan, navigable by the HBC boats and steamers for 800 miles to Lake Winnipeg ... a picture that lingers in the memory."[30] Residents of Edmonton cheered when they looked out across the North Saskatchewan from their barricades and saw the Alberta Field Force camped by John Walter's ferry, the *Belle of Edmonton*.

Walter was one of the most illustrious of the West's inland mariners, eventually the most enterprising and successful builder of all manner of water craft. An Orkneyman by birth, Walter had followed the tradition of his Scottish island people and had come to the North West in 1870 to work for the HBC building York boats for the fur trade, for $50 a year. He left the HBC and built a cabin across the river from the fort, on a flat known as Walterdale, where increased traffic from Calgary created a need for a reliable crossing on the North Branch. In 1882 he set out for Winnipeg with an ox cart and returned with half a ton of hardware to establish the first modern cable-operated ferry in all the territory between Manitoba and the Rockies. Wary of marine superstition, Walter was careful to christen his craft, and the *Belle of Edmonton* brought good fortune to him over the next two decades. Walter's ferry changed the usually dangerous task of river crossing into a reliable utility, with none of the drama of the Red Deer ford.

As Strange and his troops took the Walter ferry across the North Saskatchewan, the general noted the Edmontonians' gratitude at their arrival: "As I neared the opposite bank in the big scow that serves as ferry, the white puffs of smoke wreathed from the little guns of the Fort and the echoes of a salute reverberated across the river."[31] Lieutenant McBeth seemed to be almost a touch sentimental: "As we crossed the ferry and marched into Edmonton, we saw the picturesque town." [32]

The makeshift flotilla

In his early days as an artillery officer, General Strange had acquired the nickname Gunner Jingo. Jingo was a diminutive of jingoism, a term referring to vehement patriotism in the age of British Imperialism. Rowdy soldiers in London music halls would hoist tankards of ale and boast of the Empire's might as they robustly sang:

> We do not want to fight but by Jingo if we do,
> We've got the men, we've got the ships,
> We've got the money too.

Now arrived in Edmonton, Gunner Jingo had the men and the government's money, and soon he'd have the ships as well. After the shock of Frog Lake, he decided to build his own navy and sent the Reverend John McDougall ahead to engage the construction of a fleet. By the time the column arrived, the barge-building was well underway, supervised by the Methodist missionary who'd traversed so many miles of prairie in service to the faith.

The Field Force could relax a little in Edmonton. Local natives saw the show of force and quelled any notions of sympathy toward Louis Riel. Teamsters rested their animals and repaired their wagons. Soldiers let their boot-worn blisters heal and mended their torn uniforms. But this was only a stop, not a destination. The force was under orders to confront Big Bear and free the hostages. The plan was for the force to link with Otter's Battleford column, supported by steamboats, and unite in a common front against Poundmaker or Big Bear as the case may present. Cut Knife Hill and the steam fleet's troubles on the South Branch had disrupted this strategy, but the telegraph was out, rendering Strange incommunicado and thus uninformed of events downriver.

To the military, the government and the general public, the troubles were personified by Big Bear, though in hindsight we know the actual situation of the Cree/Chipewyan war camp was more complicated. Mindful of the problems of the Calgary/Edmonton Trail, Strange saw that the fastest and easiest way to get his column to their downstream objective may be, literally, down the stream. If you can't beat your river, join it. In so doing, the unusual general created an unusual navy, and coined a term never used before or since: "flourclad."

On May 2, Strange toured the Fort Edmonton boatyards—for generations a centre for construction of rivercraft—and selected a gigantic York boat of the classic Orkney design, 100 feet long and 25 feet wide, constructed a year earlier. In addition, four flat-bottomed scows were fastened together. He was skeptical: "To an Englishman's eye, the boats certainly looked cranky,"[33] and he didn't believe the rafts were "fit to carry a 9-pounder gun and ammunition, to say nothing of the lives of the men."[34]

The HBC reassured Strange as to the rationale for their construction methods, explaining that the boats were "made elastic." The trick was to give the barges flexibility to tolerate the river's variances "with a certain amount of give and take, as the boats constantly ran aground on the shifting sandbanks of the Saskatchewan." The British rafts Strange was familiar with were built to remain rigid, but upon explanation he realized that "double planks served better than thicker single timbers, and wooden pins were mainly used instead of nails."[35] Iron nails rust and work their way out under stress, while wooden pegs not only expand with moisture and time, but flex with the boat.

McBeth and his comrades took advantage of the Edmonton respite to do a little shopping and find something to eat other than camp food. Merchants facing a stale economy were only too glad to fill the need. "While flat-boats were being made to take us down the river, and I especially remember that with the lavish hand of the soldier of Epicurean philosophy, we spent our scanty cash in buying up the ancient stock of delicacies from the Hudson's Bay store. Dried apples and prunes, ginger bread of rocky firmness, canned fruit, and such like, found their way to our tents, and on these unaccustomed delicacies we fared sumptuously for several days."[36]

By the time supplies and provisions were brought ashore for loading, General Strange had assembled eight boats, each designated for a particular function. Five would be troop ships, carrying infantrymen and baggage, a full third of the Field Force. The largest of the scows carried 60 men, as well as the quartermaster's stores and the force's ammunition.

One scow, the "battleship" carrying the nine-pounder cannon, was more rigidly constructed than the rest, "… with a platform of stout timber in the centre, and bales of hay form[ing] a musket proof parapet."[37] The gun was lashed solidly to the boat to enable the vessel to contain the full effect of its recoil. The weapon was intended to be used at a moment's notice and would be "traversed by pointing the boat's head in the direction the gun was to fire."[38] The arrangement was unconventional but not totally unheard of, as Strange said he'd once "fired a 10-pounder gun at Shoeburyness (at the mouth of the Thames in England) off a raft constructed of casks, with a superstructure of planks. I had no doubts about the boat bearing the recoil without injury."[39] The battleship was christened the *Big Bear*, leaving no doubt as to the target.

Another ship took on the draft-horse team that pulled the big gun. This vessel was a bit better built than the others, to sustain the moving and shaking of the heavy horses. Armoured with pressed hay, it became the *Hay-Clad*. The remaining scow was actually a working ferry from the hamlet of Clover Bar that had been installed by John Walter in 1883. Strange bought the vessel and rerigged it, but it still carried the steel cables, deadman anchors, winches and associated ferry equipment. This would enable the *Clover Bar* to be landed and used as an emergency ferry should the need arise for troops to operate on either side of the river. Strange reasoned that native scouts would thus report that his force was operating on both sides of the river, without his actually having to divide the force. The subterfuge would discourage "Big Bear [from joining] forces with Poundmaker and fall upon my communications and the defenceless settlements on the south shore."[40]

By the time Strange was ready to weigh anchor, McBeth noted the cynicism of the Edmonton citizens as the fleet embarked in open flatboats. Shaking their heads, the

Tom Strange learned sketch artistry as an artilleryman, and made three cross-section profiles of the flotilla craft he organized in Edmonton. In this sketch, gunners test the nine-pounder cannon, concealed amid the armour of dozens of barrels of provisions. FROM *GUNNER JINGO'S JUBILEE*

settlers "asserted that the Indians would enjoy the sport of standing on the high banks and "potting" us as we went by."[41] Strange had already considered this, and arranged armour cladding for his fleet. But what an armour he devised. Iron would further weigh down the boats and increase their draw, as would extra timbers. What was at hand to defend "against plunging fire from the banks"[42] were the provisions and supplies themselves.

The general elaborated: "The boats were not decked, but had a narrow platform running round. Barrels of salt pork and beef, and sacks of flour were arranged along the sides, above and below the gunwale, giving a double tier of fire, loop holes being formed by intervals between the sacks, and holes cut under the gunwale. A high traverse of the same materials was constructed along the centre of the boat." The boats were double-decked, with riflemen able to line both rows of either side, and the pilots able to steer from the top deck with their long poles, called "sweeps." Recalling the U.S. Civil War battles between ironclads, Strange's boats were sarcastically referred to as "flourclads," three of them dubbed the *Nancy*, the *Bauset* and the *Roy du Bord*.

Using the scows was a stroke of logistical genius. With the scows hauling freight, there was less need for expensive wagons and teamsters. The boats didn't have to eat, which eliminated the need for teams to carry fodder. Few wagons would be needed, and they would be protected by the cavalries that would follow along on the riverbanks above. From their high perspective, the horsemen could spot any attempted ambush, and the sight of them might discourage would-be attackers.

Not everyone was enamoured of General Strange's idea. "Unfortunately my flourclads ... did not inspire the same confidence as did the steam flotilla of General Middleton."[43] Jingo was an original thinker, but his tart disposition and eccentric manner disagreed with traditional military values. Many thought him mad, including Colonel William Osborne Smith. The Irish-born Smith was an old British Army regular, having come to Canada in 1854 and raised the Victoria Volunteer Rifles in defence of Canada during the U.S. Civil War. He later went west as deputy adjutant general at Winnipeg, where he helped organize the NWMP, and stitched a microcosm of Manitoba into the 92nd Light Infantry, including the returned Nile voyageurs.

Smith wasn't impressed with the flourclads, and registered an official complaint "condemning the construction of the boats, together with a request … to try experiments on the penetration of flour sacks by rifle bullets."[44] Jingo answered the charges by appointing a board of officers to assess the craft and their vulnerability to fire. After the testimony of Edmonton's best navigators and boat builders, a few extra cross ties were hammered in, and the board proclaimed the boats battleworthy. The flour-sack armour issue was not contested further, the ultimate trial of its capabilities to be "left to the enemy."[45]

Colonel William Osborne Smith, commander of the 92nd Winnipeg Light Infantry, and no fan of Strange's homemade navy.
FROM *THE MAKING OF THE CANADIAN WEST*

Smith felt vindicated when a few civilians hired as boatmen let the craft sink in the river, which wouldn't have happened had they bailed out the seepage before it got out of control. Strange fired the civilians, but still had no pilots. He tried to hire a few capable local Métis to steer the flotilla, but none were willing to stand in the extremely exposed position atop the upper decks. Riel's rumours had got to them, as "their friends had established such a scare as to the certainty of the boats and the men in them being destroyed by the fire of Indians from the commanding wooded banks."

Finally, a veteran HBC tripman, J. Sinclair, was hired as the chief pilot for the *Big Bear*, while the boatmen of the Winnipeg infantry were ordered to man the sweeps, and orders were issued for the flotilla. "Five Infantry boats (including the *Nancy*, *Bauset*, and *Roy du Bord*), each containing a company with camp equipage, ammunition, and food supplies; One gunboat (*Big Bear*), containing an Artillery detachment, N.W.M.P, 9-pounder gun, and ammunition; One horse barge (*Hay Clad*), with forage,

Tom Strange's sketch shows the artillery horses of the cannon's gun carriage stanchioned on the craft. The oarsman, protected by baled hay, pilot the scow from a second level. This craft sank within miles of Edmonton, and the horses had to travel on land. FROM *GUNNER JINGO'S JUBILEE* and carrying the gun team; One ferry-boat scow (*Clover Bar Ferry*), carrying stores and a coil of wire rope sufficient to span the river, thus creating, in a few hours, a ferry enabling the troops to act on either side of the river."[46]

Though the planned bon voyage was delayed by heavy snow, rain and wind, the river-borne force, "the advance on Fort Pitt,"[47] finally put into the current on May 14, with the scouts and cavalry and a small convoy of wagons following along on the north bank. As space constraints precluded both infantry units—the Mount Royals and the Winnipeggers—from riding the scows at the same time, one of them had to travel with the wagon column.

Which unit would sail and which would march became a military secret. The HBC had informed Strange that the Mount Royals from Quebec were going to be seen as particular targets regardless whether they were on a boat or on land. As it was explained to Strange, it was a matter of language and appearances: "The little soldiers who spoke French like Half-breeds and did not wear red coats, could not be the Queen's men."[48] They did not command the respect usually given anglo policemen in scarlet. The Winnipeg Light Infantry troops were safe: they spoke English and wore red coats, just like the Mounties. The Mount Royals just weren't in style. Given this odd bit of cultural information, Strange devised a deception. With so many civilians in the Transport Services, many of them Métis, and scoop-hungry reporters blurting out intelligence, it was hard to keep anything secret. There were even rumours that the Quebec troops were sympathetic to Riel. Strange found that hard to swallow, but ordered the Winipeggers onto the scows and the Mount Royals to go with the cavalry on land. He didn't tell anybody he intended to swap the units' places once he reached Fort Victoria.

To hush the doomsayers foretelling disaster for the ships, Strange left his horse and personally embarked in a scow along with his staff. But he let it be known that in the event of trouble, he had "no intention of being caught in the boats while my Force was engaged on shore." Despite their disparate means of travel, Strange had every intention of keeping his land and river brigades close together and in constant

This heavily loaded scow has been arranged for the crews to be armoured against gunfire by barrels and sacks of flour, salt pork, bacon and beans. Infantryman are able to return fire from the "hold" through the spaces between the boards of the gunwale, protected by the cargo.
FROM *GUNNER JINGO'S JUBILEE*

communication via coded bugle calls. It was an excellent example of teamwork, the cavalry providing security while the "navy" did the heavy freighting. And security certainly would be a concern in places where an ambush would be possible, such as where the river narrowed, had blind bends, or presented barriers to navigation such as deadfall or sand and gravel bars.

A number of canoes headed the fleet as advance scouts for the river, warning of shallows and watching for trouble. Ed Nagle was among these latter-day voyageurs bringing their forefathers' trade back to life, and named some of his compatriots: James Grant, Charles Parley, Charles Rossiter and "a fellow named Osborne,"[49] "Half-breeds mostly, who can balance on a log going down a swift stream ... dancing in fact, keeping time to their own wild chansons. In a birch-bark canoe they will balance a portly Englishman playing a salmon."[50]

As the pilots hauled on their sweeps, they broke into their boatman's songs. Strange thought initially he should order the voyageurs hushed, so as not to attract enemy scouts. In fact, he had ordered a general silence among the riders and boats. But he just didn't have the heart to stifle the folk tunes. What the tunes lacked in stealth, they loaded with morale:

> C'est l'aviron qui nous monte, qui nous mène,
> C'est l'aviron qui nous monte en haut.

and

> À la claire fontaine
> M'en allant promener
> J'ai trouvé l'eau si belle
> Que je m'y suis baigné.
> Il y a longtemps que je t'aime,
> Jamais je ne t'oublierai.

and

> Vive la Canadienne
> Vole, mon coeur, vole!
> Vive la Canadienne!
> Et ses jolis yeux doux,
> Et ses jolis yeux doux, doux, doux,
> Et ses jolis yeux doux!

and

> Derrière chez nous, y a-t-un étang
> En roulant ma boule
> Trois beaux canards s'en vont baignant,
> Rouli, roulant, ma boule roulant,
> En roulant ma boule roulant
> En roulant ma boule!

The songs also heartened the Winnipeggers pulling on the sweeps—returnees from the Sudan who had heard about the captives from Frog Lake and Fort Pitt. Would they be too late as they had been for Gordon? A little music to soothe the soul was well worth it.

As darkness fell the first day and the fleet put in to shore for the night, McBeth was designated officer of the camp, having to contend with weather as well as paranoia: "Our flat-boats were tied to trees and we encamped in a storm, half rain, half snow, for the night … The twenty-five men fell in as best they could to be inspected in the darkness and on the sliding mud of the bank. Then we groped our way through the wet bush some distance to the rear of the camp, where we posted our line of sentries, while the rest of the picket huddled together under the dripping trees. The work of relieving sentries was made difficult by the very darkness of the forest; but the slightest movement drew out the hoarse challenge, and the sentry thus found always gladly welcomed the relief."[51]

The troops' soggy sleep ended as McBeth ordered them aboard before sunrise. "At four o'clock we came in, roused the camp, got on board breakfastless, and moved down the river in a driving snow-storm, with our clothes standing upon us like icy coats of mail." To save time, cooking and eating were done on board, the "galley" consisting of small sheet iron stoves. Dinner proved easier on the river than on the trail. While cavalrymen and teamsters had to stop and make camp in order to prepare and consume their victuals, as well as feed their mounts and teams, the infantrymen cooked aboard the barges "by placing rocks on the planks of the barges to support the stoves."[52]

First port of call was Fort Saskatchewan, where the flotilla delivered a number of prisoners captured from Riel. The accused were turned over to the NWMP's Superintendent Griesbach, as General Strange, the ranking military authority, inspected the fort and heard the stories of the area settlers that had sought refuge there. Tales included a family that had thrown their finest clothing down their well, and a new bride that had fled with her wedding dress.

At the fort, Jingo welcomed to his staff Captain Edward Palliser, a British artilleryman and younger brother of the prairie explorer John Palliser. Palliser was in Canada to design coastal defences in Nova Scotia, but when hostilities erupted in the West, he embarked on foot, horseback and canoe to volunteer for the Alberta column. A giant of a man, and an old friend of Strange, Palliser was made assistant quartermaster general and given a mission: "[Palliser] paddled himself down the Saskatchewan in a dug-out canoe, with a Half-breed guide, and restored my communications, which had been interrupted, thus rendering important service."[53] Strange also picked up a good horse Mountie from the Fort Saskatchewan garrison. Sergeant William Parker, the rider who'd nearly drowned and frozen to death to warn Edmonton, was attached to Steele's Scouts.

The leaky fleet of scows had its first casualty soon after leaving Fort Saskatchewan. The *Hay-Clad*, with the artillery horses aboard, sank into the muddy shore. The

Mounties responsible for the livestock found a small rowboat and led the animals away from the scow as they rowed. Eventually the craft was bailed out and refloated. For the sake of the horses, the team was reassigned to the land column, while the scow was lashed to another of the flotilla and towed behind as a spare.

When the fleet put in to Fort Victoria, "a very lovely place, an old HBC fort," on May 16, McBeth revealed the nature of the pervasive misinformation, noting that the store "had been recently looted … by Big Bear and his band, who were now sullenly retreating before us with all the prisoners and their ill-gotten plunder."[54] The post had been looted, for sure, but the Frog Lake Indians were nowhere near Victoria, an indication of how fear had turned Big Bear into a bogeyman, a wraith who appeared out of nowhere in the mind's eye.

Strange was jaded to the anxieties of settlers, but at Fort Victoria he was beginning to see some real effects of the rebellion, notably "poor people, who have been hiding in the woods … The young people look especially miserable, and many have died." The despair moved Strange and he decried the rebels: "The country is in a terrible state—no food and ravaged by Indians and Riel emissaries." Then Strange let loose on his own superiors: "If it were not for the amazing delay of the Militia Stores Department in sending arms, etc., and opposition from almost every source, except the enemy, I would have been through this business a fortnight ago." Strange couldn't help but compare his own ragged but proud armada with that of his well-fed rival on the South Branch: "General Middleton seems to be well supplied with regular troops, artillery, and a steam flotilla. I wish you saw my flotilla of flourclads floating down the Saskatchewan."[55]

It wasn't all drudgery and anxiety "at Fort Victoria, in the enemy's country." In spite of the conditions, and contrary to orders forbidding departure from camp, boys will be boys, and Corporal Pritchard of the 92 WLI, "an ardent disciple of Izaak Walton[,] got an old punt and pushed across the river to a likely-looking creek to do some fishing." When Pritchard returned, Colonel Osborne Smith was on the bank waiting, and ordered Sergeant Sutherland to arrest and bring the subordinate before him.

"To Sutherland's surprise the 'outlaw'… submitted good-humoredly to the arrest, but insisted on bringing his string of fish with him. The Colonel was equally surprised, Pritchard being a favorite … the very opposite of a wilful offender" who "had been of prime service to the column in crossing the Red Deer River." As a worthy "mariner and fisherman," Pritchard also knew how to back-paddle "as he moreover gravely avowed that he had been intending the best fish for the Colonel's dinner." Smith was obviously moved: "That officer, keeping his face straight with great difficulty, administered a reprimand and set the offender at liberty." No word on how Osborne Smith enjoyed his trout.[56]

On April 17, Strange met with Pakan, a Cree chief who had no truck nor trade with Riel. In fact his band had killed a messenger from Wandering Spirit. While Pakan and Strange conferred on matters of neutrality and using band warriors as scouts, members of the WLI decided to use their layover to construct kedge anchors, crude devices used by steamboaters in warping through an impasse such as a rapid or a shoal. Essentially the kedge was a deadweight, designed to be placed above the obstacle as a tie point for the vessel to haul itself up without losing ground. The kedges described by Strange consisted of "a framework of stout wood filled with stones."[57]

Jingo Strange had not forgotten the matter of the Mount Royals. Upon putting in to Fort Victoria, he ordered the Winnipeggers to camp close to the river and tend the boats, while the Mount Royals were to stay with the horses and wagons. Nobody but Strange knew that, at the last instant, the general would ring a change and order the French-speakers down the hill and into the boats, while the Winnipeggers swapped sea legs for marching orders. Journalists in the column were enraged by the swap. The general had made liars of them in their already mailed dispatches to their papers. The correspondents saw to it in follow-up reports that General Strange was branded as impetuous, "a madman who did not know his own mind for twenty-four hours." Thick-hided, Jingo had no problem with name calling, as he felt justified in the deception: "I did know my own mind, but took care no one else did, as I had reason to believe that information in the *Winnipeg Press* was conveyed to Half-breeds by sympathisers."[58]

"The character of the country continued the same from Victoria, undulating and intersected by creeks, lakes, and swamps draining into the Saskatchewan."[59] Only one hint of action was ever seen on the downstream voyage. Near Vermillion Creek, a shot was heard. The Mount Royals landed their scow and deployed in search of the night snipers, in the manner befitting Strange's orders: "In the event of an attack, the men will extend, take the best cover at hand, and open fire."[60]

The phantom attacker disappeared into the darkness, and the riflemen, "led by their gallant commander, charged up the heights with loud cheers and swept the prairie with a shower of bullets."[61] So zealous were the Quebecers that Sam Steele's Scouts nearly paid for the sniper's sins. "Five of my scouts who were out had to lie down in a deep hollow, where there was cover for themselves." Soon the infantrymen located and closed in on their quarry and "it was discovered that the sentry's Indians were young poplars waving in the wind."[62] Retreating from their brush with brush, the infantrymen had bagged only sore feet, red eyes and empty cartridges. Despite the false alarm, nervous tension was just one of the subtle signs that enemy territory was drawing nearer. More tangible proof came at Saddle Lake, when Sam Steele reported the Indian reserve empty and found a cache of supplies. Another scout reported a bullet hole through his hat.

With Frog Lake and Fort Pitt within reach, Strange finally received a communiqué from his commander, Fred Middleton. But the news was ancient, nearly a month old, the telegram having come the long way around, via Calgary and Edmonton. Sent from Fish Creek, it told of Middleton's rout and of the *Northcote* being stuck on the South Branch. Strange did not yet know the outcome of Batoche, Cut Knife Hill or anything else. For all he knew, his column was on the moon. The only relevant detail was Middleton ordering Strange to "go to Fort Pitt and restore confidence."[63]

Of course, by then Strange's column was all but at Fort Pitt. It was time to open a different line of communication in the absence of the telegraph. Jingo called for modern-day voyageurs to reach his commander and inform Middleton of his position. Two men came forward, and George Borradaile and William Scott became waterborne carrier pigeons.

On May 25, the mounted column reached the scarred settlement of Frog Lake. What they saw horrified the scouts. Every building in the town was razed. Rotted corpses were everywhere: in cellars, in rooms, in wells. Many were burnt, and all were mutilated in some way. Armed with bandanas soaked in rum to stifle the stench, the scouts of the column formed a burial detail. The flotilla soon reached the mouth of Frog Lake Creek, the village's steamboat landing that had had its future ended with the Good Friday massacre. The men of the Mount Royal chopped down a 40-foot tree and erected a gigantic cross as a memorial, on the hill overlooking the landing.

The next day, a torrential rain greeted General Strange's land and river columns as they arrived at Fort Pitt and found it "still smoking" and "littered with the debris of broken furniture and articles." They were sobered by the discovery of the body of Constable David Cowan, his heart removed and placed on a nearby pole. Fort Pitt was a shell of an outpost with only one serviceable building left. Despite the devastation around him, Strange realized the fort's history placed it at the centre of several divergent trails, including a river trail called the North Saskatchewan.

Evidence of a water trail was found on the other side of the river: a raft hidden in the brush, and tracks showing it had been used as a ferry by the Cree. Soon Superintendent Perry's scouting column found the tracks of Red River carts and the slippered footprints of female captives, the McLean daughters. There could be no doubt the quarry was nearby, and Strange established Fort Pitt as his headquarters. The *Clover Bar* ferry was unloaded and its machinery set up to enable free passage back and forth across the river.

Strange's journey to Fort Pitt left a string of armed detachments and established a line of communications 500 miles long. No teamster had been attacked, no wagon train lost. No serious altercation had harmed the column. The march and the voyage had been successful and the security of the Alberta district attained with scarcely an angry shot fired. But what Strange saw at Frog Lake and Fort Pitt enraged him. The burnt buildings, the looted stores, the putrefying bodies, and most urgently the many residents taken captive. Strange may have set up camp, but he hadn't come for garrison duty. He could smell his foe, and soon a jaunt to a nearby hilltop would bring him to his target.

CHAPTER SEVEN

The Prairie Port

Swift Current and Saskatchewan Landing

Swift Current was a typical Western name for a CPR town, like Moose Jaw or Medicine Hat, giving the railway something to call their sidings. It was an English translation of the river, Saskatchewan, that also named a nearby creek. The CPR built it as an operational centre with a rail yard, mechanical shops and a roundhouse complete with spare locomotives and extra rolling stock. By the spring of 1885, the village would also be a staging point for several arms of General Middleton's military strategy.

The strategy lay in the location. When the railway arrived in 1882, the more established town of Battleford, some 180 miles directly north, used Swift Current as a link to Winnipeg, an alternative to the tedious Carlton Trail or the unreliable riverboats. The Battleford/Swift Current trail opened another option to settlers in the North Saskatchewan country, and it attracted Métis freighters and white farmers seeking extra income.

Swift Current benefited from the South Saskatchewan, but unlike Medicine Hat it wasn't situated directly on the river. Though the reach was 30 miles away, the distance was not detrimental, and the river crossing, Saskatchewan Landing, became an extension of the hamlet. Crossing the river meant a reliable ferry was needed, and Battleford merchants got one established. In 1883, Alexander Macdonald hired Goodwin Marchand to install the *City of Battleford*, a crude, pole-driven 9' x 18' raft, just big enough for two Red River carts. It was a small start, but 20 days later when the first load of supplies arrived at Battleford, townsmen cheered as though the rails themselves had arrived.

But the merchants forgot the most basic part of a ferry: someone to operate it. Freighters ran it themselves as the need arose, but with no permanent ferryman, often the boat was left on the wrong side and was therefore useless. In the *City's* first season, a pair of unidentified but enterprising Indians took matters in hand and operated the ferry in exchange for a small fee, giving good, reliable service to round-trip freighters.

Eventually, though, the Saskatchewan Coal Co. installed a modern, cable-driven craft and the native rivermen were unceremoniously driven out of business.

Freighters were unimpressed with the coal company's service, however. Fees were high and the boat itself was dangerous. Built without sideboards, it was no match for waves that constantly threatened to wash carts into the river, which eventually happened to Goodwin Marchand himself, who lost wagon, cargo and the considerable sum of $670 from his coat pocket when the scow dumped him into the drink. The badly managed ferry was in no shape to be useful in April of 1885.

The relationship between Swift Current and Battleford was threatened by the rebellion. The flurry of military activity guaranteed Swift Current a place in the sun. The railway meant supplies and men could be transferred with relative ease and taken to the Landing in a day's travel. The military could climb aboard a steamer and sail right to the conflict. To a cash-strapped government, the river could save the expedition thousands of dollars.

On April 3, a band of 30-odd Cree appeared in Swift Current, asking for food and information. The party was well armed, so local merchants accommodated them with some flour, sugar and tobacco. But when the party demanded ammunition, storekeepers crossed their fingers and told the Indians they had none. The ammo was cached, of course, and the natives knew the citizens were lying. The band was angry but the next day they were gone. On April 5, Superintendent Herchmer at Medicine Hat was informed of the "visit," and boarded his flying column onto the CPR express. On arrival, Herchmer posted sentries at the river crossing he'd abandoned just days before.

On April 6, a pair of Battleford policemen braved the trail and the river ice to inform Swift Current and the nation that farm instructor James Payne and telegraph lineman Bernard Tremont had been murdered. Five hundred men, women and children had abandoned the town and barricaded themselves in the Mounted Police fort. Edgar Dewdney wired from Regina a caution to Minister Caron and the prime minister: "Tell Sir John; Rae telegraphs from Battleford Riel and 150 reported Saskatoon to-night, expected here shortly by Indians and Breed. Troops will not reach in time by boat."[1] The town had been looted, locals slain, and the call for relief was urgent. "The river is breaking up," came the plea; "we are anxiously awaiting help."[2]

The icy exodus of the McKay family

In the initial days of the conflict, the town of Battleford was at the centre. The past decade had been a boon for the community. With rolling green scenery, fertile loam, and river connections, Battleford was set to become a prosperous city, recognized by its selection as the territorial seat of government. It was also the location of an important NWMP post and the first newspaper between the Red and the Rockies. The

Dominion telegraph line wired the town to the world. Steamboats plied the waters, and there was no reason why the new railway would not transform Battleford into a new Winnipeg.

Sodbusters, ranchers and townspeople flocked to cash in on land speculation, homesteads and cheap grazing leases. Métis residents mingled with the newcomers as farmers, freighters, interpreters and police scouts. But all the smiles inverted when the promised railway was rerouted far to the south, through the parched prairie, its closest connection being Swift Current.

Another key to Battleford's economy was its situation among several Cree, Stoney and Assiniboine bands, whom Treaty Six had placed on reserves nearby. The arrangement would prove more advantageous to the newcomers than the First Nations, however. Many residents were employed as teachers, farm instructors and interpreters on these reserves, and the arrangement was usually amicable. But a series of shake-ups in 1884 placed the white and red worlds at cross-purposes. Bureaucratic policies that cut provisions to the reserves set native leaders at odds with their agents, and prejudicial fervour personified the problems in the form of the charismatic Chief Poundmaker. The presence of the cynical Big Bear only underscored frustrations, and in June of '84, a thirst dance turned into a shoving match and nearly an open conflict with the NWMP contingent of a hawkish Lief Crozier.

Throughout the rest of that year, the nations were on edge, and at Battleford few hands of any stripe were far from a rifle. After Duck Lake, the polarization was complete. White citizenry huddled near the NWMP fort as confused and unchecked tribesmen looted the town. Someone saw Poundmaker camped outside an Indian agency headquarters, waiting for an agent too terrified to attend to business, and jumped to conclusions. Poundmaker was unconnected to the thefts, but that didn't matter to a bigoted populace. His presence tainted him as the pariah of Battleford. The telegraph inside the fort broadcast that the once admired leader was a military strongman, his name in big, bold type alongside those of Riel and Big Bear.

Trepidation was hardly confined to the town. One family west of town remembered the days after Duck Lake with dread. Joseph McKay was a farm instructor of Métis extraction living with his family on the Sweetgrass reserve along the Battle River, not far from Poundmaker's reserve. Joseph was no direct relation to Gentleman Joe McKay, the Duck Lake police scout, but conflation of their identities would add to his family's coming ordeal.

In the small hours of March 28, McKay's 19-year-old daughter Ann Flora tossed and turned, consumed by a nightmare, and screamed out in her slumber. As her father rushed to give com-

The popular Stoney/Cree leader Pîhtokahânapiwiýin, better known as Poundmaker, drawn by circumstance and paranoia into the rebellion. LIBRARY & ARCHIVES CANADA CA 001875K

fort, the nightmare became reality. A loud knock was followed by the splintering of the cabin door. Armed natives burst into the room as Ann, her sister and her mother rushed to Joseph's side. "The noise they made was terrible, some talking and some uttering the wild, weird chant which, in the darkness, was too horrible to imagine."[3] The instructor struggled nervously in Cree, demanding an explanation. The leader identified himself, and "pressed forward dressed in full regalia with feathers and war paint."

McKay recognized the party as being from his reserve and inquired further: "My friend, what is the meaning of this visit? I have done you no harm and I am your friend. Have you not known me for many years? When I came here, several of your young men had died and their bodies lay in the snow. I helped you to give them decent burial."

The intruder replied: "I do not forget. Your wife and children must leave here with you, but you will have to give us your horses and supplies." As Mrs. McKay struggled to gather belongings, Ann Flora implored her father to hand over the horses, and went out to open the stable herself. The horses were led away and the family was rushed to a nearby reserve house. When they entered, their presence terrified the native children. When the McKays offered their hands, the gesture was coolly refused. A flustered Mrs. McKay finally lost her temper with the captors. "My friend, is this the way you show your gratitude for all we have done for you? When your children were sick, I nursed them back to health; when your little girl died, I washed and dressed her, my husband made the box and brought the priest to give her decent burial. Is this your way to treat kindness?" The leader was stoic and unmoved, and motioned the family outside.

In the crisp night air, the droning beat of drums accompanied the Indian chanting. The leader turned back to the family and explained, "Those are the Stoney Indians, most warlike of the tribes. When they come, nothing will save you. You must leave here at once and flee to Battleford."

From a shed in the rear of the house, the leader's companions produced a small birch canoe and carried it to the Battle River, where "the ice lay in the channel, but the water was running on either side." The leader instructed the family to cross the water to the ice, pull the canoe across the ice and paddle to the north bank. Upon reaching the bank they were to destroy the boat. The McKays followed the instructions to the letter, and when they reached the far side, "Father broke the canoe. He then shoved it into the water, where it filled and sank immediately."

The harsh gesture was hard to appreciate at the time, but the anonymous Indian leader had saved the McKays' lives. With no alternative but the garrison at Battleford, Joseph McKay and family set out in the night along the snow-covered banks of the Battle River. Ann Flora remembered the night as "bitterly cold and dark and when the sun rose we felt very cold and hungry. As we plodded on, our feet broke through the snow, sometimes to our knees in water." The McKays spent the morning with a nearby settler. Upon learning that messengers were canvassing the countryside warning of an attack at Battleford, the family hiked north to the Métis settlement of Bresaylor and hopefully to safety.

But the Bresaylor Métis, while not in sympathy with Riel, feared attack themselves, and complied with Cree demands for horses and supplies. When the McKays walked into the village, they were taken prisoner and placed in a tent under guard. A fellow captive, Father Louis Cochin, informed the newcomers that Poundmaker was expected soon.

When the great chief arrived on April 5, Easter Sunday, Joseph demanded an audience, and an indignant but cautious McKay strode up to Poundmaker and said "My friend, I have been despoiled of my home and goods. I was taken prisoner by your people. I was allowed to leave but am now a prisoner in the hands of the rebels. I have smoked and eaten and sat in the council lodges with you and Big Bear. Why

Father Louis Cochin.
BRENDA BURNS,
SASKATCHEWAN
ARCHIVES BOARD

is my brother now my enemy?" Ever the diplomat, Poundmaker rose and shook McKay's hand, sharing a pipe with the agent and saying to his councillors: "This man is my friend. It is my wish that he should be allowed to go. My young men are out scouting, and if he fell into their hands, something might happen before I would be aware of it."

Poundmaker kept his word, but could offer only a small rowboat as a means of escape. At sundown the McKays were summoned to the south bank of the North Saskatchewan, accompanied by Father Cochin. The stream was "running very thick with ice from bank to bank." Joseph pleaded that to put such "a frail boat in the water would mean death to all of us." But the priest was determined to get the McKays out of Bresaylor, and implored them to get in, for Poundmaker couldn't protect them forever.

Cochin didn't think Battleford would be a safe haven either, for Métis associated with Bresaylor. "I would advise you not to stop at Battleford. You might be treated with suspicion and the lives of yourself and family would be at stake." As the family prepared to embark, Cochin handed over a bag of bannock bread and urged, "You have no time to lose." The priest handed McKay a letter addressed to the nuns of Prince Albert, and when McKay waded into the icy waters to launch the boat, Father Cochin dropped to his knees, praying for delivery of the refugees to safer shores, wherever those shores may be. The McKays fled into the night, uncertain of the ice, their boat, the actions of their neighbours, even their destination.

The river was barely open, jammed with huge ice floes that could crush the tiny craft. The fearful McKays knew steamboats would not brave the river in such conditions. What chance did their puny boat have? McKay navigated around the jams, pushing away the giant chunks that crept up on the fugitives. As the current would be unnavigable in darkness, McKay tried his best to make for the north shore to spend the night. But every attempt was thwarted as ice moved underneath the boat and threatened to capsize it. With the determination of his voyageur ancestry, Joseph struggled to keep the dry side up. To overturn would be certain death from drowning and the frigid temperature. Ann Flora "looked back and saw the figure still kneeling on the wet sand. This was the last I saw of Father Cochin."

McKay finally stabilized the craft and waited for another giant ice jam to pass between them and the north bank. As new ice piled up behind it, McKay pushed ahead and got the rowboat ashore, where the family sought refuge among some willows on a wooded flat to eat some of their bannock. The night was cold, but they couldn't afford the luxury of a fire that might betray their presence. To make matters worse, they "had no blankets, and only the clothes we stood in when we left our home in Sweet Grass [a week past]." As the morning of April 6 broke, the river was still jammed with ice, and McKay refused to risk his family again. The clan spent a week huddled in the willows before attempting another passage.

In the meantime, to shelter themselves from damp spring rains, Mrs. McKay sacrificed modesty and her red flannel petticoat. The skirt was slit down the front to make a tent over top of some willow branches, as they crouched beneath the makeshift tarpaulin. Food became a concern, for they had nothing to hunt with, and the meagre rations of bannock disappeared the first day. Ann Flora explained their resolve in the face of famine: "We had no food, but for some reason or other we did not feel hungry. We were in constant fear of being discovered and I guess this accounted for the lack of appetite. We gathered gum from spruce trees and chewed this. Then father gave us the grease that he had to fix the boat with, and we tried to eat it. It seemed to coat the roof of my mouth and made me fall sick."

By April 14, the ice relented enough to open a channel. But the option of waiting for the river to open fully was lost when Joseph noticed a series of bright flashes from the top of the bank. McKay recognized it as the sun reflecting off a scout's mirror, and rushed his family to the boat, saying, "The Indians have seen us, and are using a glass to mark our position." Soon voices were heard, and soon the threat was realized.

"A party of Indians came out on the bank. They saw us and commenced to yell and brandish their rifles. There were five or six men." As a petrified Joseph struggled with the boat, the equally fearful women inside shoved on the ice with the oars in a final drive to open water. Pursuing warriors moved down the bank and hopped from ice crag to ice crag, in hot pursuit. An already hopeless situation became desperate. "We thought we were lost," but if the McKays were at all religious, God needed to intervene soon. No adventure writer or dime novelist could have stressed better the desperation than the 19-year-old occupant of that

As the military scurried about the country, Joseph MacKay and family battled fear, hunger, ice and the river. *CANADIAN PICTORIAL & ILLUSTRATED WAR NEWS, 1885 SOUVENIR EDITION*

rowboat, Ann Flora McKay: "Suddenly the ice began to move. A narrow channel formed in the centre of the river. The jam was breaking!"

Their prey escaping, the pursuers ignored their unsteady footing and levelled rifles at the rowboat. "The Indians began to shoot. The bullets struck the ice close by. We could hear the Indians yelling; the ice was piling up on all sides and the boat was pushed and bumped, and the noise of the water and the crackling of ice seemed to freeze the very blood in our veins." As the current propelled the boat out of firing range, the McKays' boiling blood staved off the cold of the water, proving the relativity of time. "Minutes seemed like hours, until finally the boat seemed to get into comparatively clear water, and as we drifted along the ice cakes became fewer." The prayers of Louis Cochin had been heard and answered, as the McKay family's seemingly eternal ordeal passed into its next phase.

As the boat neared Battleford, no doubt Joseph McKay was tempted to paddle to shore for succour at the Mounted Police post. As a government servant, the farm instructor was no doubt entitled. But the police were not alone in the stockade. Having watched their houses looted, residents had a jaundiced view of the native and Métis community, supported by prejudice, paranoia and the murders of Payne and Tremont. They were anxious and vengeful, and the McKay family's mixed blood and association with the uncertain loyalty of Bresaylor might be suspect. So, on the night of April 14, "we floated past Battleford."

The morning of April 16, now on the run for 18 days, the family reached what they thought would be their final refuge, Fort Carlton. Surely the old, trusted fort would not turn away such desperate people. In a virtual news vacuum, the McKays didn't know the fort had been abandoned. "On arriving we were dismayed to find [Carlton] burned to the ground. There was nothing for it but to go on to Prince Albert. Weak and tired, we returned to our boat."

But before they left, Mother McKay noticed a horse and wagon on the north side of the river. McKay anxiously rowed over and met William Robinson (no relation to the steamer pilot), who brought the family up to date on the evacuation of the police. Robinson too had been cut off from supplies but had salvaged some spilled flour from the post, though it'd been saturated with kerosene to keep it from being useful to Dumont and Riel. Robinson kindly offered "some bread that was made from this flour. We thanked him for it and again took to the boat." But the oil-laced flour and the sudden shock of solid food to their shrivelled stomachs made the McKays nauseous and only lengthened their ordeal.

After some hours drifting downriver, the family came upon a house where a Métis woman stood on the bank. Oblivious that he was walking into a hornet's nest, Joseph McKay and his family disembarked to ask for food. The woman eyed the stranger nervously and asked, "What is your name?"

With no reason to think it was a problem, he proudly disclosed, "My name is Joe McKay." Any friendliness the lady had shown evaporated at the answer. "You are Joe

McKay? You are the man who shot the Indian at Duck Lake?" a reference to the death of Assiyiwin, the first casualty of the rising conflict. Joe then realized his and the lady's error and sought to rectify his mistaken identity. "No, that must have been Joe McKay who is with the Mounted Police."

The lady would have no part of his explanation, and grimly cackled at what she thought was an attempt by McKay to avoid the issue. "Don't you know the rebels are looking for you?" she shot back, and then turned to walk up the hill. With two simple words, McKay made himself a fugitive again, amazed that the man who shared his handle was also a fugitive. Not believing his bad luck, he turned his family to the water, explaining, "I think this woman is a rebel. It will be safer to take to the boat again."

Six miles from Prince Albert, the family passed a house belonging to a man named Swain. A group of people outside the house shouted and cheered and waved at them to bring their little boat in. But Joseph McKay and his straggling family had had enough of being scapegoats. "We had met with so many disappointments that we decided to continue our journey," and floated on past Swain's. Four miles from Prince Albert, the ice that had dogged them thinned out in the spring sun, and soon their long ordeal too would melt away.

On April 20, Ann Flora must have sighed with relief at the sight of a "Roman Catholic Mission … [where] we were received with kindness and hospitality." Nuns came out to greet the starving family as "their little boat stopped opposite our house."[4] The mission was St. Anne's Convent, and Mother Louise Collings was as glad to see the McKay family as the McKays were to see a friendly face. "The arrival of a family from Battleford who escaped in a wonderful manner was for us a subject of joy."[5] She was ecstatic that the human spirit had triumphed and that these true believers could have a happy ending after all. That "father, mother and two daughters arrived more dead than alive from fright and fatigue after a journey of 22 days in a little boat,"[6] summed up the story. In the face of war, there rarely are happy endings. "This respectable family like a great many others now, are reminded, all is lost to them and they have only the clothes they have on."[7]

Having survived on only scraps of bannock, tree gum, hard grease and bread made from poisoned flour, the family was provided "a meal and then they went to the Chief Commissioner's [Irvine] to find food and lodging." Mysteriously, Joseph McKay turned Father Cochin's letter over to the police rather than Mother Collings. "They took with them a letter they brought addressed to us from the Reverend Père Cochin, and as yet I do not know the contents."[8] Neither did anyone else, for Irvine's report made no reference to the McKays or Cochin's letter, delivered at such an arduous cost.

Two years later, Ann Flora McKay married, and put the terror on the North Saskatchewan behind her. Her groom did the same. He too was a veteran of the uproar, the man whose identity had caused her family so much grief: "Gentleman" Joe McKay. One can only suppose the father of the bride must have had a serious discussion with his prospective son-in-law as to how their shared monikers had unwittingly endangered his family. The couple resided in Prince Albert, and Ann Flora McKay, née McKay, lived to tell this story to the *Prince Albert Daily Herald* in 1935, 50 years from the date she'd cheated the Grim Reaper.

Otter's dilemma

Help for the Battleford country was on the way, led by Colonel William Dillon Otter, though Otter himself didn't know it. Commandant of the School of Infantry at Toronto, Otter had been named by Middleton to command the second column against the rebellion. Weary from a frigid march through the unfinished railway's gaps across the Canadian Shield, the contingent received a well-deserved rest in passenger cars as a CPR express sped them to Swift Current.

A bleary-eyed Otter pulled the men of his command off the train at two o'clock in the morning on April 11, at what must've seemed the end of the earth. The units—B

Colonel William Dillon Otter had orders to ride the steamboat fleet to Clarke's Crossing, but the river and the panic at Battleford changed his assignment.
LIBRARY & ARCHIVES CANADA C-31411

Battery of the Regiment of Canadian Artillery, the Queen's Own Rifles and the Governor General's Foot Guards—fell out and set up camp, joining Lieutenant Robinson Wadmore's Infantry School Corps C Company. Meanwhile, Colonel Otter received Middleton's orders from the telegraph office: "You will eventually proceed to ferry to embark in Steamers to join me at Clarke's Crossing about Sunday next."[9]

Otter was to wait for the ships from Medicine Hat, and sail the entire brigade to Clarke's in relative ease. The flotilla would bring up the supplies from the Swift Current transport base. Combining with Middleton's force, this would concentrate a 1,200-man attack on Batoche first, after which it would be on to Battleford by river. For the plan to work, however, two factors would have to combine: that the river would be high enough for the boats to travel without impediment, and that Battleford could hold out until Batoche was conquered.

In hindsight, Battleford could probably have taken care of itself. But the wires and dispatches nagged of unknown dangers and worries. Everyone was jumpy and close to a weapon. Inspector Morris and Commissioner Irvine, respectively holding peaceful Battleford and Prince Albert, both requested assistance. Middleton grumbled to Minister Caron, but admitted his own nervousness: "Would like to attack Riel at once but I am sadly hampered by Irvine & Morris who both implore me to go to them at once. From all information I can get I believe neither of them are in actual danger but they both write about defenceless women and children. Between ourselves, I believe they are both scared and unfit but I fear the chance of their being right. Shall decide at Clarke's Crossing."[10]

Pressure came from newspapers, the Opposition in Parliament, and Minister Caron to relieve Battleford. A trio of Winnipeg merchants cabled their MP to point out the dangers in Middleton's tactic:

Report from Qu'Appelle that entire force & transport there going via Touchwood 350 miles to Battleford, distance via Swift Current only 186 miles and better trail with ferry over river. Meantime over 150 women and children in refuge in barracks at Battleford with three weeks provisions and little or no protection. Herchmer with command at Medicine Hat waiting for river to open, impossible for detachment via Qu'Appelle or Herchmer's command to reach Battleford until long after provisions exhausted. Manifestly sufficiently strong force to relieve Battleford should be dispatched via Swift Current immediately. No likelihood of collision at Prince Albert or Duck Lake until arrival of troops if then. Meantime they are well protected therefore no human reason why rush should be made to Prince Albert district while nearly helpless women and children at Battleford are at mercy of thousands of Indians and half breeds. We know every foot of the country and that it is impossible to relieve Battleford either via Touchwood or Saskatchewan navigation, only feasible way is via Swift Current. In name of humanity bring this before House immediately.[11]

In Prince Albert, a similar mood prevailed as the people mourned their dead. Under martial law, Irvine took control of the town. Mounties, volunteers and townsmen were drafted to patrol the community. Prince Albert was not built for security: it was a series of clusters of stores and houses spread over a wide expanse on the south bank of the river, with no garrison to huddle behind. But because it was a regional economic hub, the town was well provisioned, and given the police contingent and a stock of arms and ammunition in HBC stores, it was well defended. The town could also communicate with Battleford, though every message carried as much gossip as truth.

In St. Anne's Convent, the nuns were as true to their diaries and letters as to their God. Mother Louise Collings wrote almost daily to her Mother Superior, confident her words would actually reach their recipient. On April 11, Collings wrote of a planned evacuation of Battleford: "The women and children are still safe, but they implore a steamer to be sent to convey them to [Prince Albert]."[12] But the plan only remained a plan, since the ships were still frozen in the mud.

Middleton's plans were thrown further awry by the Frog Lake/Fort Pitt situation. Finally, on April 12, the general relented and imposed a new mission on Otter, who was still setting up his new camp at Swift Current. "I want you to get to Battleford as quick as you can. If the steamers are ready at Swift Current ferry within two days and can transport you, go by them to Clark Crossing and proceed to Battleford using great caution especially on right flank and wait there."[13] Battleford would be dealt with, but a riverboat ride to Clarke's was still the plan.

Otter had few career officers to consult with, so he appointed Superintendent Herchmer his chief of staff. On a bright early morning, Otter broke camp and marched to Saskatchewan Landing to rendezvous with the flotilla from Medicine Hat. But the flotilla was nowhere in sight, and Otter's men were met at the Landing only by the police guard and Captain Arthur Howard, a U.S. Gatling gun specialist. The brigade made camp on the banks, welcoming the respite to repair travel-weary gear, catch up on sleep and wash themselves and their clothing in the river. The useless Battleford Trail ferry had sunk, so a work detail recovered the raft to make it water-worthy, and a detail poled the scow across the river and set up a guard on the north side of the crossing.

On April 15, soldiers cheered the trademark whistle of the *Northcote*, as the old workhorse chugged in, towing a pair of barges. The vessel showed the scars of winching itself over endless sandbars and shoals, so after docking, Captain Sheets put the crew and soldiers to work patching up the boat and repairing its machinery.

But the *Baroness*, the *Alberta* and the *Minnow* were still missing, as "the *Northcote* was enabled to get away from Medicine Hat … earlier than Captain Davis …"[14] The lag cost the fleet dearly as river levels dropped to just inches, the *Northcote* being borne on the first of the river's heavy runs. High water would not be seen until late May, to the detriment of the Galt steamers and the dismay of the military.

Elliott Galt, reluctant admiral

As Otter and company cooled their heels, the whereabouts of the rest of the flotilla became a national worry. When an NWMP patrol from Medicine Hat passed through Swift Current on April 12 on its way to patrol the Métis camps at Wood Mountain, Superintendent A.R. Macdonnell unwittingly contributed to the misinformation by talking to the press. Citizens were eager to spread their chit-chat telegraphically, and the *Toronto Daily Mail* was only too happy to print unconfirmed stories. The paper's Swift Current correspondent was no exception and quoted the over-confident police official: "McDonnell [*sic*] says there is no doubt the water in the Saskatchewan is quite deep enough to float the steamers which have already left Medicine Hat. He heard of them fifty miles down the river yesterday. They had passed two of the worst rapids and are expected at the landing 25 miles north of here to-morrow."[15] But Macdonnell had no way of knowing anything about the steamboats' progress, or the river's true condition, as he and the fleet had long since parted company.

So where were they, anyway? Elliott Galt did his best to crack the whip on John Davis and his fleet, but with low water and sandbars everywhere, little could be done but winch, shout, curse, push, pull and send telegrams. "Elliott wishes you informed steamers are finding river very difficult and dangerous. His orders are to use every effort to get them down to meet troops."[16] To keep the government apprised of the situation, Elliott assigned a dispatch rider to the *Baroness*, to report the boats' progress and river conditions.

The South Branch from Medicine Hat to the "Bull's Forehead" at the forks of the Red Deer is a broad, serpentine valley draining an ominous, mysterious region, a shortgrass plain that deposits silt into the river in addition to glacial till from the Rockies. The stretch is treacherous to navigators in high water, impossible in low, and the fleet would have to pass through the Drowning Ford, all too familiar to Segers and Davis on the *Baroness* as the cursed reach that had trashed the *Lily*.

Elliot Galt had much on his plate. His fleet was under contract and could not be ignored, but he was not a military strategist. Besides riding herd on the boats, he had a mine to run and a railway to build. The family business was expanding, and if young Galt was to tend to it properly, he could not sit and wait for dismal news about sandbars and shallows. He wired his concerns to his father in Montreal, and Galt the elder implored Adolphe Caron to spare a reliable officer to mobilize the steamers:

> No doubt my son will officially advise you of all he has done respecting the steamboats. But as they are now away from Medicine Hat, I think it necessary to inform you in a quasi official manner that General Middleton or some other officer appointed by yourself, will have to take them in charge, and give orders respecting their movements. Elliott will now have to give his immediate and entire attention to our railway and interests … and cannot be spared for any time at Swift Current.[17]

Ever the diplomat, Sir Alexander could not resist the temptation to put a positive spin on the situation:

> Captain Davis, who has the general supervision and command of the Boats, under your orders, is I believe a very intelligent skilful man and will I trust prove efficient. Elliott telegraphs me the River is low, and navigation difficult and in places dangerous but with care and mutual aid in case of grounding, I trust all will safely reach Swift Current.[18]

Caron struggled to think of some military official who could take charge of the fleet. Then he read a message from Middleton complaining about a staff officer: "I may tell you in confidence that Lieutenant Colonel Houghton is absolutely useless, and I wish I could find some excuse to get rid of him."[19]

Charles F. Houghton was a 47-year-old British Army officer who had retired to Winnipeg after some time on the Dominion Militia staff in British Columbia. Houghton had had command of the Military Provisional District of the North West Territories, but his reputation was tainted by rumours of alcoholism. Fellow officers said he had "not much head and still less judgment"[20] In charge of arranging the Manitoba regiments that accompanied Middleton to Qu'Appelle, Houghton couldn't resist tagging along. Predictably, he annoyed Middleton, as did any officer that might usurp his authority.

"Galt telegraphs me that some Officer must be appointed to take charge of flotilla as he will have no time to do so himself." Then Caron thought of a way to unload Houghton: "About the one you refer to why not send him to Medicine Hat to take charge of boats … ?"[21] Middleton was ecstatic: "Steamers must start from Swift Current not Medicine Hat—Will send Houghton."[22] The prairie port seemed a likely place to get rid of the nuisance Lieutenant Colonel. But for reasons that remain unclear, Houghton did not go to Swift Current and remained on the general's staff.

As the river level plunged, Elliott Galt remained the reluctant admiral. Weary of the funereal pace of his family flotilla, Galt ordered the *Minnow*, which needed only a foot and a half of water to sail on, to abandon the larger boats "from [a] point thirty miles below Medicine Hat with two barges,"[23] and sail on to Swift Current. "Find it impossible to get large steamers down the River to Swift Current—have done everything I could but River has been steadily falling and now there is not enough water to navigate large steamers. Am now endeavouring to get small steamer and two small barges to Swift Current and the large steamers will follow when river rises."[24]

In Montreal, the elder Galt spun the situation: "No news under circumstances must be absolutely good news as we should have heard if any thing had gone wrong."[25] But Sir Alexander's jaw dropped when Elliott wired him that the large steamers were completely aground, scant miles from their departure point. The statesman struggled with sheepish apologies to the Defence Minister, whose head he'd gone over to get the fleet into service. His mouthful of humble pie, old Galt finally gave the minister some truthful technical facts in the form of excuses for his own inflated boasts:

My dear Caron:—I was greatly vexed by the receipt of a telegram last night from Elliott stating that he had received a message from Capt. Davis that the water was so low he could not proceed with the *Baroness*. He was then ordered by Elliott to send on the *Minnow* with two small barges. As the *Minnow* only draws about sixteen inches, I trust she will get through. With the barges she can greatly facilitate the passage of the River at Swift Current. But until the water rises, which may be three or four weeks, I fear you must consider the larger boats as unavailable. The consolation I have is the somewhat poor one that not an hour was lost after receiving the orders from you and Sir John to get them ready … Elliott telegraphs the water at Medicine Hat had fallen nine inches since the Boats started. The usual rise of water is toward the latter end of May and is caused by the melting of the snow in the Mountains. The rivers being wholly fed from the Mountains, the highest water is from the middle of May till the early part of July. I expect therefore that within a month you will be able to use the boats any where between Medicine Hat and Prince Albert. So far as I yet know no damage has occurred to the Boats.[26]

In Medicine Hat, the more practical Elliott wired General Middleton of the action taken with the *Minnow*, then personally rode out to the *Baroness* and *Alberta* to assess the situation. He wired back to his father "that very little more water is needed and he [Davis] is hopeful may get *Baroness* down."[27]

On April 17, the *Alberta* and the *Baroness* were buffeted by a spring blizzard with heavy winds and wet, heavy snows that chilled deckhands to the bone.[28] Davis realized the hopelessness, and begged Galt to call off the mission. The flotilla's progress was dismal. At this rate they were probably two weeks from reaching the Bull's Forehead, where the added waters of the Red Deer could raise the level.

With every grounding, the resultant push and pull further damaged the paddlewheel, the engines and hull integrity. Responsible for the vessels, Davis pleaded with his employers to be mindful of the possibility of a shipwreck. Resigned to agreement, Elliott Galt knew that little more could be done. Believing the fleet to be subject to military control, Caron was asked for a command decision. "Captain in charge of large steamers asks if he shall proceed downriver at all hazards as water very low and more dangerous. She has got down forty miles and is eighty from forks Red Deer after which there would be no trouble. Please reply soon."[29] Caron refused responsibility and threw the ball back into Elliott's court, advising Davis to weigh his own options. "He must judge for himself as to risk which we will not assume."[30] Without guidance from superiors, Davis's crews continued to pathetically spar the pair of dead weights downstream on little more than a mud puddle.

By April 13, Otter was weighing his options. If he waited for the fleet, his column could save the march and the cost of teams and wagons. The route from the Landing to Battleford was barren prairie, bordering the Great Sand Hills. Everything from forage to firewood would have to be packed the whole distance. But to wait for the ships, load them and hobble downriver would cost valuable time which, as far as anyone knew, was running out for Battleford. Faced with the dilemma, Otter wired Middleton for direction. Middleton, observing the disintegration of his naval scheme, snorted, "Go by land."[31]

Otter in the river

Now charged with a new mission, Colonel Otter assembled a wagon train unheard of on the Canadian prairies. Major W.R. Bell, manager of the Qu'Appelle Valley Farming Co., had been called upon earlier by Middleton to organize wagon transport for his own column. Sensing new profits from the Battleford column as well, Bell was only too happy to send his agent, E.N. Armit, to broker teams and wagons for Otter. Farmers eager for work left their ploughs and hurrahed their teams to Saskatchewan Landing to join the column. Soon, 300 wagons were in place. Now Otter had to get them across that wide river. But the sunny early spring turned into a miserable late-winter squall

BATTLEFORD COLUMN
Swift Current - Battleford
April 3 - April 17
'B' Battery, Regiment of Canadian Artillery
Queen's Own Rifles
Governor-General's Foot Guards
1/2 of 'C' Company, Infantry School Corps
North West Mounted Police
Scouts/Interpreters, Teamsters, Militia Staff
Lt.-Colonel William Otter, commanding

*His orders changed,
Otter moves overland
to Battleford*

*Baroness, Alberta
& Minnow
stranded upstream*

*Northcote ordered
to steam to
Clarke's Crossing alone*

BATOCHE COLUMN
*Fort Qu'Appelle - Clarke's Crossing
April 3 - April 17
'A' Battery, Regiment of Canadian Artillery
Winnipeg Field Battery
Boulton's Scouts
1/2 of 'C' Company, Infantry School Corps
10th Royal Grenadiers
90th Winnipeg Rifles
French's Scouts
Governor-General's Body Guard
York & Simcoe Rangers
Winnipeg Troop of Cavalry
Quebec Cavalry School Corps
Transport Service, Militia Staff
Major-General Fred Middleton, commanding*

MIDDLETON'S
REVISED PLAN

GORD TOLTON

as the same blizzard that endangered the Galt steamers also struck the Landing. As the temperature plummeted, slushy snow driven by high wind penetrated everything, and five soldiers were hospitalized for exposure and pneumonia.[32]

As comrades struggled with flapping bell tents, Charles Salyer Clapp, a private in the Midland Battalion, stood guard and endured the weather eloquently: "The storm prevailed all night, the heavens were black with clouds and neither moon or stars were visible. The wind raged, the rain poured and froze as it fell, I must confess a feeling of timidity during my hours of weary sentry go in the night which was from 12 o'clock until two, the wind was so strong that I was blown from my beat several times and glad was I when the Corporal came around with relief, but gladder still when the grey streaks of dawn were visible in the East."[33]

Colonel Otter shunned the rebuilt ferry, which was not sturdy enough to convey the heavy wagons, and instead drafted the *Northcote* as a shuttle. The crossing took two days, and the toil was miserable. Skittish horses, mules and oxen had to be coaxed onto the main deck of the steamer or its barges. Animals were held fast for the journey, and then gently eased off the boat on the north side over a gangplank that refused to stay still. All this amid the din of cursing teamsters, shouting officers and roaring boilers, and the rocking of the boat in the choppy cross-current. By the time the job was done, the *Northcote* had conveyed 745 men and 450 horses across the wide reach of the South Saskatchewan.

On Friday, April 17, Otter waved his column into formation for the 180-mile trek. The brigade made record time and were in Battleford in just six days. Otter's column saw water once again when they reached the ransacked townsite and crossed the tiny Battle River that separated the town from the fort, where the townspeople were barricaded. The bridge that spanned the river in normal times had been dismantled earlier that spring to prevent destruction by spring ice, and had not been reassembled, in order to impede an attack on the fort from the town.

There was pervasive doubt as to what the real threat to Battleford was or who actually had looted the town. Nevertheless, Otter marshalled the citizenry's thirst for revenge into an ill-advised attack on Poundmaker's camp at Cut Knife Hill on May 2. The fight was a rout, with the column retreating back to Battleford to bury its dead. After that debacle, Otter busied his men with building a new bridge across the Battle River. Built for $550, the bridge was the last river activity Otter would face until the arrival of Middleton.

Laurie takes charge

Swift Current was in full swing as a transport base. Every day, locomotives hauled in carloads of armaments, horses, provisions and livestock feed. Supplies had to be stockpiled, hauled to the Landing, then stockpiled again to await river transport, all of it moved with teams and wagons that became scarcer as the war evolved. To accomplish this Herculean task and organize transport operations effectively, a competent manager was needed. One was found in Nova Scotia, the highest ranking officer then in Canada, a major general of the British Army who outranked even Middleton.

John Wimburn Laurie was a 50-year-old Englishman, like most British officers a graduate of Sandhurst, and a veteran of the Crimean War and the Sepoy Mutiny. In 1861, Laurie was one of 5,000 British troops posted to guard Canada from attack by the United States in the wake of that country's civil war and the Trent affair. His war record was capped by service against the Fenian raids of 1866 and 1870, and he became a major general in 1882.

In semi-retirement as commander of militia in Nova Scotia, John Laurie built up a successful farming enterprise, and like many military men of the era, was supportive of the governing Conservative party. When Laurie volunteered for the 1885 campaign, Minister Caron was in an awkward situation, as

Major General John Wimburn Laurie. LIBRARY & ARCHIVES CANADA C-046828

Laurie ranked over Middleton. Things became more complicated when the British War Office in London refused Laurie for service, fearful of a conflict between the two generals.

To placate everyone, Laurie threw off rank and offered himself as Middleton's junior. The self-demotion satisfied the War Office, but still gave Laurie vast power as the militia's second in command. When Laurie reported for duty in the West, the suspicious Middleton, resenting the senior officer as a threat to his supremacy, arranged to keep him out of sight as commandant of the transport base.

Middleton's jealousy was evidenced in a wire he sent from Humboldt: "Laurie at Swift Current as reported—He will I am afraid be a nuisance and troublesome but I will try him.[34] Personal animosities aside, Middleton needed someone with reliable decision-making authority at Swift Current, and was fortunate to have Laurie on hand.

To assist, Laurie drafted Lieutenant R.W. Leonard to serve as his adjutant. A Royal Military College graduate, Leonard had given up a career with the CPR to resume the military grind, but Laurie was fortunate to have a soldier with railway connections in this tenuous situation. With the backing of country and corporation, the General rolled up his sleeves and dived into the monumental task of managing a war campaign.

When Laurie arrived on April 16 to take command, he may have wished he'd stayed home. He learned that Otter had first ordered the York & Simcoe Rangers in from Fort Qu'Appelle to guard the river crossing but then reversed the order and sent the Rangers—a unit better suited to Middleton—back to Qu'Appelle. To replace the Rangers, Laurie ordered in the Midland Provisional Battalion, a hastily assembled amalgamation under the command of the colourful Colonel Arthur Williams.[35] It was a fortuitous change: the "weekend soldiers" of the Midland had water-borne experience that would come in handy. The Midlanders were initially relegated to guarding cargo stockpiles along the Swift Current siding, but in the coming days both generals would find them to be one of the most useful units in the force.

Williams was a veteran of both militia and political circles, and Member of Parliament for the district where he'd raised his fresh-faced troops. Though an infantryman, the colonel had naval blood coursing in his veins, his father having commanded a Royal Navy vessel on the Great Lakes in the War of 1812. The Midland Battalion was his own creation, an assembly of eight local rifle militias from small rural communities (Belleville, Cobourg, Lindsay, Port Hope, Kingston, Peterborough and Hastings) in the Lake Ontario region called "the Midland." These citizen soldiers were clerks, farm boys, canal and lake workers and others whose military experience was defined only by the occasional drill. Their battle-hardening lay in the future.

The biggest problem General Laurie faced was transferring supplies to the Landing. He arrived just as Colonel Otter was crossing the river, ready to take 230 wagons north, leaving few for Laurie to use. Before Otter left, Laurie lobbied to have the entire cavalcade return to Swift Current and haul away the mountain of stores in a single trip. That would have solved most of the logistical problems instantly, but would delay Otter for at least two days. When Laurie suggested the idea to his commander, Middleton, worried about Battleford, abruptly vetoed any delay of Otter's expedition.

So when Otter pulled out, most of the Landing's stockpile and the wagons went with him, leaving absolutely no stores left to be loaded aboard the *Northcote* or subsequent ships, and no wagons to move anything from the railway to the river. With one order, Middleton had allowed envy to totally defeat his own plan! Laurie was left with a dilemma. At first he had had supplies and troops to load onto steamers, but without all of the steamers, the troops and supplies had gone. Now he had a steamer ready to move, but no supplies or troops to embark!

The ferry at Saskatchewan Landing needed attention, as well. Despite the rebuilding by Otter's troops, the cable was weak and repeatedly broke, leaving the barge to be laboriously poled to the other side. A new ferry was needed, but Laurie did not procure one.

Biding time

With only 30 teams to get supplies to the *Northcote*, General Laurie made a broad-based appeal for another hundred wagons. Farmers and teamsters from Regina, Moose Jaw, even Montana and North Dakota, plodded to Swift Current to haul for $10 a day. Still short of teams, Laurie contracted merchant Fraser Tims, who hired Métis and Indians to haul for $25 a ton, delivering 2,500 pounds per day to the Landing. Another 150 teams were needed to follow Otter's train with more cargo for Battleford.

While awaiting the freight, James Sheets assured Laurie that navigable water levels would hold until August, his confidence coloured by his zeal to get to Prince Albert and free the rest of the W&WTC flotilla from the winter ice in the midst of hostile territory. As the superintendent, he was responsible for the ships' condition, and had little desire to see them torched by rebels. Sheets travelled to Swift Current, desperate to get to Prince Albert by any means available. But Laurie wanted Sheets on the *Northcote*, and telegraphed Joseph Wrigley in Winnipeg to obtain a head-office order for the captain to stay put and go downriver with the flagship.

Fuming, Sheets sat impatiently at the Landing. To busy the crew, he ordered the boilers rebuilt, and had the carpenters repair the sandbar damage to the hull. But no sooner had the crews emptied the boilers to facilitate the metal work the engines required, but Laurie suddenly decided he needed to use the ship again as a ferry. More teams had assembled to bring up the rear as a supply train for Otter. With the ship's engines torn apart, Laurie implored Sheets to redirect the *Northcote*'s crew to remedy the rickety ferry. The hands erected a steel cable to make the ferry more functional. Donald MacIvor, the *Northcote*'s fireman, remained proud of that cable installation for quite a while, saying in 1925, "Maybe it is there yet for all I know."[36]

At Swift Current, none of the Midlanders believed they would see any action after being removed from Middleton's column. They were even shut out of the goings-on at the Landing, left to stand around ensuring General Laurie's stockpile did not walk away. The boredom was broken only when Companies E and F were dispatched to cut wood for the steamboat.

Also taking in the scenery at the river's edge was the soldier of fortune, Captain Arthur Howard. The flamboyant Connecticut national guardsman had been sent to

Captain Arthur L. Howard of the Connecticut National Guard was a representative of the U.S. arms manufacturer R.J. Gatling. The Canadian militia purchased three of Gatling's weapons at the beginning of the rebellion, and Howard came along to demonstrate their use. He took the weapon to Swift Current and rode with it on the *Northcote* to Clarke's Crossing. GLENBOW-ALBERTA ARCHIVES NA-1032-4

Swift Current to demonstrate the invention of his employer, R.J. Gatling. The Gatling machine gun was state-of-the-art military technology for 1885, and two of the prototypes had been purchased by the Canadian government. Both the Gatling company and Middleton were anxious to test the deadly new toys. The rebellion provided the opportunity, and one of the guns was taken along by Colonel Otter. Howard would accompany the other one on the *Northcote* to Fish Creek Landing, while regaling troops and crew with his U.S. Civil War stories. While waiting for the *Northcote* to depart, Howard amused himself by scanning the Indian camps in the vicinity and reporting his findings to Laurie.

On April 20, Laurie met with an irregular militia unit whose military experience was as geographers. The Dominion Land Surveyors Intelligence Unit was comprised of civil engineers who had spent recent years defining legal boundaries across the prairies. They were well experienced in dealing with the land, natives and long distances on horseback. Their knowledge of the region was invaluable, and Laurie assigned the Surveyors as a scouting party for the *Northcote*. Mindful that the progress of the boat was an integral piece of the campaign, Laurie ordered Lieutenant W. Beatty's troop to follow the steamer along the riverbank to discourage marauders and spies and stay in communication with Swift Current.

Disappointed by the Midlanders' lazy week of sentry duty, Colonel Williams lobbied to put his regiment to better use. With the *Northcote* set to sail the morning of April 23, and requests for troops upriver, Laurie urged Williams to make passage. He didn't have to ask twice, as the bored men were armed with "the burning desire of the troops to be in time for the fighting."[37]

Brigade captains of A, B, C and D Companies—half the battalion—guaranteed that their volunteers could march to the Landing in a single day, and in fact the battle-hungry soldiers gladly made the 35 miles from Swift Current in just 12 hours, the longest single day's march of the campaign. As 30 teams of wagons carried freight and the battalion's baggage, the Midlanders quick-stepped, taking "several short halts for rests, while longer ones for dinner and tea were made at which military soup and tea made from Alkalai water taken from a bog-hole, the best that could be procured, were partaken of. It was here seen what hunger could drive men to. They drank the horrid stuff readily and clamoured for more."[38] The column's happiness at doing something useful was evident as "someone struck up a familiar song which was taken up and re-echoed down the column—some marching in their stocking feet with boots hanging around their necks, some sang, others whistled, some smoked and some wrestled with a hardtack."

In the evening of April 22, the Midlanders boarded the *Northcote* and the barges. For Private Clapp, the march was nearly capped by a bath. "I was completely exhausted, and while going on board the steamer '*Northcote*' was about to faint and would have fallen in the River had it not been for two comrades ... who, noticing my weakness, hurried to my assistance, grasping my rifle and knapsack, and with one on either side they escorted me safely on board. As soon as I stepped on the Steamer I dropped my knapsack, sank upon it and was unable to rise for half an hour, when I mustered up strength enough to drag my weary frame, rifle and knapsack upstairs; here in the fore part of the cabin I threw myself upon the floor with about twenty-five others and tried to sleep, but very little of that blessing was received that night as we were so crowded and too tired."[39]

Colonel Arthur Williams, Member of Parliament and commander of the Midland Provisional Battalion. LIBRARY & ARCHIVES CANADA

One bushed staff sergeant, Walter Stewart, agreed the boys were "all pretty tired. Went on boat and threw ourselves anywhere for a sleep. We didn't want to eat, just sleep."[40] While Williams led his weary soldiers onto the *Northcote*, Laurie requested that E and F Companies remain at the Landing to prepare barges and operate the ferry. The final two companies, G and H, were left behind at Swift Current to guard the supply depot.

The Midlanders were all Great Lakes boys, and the experience they had from sailing, barging and freighting in their home territory was a welcome addition to the vagaries of the river. The dilapidated ferry received great attention from the Midlanders, who also took a liking to the *Northcote*, and employed themselves as woodhawks to keep the boilers steaming. Clapp described the ship as though he had built it himself: "Like all steamers which ply these waters, [it] was built upon the manner of the Mississippi Boats, i.e., flat-bottomed, entirely open between the decks and with a huge paddlewheel at the stern. She was of moderate dimensions substantially built, with powerful engines and cabin fitted up very nicely."[41]

One of Williams's officers, Lieutenant John Laing Weller, was transferred to Laurie's staff as adjutant after Lieutenant Leonard was reassigned as communications officer. The transport officer in Winnipeg, Lieutenant Colonel William Jackson, had sent along Lieutenant William Hudson as supply officer to go aboard the *Northcote* and take charge of stores at Clarke's Crossing. But Laurie had other plans for Hudson, and retained him to assist with the logistics of incoming supply trains. This allowed Laurie to spend more time personally overseeing the Landing and commiserating with a group of fellow officers that were going north.

Surgeon Major James Bell loaded a complete medical unit, the Number 1 Field Hospital Corps, comprised of five surgeons, six dressers, an orderly and their complement of medical supplies and appliances.

Major Martin Waters Kirwan, assistant transport officer to Colonel William Jackson, was, like Captain Howard, a soldier of fortune. Irish by birth, Kirwan had served in both the French and the British armies, most recently in the Foreign Legion. The worldly Kirwan was disgusted with the *Northcote* and didn't mind expressing his disapproval.

> The steamer we are travelling on is nothing but a scow on which a wooden house is rudely built. Her boilers are exposed, and a shot from a rifle at close range should cause an explosion. The woodwork on which the saloon is built is weak and thin, and a rifle ball would penetrate it at any of its many ports. Her pilothouse could be made untenable by riflemen on the banks unless protected by improvised breastworks made of supplies.[42]

Staff officer Colonel Bowen van Straubenzie was a 56-year-old British Army veteran, "an old soldier, [with] service in the Crimea, India and China."[43] In Canada since 1876, van Straubenzie had served as deputy adjutant general in several military districts in the East, and was sailing northward to add his experience as infantry brigade commander.

A few of the Midland troops. LIBRARY & ARCHIVES CANADA , C-2433

As loading continued, Laurie directed the teamsters to deliver baled hay and bagged oats for the cavalry horses, to be packed on the *Northcote*, its crew cramming every nook and cranny on the cargo deck and barges in an attempt to ship a heaping 350 tons of freight. The massive load was incomparable with any the *Northcote* had ever hauled. After examining the river conditions, Sheets ordered the cargo pared down to 200 tons. To make no mistake that this was a war campaign, the freight included Captain Howard's Gatling gun and 10,000 rounds of ammunition for it, plus three tons of artillery and rifle cartridges. The twin barges lashed to both port and starboard carried all manner of foodstuffs: corned-beef, hardtack flour, sugar, beans, fat pork, tea and dried apples for the troops, oats and hay for the livestock, and, more grimly, lead for the enemy. Troops were going to have to ride on the barges as well as the boat.

Five horses were put aboard, for rapid communications and for pulling the Gatling gun carriage. Kirwan had great praise for the native breeds:

> Some of them are Indian ponies, or "shaganappies," as they are called in these parts. They are hardy little brutes and accustomed to the plains. They are not fleet, but they have great staying powers, and they never stumble over the gopher or badger holes with which the prairies are honey-combed. They can subsist on tuft grass and do not require blanketing. They are docile, and for

campaigning are found more useful, in some respects, than the bigger animals we brought from Ontario or the United States.[44]

To get the steamer away faster, Laurie offered bonuses to teamsters who could deliver their loads from Swift Current to the Landing by the evening before embarking. But the wagoners did not seem to get the message, and didn't arrive until the last moment. Purser Rennie Talbot was not amused, especially after such a long demurrage at the Landing. To be "delayed for a few hours by the non-arrival of the teams with the rest of our freight" seemed only insult to injury.[45] Dawn came too early for the march-weary troops. As Private Clapp put it, "The pale faces, stiffened joints and sore limbs of the men the following morning plainly indicated that they had suffered great physical fatigue. Some were laid up for several days afterwards, but all recovered from the effects of our justly celebrated forced march."[46]

After ten days of preparations, the *Northcote* put her giant rear paddles to water as the crew "let go our lines, rounded to, and with three rousing cheers from the soldiers on shore, which were returned with interest by those on the boat, we rounded the bend and lost sight of the Crossing."[47]

The *Northcote*'s infantrymen, medics, ship's crew and machine gunner numbered around 200. "Although the wind was blowing hard, making it very difficult for the pilot to see the trees in the river, nevertheless we made a good run, and anchored in the middle of the river for the night,"[48] after a brisk 40-mile run. James Sheets announced confidently that the journey to Clarke's would take four days. But before their rendezvous, both Middleton and the *Northcote* would have separate ordeals. The ship's problems were merely anticlimactic. The general's setback would be tragic, and he would come to need the steamer more than ever.

CHAPTER EIGHT

The Passage North

Middleton in check

General Middleton wasted no time reaching the heart of the rebellion. On April 3, his column left Fort Qu'Appelle for the important ferry landing and telegraph station of

Fred Middleton
in field khakis.
LIBRARY & ARCHIVES
CANADA PA026732

Clarke's Crossing. Private Robert K. Allan of the 90th Winnipeg Rifles said that in the first 18 miles out of the Touchwood Hills, "the mud was knee deep."[1] No fewer than six correspondents accompanied the troops, including one from the U.S. and one from England. George Ham of the *Winnipeg Free Press* tagged along to ensure his newspaper a first-hand account of the attack on Batoche.

On the march, Middleton became acquainted with Owen E. Hughes, a plucky North Welshman, "the son of a leek" and a frontier Renaissance man. He boasted of having been educated in Belgium, England, France and Germany before going to seek his fortune on the raw Canadian prairie. Hughes was a linguist ("I know French and German, can understand most of the Indian language, and can swear fluently in several others when necessary"[2]) and a veteran trader and partner in Stobart, Eden & Co., the mercantile post at Duck Lake. In 1878, Hughes and the NWMP withstood an attempted raid on the store by members of the Beardy band. Hughes even tried to organize the local Métis as a regiment in Colonel Houghton's Manitoba Military District. Hughes was gazetted captain of a unit called the North West Mounted Rifles, with none other than Gabriel Dumont as his first lieutenant. The Rifles formed, drilled and trained—and were only a trip to Battleford from receiving arms and saddles—as loyal Canadian soldiers. But Houghton dismissed Hughes's unit as "inefficient," and the Rifles died on paper. The order to disband was seen as yet another insult to the Métis. Still, Hughes couldn't get enough of officialdom, and, as local justice of the peace, he loved referring to himself as "the sheriff."

Hughes was in Winnipeg on business when the "fracas broke out, ending the pristine winter silence." Concerned for his trading post stock and the safety of people he'd come to know as friends, Hughes travelled to Qu'Appelle and pestered his way into Middleton's column. To satisfy officialdom, Hughes consented to being listed as a member of the Transport Service of Colonel Sam Bedson. Whatever it took to get home.

Middleton pitched camp 34 miles from Clarke's Crossing on April 16, and added drama to the mission by genuinely expecting resistance to an attempt to secure the ferry. "Am just off to seize Clarke's Crossing. Will telegraph when I get there."[3] With Napoleonic fervour, Middleton led an advance party to take control of the crossing before the ferry could be sabotaged. On the way, they encountered the same blizzard that was plaguing other elements of the force, but the frozen scouts reached "the banks of the rolling Saskatchewan"[4] and found Clarke's Crossing safe and untouched. Middleton could hardly believe Riel would miss such an opportunity.

Clarke's Crossing was named for Mr. and Mrs. John F. Clarke, who had come to the broad valley of the South Branch before temperance colonists founded their town at Saskatoon. After establishing a ferry, the Clarkes[5] named a small nearby settlement which George Ham would later describe as "a much larger place than Humboldt. It consists of a stone house and two log ones, in one of which is the post office.[6] A later visitor to the Landing described the typical operation of the ferry "being run on a cable stretched across the river, and to this the boat was fastened with a running gear, and was operated by lowering the stern of the boat downstream but still fast to the cable so as to have the boat at an angle to the force of the running water. A wash board was lowered on the upper side to present a greater surface to the power of the stream, the water pressing on the slanting surface propelled the boat forward."[7]

Clarke's Crossing and the eastern approach to the river where the Dominion Telegraph spans the River. *CANADIAN PICTORIAL & ILLUSTRATED WAR NEWS, 1885 SOUVENIR EDITION*

Clarke's Crossing became a landmark of the region, a vast reach of river where the stream is nearly 600 feet wide and protected by high banks. In 1876 the Dominion Telegraph Service chose the location to span the South Saskatchewan, bypassing the traditional Carlton Trail route, to wire together Winnipeg and Edmonton. With the advance of the CPR's own telegraph, faraway Ottawa became connected with the West as never before. The combination of the telegraph and Clarke's Crossing's reputation as one of the few ferries not controlled by Métis sympathizers made Clarke's strategic for communications and transport as a junction of trails leading to Prince Albert, Battleford, Swift Current, Moose Jaw and Qu'Appelle.

Richard Molloy, the telegrapher at Clarke's, was charged with relaying the word to get the ferries working in anticipation of Middleton's arrival. A four-man crew from nearby Saskatoon arrived, headed by veteran sailor E. Shelton Andrews. At the outbreak of the rebellion, Andrews had organized that town's home guard, and when installation of the ferries was called for, he and his crew, which included Xavier Gougeon, took to the water. "We left here [Saskatoon] with the ferries, went down to Clarke's Crossing,"[8] wrote Captain Andrews, indicating the presence of more than one scow taken from the temperance colony.

Impressed with the captain's industry, and still intent on a naval campaign, Middleton decided Andrews needed material and had him enrolled into the Transport Service, the ever present receptacle for teamsters, contractors and any other civilian deemed valuable to the corps. The next afternoon, April 17, the remainder of the column arrived after a 198-mile march. Robert Allan was unimpressed. "Still no trees,"[9] he groused, which was an understatement given that whenever an officer wanted to build a fire, he had to pay a dollar to a teamster for a stick of kindling.

Middleton spent five days at Clarke's, plotting strategy with his officers and, by telegraph, with Minister Caron. His chief of staff, Lord Melgund, was more than a run-of-the-mill aide de camp. Born Gilbert John Elliot, a British officer who came to Canada as the military secretary for the Governor General, Melgund was the man who had scratched around Canada for boatmen and steamer pilots for the Nile expedition. Now free of his dreary desk duty, he was sent on a daring reconnaissance into the heart of his own campaign.

Melgund's party returned with a trio of Sioux scouts. On interrogation, the Sioux estimated the rebel forces at less than 200. That information, coupled with the relative peace of his march and the ease with which Clarke's had been secured, convinced the arrogant Middleton he was not dealing with military equals. He conned himself into a tragic error.

With a means of crossing, Middleton could use Clarke's as a staging point, not only in transport organization, but in attack strategy. In spite of the arguments of Melgund and others to the contrary, Middleton proclaimed, "I shall divide my force, sending half on west side of river and half on east side,"[10] proceeding to Batoche on both sides of the South Saskatchewan.

Combat engineer Captain Herbert de Haig sketched the ferry at Clarke's Crossing.
ILLUSTRATED LONDON NEWS

On April 20, the 10th Grenadiers, French's Scouts and the Winnipeg Field Battery, along with several supply wagons, were sent across on the ferry, with Lieutenant Colonel Charles Montizambert and Lord Melgund in command. Middleton would lead the remainder of the force on the east side, gambling on a double-pronged, pincer attack on Riel. With Andrews running the ferry, three days were spent in the crossing and forming up of the western column "after a great deal of trouble."[11]

His staff's protests must've had some effect on Middleton. Despite the splitting of the corps, Andrews was ordered to unhook the cable and put his scow into the stream, to float along to effect a troop transfer should either side become engaged. "Major Bedson went with me," said Andrews, as did Lord Melgund, who "preferred travelling by boat than rig,"[12] Evidently, Clarke's ferry remained in place, so Andrews must have sailed downriver on one of the scows brought from Saskatoon. George Ham called it a "steam scow,"[13] so it may have been a boiler-powered skiff, perhaps using materials from Andrews's old *May Queen*.

The wide open spaces and the successful march had lulled the general into a false sense of security. He imagined himself the master of all he surveyed, but didn't see the agents who enabled Gabriel Dumont to plot Middleton's every move and counter for it. A sympathetic teamster on the transport column, Jerome Henry, was able to draw a fairly accurate map of the Clarke's Crossing camp and pass it through the lines to the Métis. Riel and Dumont even had newspapers brought in regularly from Qu'Appelle that dutifully published the enemy's strength as reported by unwit-

Transferring the column and teams from east to west on the Clarke's Crossing Ferry. LIBRARY & ARCHIVES CANADA

ting correspondents. Apart from the captured Sioux, Middleton had no such reliable reports on his enemy. When Middleton realized the blunder, he kicked the *Toronto*

Daily Mail's regular reporter, Frederick Davis, out of the column for publishing numbers and troop movements for all the world to see, enemy included. With Davis gone, Ham became by default the correspondent for the Toronto paper.

The night of April 23, Middleton camped a few miles short of Fish Creek, known to the Métis locals as Tourond's Coulee, after a nearby settler. With a diminished enemy column on the east bank, Gabriel Dumont decided Tourond's would be as likely a point as any for an attack. The coulee was protected by dense willows, and the stream's meander offered natural offensive positions. The trail passed through open plains, flanked on either side by poplar brush. In the wee hours of April 24, Dumont set his trap: riflemen were stationed in the brush as Dumont personally rode headlong into Middleton's camp to use himself as the cheese. Initially he went unnoticed, just feet away from the camp. He finally attracted the attention of one of Boulton's Scouts, who sounded the alarm and galloped after, chasing the rebel leader into the trap.

In seconds, six cavalrymen dropped from their saddles, two fatally. The remaining troops dismounted, left their horses and withdrew to a ravine to return fire. Soon the infantry caught up, but only got caught in the crossfire. The confused artillery, with no definite target to focus on, fired on the wooded bluffs, missing the bushwhackers but dealing death to many of the attackers' horses. But the cannoneers were in full view of the snipers, and were picked off as they manned their guns. The battle lasted

"The Battle of Fish Creek" by Edward Curzon in *Canadian Pictorial & Illustrated War News*. The background shows the relative distance to the South Saskatchewan River, and to the far west bank, where half the column was cut off from the fighting by the river. LIBRARY & ARCHIVES CANADA C-002425

hours, the confusion accented by a grass fire Dumont set to add a cover of smoke to obscure his position.

Across the river, Melgund and Montizambert were four miles away, having broken camp much later than Middleton while awaiting hay and supplies to arrive from Clarke's. When the officers heard the firing, they ordered Harold Rusden of French's Scouts to investigate. For some reason, Rusden believed the battle sounds were the NWMP from Prince Albert engaging the rebels. The Scout was horrified when an officer shouted across the river, "Tell Lord Melgund we're attacked in the rear!" Even the besieged were unsure of how they were being confronted, since the assault was actually frontal. Upon Rusden's return, the western troops were moving toward the scene.

The infantrymen double-timed the four miles to the deep, icy river, which had to be forded with cumbersome cannon and supply wagons that could not be left unguarded. To move the reinforcements, "the scow which had followed us down the river was now brought up and crossing commenced."[14] Nobody had to tell Shelton Andrews what was happening: "We heard the guns firing and an officer came up and gave me orders to get the troops back across the river again."[15] The first traverse was clumsy. The scow had to be rowed over to the east bank, but somebody forgot the oars. Quickly, makeshift oars were improvised and the boat towed the cable across, where it was attached to a tree trunk. By noon the ferry was ready to use. The cannons of the Winnipeg Battery were shipped first, then the Grenadiers.

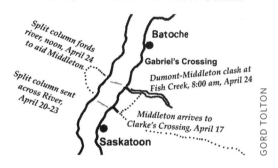

ABRUPT DELAY AT FISH CREEK

Split column fords river, noon, April 24 to aid Middleton

Split column sent across River, April 20-23

Batoche

Gabriel's Crossing

Dumont-Middleton clash at Fish Creek, 8:00 am, April 24

Middleton arrives to Clarke's Crossing, April 17

Saskatoon

GORD TOLTON

The column that previously spent three days crossing at Clarke's now made the trip in less than four hours. But it could not help Middleton: priority was given to a full and complete crossing before anyone could be allowed to join the fight. As the battle progressed, trooper Rusden noticed a few rebels not engaged in the battle. "We saw the halfbreeds clearing out in numbers and begged to be allowed to chase them."[16] Melgund denied the request, not wanting to draw protection away from transport wagons yet to be ferried from the west bank. Melgund was correct, for it was still some distance to the battlefield, and a broken string of infantrymen would've created a shooting gallery, and a second front.

Soon the very appearance of fresh troops had a stilling effect on the Métis. Ham correctly assessed that Dumont was aware of the late arrivals, "evidently on the look-out for the appearance of Colonel Montizambert's force from the other side of the river." The rebel tactician's response was to live to fight another day. "Dumont was greatly afraid that Colonel Montizambert was crossing the river with the left column to strike him in the rear." When the Grenadiers appeared, "Dumont … began to draw off his little force, keeping a few of his best marksmen to cover his retreat."[17]

Lord Melgund, aide de camp to General Middleton, led the west bank column back across the river to the Fish Creek battle site. LIBRARY & ARCHIVES CANADA

By the time Montizambert arrived, the battle was all but over. The Winnipeg Battery made a show of some shelling of cliffs, more for psychology than strategy. The Grenadiers fanned out into the rebels' former ground, but the guerrillas were gone. A perplexed Middleton threw up his hands, ordered a ceasefire and denied Montizambert permission to pursue.

That evening was one "no one on the campaign is likely to forget … Everything was in confusion … A more miserable look-out could not be possibly conceived." As wounded and dead were tended to, troops found their own means for supper. To make an end to the deadly day, nature called up a spring squall of wet, slushy sleet that endangered Captain Andrews's boat crossing, as he and crew "had a time keeping the ferry off the rocks."[18] Trooper Rusden, wracked with guilt from missing the action and sickened by the despair painted a bleak scene: "Tired out, cold, hungry, and miserable; on one side of the river the groans of the wounded and dying … on the other, confusion, a large transport guarded only by a handful of men who might be attacked, cut off, and destroyed before help could arrive from the already worn-out troops on the other side."[19] The next morning, all transports were brought across the river. On that "never-to-be-forgotten day," drenched guards accompanied the teamsters, while grave diggers tended to their sad duty.

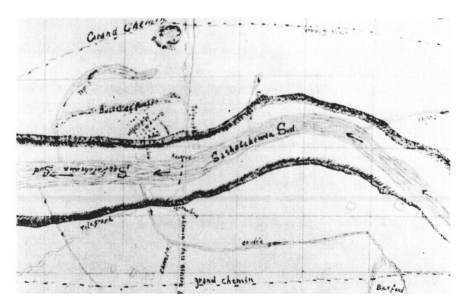

Clarke's Crossing and Middleton suffered from a lack of security, as evidenced by this spy map found among Riel's papers, drawn by Jerome Henry, a teamster in the military transport column. LIBRARY & ARCHIVES CANADA

Despite the setback dealt the opposition, Dumont's hunters too were fatigued, and retreated to Batoche. They had inflicted serious damage, but in many ways Dumont's command was in worse shape, with six dead, countless wounded, and many of the unwilling Sioux abandoning their shaky alliance. Most critical was the loss of 55 horses captured or killed by the government troops. There was also collateral damage: the Field Force, vengeful in defeat, embarked on a spree of unbridled destruction. Houses of Métis and white settlers alike were looted and burned indiscriminately. The Tourond house, near the battlefield, received particular attention by the wrecking crew, as they broke furniture and set the house ablaze. Cattle were rounded up, slaughtered and turned into meals for the troops.

Owen Hughes got a first-hand look at the battle effectiveness of his neighbours against the government that had called his militia "inefficient." The "sheriff" couldn't resist rubbing salt into Middleton's pride. "What do you think of my men now, Middleton?" he taunted.

"What men?" came the brusque general's reply. "What the devil are you talking about?"

"Why, my men, of course," shot back Hughes, his chest full of pride at the damage his former recruits had done. "The men Houghton disbanded—Gabriel Dumont, my lieutenant, and my half-breeds who have just driven your army back. Great Scott, had I been there to lead them, we'd have driven you out of the country!"[20] History does not record Middleton's reply, but one might guess it was uncomplimentary.

Middleton was personally devastated. He couldn't believe "primitives" could be capable of this. Eleven of his men were dead, 40 wounded. Even his hat had been shot through, an act of bravado Dumont himself took credit for. Though Middleton still held the field, he knew privately he'd been checked. Officers and troopers lost confidence in him and in the campaign. "To call the action a decided victory is absurd."[21] said one newspaper. The general admitted he was in "an embarrassing, but not a novel position,"[22] and was seriously thinking that the prime objective of Batoche should be bypassed and the column should march around to Prince Albert and reconnoitre with Irvine's Mounties.

Correspondent Ham reported that perhaps the "command [should go] to Hudson's Bay Company's ferry," past Riel's stronghold, and take control of the lower portion of the river. That notion was tempting, but Middleton could not move anywhere just yet. So many critically wounded men could not be transported overland without killing them. Leaving them behind was not an option. The HBC ferry would have to remain as it was for now. What Middleton needed was the *Northcote* to move his patients. "Here I am, with nearly forty wounded, and the long expected

Gabriel Dumont's innate intelligence outfoxed Middleton's classical British tactics. L.M. MULVANEY, *THE NORTH-WEST REBELLION*

boat is not even within hail a hundred miles southward."[23] Until the boat arrived, the soldiers were going to have to mend under canvas.

Middleton's pomposity had been burst, deflated not only by a band of wilderness-born hunters, but also by the river he had allowed to fool him into dividing his force. Subordinates lost faith in his command, and he became gun-shy, unsure of himself and very vulnerable: "The enemy are boasting that we are afraid to move, and are given ample time to make further preparations for escape and defence. I know the edict of delay is bad, yet what can I do?"[24]

Camp was pitched a short distance from the battlefield, near the river where *Northcote* and company would land the essentials for Middleton's comeback. "General Middleton cannot move another mile without supplies," wrote Ham, assuring military capability that would be added on arrival. "[He] has the utmost confidence in Colonel Williams and the Midland wing with the *Northcote* but is evidently extremely anxious to hear from them."[25]

Just moving on depended on the *Northcote*'s cargo of flour, hay, pork, beans, biscuits, rifles, ammunition, troops and the Gatling gun. "Everything depends on the supplies,"[26] Ham wrote, fearing failure would result in falling back to Clarke's Crossing. Without the boat "we have driven off the enemy, but by this enforced wait we are losing all the fruits of victory." As Middleton prayed for the *Northcote*'s safe deliverance, he cursed it: "I can no longer trust to the boat."[27]

After Fish Creek, telegraph operator Richard Molloy became the most important man in Canada. From his office at Clarke's Crossing, he was tapping the key 16 hours a day to let the outside world know of the reversal. The day of the battle, Molloy was joined by J. Stuart Macdonald, a fellow Dominion Telegraph worker, and was glad for the help. Reporters demanded the wire to file their stories, "each correspondent naturally desirous of obtaining priority."[28] The telegraphers were also popular with Middleton and Minister Caron, as military couriers burned a rut between Clarke's and Fish Creek with official dispatches. As the battle became newsworthy, relatives with concern for their boys kept Molloy and Macdonald's fingers dancing.

J. Stuart Macdonald, the telegrapher at Clarke's Crossing, was kept busy relaying the news of Fish Creek and the *Northcote* to the outside world.
BRENDA BURNS, SASKATCHEWAN ARCHIVES BOARD

The *Toronto Daily Mail*'s armchair "Old Soldier," Robert McManus, correctly assessed that "the abandonment of the river route from Swift Current and the famous dash of Otter's brigade across the prairies for the relief of Battleford, have materially changed the phase of the campaign."[29] George Ham agreed: "The tug *Minnow* with barges is trying to get up from Medicine Hat, but it is evident the water route must be abandoned."[30]

E.R. Johnston witnessed Fish Creek for the *St. Paul Pioneer Press*, and saw the anguish in Middleton. The correspondent boiled the camp's condition down to a single statement: "Now we are waiting for our wounded to get into condition to travel, and for the arrival of the *Northcote* from Swift Current."[31] But soon, scouts brought dismaying news to the command. "Word has just been received that the *Northcote* ran ashore here two days ago on a sand-bar 90 miles south of here."[32] Jim Sheets's roosters were involved in their own psychological battle against the South Saskatchewan.

Warping off to war

In a cramped stateroom, Major Kirwan scrawled an open letter intended for publication: "My hand is unsteady, and the table on which I am writing is shaking, for I am scrawling this letter on board the steamer *Northcote* as we are going down the South Saskatchewan. Our destination is General Middleton's headquarters, to whom we are bringing supplies and reinforcements."[33]

As Kirwan wrote, the *Northcote* was subject to a plague of river variables. The brief spring floodtide was gone, and the high flows were not due to return for another month until warm rains and sun could release the snow pack from the Rocky Mountain watershed. The *Northcote* could only aid Middleton if it met the column. "All told there are about 100 tons of supplies on board the two barges, and scouts have come from the front to tell us that man and beast at head-quarters are short of food and ammunition, and urge us to hurry on over a river choked with sand bars and crossed by barriers every few miles of the way."[34]

Kirwan detailed how the barges were arranged to provide both accommodations for the men and defensive measures against the enemy:

A barge is lashed to each side of the steamer, and oats, hay, canned meats, hard tack, tea, sugar, ammunition and other necessaries for an army in the field are crowded on board. The boxes and bales have been arranged so as to form breast works on the outer side of each barge, for we are told that the hostile may make it merry for us at certain points along our way. A few bags of oats have been placed in the centre of each barge and from these an awning has been stretched to the sides. At night this answers for a tent and in daytime it is rolled up in the centre of the barge and wind and weather flit across the bronzed features of the men who lie exposed on the open boats beside us. In some places bags of oats and bundles of hay have been built into the form of huts and a few comrades crowd into the little shelter and rejoice at their good fortune. In other places water-proof sheets have been placed over walls made of sacks of oats, and with bags of flour for a floor, squads of men nestle underneath and eat, sleep and take their turns at duty, looking healthy if rough, and strong if stained with the soil and dust of travel.[35]

Further sleeping and dining arrangements aboard the main ship were spartan and haphazard:

On board the steamer the officers have berths in the cabin, and share with the crew the comforts of a state-room large enough to accommodate about half the number which is now crowded between its thinly panelled sides. The assistant-surgeons and dressers of the ambulance corps sleep on the floor, and we take our meals in relays, the "roustabout" crew being served first and then the staff and field officers, while the company officers follow in regular rotation. Our rations are simple, and I hope wholesome. We have plenty of hard tack, canned meat, sugar, and an occasional slice of soft bread, a piece of pork, some beans, and plenty of tea. Our orderlies manage, by means unknown to me, to scrape up some pieces of pudding or "stick-jaw," as it is called. Once or twice Dr. Horsey, of Ottawa, shot some duck, and there was rejoicing at his mess board, to which the staff of the Midland battalion were allowed to approach.[36]

The troops were ready, as the wordy orator Arthur Williams issued written orders to his footsore Midlanders that "in the advance down the river the strictest discipline and watchful steadiness will be evinced and if called upon to meet the enemy as a probable all will stand shoulder to shoulder and the utmost steadiness and calmness exhibited in carrying out such orders as may be issued."[37] To ensure order, Williams kept his men in barracks routine:

At six o'clock every morning the reveille sounds and the blankets are packed away for the day. The men come from their nooks and corners of the barges, fold up the awnings and put the kits to order. Their rifles are placed against the breastworks and stand ready for use. At 6:30 they get their breakfast of hard tack, tea, canned meat, and any nicknacks they can scrape together in the way of bash or extras.[38]

In spite of the Midlands' battle readiness, the only enemy in sight were the protruding sandbars, and soldiers' duties turned to assisting the steamer crews. Sergeant Walter Stewart diarized that the good start was short-lived. "Got stuck on a sand bar before we got five miles, but with heaving and twisting about got clear. Went through similar operations a dozen times during the day. Anchored for the night only 15 miles from where we started."[39]

Discipline seemed not to extend to the troops' language, however: "The soldiers assisting by pulling on the ropes and cutting and carrying wood when we required them to do so. The army in Flanders shows signs of swearing."[40]

April 24 brought another day and more toil, and a torment of rain to irritate those dealing with freeing the boat. "Wooded up early and started off, but still did not go far before the old *Northcote* found another sand bar to run into. Had heavy rain storm lasting about three hours, during which time we ran on to another sandbar; got off only to get high and dry on another. Only made about eight miles today." But ignorance was bliss, as the "boys [were] all in good spirits, as usual, singing and joking all day long, but feeling sorry for the old boat."[41]

The river would be problem enough, but the soldiers and crews were also afflicted by nervous tension. Colour Sergeant William Wrighton held his rifle at the ready as he eagerly succumbed to the rumours. "I am told it will be a very dangerous journey as the Banks of the River are very high and in some parts narrow, also the whole country along its Banks are occupied by the Rebels, so there is every chance of having some sharp work. The men all appear very anxious to proceed." [42]

A rotation of sentries aboard the boat was effected and a plan of readiness put forth for nightly layover and in the event of attack.

THE ROUTE TO THE WAR ZONE

Batoche
Fish Creek
Gabriel's Crossing
Clarke's Crossing
Saskatoon
Moose Woods

Left Sask. Landing April 23
Arr'd. Fish Creek May 5
200 tons of cargo
Cos. A,B,C,D - Midland Battalio
No. 1 Field Hospital
Militia Staff Officers
Capt. James Sheets commanding

The Elbow

Saskatchewan Landing

GORD TOLTON

> At nine the guard is mounted; two sentries are posted, one over the quarter-master's stores, and the other over the Gatling Gun, which grips with its ten teeth on the stern of the steamer. At 12 o'clock they get their dinner; at 6 p.m. supper, and at seven the retreat sounds. A picket, composed of a captain, a subaltern, a sergeant, two corporals, and twenty men, is told off every day, and at night the sentries are doubled. When we can we anchor in mid-stream, but when [it] is not practicable outlying pickets are placed on land, at some distance from the steamer, and every precaution taken against surprise. Then the Gatling is pointed so as to play on an attacking force if the men are obliged to retreat to the boat.[43]

As Charles Clapp summarized, "We knew not at what moment we would be attacked by Indians from both shores, in fact we expected it and were fully prepared to give them a warm reception should they have done so."[44] Few of the bands had much sympathy with Riel, despite their wariness and curious contacts with settlers. But vivid imaginations saw a "Red menace" behind every sagebrush. The citizen soldiers' steely bravado would have to go untested for the moment, and "we proceeded to our destination unmolested by the redskins."[45]

Kirwan was losing interest in the territory: "On each side of us the land rises in irregular and jagged outlines, hillocks, and deep water ways cut through the soil, and denuded of its scanty verdure."[46] To his globetrotting mind, there seemed little reason for life to exist here:

Wild fowl are not as numerous as we were led to expect, but an odd flock of pelican or swan float gracefully above us. Geese and duck are not in these parts found "by the acre," as we were told they did when we were leaving civilization; and of big game we can see nothing but the bleached bones of the buffalo which dot every few yards of the banks back from the water line. When we stop for wood we can see the tracks of antelope and wolves, but we see nothing larger than prairie dogs when we hunt along the shore. It is a weary waste of sandy, almost barren soils, sloughs and tuft grass, looking as lonely as the ocean and as silent as the grave. No fish can live in these muddy waters, and a few rabbits are the only edible four-footed creatures which we can beat up in the sedge and scrub which cover the gullies.[47]

Kirwan seemed to be entertaining serious doubts as to exactly what everybody was fighting over.

The *Northcote*'s layover cost her crew and the military dearly. Any advantage gained by the early spring runoff was lost, "delayed fully two-thirds of the time in endeavoring to get loose after having run aground."[48] That didn't do justice to the misery that the steamer's crew endured. Clerk Talbot was close to the nerve centre as a tough headwind and the low water tested his mettle. "Another very blowy day. Made very little progress today. Captains Segar and Sheets worked like very Trojans, forcing the boat over places where the water was only 30 inches deep, and the boat was drawing 34 inches. Swearing systems aggravated."[49]

Rennie Talbot loved to discuss the weather of the day as well as its events, and poetically saluted the first Sabbath of the voyage. "Sunday, 26th—A lovely day—'In gentle sighs the softly whispering breeze, Salutes the flowers, and waves the trembling tree' … No bad language used out of respect for the day."[50]

The crew could not afford to do more than casually observe the Lord's Day. Every lost travel minute threatened progress. Sergeant Stewart expressed it this way:

Sunday was no day-of-rest for us. We spent the day, all hands working hard unloading scows and boat, taking everything ashore. The only way of releasing the old tub. The worst stick-stack-stow we have had yet, deep in mud. We got steaming away again, but only ran a mile, when we got stuck fast again. All hands went ashore with a long rope and after a great deal of long and strong pulling got her off, but it was nearly dark and had to anchor for the night.[51]

In spite of pre-dawn starts at 3:30 a.m., the *Northcote* was always, by afternoon, "hard aground, and there we remained, sparring and pulling until 8 o'clock at night," when finally the large towing winch gave out and more. James Sheets finally threw up his hands. "Not being able to do anything more for that night" as "the soldiers mounted guard, and the rest of us retired to sleep, perhaps to dream that: 'By torch and trumpet fast arrayed' they were dealing out death to the rebels."[52] Talbot proved prophetic, for none knew that on that very day, death had in fact been dealt at Fish Creek.

The next morning, April 27, proved to be "a beautiful day,"[53] and the deckhands repaired the winch enough to work with a single pulley. Some mechanical advantage was lost, but as the *Northcote* was far from a repair shop, the fix would have to hold, for the winches were needed. Every twist and turn in the meandering river exposed yet another sandy shallow. "Our progress was greatly impeded by the presence of the numberless sandbars which characterized that branch of the Saskatchewan."[54]

Every time the watchmen failed to call out a shallow, the *Northcote* would stop dead. And so the men at the bow of the ship and barges were both revered and reviled along the journey. Charles Clapp articulated the watchmen's role:

> The depth of the river had to be poled all the way and to this effect two men were stationed, one on the bow of the steamer and the other at the bow of the large barge, with sounding poles in their hands, on each of them was marked a scale of feet, and which they continually dipped in the river, drew them out and from the height of the water mark knew how deep the water was . . . Every time they drew the pole from the river they would roar out, in stentorian tones, the depth of the water to the mate who, seated on the hurricane deck, passed it on to the Captain in the Wheelhouse.[55]
>
> Six feet—four and a half—no bottom—two feet—three feet—one feet. Being so accustomed to call out "feet" they would roar it out in a louder tone, for, of course, it meant grounding.[56]

Invariably a call would be missed, as the watch could not possibly catch every unknown rise in the riverbed. When everyone aboard lurched forward, all knew the watchmen had failed, and "about twenty times a day the cry was by the officer of the day, 'All hands on the flats.'"[57] "Then the spars would be set to work to try and push and raise her off. The engines were put back, the steamer throbbed from stem to stern, the steam hissed and roared in the escape pipe, the sand was stirred up from the bottom of the river until the water grew thick and yellow, and if she was not very hard aground, after a few minutes of this kind of thing she was loose."[58]

Victorian travellers on the river always marvelled at how the roosters could manipulate a ship to walk itself out of an abject coma. Dr. Edmond King was utterly fascinated. Veteran steamboaters and most everybody else aboard found the process routine. Troops found it tiresome, and it made officers chew the floorboards. But wide-eyed Dr. King had never seen anything like grasshoppering, and was totally enthralled with the boat's machinations:

> It seems strange. But one soon gets used to it and can sit on deck and be
> amused at the different intonations that these fellows give to the varying
> calls … When the boat gets stuck the fun begins. The ropes are run around the
> [capstan], the spars dropped, the derricks put to their utmost strength, and at
> last the boat slowly raises herself, and, slowly clearing the obstructing sandbar,
> glides off. [59]

Frequently, even this monumental effort was hardly enough to "de-beach" this particular whale, and it took a lot of manpower. A frequent athletic event popular at drills and sports days was the tug-of-war, and at various points in this particular war, a tug was needed. "In the great majority of cases we were high and almost dry on a bar, the tow line was thrown out and the services of the Midland were called into requisition when they generally made short work of it." Their military trousers muddied and their fingers blistered, "the strength of the gallant Midlanders was fully tested." [60] Among the Midlanders, one Major Hughes inspired his wet, gritty troops, "proving himself a brick by throwing off his coat and setting the men a good example by working as only he can. All praise to him." [61]

When winch or manpower failed to budge the boat, all hands available were required to lighten the load. So roustabouts and militiamen alike would manually shift the tonnage from boat to barge until the *Northcote*'s wheel kicked up water. But "the barges had to be poled ashore and relieved of their loads, brought back to the steamer and her cargo transferred to them and she then being light floated off easily. The work of the reloading being concluded we resumed our trip." [62]

Back and forth, at each and every sandbar did this monotony continue. On "one occasion … we ran on a bar which caused a delay of twenty-four hours."[63] It's too bad those aboard never recorded verbatim some of the conversations. The colour and intensity of the language were no doubt considerable. Clapp tried to be diplomatic: "Before we reached our destination patience had nigh well ceased to be a virtue." [64] Dr. King attempted polite accuracy in recounting Sheets's pilot-house orations to his crew:

> Did you ever go down the river on a boat commanded by an "only original"
> river captain? The only original must be capable of using a very big "D" at the
> proper moment and with a peculiar emphasis only to be acquired by a Yankee
> and, by him, only after several years cultivating the proper nasal intonation.
> When such a one speaks as he does so with authority; his voice gives forth no
> uncertain sound and he means business from the word go, or to be more literal,
> "d—n." Such a person is the captain of the steamer *Northcote*. [65]

When the *Northcote* reached the "Elbow," where the northeasterly course turns abruptly northward (local natives called it "the river that turns"), the tone of the trip turned as well. The sentries spotted something, and two hundred pairs of legs scurried about for skirmish.

> Officers rush from the saloon and I know something unusual has happened. Field glasses are out, for there is something moving on the horizon. Friends or foes we cannot tell at this great distance, and the bugle sounds the assembly. Then there is the rush of many feet and the men fall in at their appointed posts on the barges. The company officers go down too, and the click of rifles is heard as the men examine the springs and move the breech blocks backwards and forwards. Then the rifles are placed horizontally on the breastworks, and the men stand behind them. The deck hands move about uneasily, and the captain of the steamer, up in the pilothouse wears an anxious expression on his well bronzed face.[66]
>
> Some of the officers have gone to their staterooms and return with their revolvers buckled on, or with Winchesters slung over their shoulders. There is no hurry and everything is business-like and easy. Colonel Van Straubenzie is still looking through his field glass, and the moving figures in the distance come nearer and fringe the horizon like a mirage. Captain Howard has readied his Gatling, and his gunners are at their posts. The surgeons have unpacked their instruments of torture, and saws and knives and bottles with strange labels are placed on the tables of the saloon. Officers' baggage has been piled in one part of the cabin where the hospital is to be, if required.[67]

It was the excitement Sergeant Stewart had been praying for: "Wishing some of the rebels would show themselves to vary the monotony."[68] The call was soon answered, when the unmistakable sight of armed riders charging headlong boiled the blood of amateur and professional soldier alike.

"The moving figures on the plains converge to their centre, and they look as if closing for consultation. They now dot the horizon like moving balls of ebony on a brownish-emerald lawn, and Colonel van Straubenzie is still looking at them through his field-glass, while around the steamer and down in the barges officers and men are standing ready for emergencies." Then, "as they come closer we see the wide awake hats of the men and their long boots, bandoliers full of rifle and revolver cartridges, and their sleek ponies, all looking comme à la guerre."[69]

When Colonel van Straubenzie quietly lowered his field glass, the apprehensive calm turned into outright laughter when the old officer said simply, "Scouts."[70]

The scouts were the Dominion Land Surveyors, come to assess the pathetic progress of the luckless steamer. "Captain [John Stoughton] Dennis ... came to find out what delayed us on our way"[71] and to break the news of the incredible reversal at

Globetrotting British warhorse, Colonel Bowen Van Straubenzie. L.M. MULVANEY, *THE NORTH-WEST REBELLION*

Fish Creek. They also passed along intelligence as to where the ship might encounter danger. "We were told that if attacked at all we would probably catch it at the Moose woods, a few miles south of [Saskatoon]. And then we should hurry on. The men at the front were short of ammunition, the wounded wanted medical comforts, the horses had no oats, and we could supply all of them."[72]

But progress was hard to make on a river that did not want to be navigated. While in the vicinity of the DLS camp, the *Northcote* got jammed on another bar in the change of the channel, where "the river being low and full of sand bars, we were aground again at 5 o'clock."[73] Captain Howard tired of watching the *Northcote* suck itself north. As van Straubenzie and Kirwan vainly protested, Howard decided he wasn't missing much and climbed off the boat and went ashore to visit the scouts' fire.

In the DLS camp, Lewis Redman Ord, a sarcastic surveyor with little love for Middleton or British officers, and Captain Howard traded news of the Fish Creek surprise. All were anxious to get to the front, but few more than Howard, eager to demonstrate his lethal Gatling. He requested permission to take horses from the Surveyors and haul the Gatling to Clarke's Crossing himself. Ord agreed, but the plan fell on van Straubenzie's deaf ears, giving the wry-humoured Ord fodder for his future critical commentary of the campaign.

The gun could have reached Clarke's crossing by land in two days but the officer in command of the steamer, having orders to take it down in that vessel, appeared determined to carry out his instructions if it took him all summer; and there seemed to be a chance of a considerable part of the season slipping over, she got along so slowly. The captains of the boat, old river navigators both, then wished him to land a part of the stores, leaving a guard over them, so as to lighten the steamer, and guaranteed to take her down to Clarke's Crossing in very short time.

Then Ord let van Straubenzie and his favorite target, Middleton, have it: "But this hardy soldier aforesaid was either an extraordinary slave of red tape, or afflicted with all of his senior's caution, and refused to be guided by this sensible advice. How dare they advise him?"[74]

For the soldiers the only relief for boredom or bloodlust would be an opportunity to send a message to the outside world via the DLS couriers. "We were able to send letters from this point, which opportunity was seized by all and quite a large mail was sent ashore."[75] Leaving the Elbow, the *Northcote* faced a stiff headwind that impeded progress. "Blowing very hard and cold. A very disagreeable day, and one in which it was nearly impossible to run."[76] The day was miserable for Rennie Talbot, as even the night's slumber was interrupted by an ungainly shipmate on watch. Both his poetry and his subconscious bore ill will:

As we were now in the enemy's country great care was taken in posting guard, and one sentry was posted on the roof directly over my head, all through the silent "watches" (the man was a jeweller) he kept me awake with his heavy tread … I lay there in my "little bed" wishing he would fall overboard, or get paralyzed in the legs, or do any thing in order that I might woo the fickle god of slumber, or in other words, less elegant but more forcible, "pound my ear." At length I fell into a fitful doze, and dreamed that I saw that unfortunate sentry flying across the prairie pursued by a hundred bloodthirsty Indians while I stood by and cheered them on. So thus I had my dire revenge.

Talbot qualified his insomniac fantasy, though: "I'm a bad man from way back."[77]

The tedium and labour continued. As if running aground were not laborious enough, there was the matter of fuel for those massive, hungry boilers. While the prairie above was quite barren, a fact not lost on Major Kirwan, bored as he was with the wide open spaces, "there is not as much timber as would shingle a cabin. For hundreds of miles on these dreary plains and on the trail travellers carry fuel; or pick buffalo chips with which to cook their food as they move across these desert wilds."[78]

But the river valleys were abundant with large cottonwoods, the supply limited only by the amount the *Northcote* could carry. The lack of strong current weighed heavily on the steamer's fuel economy. "Two or three times each day we had to stop and wood up when about thirty men with axes would be detailed to chop while the remainder of the detachment carried on board the wood."[79]

Woodhawking took a toll on the soldiers' poorly tailored uniforms, which were

… stained with carrying wood on board the steamer, as she stops two or three times a day to wood up. Their boots are brown and unpolished, and their accoutrements bear the stains of labour on every inch of their surface. The officer commanding insists on making the soldiers wash their under-clothing regularly and on keeping their arms in good order; beyond that the men are allowed to appear much as they please, as long as they keep in uniform.[80]

Even the officers were becoming threadbare for the experience, "wearing their oldest uniforms … dressed in hunting breeches of buckskin or corduroy. Like the men, they look rough and ready, although many of them are from the lap of luxury. Colts or Smith & Wesson revolvers dangle from their sword belts when they have their war paint on."[81]

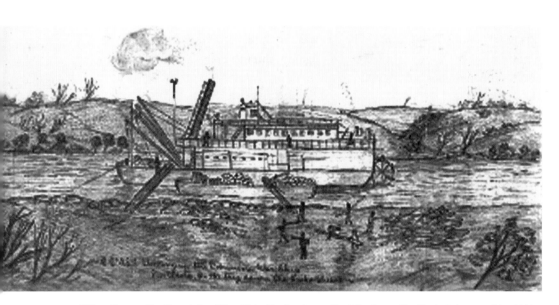

"Wooding up the DomInion War Ship *Northcote* on the trip down the Saskatchewan," by J.W. Craig, May 7, 1885. UNIVERSITY OF SASKATCHEWAN ARCHIVES, JEAN E. MURRAY FONDS

As the river dried up beneath the steamer, so did morale, as all grumbled mutinously. "A fearful time, stuck half the days at a time, river very, very low and everybody kicking like a steer."[82] Even the livestock took a surly tone as the draft horses and the Indian ponies began to tussle on the boat. "The larger horses are jealous of our shaganappies, and they kicked and fretted at the little creatures so much that we were obliged to board them off for protection."[83]

But as cool April turned to a warm May, "the sun blazing down upon us,"[84] the snowpack melted and the river rose again. The *Northcote's* loathsome delays became fewer and fewer as it once again resembled a watercraft. Fuel economy improved, as did the general mood. Groundings became less frequent, and those soldiers blessed with singing voices struck up a choral group. "We made a good run to-day, and everybody is correspondingly good natured and happy."[85] The music did not soothe the savage breasts of the horses, however. "As I write I hear the big ones kicking in their stalls beneath me, and the voices of the orderlies are shouting hoarse oaths at them to be still. The noise blends with the chorus 'Hold the Fort,' which the glee club has started."[86]

As "the boat took a notion and ran all this time without getting stuck,"[87] the voyage entered one of the most beautiful valleys on the Canadian prairie. In 1885, it was pristine and untouched by the sodbuster's plough. The tranquility stirred the creative spirit in Clapp's soul, as he found his surrounding "abounds in scenery, stern and wild, and many excellent views would have delighted the most fastidious artist; while the forest and the prairie would prove a veritable paradise for the sportsman as every variety of game is plentiful from the moose to the gopher and from the eagle to the prairie chicken."[88]

Even the fastidious Kirwan now praised the landscape:

A solitary bird of prey now and again floats by or rises screeching from its nest
when we disturb it as we go puffing, whistling, and blowing down the stream.
An old, small bird twitters on a bough often enough to let us know that the
desolation is not absolutely complete, and one or two butterflies are seen, their
beautiful plumage lending a charm to the dull background of sandy loam …
An odd eagle rises from its nest and hovers about until we pass by, and pelican,
"wavies," and cranes float, on gracefully pinioned wings, above and around us.[89]

On the warm Saturday night of May 2, the *Northcote* anchored near the parkland
forest of Moose Woods, in the domain of Whitecap and his expatriate Sioux from
Minnesota. The Whitecap had left the woods and gone north to join the Métis at
Batoche, and most were unsure about their degree of belligerence or their whereabouts.
Paranoia returned, and the night guard was doubled. Through the night, few aboard
slept, all soldiers having been ordered to have arms at the ready and clothing handy in
the event of a night assault.

Migration of the medicine man

On a sunny April morning, a telegram breaking the news of Fish Creek reached
the table in a CPR caboose in Swift Current that served as General John Laurie's
headquarters. As staff officers digested the news with their breakfast, Laurie briefed
the personnel responsible for medical operations. Heavy on the coffee talk was the
recently departed *Northcote* and its mediocre progress.

At the table was the Field Force's deputy surgeon general, Dr. Thomas Roddick,
a Newfoundland native who had apprenticed with a Truro, Nova Scotia, doctor at
the age of 14. As a 17-year-old McGill University intern, he had treated victims of
a horrific railway bridge disaster at St.-Hilaire, Quebec, and established himself as a
leading expert in trauma. At 29 he became McGill's professor of clinical surgery, "most
skilful as an operator, and renowned as a teacher . . . a wonderful facility in diagnosis
and treating fractures, and his bandaging was a work of art."[90] Now 39, Roddick had
set out to try his hand at combat medicine.

Concerned about the Fish Creek wounded, Roddick dismissed any notions of
river passage for his own staff. His doubts were confirmed by "the arrival in camp of
a scout who reported [the *Northcote*] grounded ten miles from the Elbow of the South
Saskatchewan, and with very little prospect of her getting off."[91] A number of useful
medics were already stuck in the river, useless to the Field Force without higher water.
So Roddick and 10 medics decided to set out from Moose Jaw by wagon to Saskatoon,
where a hospital could be established.

Another doctor at the breakfast table hated wagons and horses, however, and had the means to ignore both wagon and steamer. Surgeon Major Campbell Mellis Douglas decided he'd employ an all-Canadian mode of transport to bring his services to Saskatoon. For some vague reason, Dr. Douglas just happened to have such a means at hand. "A happy thought occurred to me. Why not go down the river in a canoe I had with me?"[92] Campbell Douglas would paddle his way to Saskatoon in a craft of his own design, and thus become the "Lone Canoeist of the Saskatchewan."[93]

A solo venture through the middle of an uncharted war zone may seem conceited, foolhardy or naive. But such judgments would be unfair, given the character of Dr. Douglas. He was born into a family of healers in 1840. His father, Dr. George Douglas, was in charge of the quarantine hospital at Grosse Isle, the island in the St. Lawrence that was the immigration centre for newcomers to British North America. Douglas grew up watching and assisting his father amid the squalor of refugees fleeing the Irish potato famine, assisting their recovery from hunger, cholera and the Atlantic crossing. Many did not recover, and the younger Douglas became steeled to death as the elder Douglas struggled with new concepts in sanitation to reduce mortality. Campbell Douglas entered the British Army in 1862 after a medical education at Laval and the prestigious University of Edinburgh. His greatest act of life-saving would occur in the Bay of Bengal, near faraway Burma.

The action took place on Little Andaman Island, where in 1867, eight British sailors had gone missing and were presumed dead at the hands of indigenous inhabitants. A squad of 17 soldiers had landed to track the vanished seamen, but were themselves attacked and trapped on a beach between hostile bowmen and the pounding surf of the Indian Ocean, their launch swamped by the tide. All seemed doomed until, at the symbolic 11th hour, a boat rowed by four soldiers of the 24th Regiment thrust through the breakers to the rescue. Standing in the bow in command was an ardent, 26-year-

Campbell Mellis Douglas as a young medical officer in the British Army. LIBRARY & ARCHIVES CANADA

old Canadian assistant surgeon named Campbell Douglas. In three trips, Dr. Douglas's amphibious crew successfully extracted all of the trapped soldiers, and his skill also saved his own crew from drowning. He was awarded not only the Silver Medal of the Royal Humane Society, but also, along with his oarsmen, the Empire's highest military award for valour, the Victoria Cross. He was only the sixth Canadian to have achieved such honours up to that time.[94]

A man of both action and dreams, Campbell Douglas left the army in 1882, and retired to the placid surroundings of a farm at Lakefield, Ontario, where the Kawartha Lakes lie still as a calendar painting. At 42 he turned his back on medicine and Empire to fill his days designing and market-ing, of all things, sporting goods. In 1880, he filed Canadi-an and U.S. patents on a collapsible canoe, and whiled away his days testing his creation on the lake. But on March 27, 1885, Douglas's placidity was rippled by news of events in the West. He was requested to return to service as surgeon general and to take charge of medical arrangements for the mobilizing force.

Despite his experience in military medical affairs, Douglas saw the task as impossible. Seeing little to work with and little time to do it, a dejected Douglas resigned his short command, and threw arrangements back to the Defence Minister. Caron in turn appointed Darcy Begin as surgeon general, Roddick as his deputy, and Michael Sullivan to the post of purveyor general. But Douglas was not off the hook; he was reactivated and put in command of Number 1 Field Hospital. He was almost comforted by the demotion, and transported the field unit to Swift Current by rail via Chicago and Minneapolis. But besides his medical gear, he just could not resist packing a secret bit of cargo. Landing the hospital staff at Swift Current, Douglas continued with a small staff to Calgary, and assigned them to General Strange. That done, he returned to Swift Current to find his unit had shipped out without him on the *Northcote*.

But now the vessel was out of communication, rumoured to be floundering with his medics stuck on board. The *Toronto Daily Mail*, that faraway bastion of rumour-mongering, questioned the vessel's fate in a headline, "The Northcote Still Missing,"[95] an inflated extrapolation from a story filed by George Ham, which in smaller print read: "It is possible that an accident has befallen the steamer … though the river is very low, and she may not have made as good time as was expected." Ham's editor, needing more drama, had written his own banner for the story.

Faced with such news, Douglas felt like so much deadwood in the middle of the prairie. So, at that fateful breakfast meeting, he looked up from his tea and sought further details from General Laurie. "How much water does she draw?" inquired Douglas of the steamer. "Four feet aft" was the reply.[96]

Campbell Mellis Douglas as a military medic in his field hospital tent. LIBRARY & ARCHIVES CANADA C 62595

"A happy thought occurred to me," said the doctor, who, for reasons known only to himself, had brought along his folding boat. "Why not go down the river in a canoe?"[97]

"I would be such an insignificant object that if there were hostile Indians along the bank I would probably pass without being seen. I would see what the river was like and how the steamer was getting on." Perhaps imagining that someone should argue him out of such a far-fetched scheme, Douglas was stunned when Laurie shot back, "That's very public spirited of you, Douglas."[98]

That did it. "I felt that I was nailed." Laurie took the flip remark seriously, and little wonder. With those tempestuous riverboats, Laurie was probably glad to hear any fresh idea, no matter how ludicrous. "It was not without inward qualms that I set to make preparations for the voyage," wrote Douglas. "I had mental visions of wily Indians in ambush taking a potshot at the solitary navigator and sending him to the happy hunting grounds to paddle his own canoe at his leisure."[99] The officers didn't calm his trepidation when they asked for locks of his hair to remember him by. But the doctor was a VC winner, and honour forced out of his mind any thought of rescinding his offer. Just getting the little canoe to Saskatchewan Landing would be chore enough.

Borrowing a small cart and pony, Dr. Douglas loaded up his compact boat, his baggage and his medical kit. He may have been an accomplished surgeon and canoeist, but he was no teamster. A few miles out of town, Douglas dropped the reins to shift his shaky load, taking the canoe out first. But when he looked up, the wagon was no longer there: the pony had bolted and circled back to Swift Current, scattering his effects on the prairie.

Dragging his beloved 45-pound canoe pack, Douglas chased the wayward cayuse for three miles. When the rig trotted past a teamsters' camp, the drivers unsuccessfully attempted to catch the runaway. Huffing and puffing, Douglas was advised to stop running and "take it quietly," as the horse would eventually tire. So Douglas quit the chase, regained his wind and prepared to drag his canoe back to town. Another mile down the trail, Douglas was ecstatic to find the pony tied to the wheel of a freight wagon. "[The pony] looked as sleepy as ever, and immediately coughed as if to hint his chest was delicate."[100] The following morning a stiff Dr. Douglas reintroduced himself to the skittish pony and started again for the Landing. This time, horse and surgeon reached both a consensus and the riverfront that afternoon, without incident.

Now the doctor could tend to matters more within his ken, as he assembled his boat. The canoe had been built for him by some Peterborough, Ontario, craftsmen the previous year, "of the Canadian model," 12 feet long, 2½ feet wide and 1 foot deep amidships. For transport, the ribs could be released and each side folded lengthwise into a portable pack. Douglas's innovation had no name yet, but before duty's end he would christen it the *Saskatoon*.

The night before embarking, the doctor examined his river, dismissing it as "a dull-looking stream flowing between sandbars in a bed much too large for it." Time and practice would change his view: "the water was low; the stream ran between sand banks at the rate of about two to three miles an hour and its depth was variable."[101] When Douglas was ready to go he packed two weeks' provisions and a cooking pot. With the current and his own muscle power and a single double-bladed paddle, he attained a speed of 5 miles per hour.

Small wonder the heavily laden *Northcote* was having such difficulty, for even Douglas was at times forced to portage. "The river wound among the sandbars in a way that was confusing, and unless I watched carefully the set of the current I would suddenly find myself with only about two inches of water under my keel."[102] Whenever he attempted a shortcut, the result was usually a bare-legged medic wading through sand and ice-cold water, towing his lightened craft through a quarter mile of shallows back into the main stream.

When Douglas stopped for sustenance, he would dip into his ditty bag of hard tack, canned fruit and meat, tea, chocolate and sugar. At night he camped beneath the upturned, propped-up canoe with a waterproof sheet forming a front wall. Despite the warm spring, the doctor would awaken to find his tarpaulin covered in ice. Douglas reached the Elbow of "the river that turns" in three days, and hadn't seen a soul. Not even a shack on the hill near the Elbow bore any sign of life.

After turning north with the river, the doctor was stalemated by a stiff headwind, so he put in to shore and made camp, spending the day reading and resting from the past few days' activity. The following morning, the river was glassy and calm. Fit and rested, Douglas re-entered the stream and gained an amazing 20 miles. Then the calm of the wilderness was broken by the shrill of a steam whistle, inspiring a fury of paddling. Soon the doctor was heartened by the "sight of the smokestack of a steamer, without doubt the *Northcote*," beached again. Douglas could not believe the boat was so tardy, and initially thought it was on the return trip.

The sight of the paddler broke the tedium for the soldiers aboard the *Northcote*. They'd heard of Douglas's journey from a Surveyor, who, unnoticed by the doctor, had spotted him at the Elbow and brought the intelligence to the steamer. Miles Kirwan wrote that "we saw something moving on the river behind us. It was a long way off, but we soon found it to be a canoe, and then we knew that Dr. Douglas, VC, was in our wake, and that aided by the current, he would soon be on board."[103] The sight of the doctor provided a much needed boost to the morale on board. "On he came with his double paddle moving like a windmill, and we all gathered on one side of the barge to give him a welcome."[104] As the craft made its way "under the lee of the steamer," the red-coated Midlanders gave him a hearty tiger cheer.

Douglas was glad to come aboard for a clean bite and some conversation, wanting to ride the *Northcote* for the rest of the journey, but "soon tired of the monotony of seeing the ship, heavily loaded, with two barges alongside, warped or lifted from one sandbar to another by means of her 'grasshopper legs.' So after dinner I launched my canoe again and left the *Northcote* as I had found her, stuck on another sandbar."[105] As Douglas paddled effortlessly past the steamer, no doubt many a weary soul wished

Douglas had brought more of those remarkable little canoes. He probably could have made a small fortune selling them just then.

Douglas felt little false bravado about his personal security. "The thief doth see in every bush an officer," he thought. Knowing he could be ventilated by a rebel sniper at any moment, he steeled himself by sticking to his paddling and trying not to think about it. Soon his mind's eye was occupied with forming imaginary pictures from the accumulations of clay and sand in front of his bow: "pinnacles and round towers, forts with moats, came successively into view." The doctor hinted that his imaginings were akin to the mirages of the desert traveller. "Desolation is the chief impression I have carried away of the South Saskatchewan."[106]

As Douglas passed the Moose Woods, he noticed the abundance of wildlife in the river valley, not yet used to mankind enough to fear it, as "evidently canoes were a rarity on the river."[107] Swans, geese, ducks, beaver and deer escorted him through the marshy mid-river islands and sandbars. One could hardly believe there was a war on. The next day, Douglas noticed the first inhabited dwelling he'd seen in days, and a pair of gawky farmboys came to inform him he was nearing Saskatoon. Three miles farther, he put in to the temperance colony's ferry landing, and lugged boat and gear ashore.

Campbell Mellis Douglas found the town in alarm. Riel had threatened the colony, and the army come to defeat him had itself been defeated. Unable to wait for the *Northcote*, improvised ambulance wagons were bringing in Middleton's casualties the same afternoon Douglas landed. There was barely time for the medic to stow his paddle and grab his scalpel and bone saw.

Into the war zone

The HBC Commissioner was fighting pitched battles of his own, with papers, ledgers, telegrams, orders and bills of lading, as he struggled to maintain the company's supply lines by rail, land and river. At one point, Joseph Wrigley even had to stand in for the military transport officer in Winnipeg at the height of the teamster shortage at Swift Current. By May 2, the teams and supplies were in hand, and Wrigley put on another hat as president of the W&WTC. The *Northcote* was on its way, but in all the excitement the matter of who was paying the bill got overlooked. Negotiations began with a telegram reading: "Would you prefer to charter her or leave for present question on understanding she is on Government service."[108] Finally, Wrigley and Minister Caron agreed the *Northcote* would be taken on at the deficit rate of $250 per day, expenses included. With the ship already engaged, the government got the upper hand.

As the ambulances rolled into Saskatoon, Campbell Douglas put the temperance colony's settlers to work as corpsmen and nurses. On May 3, an exhausted Douglas was pleased to greet his colleague Dr. Roddick, newly arrived by wagon team. Douglas had beat him in by half a day, but the extra medics and supplies Roddick brought were welcome. Roddick himself couldn't have been happier to see Douglas, as "he was the first to bring tidings of the whereabouts of the *Northcote*,"[109] and praised him with "due credit for his pluck and endurance."[110]

On the ship, another "twenty-four hours stuck in the middle of one spot, struggling to wrench her out of the sand bank into which the more we struggled the more she sank, until we tore out the thwarts and stanchions in our efforts to get free."[111] The Midlanders "had [a] church parade in the morning on the port side scow, Colonel Williams reading the service."[112] Soldiers found new ways to keep busy. Kirwan was surprised that amid the cursing of the captains and the squeal of machinery he could "hear the sound of harmony, and I detect the voices of a glee club which has been formed among the men singing the song, 'When the Clouds Roll By.' There is a touch of pathos in the music, and it visibly affects some of the men, many of whose faces are shaded by lines of drought and care."[113]

With little to do to help the roustabouts, soldiers found other ways to pass the day. "A barber is at work cutting hair, which he crops into the scalp, leaving the stumps to stand erect like stubble in a harvest field. In another place men are reading while under one of the improvised shelter huts made of bags of oats I can see, from where I write, two men making entries in their note books and then putting them carefully away in their knapsacks. Some are washing their underclothes, others are sewing, while the cooks are busy in the galley preparing the evening meal."[114]

But the officers were fearful for those so desperately awaiting their arrival, and Kirwan "knew that we were slowly consuming the supplies that our comrades so badly needed at the front … The General is campaigning in a desert. He has to draw his supplies from a base 200 miles away. There are no friends to buy from, and no enemies to requisition, and here we are with the stores he so much requires navigating unknown waters and floundering about in a river down which no steamer has ever ventured before."[115]

Unknown to the crew, a mission was afoot to rescue the *Northcote*'s cargo, "the intention being to lighten her, so that she might be enabled better to cross the various sand bars which were constantly impeding her."[116] This would be accomplished by some 50 teams led by Colonel Sam Bedson, whom Dr. Roddick had come upon as he was approaching Saskatoon.

The frustrated Kirwan, having left the stranded boat for an evening stroll among the coulees, saw a cloud of dust, and through his field glasses he "discovered teams away in the distance upon the hills."[117] Deducing that it was the relief wagons heading to unload the *Northcote*, he returned and ordered the boat, once under way again, to make a series of landings downriver, in hopes of attracting Bedson's attention. But the connection could not be made and Kirwan could only painfully wince as the perplexed teamsters crisscrossed the prairie trying to find the ship.

That same Sunday, a settler some of the Midlanders recognized as "Pete Robertson of Port Hope came aboard with Col. Williams and stayed all night. He is farming here near Saskatoon." Unimpressed, Sergeant Stewart said "he looked like a tramp."[118]

But Robertson "gave us some particulars of the fight the 90th had, and told us the wounded were at Saskatoon."[119]

The scuttlebutt was that Middleton was mobilizing for action. That would mean more wounded bound for Saskatoon, and Douglas and Roddick wanted them in better shape than wagons were delivering. To accomplish that, they would have to stabilize the wounded in the field, which in turn meant that that damned steamboat and the field hospital it carried would be indispensable. So, when the relief wagon teams arrived back in Saskatoon empty-handed, Bedson and Roddick mounted some fast horses and went out to find the *Northcote*. They found it only five miles from town, stranded on yet another infernal sandbar. Finally, "about a dozen teams came and met us from Middleton's camp, wanting oats and hay. Told us that all were anxious about us, thinking we had fallen into enemy hands. Ran boat ashore and tied up for the night. Teams loaded up and went back to camp."[120]

Soon after Bedson and Roddick's visit, the ship freed itself and after a "very blowy and disagreeable" day,[121] the *Northcote* put in at Saskatoon at eight o'clock in the evening, "thirteen days in accomplishing a distance of 200 miles."[122] The town turned out for the customary greeting, and a farmer named Eby waded out into the river to offer a basket of freshly caught jackfish.

The field hospital was unloaded, and the majority of the surgical staff was to occupy the makeshift brigade hospital, "several sheds put up of rough boards,"[123] now chockablock with the medical stores and supplies delivered. Every facility would be needed, for the attack on Batoche was nigh.

The crew wooded up the ship as soldiers stretched their legs. Eager for battle, they had a sobering sight before them: "Several of the wounded walked to the boat to see us."[124] The combat-scarred veterans of the rout at Fish Creek hobbled down to the waterfront to meet the ship, "some with crutches, some with heads bandaged, others with their arms in slings, while one young felloe, a mere boy, belonging to 'A' Battery, was minus his right arm."[125] The stirred troops reboarded, wondering if any of them would soon join the convalescent or have their names appear in a new list of fatalities.

With a new battle imminent, Roddick and two dressers, William Pringle, a medical student from Cornwall, and John Alexander Kinloch of Montreal—assigned respectively to Boulton's Scouts and the 90th Winnipeg Rifles—boarded the *Northcote* as it left Saskatoon. Shortly after their departure, a rider was sent to Fish Creek, and soon the word had gone all through the ranks, as reported by Minnesota newsman E.R. Johnston: "Everybody is surprised at the news received in camp that the steamer and barges, after the long troubles at the Elbow ... had reached Saskatoon, and would probably be here at 2 p.m. ... The boat is expected hourly, but up to 8 to-night had not arrived."[126] The camp would have to wait until the next afternoon, but the *Northcote* was a distant dream no longer.

After a few more groundings, the troubled steamer arrived at Clarke's Crossing mid-afternoon on May 4, and emptied its provisions and supplies. Middleton sent word to Williams to leave a few of his Midlanders at Clarke's for guard duty, and with the extra picket of B and D Companies, Clarke's was deemed safe from the enemy and designated as the supply base. "There were literally thousands of packages of canned beef, sugar, tea, flour and other provisions piled to a height of three to five feet on the west bank of the river."[127]

The ship didn't stay long, as it was wanted at Fish Creek. Clerk Talbot wrote that, as the boat departed, its crew "had to cut one of the telegraph wires across the river before we could get by."[128] After the *Northcote* had passed, the wire was spliced back together by repairman Joe Labelle, who would stay aboard to repair the wires that would be cut between Battleford and Edmonton.

Shelton Andrews saw little excitement in sitting around the supply base, and joined the steamer crew "… as they had no-one else to splice their wire ropes."[129] He was taken on as a liaison from the army's Transport Service. Hiring Andrews meant hiring his sidekick, Xavier "Louis" Gougeon, the Métis ferryman from Saskatoon. Gougeon signed on as a deckhand, having been fired from the service by Major Bedson for the heinous offence of refusing to clean his boots. At seven o'clock the next morning, May 5, the *Northcote* finally made Fish Creek Landing, where the bivouacked column had spent nearly two weeks lodged at "Camp Middleton," licking wounds, burying dead and more closely scouting the area.

Having spent two impatient weeks waiting for the *Northcote*, and fearing another ambush, General Middleton and scouts explored downriver and found a deserted Gabriel's Crossing, near the abandoned farm of Gabriel Dumont. The desertion was very recent, however: stoves were still stoked, a kettle still steaming, a fresh hand of draw poker still on the table, "the deuce of diamonds and the jack of clubs … faced up."[130]

Dumont had long since sold his ferry and store to Joseph Vandal (who had harboured the Kerr brothers), and retired to the farm. Gabriel's Crossing was more primitive than the newer ferries, and was never able to compete with Xavier Letendre's modern craft. Journalist George Ham, along for the ride, described "the ferry boat lying high and dry and needing oakum and pitch, [and] resembl[ing] more

Gabriel Dumont's homestead near his ferry landing. These buildings were ransacked by the Canadian military, and boards from the house cladding and the corrals were salvaged as armour for the *Northcote*. TORONTO DAILY MAIL, MAY 29, 1885

a stoneboat … than … a vessel. Close by are the long wooden sweeps by which the ferry is propelled across the river."[131] With all the local excitement, Vandal had not launched the scow, probably on Riel or Dumont's orders to have ferrying activity confined to fortified Batoche.

According to Major Boulton, "the General gave orders that we could allow nothing to be touched, and turned all of the men out of the building, not, however, before some mementoes of the campaign had been secured."[132] Ham confirmed the pilferage. "I fear some of the articles needed in camp, mysteriously disappeared into the haversacks of the boys while the General wasn't looking." Ironically, Middleton committed his own larceny, as he assessed that Gabriel's barn boards would probably suffice as armour against rebel bullets.

Just as Middleton returned to camp, "the steamer *Northcote* arrived at 7 a.m." His relief guarded, he huffed that the *Northcote* had come "mostly by land." But at least the mass of supplies had finally arrived, the half-month delay forgotten as the goods were brought ashore. Eager for interviews, Ham met John Segers, "one of the Canadian Voyageurs who went to Egypt last fall … who is now employed on the *Northcote*." Ham admired both Segers and Jim Sheets, praising them as being "of the 'Git Thar' stamp," as rivermen "known both to pull their boat through a couple of inches of mud, and it seems they had to do it on this trip."[133]

Ham was glad to talk to someone other than pompous officers for a change, and his conversation with Segers was amiable. Unable to resist the urge to jibe the British, Segers' recent employers, Ham asked the pilot about the calibre of food provided to

Better late than never, the hapless *Northcote* arrived at Clarke's Crossing on May 4. Middleton needed the ship desperately a few miles downstream at his camp at Fish Creek Landing, and it moved there the next morning. GLENBOW ARCHIVES NA 363-50

the boys in the North West from his boat. Sassed the grizzled folk hero, "'Why, your hard tack is plum pudding compared with what the British Government served out to us. Why, you could soak one of their hard tack for two weeks and the bark wouldn't be wet.'"[134]

Besides reporting the wisecrack, however, Ham pointed out a significant logistical accomplishment: "We have fifty days' supply for 1,000 men, and about twenty-five days' forage for the horses—over 600 in number. In fact, it taxes the admirable Transport Service to the utmost to 'tote' the baggage and supplies along with the command."[135] Late or not, the river connection had ensured that the campaign would be a well-provisioned effort.

In addition to the supplies, the ship had reinforced the column's strength with Captain Howard's Gatling gun and the remaining two companies of the fractured Midland Battalion, A and C. Middleton apologized to Williams for having split his regiment, but welcomed van Straubenzie and Kirwan to his staff, having lost officers to combat injury and Lord Melgund's sudden recall to England. A general parade was assembled two hours after the boat's arrival, a military spectacle that excited Ham to write that "we may move this afternoon or tomorrow."[136]

But Middleton remained tight-lipped, only conferring with his officers on utilitarian matters such as medicine. Dr. Roddick used the opportunity to clarify medical arrangements and how the river would be utilized in that respect. The field hospital at Saskatoon was to remain more or less as it stood. The location of a larger base hospital remained up in the air—either Swift Current or Moose Jaw—depending on the river. Satisfied that the steamboats would be used only for ambulance duty, Roddick returned to Saskatoon. Any other agenda the general may have had for the *Northcote* and the rest of the fleet was really still in his head.

Unknown to James Sheets, Middleton did have greater plans for his craft. The *Northcote*'s job was supply and transport. To Sheets, the military was just another commission. Forage and ammunition were just cargo, and whether passengers wore uniforms or not, they were just passengers with fare paid by Ottawa. But his suppositions were simplistic, for where a government is concerned, nothing is simple.

As he left the *Northcote* to join the land column, Martin Kirwan noted the northern lights. "At night the aurora forms tremulous streams of light up to the zenith, where they sometimes join like rings of electric light flashing in the darkness."[137] Soon the prairie too would flash—with the drama of gunfire.

The second wave

Four days after the *Northcote* chugged north, the *Minnow* appeared at Saskatchewan Landing. Despite its shallow draft, the tiny craft had run aground many times in the long voyage from Medicine Hat, damaging its hull. The constant running aground, or "high-centring," had caused its crew to abandon two barges. Repairs were soon made and General Laurie presented a new mission for the *Minnow* and its pilot, Captain Maloney.

Concerned with the *Northcote*, Laurie ordered Maloney to steam on to the Elbow with an empty barge to take on the Medical Corps, Howard's Gatling and the nine-pounder cannon ammunition, and proceed to Clarke's Crossing. That would deliver the militarily sensitive essentials to the column much faster and might have changed Middleton's strategy. But there was one hitch: the *Minnow*'s commander. Little is known about Captain Maloney, not even his first name, but he was no steamboat legend. Like many in his trade, Maloney was noted for his imbibing, and according to Laurie, he was a "thoroughly incapable Captain."[138] He apparently also had a problem with money and a misguided sense of duty. Despite the urgency of his mission, the errant captain insisted on taking on a more lucrative commission.

Cavalry horses needed oats, and a Métis trader from the Red Deer River forks, George Gunn, had contracted to take a scow-load of the feed downriver to Middleton's camp. With the assistance of a roll of cash, and probably a bottle of the finest rotgut, Gunn persuaded Maloney to tie a line to his barge and take it downriver. Though Laurie suspected this was detrimental to the *Minnow*'s express purpose, he grudgingly acceded to Maloney's side deal, and the *Minnow* left with 45 tons of stores, including 10 tons of oats for Fish Creek.

But Maloney didn't get 15 miles when his barges ran aground in rapids at the mouth of Swift Current Creek. He abandoned the barges and proceeded upriver, supposedly to relieve the *Northcote*. But Jim Sheets never saw the little tug that could have helped his ship so much. Without a military representative aboard to pester him, Maloney dawdled up the river, and government troops would not see the *Minnow* until the war was nearly won.

When word of the desertion reached the base at Swift Current, Laurie tried to arrange for a group of civilian freighters to salvage the wrecked scows and pole the freight downriver. But the civilian crews were aware not only of Laurie's dilemma, but also of the potential for ambush. Imbued with a touch of profiteering, the crews held out for higher wages and demanded a military escort. Their strike was foiled by Laurie's adjutant, Lieutenant Weller. Knowing he had marine experience in the Midland at his disposal, Weller "zealously volunteered to take the loaded barges to Clarke's Crossing."[139] At dawn on May 1, Weller and his boatmen marched out of the Landing camp, bound for the barge wreck, and the civilian rafters awoke to find they'd bargained themselves out of a job.

When Weller reached Swift Current Creek, he found both abandoned barges, one still stuck in the rapids where the waters merged. So the Midlanders rolled up their pants and waded in. One of the scows was crushed beyond repair, so salvageable cargo was transferred to the undamaged barge. Before embarking for Clarke's, Lieutenant Weller reported to Laurie his thoughts of using the barges as a transport on their own.

Wrote General Laurie, "I had instructed Lieutenant Weller to furnish a report on the possibilities of utilizing the river for our regular transport service … he was strongly of [the] opinion that with proper appliances and trained men, no serious difficulty need be experienced."[140]

Weller's optimism was fuelled by the rising water level during that first week of May. Inspired by an idea from Joseph Wrigley, Laurie ordered construction of an entire flotilla of barge craft that could take Swift Current's accumulated supply backlog downriver to where it was needed.

Soon the CPR delivered an army of carpenters and labourers unloading timber and tools, planking and kegs of nails. The woodworkers were from the Winnipeg firm of Boyd & Crowe, contracted to build a fleet of 10 flat-bottomed scows, each designed to convey 20 men and 10 tons of supplies. The workmen and materials were forwarded to Saskatchewan Landing and assigned to the supervision of the supply officer, Lieutenant Hudson.

Like everything else that had gone wrong in this quirky campaign so far, however, new foul-ups and blunders arose to haunt General Laurie. The Boyd & Crowe crews, in their hasty departure from Winnipeg, had neglected to bring along the tools and experienced caulkers that could make the barges watertight and seaworthy. Swift Current, not exactly a hotbed of shipbuilding technology, lacked such materials. The old axiom about "for want of a nail, the war was lost" must have raced through Laurie's organizational mind. But disaster was forestalled by a fortuitous coincidence.

The Halifax Provisional Battalion finally arrived by train, but since there was little for them to do but guard stations along the railway, a contingent was posted to Swift Current along with Companies E and F of the Midland. Among the Halifax militiamen were craftsmen of shipbuilding. A machinist from Halifax, Lieutenant A. Anderson, fabricated a set of caulking irons, and soldiers from both troops took to the job.

As the barges were being built, the second crest of spring meltwater lifted the *Alberta* and the *Baroness* from weeks of paralysis. The *Baroness*, with John Davis at the helm, pulled in on May 5, after 25 days' passage in substances few could call water. Josephus Todd's *Alberta* straggled in the next day, each steamer with a single barge in tow.

There seemed no point in trying to catch up with the *Northcote*. Nevertheless, Laurie introduced himself to Davis and planned strategy. The only clue as to their conversation came from the ship's clerk, whose journal reported: "Capt. Davis told me firemen to be paid $50 per month."[141] For that fortune, the ship's master was expecting peak performance.

His ships landed but not loaded, Elliott Galt thought it an excellent time to negotiate with the government for the cost of their services. Whether he or his father knew of Wrigley's contract for the *Northcote* is unclear, but the Galts were influential enough to cut a separate deal. When negotiations finished, the NWC&NC received $1,000 per day ($600 plus expenses) for all three steamers.

That aside, the stevedoring of General Laurie's stockpile began, the pair of sternwheelers being loaded first. The Midlanders left their carpentry to stow over 354 tons of supplies on the steamers and barges, directed by Major Henry R. Smith.[142] The Boyd & Crowe labourers fashioned gangplanks and loading chutes to expedite the work. Consigning and securing a wartime payload had become a science as soldiers and hands shunted the cargo into place. The only complication came from the variable spring weather, as ice formed on the deck of the *Baroness*. John Davis took a nasty fall on it and broke his collarbone. Nursing the fracture in a sling, he struggled to perform his duties.

Though Davis assured Laurie of a successful voyage to Clarke's Crossing, his injury may have been a factor in his request for a military escort. With the *Northcote*'s relatively safe journey, Laurie did not agree there was any violent threat on the lower river. Not totally unsympathetic, however, Laurie realized extra help was needed to cut firewood, so he assigned the remainder of the Midland Battalion to the *Alberta* and the *Baroness*. On the morning of May 8, the sternwheelers, towing their barges, left Saskatchewan Landing. The Reverend Pitblado, chaplain to the 90th Winnipeg Rifles, took passage to join his unit at the front. Maybe Davis asked the parson to lobby the higher power for some higher water.

The divine intervention may have worked. Though the *Baroness*'s clerk reported "constantly aground,"[143] the boats still made better time than the *Northcote* had done, averaging 23 miles a day, and 50 miles on their best day.

Davis and Todd were probably glad to be going anywhere. Could they have known how fortunate they were not to be upstream with the *Northcote*, where Middleton was about to send their colleagues into hell?

CHAPTER NINE

Glory Denied: The Naval Raid on Batoche

The general's grand plan

When George Ham strolled down to view "the Good Ship *Northcote*," he found it a beehive of activity. As roosters unloaded supplies, soldiers directed by Captain Herbert Haig, combat engineer, were armouring the steamer. "She is being bulwarked as I write, with two-inch plank, doubled around her lower decks, protecting the boiler. The pilothouse is also to be protected. And two barges on either side will be partially laden, and in such a manner as to be veritable 'iron-clads,' and in them men will be stationed. In the steamer's bulwarks portholes have been made."[1] Middleton's intent was becoming clear. The attack he originally intended had been upset by the failure of the Galt fleet and the trouble at Battleford. Fish Creek ended his other plan for a two-pronged assault, but he never got past the dual-attack idea.

Had James Sheets known what he was getting into, he might've thought about relocating to the Missouri. The captain was still single-minded, enthusiastic to get to Prince Albert, and he protested his fleet's involvement in war games. But in such times, even he was subject to military authority. Sheets could get angry, but it would do no good when the following order reached him at Fish Creek: "To the captain of *Northcote*: You will proceed to Gabriel's Crossing, there to communicate with the forces. To-morrow, the 8th, you will proceed to Batoche at an hour to be decided upon in the morning. If the captain of the boat should feel himself pressed, he must go straight on and anchor when out of danger, and await communication with the force."[2] Clerk Talbot filed the order, recalling that "there was something else about blowing signal whistles, but what I have written is the sum and substance of the order."[3]

For reasons unknown, no officers were consulted, and few outside of the staff knew about the order. Though in contact by telegraph, Middleton never even informed his superior, Defence Minister Adolphe Caron, of his intention to use civilian property in such a manner. Strategy and tactics were kept confidential, to the exasperation of subordinates, including Major Charles Boulton: "Nothing of the General's intention was known until the following day, and I may say here that I never met a man who was so thoroughly able to keep his own council, no one knowing until orders were issued what the projects were."[4]

Eventually Middleton informed his officers about the full scope of his plan. A two-pronged pincer attack would be implemented, coordinating the attack of the *Northcote* from the river, where "Major [Henry] Smith, of C Company … with 31 men, will be detailed to accompany the steamer, and cut off the retreat of the rebels should they attempt to cross the river after engagement."[5] The idea was to hit Batoche from two sides with full force. The ground force would be on the hill above the town, attacking from the ridge to the southeast. The *Northcote* would sail in behind the town, and Major Smith would await the signal from Middleton's cannons atop the hill. At that time, Segers would dock the vessel to deploy 31 troops on shore. By then, Middleton would be charging down the hill, infantry and cavalry 800 strong. The strategy would force Dumont to split his meagre forces to cover both flanks.

If there were any objections to this plan, they were not noted for history, but there almost should have been. The landing party would be overwhelmed ten to one by those defending the town—hardly a realistic offensive. The locals on the ship should have been able to warn of the overhead ferry cable installed the year before, and been able to predict with some accuracy the number of resisters in the village.

Gabriel Dumont and his beloved "Little Petit" rifle. This photo was taken some years later, but Dumont used this weapon against the *Northcote* and the militia as he directed the defence of Batoche. LIBRARY & ARCHIVES CANADA PA 178147

All Sheets could do was make a professional protest. "Sitting ducks, that's what they were, Captain Sheets grumbled, and no one aboard dared to contradict him."[6] River level tolerances would be marginal: at the very deepest, there would be only 36 inches of water for a craft that drew 30. The *Northcote* could bottom at any time, leaving crew and invasion force at the enemy's mercy. In addition, the ship would still have to tow two barges full of supplies through this gauntlet, crippling what little manoeuvrability the sternwheeler retained.

Finally, even the most amateurish tactician would have realized that indigenous fighters, born and bred in the area, would not allow such a huge target to move into their midst with ease. The Métis and their Sioux allies had covertly observed the vessel moving upriver, and knew its every detail. A counteroffensive against the *Northcote* had been foretold as early as April 20, when the mystic Louis Riel scribbled a prophetic little prayer into his diary: "O my God! I beg You, in the name of Jesus, Mary, Joseph and Saint John the Baptist, please use our ferry cable to overturn the steamboat so we may gain possession of all the provisions and useful things in the boat, like weapons and ammunition."[7] Capturing the vessel would also yield prisoners to use as bargaining chips.

Gabriel Dumont realized the role of the *Northcote*, and lined both banks of the South Branch with 30 crack sharpshooters. A further 150-odd defenders were entrenched around the townsite, ready to pick off anyone unlucky enough to make a landing. "When I learned that the enemy had torn down my stables to strengthen their steamer, I concluded the steamer was descending to Batoche to take part in the impending attack and to divert the attention of a part of the defenders. These were in fact the orders Middleton had given."[8] In light of Fish Creek, the general should have been more aware of the rebel leader's penchant for countering tactics. George Ham anticipated that "we may expect that with the military genius Dumont possesses he will not lose any such advantage as this second almost impregnable fastness will give him."[9]

Ham was the first published, though guarded, skeptic. "It would be idle to speculate at this time on the probabilities of tomorrow."[10] A seasoned investigator, Ham sought opinions from locals who knew the area, those who wondered whether the boat would even get to Batoche. "If we have a fight at all, I am told by those acquainted with the country it will be about halfway between Gabriel's and Batoche's, at a spot where there has been a landslide in the riverbank, close to where the trail passes, and on the right are dense heavy woods."[11] Doubtless Ham's source was the crew of the steamboats, most likely the returning fugitive George Kerr. The informant was sure of an ambush at a spot even more favourable than Fish Creek.

Was the general being incredibly optimistic? Was his Sandhurst training unable to contend with guerilla strategy? Was he, under the pressure of criticism, unable to devise anything else? It seems a mystery why Middleton used a steamboat as the bait in a trap. Or more poetically, was this an attempt by the general to woo the South Saskatchewan into his camp? In the days leading up to Batoche, Trooper Harold Rusden noted that Middleton was to be found seated on a hay rake, eating his lunch while he "whistled his favorite tune, 'There's One More River to Cross.'"[12]

Battle stations of the crew from hell

Military jurisdiction over the *Northcote* was assigned to Major Henry Smith, battalion commander of C Company of the Infantry School Corps. Smith would direct the river-borne attack. Fireman Donald MacIvor waggishly called the unit "the Toronto Sea School,"[13] a sardonic three-way pun on "C" Company's name, the fact that they were part of a "school corps," and of course their Ontario landlubber inexperience

Samuel Bedson, militiaman, prison warden and the commander of Middleton's transport service.
ARCHIVES OF MANITOBA N 10717-P

with matters marine. From the numbers on the troop rolls, Smith must have left behind the six of his infantrymen that were injured at Fish Creek. To round out the complement, Smith and Middleton collected an odd mixture of combatants.

Samuel Lawrence Bedson, the transport officer, was aboard to assess the impact of steamboat service on the military. According to Smith, Bedson was placed in charge of the boat and supplies, with James Sheets reporting to him. Several of Bedson's Transport Service were aboard with him, as was Supply Service officer John Vinen, and Owen Hughes, the Duck Lake trader who'd rubbed Middleton's nose in the mess of Fish Creek. Middleton was glad to get rid of the vocal pest, perhaps hoping Hughes' own vaunted Métis would finish him off. To counter Sheets and Segers, Bedson decided to bring along Shelton Andrews as a ringer, perhaps expecting the seaman to be the militia's eyes and ears in navigational matters. Six members of the 90th Winnipeg Rifles were attached, possibly taken on because of steamboat experience such as one Private William Eccles possessed.

Since neither rain nor snow nor time of war keep the postman from his appointed rounds, stagecoach driver Jack Art, his Qu'Appelle/Prince Albert route cut off by the war, threw a six-week backlog of mail into one of the barges. Telegraph repairman Joe Labelle was along to restore telegraph lines, with equipment that would enable temporary service where possible.

Two medics, Dr. F.A. Moore of the 90th Winnipeg Rifles and Dresser W.R. Mc-Intyre Pringle, would deal with casualties. Middleton's own aide de camp, Captain Henry Ellison Wise, was badly injured when his horse was shot out from under him.[14] Lieutenants G.P. Elliott and A.C. Gibson of the 10th Royal Grenadiers were sick with unspecified illnesses. A lieutenant in the 90th Winnipeg, Hugh John Macdonald, who had hoped to advance with the ground force, was stricken with an inflamed eye from erysipelas and ordered aboard to recuperate. Doubtless the order was influenced by the officer's high-profile identity, for he was none other than the son of Prime Minister Macdonald.

Despite his famous father, Hugh John Macdonald was no prima donna. He'd served against the Fenian raids and in the Red River expedition of 1870. At Fish Creek, he was the first officer to offer to lead a bayonet charge. Now he lay on a sick cot on a boat, far from his unit. But Macdonald had good company. Growing up in Kingston, Hugh John had been a childhood friend of George Ham, and the journalist pledged to watch over him.

By the time Smith had organized his eccentric band, about 50 men had been placed on the *Northcote*, in addition to the craft's regular crew commanded by James Sheets, with battling riverman John Segers as pilot, experiencing his second military action in less than five months. Sheets and Segers boasted a crew of 35 hands, including engineer Arthur L'Heureux, assistant engineer Daniel Hurst, clerk Rennie Talbot, and assistant clerk Donald McDonald, a 22-year-old Métis with deep family roots in service to the HBC.[15] The rest of the crew was made up of a first mate, 18 deckhands, two carpenters, two firemen (or boiler tenders), two watchmen, a steward, a cook and even a couple of waiters.[16] George Kerr, the refugee storekeeper from Batoche, offered assistance in locating the twists and turns of the river and detailing distances along the route, while signing on as a deck hand. Kerr had a personal stake: Riel's men had looted his store, friends of his were prisoners in the village, and there was a price on his own head. Xavier "Louis" Gougeon, ferryman turned rooster, could also add some local colour, if the planners would only listen.

Under the supervision of Haig, the *Northcote*'s crew and attachments transformed the craft "into a man-of-war."[17] The vessel's new role called for the upper deck to be reinforced with whatever lumber could be scrounged. The pilothouse was covered with three-inch boards, with small loopholes notched out for sights and to stick rifles through. As additional cladding, various provisions were stacked up on deck: cordwood, sacks of oats and flour, boxes of meat. Mattresses looted from houses surrounded the windows on all decks. Curiously, the hull itself was left unprotected, as noted by fireman MacIvor: "Remember that it was only half-inch board that was in the ship … [it was] not a steel ship."[18] On May 7, armed, armoured and loaded with 85 men of all persuasions, the *Northcote* spent a bright afternoon sailing to the final staging point, at Gabriel's Crossing.

George Ham's first ride on the boat left him a little bored, but tranquil:

The steamer *Northcote* … left Fish Creek at 1:45 p.m., having been detained to take the temporary telegraph line running into camp down the river, and reached the crossing which boasts of Gabriel's name and fame after a slow run of two hours. If the land force had an uninteresting march, this trip on the boat was not less so, only it was a more pleasant one. There was a strong headwind, and there being two heavily laden barges in tow, the boat required all skill of the experienced commanders, Captains Sheets and Segers, to control her. Along the river it was seen that while there were numerous houses on the east bank there were only two on the west side.[19]

Those houses were abandoned, the locals having gone to Batoche to prepare the defence. "Agricultural implements, mowers, reapers, seeders, a thrashing machine, etc., were lying exposed to the elements, and in one place there were a number of old Red River carts left, as if from last year's first snow fall."[20]

Earlier that morning, Middleton had started moving his ground force, a column totalling 886 men, toward Batoche. By afternoon, the column had marched 13 miles from Fish Creek. They arrived near Gabriel's Crossing at 6 p.m., where they met the *Northcote*. As Middleton scouted the Humboldt Trail, the Field Force looted Gabriel

Dumont's abandoned farmstead and trading post. A barn was torn down, and its boards were used to enclose the upper deck and add to the pilothouse cladding of the *Northcote*, which Major Smith had kept anchored at Gabriel's all that day, awaiting the order to sail for Batoche.

In a final insult to the Métis adjutant, Dumont's house was torched in a rude symbolic ritual: "Scarcely had the troops this morning arrived and moved towards the open in the east when flames were seen issuing from what is known as Gabriel's place, a fine large double house connected by a passage way six or eight feet in length. The 'fire fiend' burned fiercely and after a few minutes visited the store, a dozen yards away. Then a stable in the rear of the residence, and a store house on the south."[21] Before the tinder was lit, Dumont's prized billiard table was carried out and used to further increase the armour coverage on the steamer.

As the soldiers rampaged under Middleton's nose, Ham noticed the fire had attracted company. Across the river, insurgents watched their leader's property burn. They did little to conceal themselves, in defiance of the soldiers. "In a short time the bright flames and ascending smoke brought out the lurking enemy across the river, and here and there could be seen half-hidden half-breeds curiously watching the destruction of one of the leaders' homes. As I write the flames are still at work, and before many hours the buildings at the Crossing will have gone up in smoke. The reason of the destruction of this place is to show the rebels that only such men as Dumont are being punished, while the rest of their places are untouched."[22]

In spite of the supposed singling out of Dumont, the observers were unmoved by the government's implied humanity. Métis spies kept Dumont informed of the Canadians' ravages: "The English were camped at my homestead. They burned my house and tore down my stables to reinforce the *Northcote* and protect it from gunfire. The Métis scouts saw them and we knew that the *Northcote* was going to come downriver to surround us."[23] The ravaging of the homestead only strengthened rebel resolve.

Some sources even say Madeline Wilkie Dumont's pedal-operated washing machine, prized as one of the few such conveniences in the area, was stowed aboard the *Northcote*. The mind boggles at just what possible military use, offensive or defensive, a washing machine could possibly have.[24] Smith judiciously made little mention of the plunder in his official report, documenting the looting as "preparations for battle." Still not satisfied with the ship's armour, Smith ordered further fortification: "After embarking, I found that the vessel had been partially prepared for defence, but not as I considered, sufficiently: so the 8th was employed in adding to the defences by piling up sacks of oats, boxes of meat, etc."[25]

The commandeered lumber was nailed to the main deck's walls, now a quadruple layer against bullets. The feed sacks and crated provisions were stacked around the promenade of the saloon deck, and reinforced with hay. Talbot wasn't that impressed: "All the protection we had in the pilothouse was a few bales of hay and one or two …

planks in the front leaving both splash boards open, and thus when a man stood up he was exposed from the middle of the breast to the top of his head."[26]

After Dumont's house was in ashes, the troops boarded and moved the ship to anchor in midstream for the night, to prevent approach by enemy agents. But the cable on the anchor split, and the vessel drifted to shore. Fortunately it landed on the east bank, for the spies were still on the west. Talbot complained, "We spent all day in fishing for our anchor, and as we saw about 26 Indians watching us from the opposite side of the river, we were therefore put upon our guard and C Company fixed the load in better shape for protection … Well, we found our anchor, and were ordered to proceed the next morning and be at Batoche at 8 sharp."[27]

Some accounts say a cannon was placed aboard the ship, but likely this was only a small ship's cannon, used mostly for ceremony. One story even says a Gatling gun was aboard,[28] but this is erroneous, for Captain Howard was with Middleton's column, which had marched 16 miles to the open prairie to spend the night of May 8. That evening, only eight miles from Batoche, Middleton and Boulton made another final recon, to within a mile of the village.

Dumont, meanwhile, was doing some scouting work of his own, as his observers continued to watch his occupied property. Ham was told the boat's guard could hear the scouts taunting them. "The rebel spies watched the steamer the previous night on the opposite bank from Gabriel's, and the sentry could hear them shouting, one boastfully singing out to us as he departed, 'Now come on you _____!'"[29] Ham suppressed the expletive, but one can use imagination. The night was fraught with anxiety, a sort of nervous calm. "At six o'clock one sentry reported having seen two Indians come down to the river and the opposite bank, a couple of hundred yards down stream, and get a drink of water. In an instant they were gone. Another sentry reported at nine, that he had heard Indian whoops, but the patient listening of other extended ears failed to hear them again. The night passed quietly."[30]

Captain Howard and his Gatling gun, used shortly after the *Northcote* attack. The gun was not on the steamboat during the attack as some histories report; Howard was with the ground force. *CANADIAN PICTORIAL & ILLUSTRATED WAR NEWS, 1885 SOUVENIR EDITION*

The eve of invasion

George Ham could not leave well enough alone, and decided to make a weird little reconnaissance of his own. He'd finished the story of the fire at Dumont's and was anxious to forward it to his newspaper. On hostile turf, this might be his last day on earth and the last story he would ever file. "The courier is just about leaving, and as Indians are within 400 or 500 yards of us across the river and may open fire at any moment, I have not time to say more than that we have arrived here."[31] Many aboard the ship had the same idea and desired to post their mail home.

But the civilian mail carrier in Middleton's column feared for his life and would not make the trip over to Gabriel's Crossing before continuing on to Clarke's. A deckhand, George Macleod,[32] was called upon to make the trip to main camp and return with the day's mail and other items requested by soldiers. Macleod, protesting that he and his horse could not possibly carry all the requests, was issued a buckboard belonging to interpreter Peter Hourie, and a travelling companion, George Ham. When they arrived at camp and loaded the mail, they were forced to switch their tired horse, and the wagon was soon bouncing along the prairie behind a captured Métis mount.

On the twilight trip back, the spirited pony led the wagon astray, and in the darkness they were soon lost. Ham and Macleod spent the rest of the evening desperately trying to avoid one Indian or rebel camp after another. The pair separated while trying to locate the trail, Ham almost shooting Macleod as a rebel in the process. At 3 a.m., they drove right through the middle of a rebel rendezvous camp that fortunately was vacant. The sun was already rising when the wayward mail carriers finally got back to the *Northcote*. The disgruntled collection of troops grumbled at the delay, for the boat was only a couple of hours from sailing.

The men in Middleton's camp were up and marching at 6:00, their spirits raised by distribution of the contents of a package that had arrived by transport that morning. Samuel Davis & Sons, a Montreal tobacco firm, had shipped 10,000 complimentary cigars for the men, who happily smoked and marched their way out of camp. After 14 days in camp, they were probably glad to be going anywhere.

It is not known whether the men on the *Northcote* received their share of the cigars, but the sternwheeler was already making its own smoke as it chugged down the six miles of river between Gabriel's and Batoche. "According to General Middleton's preconcerted plan, the *Northcote*, with two heavy-laden barges, left Gabriel's Crossing at six a.m. today "[33] Donald MacIvor, the ship's fireman, said they got the signal to progress from a man ... on the East bank of the river waving a white flag for us to go down."[34] Rennie Talbot confirmed the 6 a.m. start, with "myself, Captain Sheets and Captain Segers being in the pilothouse."[35]

Charles Clapp of the Midland Battalion was off the *Northcote* and approaching Batoche on foot. He was sentimental about the boat and observant when Middleton tried to communicate with Henry Smith by the artillery: "Within three miles of Batoche we halted and one of the guns was placed on a slight knoll nearby and a blank shell fired as a signal for the *Northcote* to proceed."[36] A couple of miles downriver from the Batoche ferry, Major Smith heard the signal, checked the time and realized they were far too early for the coordinated attack. The *Northcote* replied to the shell blast with a signal flare, "a rocket."[37]

Not wanting to proceed ahead of schedule, Smith ordered the vessel anchored. Shelton Andrews spied scouts moving about in the thickets and observing their short layover. The spies "followed us down two miles before opening fire on us,"[38] giving credence to Ham's mention of a possible attack before Batoche. Ham then recounts that "after anchoring a short time so as not to anticipate the arranged time of arrival at Riel's headquarters, reached within one and a half miles of our destination, where we were to remain until the bombardment of the rebel stronghold by General Middleton was heard, he starting at daybreak from the camping ground reached on the previous day, nine miles east of Batoche's."[39] At 7:40, the *Northcote* moved on from its mooring, still too early, and rounded the bend just before 8 a.m. It would be an hour before Middleton would arrive.

Near the village, anxiety reigned supreme as the gunboat approached. The arrival was a signal that the wrath of the Canadian government would soon be upon the rebels. Louis Riel saw the *Northcote's* bright phosphorus rocket flare, and used it to taunt his oblivious followers, telling them "it was a thunderbolt from the Almighty to destroy their enemy."[40] Gabriel Dumont prepared to channel the apprehension into a carefully planned ambush. Winchesters, Sniders, Sharps buffalo guns, even ancient Hudson's Bay muzzle loaders were at the ready with Métis and Sioux gunmen alike. "I had placed some Métis on the right side of the river, below the cemetery where the river channel passed a long beach. I thought the *Northcote* would pass close to the side of the river and almost touch the shore. I had also placed, on the other side of the river, some Métis who could fire on the *Northcote* right after it had been fired on from the left. It would be very difficult to get past these two."[41]

On the hill overlooking Batoche sat the Catholic church, St. Antoine de Padoue, and alongside it the rectory. That morning, Father Vital Fourmond nervously dreaded the beginning of hostilities. The priest was getting ready for his usual morning walk with Mother Mary Greere, one of the nuns ordered in by Riel. Fourmond tried to mask his fear: "Well, Mother, are you ready to leave? There is a steamboat coming to get us all!"

"But to go where, Father?" Mother Greere inquired. Fourmond knew the boat was not coming for a pre-battle rescue mission, but still he half-jokingly tried to reassure the Sisters. "To Winnipeg, I suppose, but we shall have to have lunch first. Then we must gather our belongings and be ready to leave." The nuns were in the garden, watching the *Northcote* as it anchored. The whistle soon announced that there would be no lunch, no packing, and no passage to Winnipeg for the clergy. A rebel sentry who'd been stationed on a hill came running past the rectory, shouting, "There they are! There they are!"[42]

Soon Fourmond's keen ears picked up the advance of the *Northcote*, and comments in his memoirs indicate that everyone was well aware of the military implementation of the ship. "Around 8 a.m. we were out on the plateau of the mission, getting more and more worried … Suddenly a terrible howl came to my ears, coming from upstream. We looked at each other: it's the steamboat. It seems like a signal. The sound gets closer and closer. No more doubt. It's the steamboat arriving and whistling war. We expected Middleton's soldiers to arrive from the prairie; we assumed an understanding between boat and army."[43]

Soon Fourmond could see the *Northcote* as well as hear the chilling shriek that declared war. Beside the little cemetery, a few yards in front of the building, a band of Sioux warriors had prepared to be among the first combatants to engage the reinforced steamer. "Boat arrived in front of the mission, we see it going down and advance between the two camps along the riverbanks and force passage. No firing heard anywhere. The attack starts by a group of Sioux camped close to the mission; we see them getting rid of their blankets and leggings in haste, done very fast. Immediately take guns and run toward boat through the bushes. Hiding as best they could so as not to attract the attention of the defenders of the steamboat. They were barely out of our sight, when we heard some gunshots, followed by many more, mixing with the sound of the boat whistle. The battle had started."[44]

Assault and counter-assault

Miles upriver from Batoche, a telegraph key uttered its staccato signal to the nation. "Clarke's Crossing, May 9 … Weather calm and warm. River still rising." As danger loomed about Batoche, as priests and nuns shuddered, warriors and rebels waited, armies marched and a boat sailed, a single voice was available to alert the world that hostilities had broken out. Richard Molloy, even from his remote location, could hear the echoes and boom bouncing from the high cliffs of the river and knew the meaning. "Loud reports as of distant cannonading are being heard here this morning, It is supposed a battle is in progress."[45]

The first shots belonged to the Dakota Sioux of Whitecap, one of the few native leaders who had come to Riel's assistance, though some debate and good evidence indicates that Sioux participation was involuntary. Whether willing partners or merely fulfilling a ransom, the Sioux were at Batoche,[46] pouring fire on the *Northcote* from the east bank. Philippe Garnot, Riel's secretary, remembered that "some people who were on both sides of the river in order to prevent a landing of the troops from the vessel opened fire."[47] Rennie Talbot knew the tune. "All three of us standing up, thus making a splendid target of ourselves, when bang, bang, whiz, whiz, a volley came pouring into the pilothouse upon us. We immediately dropped to the floor, and then came one of the most continuous fusillades it was ever my luck to witness."[48]

When the whistle sounded, George Ham was taking the air, leaning over the rail smoking a cigar and reading a newspaper, when he chuckled at a particular humorous passage. To share the joke with Sam Bedson, he strode down to the barricaded lower deck. By the time Ham made it downstairs, he was dodging bullets and scrambling for cover. "The rebels, however, materially interfered with the carrying out of these plans

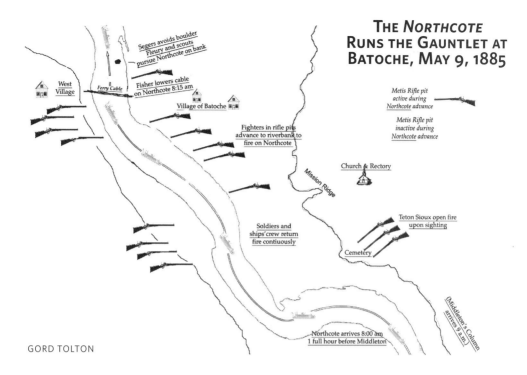

THE *NORTHCOTE* RUNS THE GAUNTLET AT BATOCHE, MAY 9, 1885

Segers avoids boulder
Fleury and scouts
pursue Northcote on bank

West Village

Ferry Cable

Fisher lowers cable on Northcote 8:15 am

Village of Batoche

Fighters in rifle pits advance to riverbank to fire on Northcote

Metis Rifle pit active during *Northcote* advance

Metis Rifle pit inactive during *Northcote* advance

Mission Ridge

Church & Rectory

Soldiers and ships' crew return fire contiuously

Cemetery

Teton Sioux open fire upon sighting

(Middleton's Column arrives 9 a.m.)

Northcote arrives 8:00 am 1 full hour before Middleton

GORD TOLTON

by opening fire on the steamer at ten minutes past eight, just after she had got under headway. The first bullet passed through the pilothouse. This first shot was evidently the signal to the rebels of our boat's approach, and as we rounded the bend a moment or so later we were raked fore and aft by a fierce storm of bullets coming from both banks. From almost every bush rose puffs of smoke, and from every house and tree came bullets buzzing."[49]

Soldiers did not return fire instantly, and soon the volleys increased heavily from both banks. Donald MacIvor became acutely aware of the situation. "The rebels were pounding at us on each side from the shore."[50] As the ship inched closer to the village, it was caught in a deadly crossfire. One of the first men hit was the medic, McIntyre Pringle, "knocked out by almost the first shot."[51] Desperate soldiers and sailors alike shouldered rifles to return the compliments through the loopholes in the barricades. Those civilians not armed sought refuge in the well-timbered bottom deck or in the hold. Smith recounted: "For a time we did not reply, but the Rebel fire soon became hotter, and we commenced both independent and volley firing, and this we continued without intermission till some distance below Batoche, partly to keep down the opposing fire, and partly to lead the enemy to believe that our force was much larger than it really was."[52]

Owen Hughes related that "the only way to keep down the enemy's fire was by firing alternate volleys at both banks."[53] Even Ham had to trade pen for sword, if clumsily: "Part of the *Northcote* was barricaded with bags of flour so arranged as to make port holes. My old friend, Hugh John Macdonald, was seriously ill, and I grabbed his gun and shoving it through the porthole, banged away, only to set fire to the bags. Quickly extinguishing the burning bags, I hastened to another porthole in the bow of the boat, not barricaded, and fired away, until a lot of splinters struck me in the face—the splinters being the outcome of a fairly well-directed rebel shot. Discretion being the better part of valour, just then, I moved to another porthole, and a soldier came up and with his fingers easily picked a bullet from the tendrils of the wood, and quietly remarked, 'Pretty close shave.' It was pointing straight for my heart."[54]

Officers were not immune to the random fire, which did not discriminate among classes. "Captain Wise, who'd been unable to take part in the land engagement owing to the wound he received at Fish Creek, remained with Chief Transport Officer Bedson, who was in charge of the boat, in the cabin, and both had several very narrow escapes, the latter having a bullet graze his thigh. [Bedson's] state-room was pierced by seven balls, which he returned with interest."[55]

Even the wounded on board stood up from their convalescence to defend the position. Patients rolled out of their bunks and barricaded their mattresses against the cabin walls to baffle the impact. Even Hugh Macdonald left his bed and "took his place in the ranks rifle in hand"[56] to take aim at the bank. Despite his painful facial paralysis, the prime minister's son "stood up like a little man at a port hole whenever he could, as indeed we all did."[57]

Eventually the soldiers found their mark, Ham observed. "Notwithstanding that the rebels were protected by the brush and timber which covers the banks, apparently some injury was inflicted upon them. Volley after volley was fired, and several of the lurking enemy were seen to drop headlong down the sloping banks. So the fight went on, fierce and hot as we approached Batoche's."[58]

Despite criticisms of the ship's crew, Ham's vantage point slanted his view differently. "The troops on board implicitly obeyed instructions, while the few civilians rendered excellent service in replenishing cartridges in boxes, and also in handling rifles."[59] Some say the crew cowered in the hold. Another account says crewmen Arthur L'Heureux and William McEwen, at least, took a perverse delight in the symphonic din orchestrated by the rebel assault on the power source: "A little Frenchman and the engineer and the cook seemed to enjoy it as the bullets kicked up a regular tattoo on the boilers."[60] Fireman Donald MacIvor thought that "the sound of the bullets on the ship was like a heavy hail storm on the windows."[61]

Father Fourmond watched as captains like Philippe Garnot directed Métis and Indian combatants to leave their stations in the rifle pits to take vantage points along the river. "The shooting became heavier as the boat came downriver and neared the camp. We feared for the poor people caught between the two fires. We thought the cable could turn it over and sink it."[62]

Ham had occasion to peek out from cover and admire the scenery amidst the battle. But as if the bullets whizzing past his head were not enough to bring him back to reality, he glanced over to the west bank to an even more unsettling sight. "The pretty little church of St. Antoine de Padoue lifted its cross-crowned steeple high above

Artist's conception of the *Northcote*'s running of the gautlet at Batoche, May 9, 1885. THE
CANADIAN PICTORIAL & ILLUSTRATED WAR NEWS

the other buildings on the eastern bank. A horrifying spectacle met our gaze on the
opposite bank. A man, presumably one of Riel's prisoners, was dangling by the neck
from a branch of an almost limbless tree—a victim of rebel rage and vindictiveness."[63]

Dumont and his fighters were prairie-born hunters, having lived for generations
from nature's bounty, for subsistence and commerce. Be the prey a beaver, a buffalo,
a rival hunter, a government soldier or even a steamboat, this was their territory.
The military were strangers fighting for glory, but the Métis were fighting for their
ancestral home and way of life. Desperate times call for desperate measures, and
Dumont had devised a trap using the ferry cable that spanned the river. Because the
Northcote had to "pass through a rapid caused by a bend in the river, before it could
continue on its way, I had suggested that at this spot we cripple the helmsman, so as
to set the boat adrift, and that an iron cable, thrown across the river, would make the
vessel capsize."[64]

Correspondent Ham noted that a definite military organization was in effect on
shore, as a few Métis horsemen raced back and forth along the bank to organize the assault and counter-assault. "Near at hand the rebels, who lined both banks for a couple
of miles, were running swiftly and keeping pace with our progress. Several mounted
men, evidently leaders, were directing their movements. A few volleys quickly dispersed them to their hiding places, where they fought the customary bush fight. They
completely riddled the steamer with bullets, but it was strongly bulwarked on the boiler deck where the soldiers were standing and our casualties were consequently very
light."[65] No doubt one of the horsemen was Gabriel Dumont, driving the offensive as
handily as he would have directed a buffalo hunt.

In the pilothouse, Jim Sheets and John Segers kept incredibly cool despite the circumstances. Perceptive rebel marksmen made the pilothouse their target, knowing
control of the boat was maintained from the tiny structure perched atop the vessel.

Segers's usual wide field of vision from the helm was severely restricted by the three-inch planking nailed to the windows.

Rennie Talbot had bulletproofing problems as well. "I seized the pilothouse stove-pipe to try and remove it out of my way, when in doing so I exposed my head nearly to the shoulders, when immediately a perfect hail storm of bullets flew about, two of them piercing the pipe, which was very small, being a piece of exhaust pipe. After moving the pipe, which I did much quicker than it takes me to tell it, I seized the stove and held it up in front of my breast and head, and only in time as bang, bang, came two shots in close succession upon it, which certainly otherwise must have hit me. In the meantime Captains Sheets and Segers held a bale of hay in front of them, which must have at least received 20 shots."[66] The pilothouse was "a special target of the rebel marksmen, they being fully aware of the disaster which must overtake us if we were disabled in this vulnerable point. Dozens of bullets had pierced the wheelhouse." [67]

The trio were finally overwhelmed by the fusillade, and sought refuge on the floorboards to avoid a bullet in the head. Seventy-five to 90 bullets passed through the pilothouse, but despite being on the floor, Segers was able to keep control. Realizing that letting the ship freewheel through the passage would be suicide in the shallow waters, he took unique action.

Probably not realizing he was inventing the technique of remote navigation, Segers shouted to a crew member stationed on the saloon deck beneath the pilothouse to relay directions back to him. With his guide acting as a frontier radar, Segers lay down on his back on the floor, protected between a pair of cast iron box stoves. "Segers once more crawling upon his hands and knees seized the wheel and turned the boat once more to head downstream. In doing so he received a bullet in the sleeve of his coat." [68]

The climax of the attack as the barricaded *Northcote* careens directly toward the lowered Batoche ferry cable. At this point, the ship has been under heavy fire for some 15 minutes.
CANADIAN PICTORIAL & ILLUSTRATED WAR NEWS, AUGUST 29, 1885

Seemingly invulnerable, Segers conjured up yet another riverman trick by placing his feet up on the wheel and actually steering with his toes.[69]

Despite the hundreds of rounds fired at the *Northcote*, a lack of good weapons was evident, as many of the guns simply did not have enough range. The river was wide enough here that Segers was able to keep the ship exactly midstream, several hundred yards beyond the capability of many of the antique firearms shouldered by the Métis. "Many of the enemy's bullets fell short of the mark when we were midstream, shotguns with common balls being their weapons, although without doubt some had Winchesters and Snider-Enfields. So fast and furious was their fire that it was evident the whole rebel force had gathered here to make a determined stand."[70]

In his dispatch, George Ham tried to estimate the numbers of the defenders of Batoche, "The rebel strength is not known, but from the fury with which they fired, their force must have reached probably four hundred or five hundred, Indians predominating, except at Batoche's, where the Half breeds had congregated."[71] In the thick of the frenzy around him, Ham inflated the count somewhat. The highest estimates placed the number at 322, listing 282 Métis, supplemented by 35 to 40 combined Dakota Sioux and Cree.[72] The defenders' commander, Dumont, placed the number at "about 175 men, besides the squad of 30 men who were watching the *Northcote*."[73] Some Métis memoirs say there were about 150 fighters, "who were the inhabitants from the west side of the river—Duck Lake, Carlton"[74] region. The east side at Batoche accounted for another 150. Ham could be forgiven his crude statistics; he was too busy trying to stay alive.

The crippling cable

Dumont's tactics called for the cable that guided the Batoche ferry to be lowered to impede the *Northcote*'s progress. A taut cable could do untold damage: it could stop the boat, capsize it, maybe even slice its higher decks right off. If the boat could be stopped, the Métis could board and capture the supplies, guns, ammunition, medical supplies and food.

The men in command of the sternwheeler were conscious of the danger posed by the ferry cable and its offensive use. Major Smith, with perfect hindsight, remarked that: "[Captain Sheets] was aware that a wire cable was stretched across the river at that place, and he knew that there was a danger of its catching the boat, and he was warned to be on the lookout for it."[75] As the *Northcote* crept closer, Sheets, Segers and Talbot were keeping vigilant. "Hundreds of the rebel devils were lying near it ready to rush upon us and have it hand to hand."[76]

The Métis hurried to marshal forces on both banks to unfasten, lower and refasten the cable. The ferry operator, Alex Fisher, assisted by Pascal Montour, directed the dismantling. But despite the ample lead time Dumont had on the steamer's approach, work on moving the cable had still not begun. Perhaps the delay was caused by the movement of fighters and munitions to and from the west side of the river up to the time of the fight. With time running out, Fisher and Montour miscalculated and the cable was left set too high.

Still, the ship would not pass unscathed. Talbot was closest to the potential disaster. He hit the floor of the pilothouse and prepared for the eventual decapitation of the ship:

> We struck the rope, it catching upon the derricks and spars, the boat slacked up, quivered all over like a living thing, and for one brief, agonizing, fearful moment appeared to stop, when with a fearful crash the derricks and spars fell to the deck, and we poor devils in the pilothouse gave a sigh of relief, but only for a moment. It had caught the smoke stacks. I shall never forget with what anxiety we watched to see if we were caught; but no, they commenced to fall slowly backwards and one of the guys catching on the big bell rope it charged out what I fully believed to be my death knell. For even if the smoke stack did fall, the line (which was wire rope) would catch the pilothouse and they—well, I hate to think of it.[77]

There was little time to think of anything. To the dismay of the ferrymen, and to Dumont and Riel, the only immediate result was the severing of the smokestacks that "fell on the barge and the other on the forecastle [upper deck]."[78] The collision also removed a mast and ripped the giant loading spars, the "grasshopper legs," from their upright mountings, scattering them across the decks with a crash. The rebels began to prematurely savour a victory, figuring they'd snared themselves a gunboat. As Ham recounted,

> Our misfortune excited loud cheers from the Métis, mingled with fiendish war-whoops from the Indians. The cable … was lowered just as we approached it, the intention of the rebels being to corral the steamer and, in the confusion expected to ensue, to capture the boat and massacre its human freight. Very fortunately for us this scheme failed, but only by the merest chance, for had the cable caught in the pilothouse, which it had barely missed, the wheelsman, exposed to the enemy's fire, would have been shot down and the steamer rendered utterly helpless.[79]

The failure to ensnare the *Northcote* disheartened Gabriel Dumont: "I had also given the order to lower the ferry cable, but the men thought it was low enough and didn't move it. The cable barely touched the steamboat. It drifted by."[80] Talbot had spotted Fisher and Montour fiddling with the settings. "Even while the line was pressing against the smokestacks, one of the rebels noticing, or at least thinking, the line too high to catch the pilothouse, rushed to the windlass and tried to lower it. In doing so the smokestack fell with a crash, and the ferry line surging caused it to fly over the pilothouse, only tearing off a small piece of the roof and a pair of deer horns, and the whistle."[81] The *Northcote* refused to be trapped, forging on by sheer inertia.

The good fortune was not noted by Smith, however, as he honestly believed the ship was coming down on his head. Still under attack, soldiers and crewmen scrambled to put out a fire caused by sparks from the toppling smokestacks. Smith thought the destructive noise a sign that the entire upper deck was being sliced off by the cable. Only later did he learn the exact extent of the damage. "As we passed Batoche the fire was especially heavy, and I heard a crash as if a portion of the upper deck had been carried away."[82] The terrific din distracted the troops from the immediate problem: "when they heard the crash of falling derricks and smokestacks they ceased firing, not understanding the cause." The Métis noticed their lapse and left their rifle pits to rush the boat. Ship's crew and others were more attentive and kept the cover fire going until the soldiers regained their composure and "whaled it to them, causing them to fly to their pits again."[83]

Whether Dumont's men knew or understood the physics of steam-powered propulsion is not known, but their tactic with the cable dealt a crippling blow regardless. Like removing the lid from a boiling pot; the boilers' capacity to create steam was drastically reduced. Without the tall stacks to maintain pressure and regulate operating temperature, the boilers couldn't produce steam or run at peak efficiency.

Besides the damage to the vessel, there were human casualties as well. Owen Hughes and John Vinen were at the front of the boiler deck and bore the brunt of the falling funnels. Shaken, they climbed out from under the stacks and "sought the seclusion which a cabin grants, but it was worse in there," meaning the stateroom where Bedson and Wise were barricaded.[84] As they reached the cabin, with Shelton Andrews on their heels, a fresh volley of rebel fire rained upon them. "Both managed by the skin of their teeth to escape but after Vinen had entered the cabin and was helping to barricade it, he received a bullet in the thigh."[85] Andrews, Hughes and the now crippled Vinen were trapped: "The cabin was riddled and we could not either get downstairs or up."[86]

The crashing spars created a hazard for Sheets, Segers and Talbot, striking the wheelhouse and blocking the door. The careening gear also broke the ropes that connected the wheelhouse with the engine room, the only communication the pilot had with his engineer. The three men prepared to go down swinging confined in their personal Alamo. "I was so positive that it was all up with us in the pilothouse, as it was impossible to escape out of it, that I grabbed my rifle, Sheets and Segers also doing the same, and saying good-by to one another, prepared to sell our lives as dearly as possible, and even amidst all this excitement we thought of what a terrible slaughter must even then be going on deck."[87] As Talbot's cool was completely gone, he stationed himself and his rifle, firing blindly, and peering out occasionally to line a target into his sights. Segers shook his head and remarked, "My, God, what a terrible lot of our boys must be dead 'ere this."[88]

The loss of the stacks made a firetrap of the wooden ship. "I expected the old *Northcote* to go up in a chariot of fire at any moment"[89] Without the chimneys, the wood of the lower decks was exposed to the hot cinders and smoke bellowing from the boilers. Smoke from the truncated funnels billowed into the pilothouse, creating yet another peril. Crewmen and soldiers manned a bucket brigade to keep the decks moist, dodging gunfire while stamping out fiery embers. Dumont's sharpshooters showed no mercy when "a fire started. The crew however extinguished it, although my men fired on any that showed themselves on deck."[90]

The infantry's belated arrival

While the battle raged, Métis and Indians were all drawn to the river to join the attack. But a perfect opportunity for Middleton was lost. His ground force was still an hour away, as stressed by Fourmond. "Watching the battle from this site, we often looked out at the prairie to see red coats, expecting every instant for the shooting to start on this side. Strangely, inexplicably, no one appeared and for about an hour only the boat was involved in the shooting."[91]

As the boat passed Batoche, Ham saw a priest making a vain attempt to halt the carnage. In light of the holy man, and the words of concern written by Fourmond, it would seem that the boatmen had a much "higher authority" riding with them that warm spring morning. Likely, many of the men on board had hasty private conversations with their deity. "One man in priest's garb was seen near Batoche's waving his hands as if in despair, and apparently endeavouring to keep the breeds from firing at us, but their bullets poured around him and he disappeared. Some women were also there."[92]

As the land column prepared to advance on the village, they realized their comrades were already in the fray. "The firing got heavier and heavier and it seemed as if the whole rebel force was pitted against the jinxed vessel"[93] Middleton could hear the noisy din of the combat taking place on the river. "As we got near the river, much to my annoyance we heard a rattling fire and the steamer's whistle, showing the latter was already engaged."[94] Soon the whistle would be silenced by the slicing cable: "At intervals before this we had been blowing our whistle to let the General know where we were, but as the whistle was torn away we could do so no longer."[95] The Métis cable trap had cut off "our communication with General Middleton by our code of whistling signals previously arranged upon, the whistle being carried away with the pipes."[96]

The *Northcote* still had enough steam left in its pistons to produce limited power. That together with the current and the momentum of the barges was enough to keep the craft moving. And movement was a priority in the crew's mind, as the steamer was still under heavy fire from both banks. Soon, as if the river herself were an ally of the Métis, a new problem literally poked its head out of the water.

As the *Northcote* passed the ferry, it encountered a series of mild rapids, exposing rocky shoals that nearly succeeded where the cable had failed. "Just above Batoche's the rapids commence, and a big rock covered with sand juts out into [the] stream, leaving a narrow channel immediately on the western side, the head of which is at a sharp bend, to round which the boat had to run her nozzle almost on the bank. Here the firing became terrifically hot from a favourably located ravine directly in our front in which the rebels were hidden. The rapids were passed safely, notwithstanding that the pilots were totally unacquainted with the river and that the two heavy barges handicapped them in handling the steamer. Fortunately there was no wind to render their duties still more arduous in controlling the boat's movements."[97]

Recent photo looking north from the ferry landing on the east bank. The boulder Segers avoided by steering with his feet is still there (beneath arrow). GORD TOLTON, MAY 1995

The *Northcote* passed the rapids, but rocks were still a problem as the crew tried to maintain some semblance of control while still under fire. Ham noticed the boat swerve, thinking the manoeuvre was a controlled tactic "to avoid two large boulders directly in her course"[98]

With the helm still held firmly by Segers' feet, the impact with the cable had swung the boat sharply sideways, pointing the ship in to the shore. To turn and get headed back into the main stream, the paddlewheels would have to be instantly reversed. "Segers rang and rang a dozen times for [the engineer] to start the engines, but with no response, and the boat slowly swung around bow in, and slowly drifted downstream, thus affording the rebels, who lined both banks of the river, and who were nearly five hundred strong, to rake us fore and aft and as the banks were very high, and they could see our heads, every little time they poured hundreds of shots into the pilothouse which lodged in the bales of hay behind us (against which we were leaning)."[99]

But the ring went unheeded: the signal-bell ropes to the engine room were broken and engineer L'Heureux was nowhere in sight, having deserted his post and gone for cover in the hold. With the engines sputtering, "the result was that the boat twisted round and would strike on the shore, the current would then swing it back, and would then strike again."[100]

As Segers steered with his feet and prayed for full reverse, the *Northcote* "was allowed to swing around, and floated down stream stern foremost for a while."[101] The pilot struggled to keep his ship from climbing the bank, as unwelcome passengers tried to jump the barges, and soldiers struggled to prevent the boat from being overrun by would-be pirates. "One barge barely grazed the bank, and the boat would have been boarded by the rebels but for the steady volleys our men poured at them."[102] Soon, L'Heureux's assistant, Daniel Hurst, saved the day and ducked bullets to reverse the engine in time for Segers to right the ship.[103] Andrews said his friend Xavier Gougeon also "was called to take care of the engine … and stayed there till everything was over."[104] Talbot praised both Hurst and Gougeon, who "flew to the throttle valve and started the engines, and only in time, as in another moment the boat would have grounded and been boarded, and a great number, probably all, of our little command slaughtered."[105]

The battle was winding down, though "a withering fire was still maintained from some rifle pits which the enemy had dug at different places, and this was hotly returned until nine o'clock, when the rebel firing ceased, save a stray shot or two. We had run the gauntlet of their fire for five miles."[106] The Métis could savour their victory, but didn't have long to celebrate. Firing on the *Northcote* ceased just in time for them to return to their rifle pits and turn to the defensive. Gabriel Dumont still feared that the *Northcote* would land the soldiers, so, to protect Batoche's riverfront, he organized two scouting troops to flank the riverbanks: Patrice Fleury in charge on the west and Ambroise Champagne on the east. Around 30 scouts continued to follow the ship for miles, pestering the crew throughout the night and the next day with sporadic sniping. "Opposite the home of [Dumont's] late brother Isidore, the boat dropped anchor about 9 in the morning of the tenth. They were kept there in check all day long, and in spite of the bugle calls, no one came to their aid, and it was not until 6 at night that they raised anchor and went a few miles further downstream to moor for the night."[107]

As the crippled steamer passed Batoche, the soldiers on board noticed the arrival of Middleton. "As some of the red coats were seen coming up in skirmishing order in the distance, our small force gave three lusty cheers. This was the only glimpse we had of the troops."[108] Talbot heard the cheers and knew they were for Middleton's column, but was more concerned to see "the rebels rushing away from the river, and then I knew the General must be approaching their rear, but even then we came near rising up too soon, for several shots were fired up at us. We were comparatively out of danger and we anchored two miles below the ferry. We waited here all day to hear from the forces, but heard nothing."[109]

Recent photo illustrating Gatling gunner Howard's field of vision from the cemetery toward St. Antoine de Padoue and its rectory. Howard opened fire on the rectory, but there were no combatants inside, only church staff, and some were wounded. GORD TOLTON, MAY 1995

Fourmond and his fellow priests and nuns in the rectory would soon cease to be observers and instead become targets. As the morning progressed, Middleton dismissed the *Northcote* and its defenders from his concern. He'd heard a whistle as it moved upstream, and then turned his attention to the bigger issues of preparing to seize the village. The ground assault began as Captain Howard opened fire with his Gatling gun on the rectory next to the church.

Middleton's forces were turned back the same day from Mission Ridge, the hill overlooking the town, by the same marksmen that had attacked the ship. Safely entrenched in rifle pits, Dumont's men were able to fire on the troops at will and unseen. That the troops got as far as Mission Ridge at all should be credited to the action of the *Northcote*. The ship distracted the full Métis force away from the area of the church and cemetery where the ground force approached. Were it not for that distraction, Middleton may have been ambushed much further back on the trail. The only contact the land force had with the river that day was from the artillery. Major E.W. Jarvis of the Winnipeg Field Battery and Lieutenant G.H. Ogilvie of A Battery bombarded Métis houses and positions on the west side of the river. One lucky shell even struck Alex Fisher's ferry, "preventing the enemy's communications by the scow."[110]

Retreating to a camp the military called a "zareba," Middleton plotted strategy and reconnaissance for the next three days, while his troops tended their wounded, picked up their dead and grumbled about the general's inaction.

Duelling commanders

As the rebel combatants regrouped to resist the ground attack, the battered *Northcote* limped downstream to a safe distance. Segers was able to use the current to make course corrections, but even after dropping anchor, the craft continued on from sheer inertia until the hook found something solid enough to hold, some two miles past the village. It was as though the ship had a mind of its own with no intention of staying in the war zone. The crew and the soldiers were remarkably fortunate to be alive, and despite the cable's ravages, the ship was still in one, albeit fragile, piece.

Deckhands, firemen and engineers clambered clumsily from their improvised barricades and shook themselves into action to repair the damage. Sheets, Segers and Talbot were trapped in the pilothouse by the fallen debris. To extricate them, a hole had to be cut through the shack's roof, a task that fell to carpenters Roderick Smith and John McDonnell. But there were still snipers left on shore just waiting to pick off anyone that stuck their head out. To protect themselves, Smith and McDonnell had the ship's blacksmith, Donald McIvor, haul out some sheet tin to hastily fashion two crude suits of armour. Thus suited up, the sawyers ventured atop the steamer and went to work.

A few of the crew had gone ashore to gather wood for repairs, but were chased back aboard by a peppering of shots, while the luckless tin-clad carpenters drew the brunt of the fire. One rifleman "gave a parting shot to the steamer,"[111] striking McDonnell in the ankle and shattering his foot. Smith's pants showed signs of several grazes. McIvor saw the firing was coming from "the half breeds on the west side running down on horseback. They looked like crows."[112]

The gunmen had been assigned to the downriver location to guard the camps' herd of ponies. Dumont had sent the horses away from the village to keep them from being driven away or killed by the enemy, as he had lost a significant number of mounts at Fish Creek and couldn't afford to lose any more. "Near by are about fifty Indian ponies quietly grazing."[113] Captain Andrews located the snipers' positions on a "bluff on one side of the river and in a stable on the other, and they kept continually firing on us."[114]

Everyone aboard the *Northcote* knew they were being followed: "A number of hostiles are skulking down north,"[115] and after McDonnell's wounding, the crew refused to go out on deck. "When they got [McDonnell] down they said they wouldn't go back there again."[116] Crew and military alike could only count their blessings. The onslaught had been successfully repelled, and the word "miracle" was hardly strong enough to describe their good fortune. McIntyre Pringle had a flesh wound in the shoulder, John Vinen a similar graze in the thigh. "Our casualties are trivial,"[117] wrote Ham. There had been a gain as well: "In our engagement this morning eight rebels are reported to have been killed and there must have been a large number wounded."[118]

That estimate is difficult to confirm. The extant accounts of Batoche defenders killed take in the entire four-day action. Fifty-three bodies were found on the field, but there was little evidence to distinguish how many were killed during the steamboat attack. Hugh John Macdonald boasted downing five himself, but this is likely just so much folklore.[119]

The gauntlet behind them, the crew threw their backs into getting their bullet-riddled ship back into working order. The smokestacks were a priority. As crewmen picked up the crumpled metal, Donald MacIvor took steps to jury-rig replacements: "I cut the rivets in the middle of one of them and put a piece on each stump of the boiler as the boat was taking fire."[120]

George Ham sat down with pencil and paper, with the fight still fresh in his active mind:

Dropping below Batoche's nearly three miles, anchor was cast in midstream, but the steamer drifted another mile before the anchor firmly caught. The work of repairing damages was begun, and in a short time the smokestacks which were reduced in length, were re-erected: but scarcely had this been accomplished before firing disturbed the workmen, who were working behind a barricade of boxes … and in the cabin in which I am writing a scene of wild disorder prevails. The skylights are smashed, and the flimsy material of which the upper works were constructed offered no resistance to the enemy's fire, and are punctuated here and there with bullets. Later in the run, however, mattresses and bolsters were piled around the sides of the interior, and the place made fully secure.[121]

According to Owen Hughes, Ham also lived up to his name, as he took on the role of morale officer and "divided his time between telling anecdotes and carrying around ammunition. He was a great entertainer."[122]

Out of communication with Middleton, Major Smith realized the ship had to somehow signal its position to command. But the steam whistle lay on the deck, sheared off in the chaotic crumbling of the *Northcote*'s smokestacks. Amid much activity, the whistle eventually got replaced by an unnamed crewman and Private Coombs of the Infantry School Corps, "… a dangerous task which two men could only be induced to undertake on the promise of a reward of fifty dollars each."[123] The payoff was well earned, as the bullets whizzed around them amid their appointed task on the lofty perch. Smith was impressed: "This they did successfully under fire from the banks, and without, I am glad to say, any injury to themselves."[124]

By 6 p.m., with the stacks repaired, steam pressure was restored somewhat, although the boilers were going to need work to return to full operation. The whistle was working again, and the shrill wail pierced the valley, skirling the end of the ship's role in the battle just as it had piped the beginning. "Our signals to General Middleton were resumed; but although we could distinctly hear the sound of cannonading, no answer to our shrill whistle was given. The scouts evidently could not reach us owing to the presence of ambushed rebels secreted in the bluffs between us and the General's headquarters."[125] The land force heard the whistle, But there was little anyone could do about it. "The boat is down the river and has been whistling all afternoon,"[126] but the *Northcote* was on its own.

As Batoche's Métis defenders left the waterfront to repel Middleton's ground force, Patrice Fleury led a band of scouts to follow the *Northcote*, harass it with gunfire and keep its occupants away from hidden horses. GLENBOW ARCHIVES NA 935-11

With the situation stabilized, the commanding officers fell to bickering and pointing fingers. Sheets and Segers were taken to task for allowing the craft to hit the ferry cable. Sheets argued back that a steamship by that time is a pawn in the hands of inertia and does not stop or change its course on demand, in spite of the Queen.

The military officers—Smith, Bedson and Wise—enthused by the successful repairs to the smokestacks and whistle, "held a consultation and decided to return up the river." With Middleton on the hill, the commanders wanted to turn the boat around and continue the mission to land the soldiers. But James Sheets "adamantly refused to do so, claiming that not only was it certain death to the pilots but contrary to the written orders given him by the General."[127] Sheets had had enough. His craft was not built to withstand combat, and the crew had signed on for the purpose of transporting men and supplies, not to be shot at. Sheets had reluctantly lent his vessel to the attack only under orders from his employer, and in light of his ship and crew having been placed in such peril, he exercised his own authority. As commodore, James Sheets had complete mastery over his boat's destiny, and that pointedly did not include another bout of gunplay.

John Segers, who'd dodged bullet after bullet in the wheelhouse, refused to turn the bow, and would not even man the pilothouse until it was reinforced. No fewer than 90 slugs were embedded in the pressed hay that clad the exterior of the shack. "When the bullets would strike, they would go right through,"[128] and holes were everywhere. Even the "mail bags were fairly riddled by the rebel fire."[129]

Bedson asked his own pilot, Captain Andrews, to reinforce the shack, and Andrews in turn "asked my men [six soldiers of the 90th Winnipeg] if they would go with me and they said Yes and we went up a ladder"[130] to add extra planking to Segers' perch. Even at that point, the plucky Andrews took a bullet in his hat and one through the coat.

Faced with Segers' intransigence, Bedson pulled his ace. He asked Captain Andrews to helm the ship and steam back to Batoche. But the tactic backfired. Citing the lack of firewood on board, and the danger to woodhawks, Andrews refused the wheel. Likely, he had professional courtesy in mind as well, refusing to supplant a fellow navigator. But the military men still had glory on the brain, and tried another tack.

Perturbed with the stalemate between Smith and Sheets, Bedson polled the men and found a member of the 90th Winnipeg who had worked as a Red River pilot, and asked him to steer the ship. "Private William Eccles, of E Company, 90th, who had some experience in steamboating, volunteered to pilot the steamer up."[131] The proposal was put to Captain Sheets, who considered it but faced a mutiny of his own men if he allowed it. The boat's engineering crew, particularly Arthur L'Heureux, would not work with Eccles, so that idea was scrapped. Smith puffed and brooded: "After another consultation it was decided not advisable under the circumstances to take advantage of his manly offer. Hence we remain now out of the fight."[132]

The *Northcote*'s adventure at Batoche should have sealed its place in history, but Smith's unfortunate report scathingly criticized Sheets, Segers and the crew, dismissing them as U.S. "aliens." "Our weakness lay in the fact that the master, pilot and engineer were aliens, and that the crew were civil employees and not enlisted men."[133] Smith had nothing but high praise for his own troops, while spewing venom on the crew. His criticism contained only a grain of truth, considering that the firefight had been endured by all. The militia troops on board had as little combat experience as the ship's crew. Smith did not mention the crewmen who had returned fire, the pilot and assistant engineer who had held the ship's course and prevented capture, or the carpenters who had donned makeshift tin armour to free their shipmates from the pilothouse wreckage.

Civilian trader Owen Hughes had similar barbs for the roosters: "They kept themselves under the water line as much as possible."[134] A rumour later reached Private

Robert Allan of the 90th Winnipeg that engineer L'Heureux had been detained for abandoning his post during the battle. "Our men had to bring him in and stand guard over him," and though there is no record of any actual arrest, L'Heureux's behaviour got the entire crew painted as cowards. The crew were none too happy with him themselves, and Donald MacIvor didn't mind saying that "as far as I know everybody was a man except the first engineer … He left the engine room and went below."[135]

The river fight itself was overshadowed by the subsequent four-day standoff and the eventual final siege of the town by the ground forces. Smith's denigration of the *Northcote*'s crew probably reflected his own bitter disappointment at having missed the final charge, and something of a colonial prejudice against Americans. A contemporary armchair critic of General Frederick Middleton, safely screened by the veil of time, distance and hindsight, complained that "General Middleton's navy project did little more than imperil many valuable lives and withdrew from his forces a considerable number of men who were badly needed on Saturday, Sunday and Monday."[136]

But despite having been unsuccessful at landing any infantry, the ship nevertheless furthered Middleton's objectives by drawing the Métis to the river. It was not the fault of Sheets, Segers, Smith or Bedson that the ground force arrived when it did. Historians have argued for a century over whether the *Northcote* was early or Middleton was late.

With her thankless task as a warship on "the Gilbert-and-Sullivan engagement"[137] over, the *Northcote* had but a day or so to lick her wounds and return to her intended mission as a transporter of men and supplies. The running of the Batoche gauntlet became a mere footnote, unfairly spoken of in short, choppy sentences and dismissed as "a comic opera engagement."[138]

Only Ham fleshed out the fullness of the drama, in his newspaper accounts and his autobiography. And even he, with the temperance of time, applied only personal ruminations and never tried to turn the *Northcote*'s experience into an epic. With tongue firmly planted in cheek he wrote: "I kept up a steady fire at something unknown. I don't know whether I hit any clouds or not, but I am assured of one thing: if any lead mines are ever discovered on the banks of the Saskatchewan, I should have a prior claim over anybody in their ownership. This was the first naval battle in the Canadian North-west, and I imagine it will be the last. At any rate, it will be as far as yours truly is concerned."[139]

CHAPTER TEN

Picking Up the Pieces

From out of the ice

Archie Ballantine was one of those all-purpose wanderers who characterized the Canadian plains in the 1880s. He was a jack-of-all-trades kind of frontier character, never colourful but always functional and a hard worker. He'd worked his way west to Prince Albert in 1879, to the edge of a wilderness booming with excitement. He cut timber, did odd jobs and worked the slippery decks of the steamboats, as a fireman and an engineer on the *Manitoba* and as a woodhawk and watchman on the *Northcote*. At the outbreak of the rebellion, his repertoire grew yet again when he joined the Prince Albert Volunteers relief team as a medic and horse doctor.

Ballantine spent a number of uneventful but nevertheless nervous April nights on sentry duty in the town. Soon, word was that the three steamers in nearby winter port were to be commandeered. The *North West* was to be awakened from its slumber, for "in the event of the town falling into the hands of the rebels, the women and children could be taken on board and carried down the Saskatchewan out of reach of the enemy."[1] Laid up on Prince Albert's banks, the *North West* had been under heavy guard since the beginning of the troubles. Anglican minister John Hines was one of those set to guard the vessel in response to a threat to burn it.

On his very first night, Hines was to share sentry duty with a Mountie corporal, "but, alas! my brother in arms did not turn up, and I spent the whole night alone marching up and down the boat, lugging about with me an antique American rifle, almost heavy enough to require a gun carriage to move it from one end of the boat to another."[2] Hines was probably not the best man for the job. The weapon he found so heavy was a single-shot rifle which had to be loaded for him, and which he hadn't the slightest notion how to reload. Fortunately, the reverend's first night of duty was uneventful.

Eventually, Hines sought out his absent sentry partner in the detachment that was set up in the HBC's kitchen. There, he found "all the brave fellows engrossed in sleep,

194

having sat up late studying the tactics of war with a deck of cards, and as many of these were scattered about the floor, we understood these as representing the dead among the enemy." The corporal was reported and disciplined, and "after this event, [Hines] always had company"[3] on *North West* watch duty.

The other two steamers at Prince Albert, the *Manitoba* and the *Marquis*, were still in drydock in the mouth of the Sturgeon River, where Captain Julian Dougall tended them as he bided his time in his small cabin. As the rebellion called the boats into service, Dougall hired a work crew to prepare them to sail. With tools and equipment in hand, the labourers, including the ever reliable Archie Ballantine, travelled the five miles to the Sturgeon to assist the crusty old pilot.

But the workmen discovered both boats frozen into the river mud, and too little water to refloat their bulk. With little else to do, the crew took to battening down all the hatches and holds and making any necessary repairs to the boilers. Eventually the hands ran out of work, as there wasn't even enough water to fill the boilers.

Dougall sent his boys back to Prince Albert for a well-deserved Saturday night and Sunday off, ordering them to return Monday morning, on the chance that some miracle might grant some meltwater. Ballantine decided to stay with Dougall at the cabin. On Sunday morning, they awoke with a start to find their beds nearly underwater. The channel had risen by more than four feet overnight, and the current was flowing on either side of an ice jam in the centre of the channel.

The captain and the deckhand clambered into an old canoe and paddled to the ice to see how the *Marquis* was affected. They discovered the flood had jarred and lifted the ship, but the bottom-mounted rudders were still frozen into the mud, preventing the boat from breaking loose altogether.

The stern of the *Marquis* and the bow of the *North West*. The ships are shown in winter drydock, their paddles removed, in the spring of 1884 at Cumberland House. The two vessels were in similar storage condition in the spring of 1885, the *North West* at Prince Albert, and the *Marquis* and the *Manitoba* at the mouth of the Sturgeon River. ARCHIVES OF MANITOBA

The nearby *Manitoba* was in even worse straits. The river had found a hole in the hull, and with water in the hold, there was little hope of raising her from the mud. As the waters rose, Dougall's shack was endangered, and the pair had to evacuate their belongings before the cabin flooded. With a tarp they built a crude shelter and waited for the ice breakup. Only then could anything be done.

The ice finally ran out on April 10, as Dougall and his crew cut and piled wood so as to be ready when the *Marquis* could float out to the North Saskatchewan. But things got progressively worse for the stranded *Manitoba*. Ice floes caught on the hulk and piled up a menacing 20 feet above her.

The *Marquis*, while not as bad off, was still of concern. Mud clung tenaciously to her rudders, and a 45-degree list put the hold in danger of being swamped. When the mud finally released its grip, the ship snapped all its reinforcing tension lines, or "hog chains." Also, the ice had split a massive iron clevis, a yoke-like pulling point vital to the steering gear. To retrieve the broken-off piece, Ballantine waded into the frigid stream and laboured beneath the stern in a bitter, 2½-hour ordeal to attach a tow chain to the clevis. The piece was retrieved, and a blacksmith repaired the yoke while Ballantine chattered before a fire. When the repair was done, Archie dived right back into the icy pool again to reinstall the clevis.

Three of the ship's four wooden rudders were still mired, however, and finally it was decided to cut them off at the posts. The carpenters could build new ones once the vessel was afloat. By the end of April, her boilers filled from homemade siphon tubes, the *Marquis* was ready to back out into the North Saskatchewan. Since she had only the one rudder left, Dougall brought in the *North West* to tow the *Marquis*'s rear end off the bottom of the Sturgeon. Once she was put into a proper landing, the stern

The *Marquis* tied up at an unidentified warehouse on the Saskatchewan River, 1884. ARCHIVES OF MANITOBA

was raised out of the water and the carpenters went to work. On April 23, with new rudders installed, the boat made a trial run to Prince Albert.

The *Manitoba* would not fare as well. The flood and ice had taken their toll and smashed the bottom of its hull. The hold and lower deck were covered in silt and mud. All that remained was for the W&WTC to write her off and salvage the remains. It fell to Ballantine to tour the rotting decks and recover furniture, laundry and cabin fixtures.

> I took the bedding, blankets, sheets and pillows outside and hung them on the willows and some stretches of line tied to the trees. The weather was fine and things dried fast. As they dried, I shook sand and mud out of them and stacked them in a pile and covered them with canvas. Then I carried ashore all that I could of the heavy things, and after that, cleaned up the boat. This took about six days.[4]

As Ballantine diligently cleaned up the wreck, his mates and his captain left to join the war service. On May 1, the *Marquis* was steaming down to the Forks to ascend the South Branch, intent on assisting the *Northcote*.

As Batoche rages, the nuns wait ...

When the fighting at Batoche began, Mother Louise Collings at the Prince Albert convent grew fearful for her colleagues. Scouts told her of the abandonment of the St. Laurent mission, and she did not know the Sisters were at St. Antoine's. The churning rumour mill told her that "the rebels still had possession of the raft,"[5] the Batoche ferry. Private Robert Allan confirmed the barrage on the river: "Our cannon is shelling the Indians down by the river, and making them scramble up the bank."[6] When a Canadian ball hit the ferry, "some were shot and some were drowned."[7] Another anonymous letter confirms the destruction of one of the ferry scows and the fate of riverborne rebels: "A party of half-breeds endeavoured to escape across the river, but … in the midst of the stream [they] were drowned. A shell from the battery was laid upon one scow, and when the smoke cleared away the empty barge was seen floating helplessly down the river, the cable being broken and those on board the scow either killed or thrown into the river."[8]

The nuns were finally able to learn the facts of Batoche: "The steamboat bringing a regiment from Winnipeg for General Middleton by way of Medicine Hat on the South Saskatchewan by St. Antoine's … was fired upon by the rebels."[9] But there was no way the sisters could know of the *Northcote*'s perils, or that it was still being stalked by Fleury and Champagne's scouts on May 10, the day after the battle.

... and the Northcote regroups

Downstream from Batoche, though the *Northcote* was out of the main action, the ship's crew and military contingent were far from out of danger as they continued to cope with their situation. The soldiers were put to work reinforcing the pilothouse, so that pilot Segers would stand behind the helm. Sheets had anchored the boat in midstream through the night. The boiler had finally given out, overstrained from trying to maintain pressure after the funnels were clipped, and the engineers and firemen worked through the night to repair it. With little sleep, crew and soldiers were roused to breakfast at 4 a.m. to try to get the ship underway. But the rank and file steamer men had had enough of being targets. Engineer L'Heureux refused to remain at his post and tried to incite a strike among his mates, who "spent most of the time skulking in the hold." L'Heureux was making few friends, and even George Ham said the engineer "acted in a most cowardly manner."[10] Finally L'Heureux was relieved, and Shelton Andrews and the 90th Winnipeg rivermen, filled the gaps in the crew.

The perilous overnight stay did bring Major Smith and Captain Sheets to an agreement over returning to Batoche, however. "The Master said that he could not with safety go [back] with the barges in tow, and that he was getting out of wood and must take on more before he could remain anywhere long. We then decided to run down to the Hudson Bay Ferry, leave the barges there, take on wood and sufficient supplies for the Column, and return at once to Batoche."[11] The *Northcote* would return, but it needed to regroup and refuel.

The Hudson's Bay ferry was only 22 miles downstream, but in the steamer's condition it might as well have been a hundred. The entire morning and afternoon of May 10 were spent patching and priming the boiler and timbering over the wheel house. By 6:30 p.m., they were ready to embark, but as the paddle began to churn, the *Northcote* found it still had unwelcome company. The Métis scouts had continued to observe in stealth. "the rebels, who had been hiding, poured in a broadside, the soldiers returning it by volley firing. They followed us for some distance until cut off by dense woods."[12] The scouts finally lost interest and the ship continued downstream unimpeded. They made only nine miles before darkness forced anchorage for the night.

At the crack of dawn, the *Northcote* weighed anchor and started out for a known woodpile some 11 miles distant, hoping the Métis would not think to have plundered it. After losing four hours poling off a sandbar, they found the cordwood unharmed. Hoodoo and other Métis settlements nearby were found empty, the inhabitants having answered the call of Riel and Dumont. This included Maxime Lepine's house, where Lepine ran a ferry that Major Smith intended to destroy. But even that bit of fun was denied the soldiers, as Lepine's scow was already at Batoche, hauled upstream on Riel's order.

At 3 p.m. on May 11, the *Northcote* arrived at the Hudson's Bay ferry, also known as Fort Campbell, "where we were received with loud cheers"[13] from 25 Mounties and, more to the liking of Sheets, from a fellow steamboat crew.

They were pleasantly surprised to find that not only was the HBC ferry safe, but the *Marquis* had arrived. Commissioner Irvine had ordered Dougall to the Landing with an escort of Mounted Policemen headed by Inspector M.H. White-Fraser, to secure the ferry and lend assistance at Batoche. To tend to the wounded, White-Fraser had brought Hospital Sergeant Edward Braithwaite, who pronounced the patients Pringle, Vinen and McDonnell to have "not been wounded badly."[14] Braithwaite authorized them and the ship's sick transported to Prince Albert by wagon. McDonnell would eventually have to have his wounded leg amputated.[15]

Nobody could have been happier to learn of the ice breakup than Sheets. The disgruntled captain had had enough of tin soldiers, Batoche and the *Northcote*, and wasted no time climbing aboard one of the wagons bound for Prince Albert, where he could finally perform the task he'd come to do. Captain Sheets bade a hearty goodbye to his faithful crew and good riddance to the military mindset.

Unfortunately, it may have been this attitude of Sheets's that resulted in calumnies such as that "the captain of the boat was as frightened as any and was put off at Hudson's Bay Crossing,"[16] a bald-faced lie repeated by Robert Allan, who, it should be noted, was with the land force at Batoche and had nothing to do with the *Northcote* whatsoever. Had Sheets known of such vicious gossip, the veteran riverman might have provoked a good old-fashioned Mississippi duel with Major Henry Smith.

Having unburdened the heavy barges, the crew of the *Northcote* "got up to the rope again and ready for action,"[17] to avenge themselves. Colonel Bedson commandeered the *Marquis* to accompany the *Northcote* back upriver to the fighting. George Ham filed his lengthy dispatch and sent it with a courier to the Humboldt telegraph station. A couple of days later it was published in the *Toronto Daily Mail*.

The *Marquis* poles off a shallow, accompanied by an unidentified steamer. The battle-scarred *Northcote* accompanied the ice-damaged *Marquis* to return to the fighting at Batoche. *CANADIAN PICTORIAL & ILLUSTRATED WAR NEWS, 1885 SOUVENIR EDITION*

Smith ordered White-Fraser to spare as many Mounties as he could to escort the return excursion. White-Fraser and 24 patrolmen climbed aboard, along with Braithwaite, who "requested leave to go." A puzzled Fraser refused, believing the medic's place to be with the wounded in the wagon. But Braithwaite protested, "Excuse me, sir, I do not think you have any right to take our men upriver without medical aid."[18] White-Fraser finally consented, but only if Braithwaite "would do regular duties until I was wanted medically." Major Smith ordered a daybreak embarkment for the morning of May 13, but sailing was delayed until 8 a.m. En route, the *Marquis*'s steering gear, still damaged, got twisted on a sandbar. The *Northcote* extended a tow cable, and the flotilla progressed upriver slower than usual.

Archie gets a rest, then ships out again

Back at the Sturgeon, Archie Ballantine cooled his heels for nearly 10 days salvaging the *Manitoba*. He knew there was a war raging all around him, but though the ship he'd done so much to bring back to life had been pressed into war service, he "had not heard a word of what was going on, nor had I seen a soul. Everything was as still as death, except for the chatter and song of spring birds."[19] But as lonesome Archie sat on the riverbank cooking dinner, his paradise stillness was shattered by the familiar noises of the *North West*. Soon the workhorse hove into view and put in near the wreck of the *Manitoba*. A work gang of deckhands swarmed off and began loading the booty of Ballantine's toils for transport to the nearest HBC post. Ballantine, after a month at his forsaken post, gladly climbed aboard for Prince Albert.

On the way, Ballantine could not help but admire the refurbishing job on the grand vessel. As he strode across the freshly painted deck, a tall, assuming figure approached him. It was Captain Sheets, again in command of the *North West*. Sheets had heard of Ballantine's long, undignified service and asked the handyman if he "would like the job of night watchman." Nonchalant as always, Archie replied, "It would be all right,"[20] and took his post on the bow of the *North West*.

Assembling a flotilla

Swift Current's railway siding remained busy as supplies poured in from Winnipeg to be loaded aboard rivercraft. Busying themselves with drill and camp work, G and H Companies of the Midland Battalion also guarded the depot, having stayed behind when their compatriots marched off to Batoche. On the drizzly, snowy afternoon of April 24, the abandoned Midlanders welcomed the arrival of the 7th Fusiliers from London, Ontario.

Too late for either boats or columns, the Fusiliers resigned themselves to garrison duty at Swift Current, while awaiting orders. They were hardly needed, as, with three regiments in town, no supply depot was ever so safe. Hospital Sergeant Alexander Campbell reported their duty to be one of finding out just how many different sporting matches they could organize with other passing units: "Games were arranged when we had the material to play with, but between us we were able to rake up enough for Boxing, Rugby and Association Football, and we had the pleasure of winning both the Rugby and Soccer games."[21] But with the news of Fish Creek, the Fusiliers' games were set aside, for General Laurie had a more important contest for their backs and minds.

Meanwhile, the fleet of flat-bottomed scows being assembled at the Landing were nearly complete and ready to be loaded. After the planned 10 craft were built, there remained enough lumber and nails left over to build another 2, and since there was a brief delay in the arrival of cargo for the fleet anyway, General Laurie authorized the extra 2 scows. Though he wrote that 12 barges were constructed, however, only 11 left the Landing, and apparently no accounting was ever made for the 12th one.

By the night of May 11 the homemade flotilla was loaded and ready to sail. An incredible 249 tons of supplies had been squeezed and prodded onto the barges, nearly 10 tons more than planned for. Between the scow fleet and the departed *Alberta* and *Baroness*, over 400 men plus all their kit, camp equipment, arms, ammunition and 600 tons of war supplies would be on their way to Middleton.

Word came down ordering the remainder of the Midland Battalion and the 7th Fusiliers to join Middleton, who wanted the fresh troops to either march north via Moose Jaw and overland or retrace the trail from Fort Qu'Appelle. Laurie had difficulty complying, as he had precious few wagon teams left that could accompany any troops anywhere.

Before his barges could sail, however, Laurie had another civilian labour problem with the Boyd & Crowe crew. The Winnipeg contractors contended that the original agreement with Joseph Wrigley provided for workers to man their barges, but only if 20 soldiers accompanied each craft. The General agreed, but countered with a notion to provide each of the civilian sailors with a rifle.

Then Laurie realized he could solve all of his transport problems in one fell swoop with means that were readily at hand. The 400-odd soldiers requested by Middleton could most easily, most swiftly and—most

An unidentified steamer is photographed pushing a barge toward a military camp. The boat could be either the *Baroness* or the *Alberta* delivering badly needed stores to the Clarke's Crossing supply depot.
GLENBOW ARCHIVES NA-363-11

important to Laurie's government masters—most cheaply be transported, supplies and all, via the two steamers and the free-floating barges.

Boyd & Crowe were ecstatic. Not only would they receive free military escort, they would be paid a bonus for transporting the government troops. Then the contractors pulled a double-cross on the general. Realizing that many of the troops were also experienced bargemen from back east, Boyd & Crowe laid off nearly all of their boat crews to make more room for troops. Leaving only one of their own rafters per barge to act as navigator, the canny contractors were in the enviable position of being paid by a client and having the client do the work! Only a government could engineer itself into such a scenario! To be fair, Boyd did offer a cash donation to the 7th Fusiliers, but Laurie disallowed the payment as improper.

The little navy would have no hope of getting in on the main fight, though. As they sailed north, the Battle of Batoche was already raging and would be all but resolved before the *Baroness* and *Alberta* would arrive. Nonetheless, the supplies and relief they carried would be much appreciated by hungry horses, battle-scarred soldiers and isolated settlers. What's more, details of the remainder of the campaign were sketchy and plans to resupply Middleton had to continue.

The entire complement of the Fusiliers, officers and staff, would ride the river the 320 miles to Clarke's Crossing, though "there was not a riverman in the whole battalion."[22] Also boarding the rickety fleet were the final two troops of the Midland Battalion—the Peterborough and Hastings Companies G and H—who had been recalled from patrolling the Cypress Hills, where they'd been diverted some days earlier.

To command this armada, Laurie assigned the highest-ranking officer of the Midland Battalion, Lieutenant Colonel J. Deacon, to assume command of "the Saskatchewan Brigade." The company captains were consulted to see if their commands were amenable to overcrowding in order to avoid having their units broken up. Anxious to join the fighting, the captains zealously volunteered to cram themselves aboard and perform all the necessary work on the barges. Rafts originally designed to carry 20 men apiece were crowded with as many as 35.

Self-portrait of Alexander Campbell, a London, Ontario, medic who documented in words and pictures the toil and boredom of his unit, the 7th Fusiliers, during the North West Rebellion, in "An Account of the Advances of the 7th Fusiliers of London." UNIVERSITY OF SASKATCHEWAN LIBRARY SPECIAL COLLECTIONS MSS 49 #17

The Fusiliers' medic, Sergeant Alexander Campbell, described the boats and their freight as "large flat bottomed scows, with the only means of control a large unwieldy sweep fore and aft."[23] Officers of the 7th were put in command of each barge, and they were sailing under sealed orders. To purge maritime superstition, each scow was duly christened and named after respected officers, the prime minister and even the contractors. Thus did the fighting fleet grow by the addition of the *Major Smith,* the *Captain Evans,* the *Sir John Macdonald,* the *Captain Leonard,* the *General Middleton,* the *Captain*

Kelly, the *Lieutenant Nelles,* the *Boyd & Crowe,* the *General Laurie,* the *Hard Tack,* the *Smith & Evans* and the *Captain Kerr.* Major A.M. Smith of the 7th Fusiliers was doubly honoured by being the namesake of one of the barges while himself commanding the *Lieutenant Nelles.* Except for the *Captain Kelly,* each barge towed a rowboat to enable the ships to communicate with each other if separated, and to scout out the channels.

Sergeant Campbell sets the tone for the whole barge journey: "We were anxious to get on but had to wait for the river to rise which it didn't after all,"[24] as the Fusiliers would grumpily discover. In fact, as a dispatch to the *Winnipeg Daily Sun* reported, "The river is still falling."[25] The barges left Saskatchewan Landing at eight o'clock on the morning of May 11, "... loaded with tons of supplies including Hay, Oats, Tea, Sowbelly, Hardtack, some flour and some canned meat, but unfortunately the supplies for the crews were not equally distributed."[26] All rations were placed on the *Captain Kelly,* to encourage the squadron to stick together for safety and general expediency. Some civilian navigators were aboard the barges, but the pilots' names are lost to time. Officers' reports do mention the names of a few of the Fusiliers that navigated, however: Private M. Seevy on the *Captain Kelly,* and Major Gaitshore and Sergeant Jacobs on the *Lieutenant Nelles.* One of the contractors, Nat Boyd, navigated aboard the *Captain Kerr.*

The barges met with varying degrees of success. The crews made good time downriver by dint of the zeal of commanding officers, who, sometimes overzealously, would lighten their craft by tossing badly needed supplies overboard or setting them ashore. Putting all the rations on one barge proved disastrous, and the haste in construction and planning showed, as reported by the troop captains.[27] One of the biggest problems was, as usual, the shifting nature of the channel. The deposits of sediment seemed as fluid as the river itself. The aptly named *Hard Tack* ran into "a pocket formed by three sand bars on the three sides of a square, and on these bars not a foot of water could be found."

The boats had to fight for every mile of progress downstream. "We only find the sand bars and shoals by running aground on them," said Lieutenant Fred Bremner of the *Captain Kelly,* bemoaning that he did not have a rowboat to scout out the shallows ahead of his barge. But no one else was having any great success, either, pilot rowboats or not. The *Lieutenant Nelles* got into trouble right away, "stranded on a sand bar within sight of the Landing."[28] Initially, many of the barges were chained together, a noble effort, "the idea being that if one ran on to a bar the free boat would cut loose leaving a slack line on the stranded boat and the weight of the free boat was supposed to pull the other off."[29] The trick didn't work, and after myriad groundings on sandbars the boats were separated.

Captain Thomas Tracy, on the *Sir John Macdonald,* also got into trouble early. When his craft struck a sandbar, the other barges followed right along into the hazard, "the men having to jump into the water and work very hard" to free their vessels. Tracy's comment somewhat understates the toil it took to keep the Saskatchewan Brigade afloat.

The Saskatchewan Brigade embarks in the transport scow *Lt. Nelles*. The troops' physical appearance and morale would soon deteriorate, according to Alexander Campbell in his "An Account of the Advances of the 7th Fusiliers of London." UNIVERSITY OF SASKATCHEWAN LIBRARY SPECIAL COLLECTIONS MSS 49 #17

The worst luck of all, though, was that of Captain Dillon, on the *Captain Leonard*. His craft grounded twice the first day. The second time, 20 miles from the Landing, Dillon threw up his hands and pitched camp for the night. The next morning's fresh start did little good, and the entire day was lost. Colonel Deacon, on the *Lieutenant Nelles*, sent a rowboat back to ascertain the trouble, and discovered a rampaging Dillon threatening to throw the whole load in the river if he didn't get help soon. The next morning, his dejected crew made a fort out of their cargo of hay bales and oat sacks on the shore and set out again. From there on, their "luck" improved somewhat, still "getting stranded four to six times each day" but at least making progress due to the lighter load that made working around the shoals easier.

Three miles downstream, the *Nelles* stopped, not for grounding but to wait for Dillon. When the *Leonard* finally caught up, Major Smith ordered the barges lashed together, but again the concept proved futile. When the *Nelles* ran into yet another sandbar, Dillon cut the line and sailed on while Smith's crew hit the water to extricate the *Nelles* from its latest predicament. "I now estimated that we were a day's run behind the main body," Major Smith admitted.

The work of freeing the boats often took hours, and they "stranded, on the average, two or three times a day." Although these groundings resulted in separation from the flotilla, all of the barges faced the same conditions and thus did not become very far separated overall. Often the boats would high-centre simultaneously, so the crews could pool their resources to free each other, as when the *Sir John McDonald* and the *Leonard* spent over six hours cooperating. In freeing the *Leonard*, the *McDonald* took on water and had to be bailed out.

Eventually, befuddled captains had to face their cranky, half-naked soldier crews and come to terms with the fact that the barges, well built as they were, just could not haul the tonnage that had been loaded aboard. Sixty miles from Saskatchewan Landing,

Captain Frank Peters reluctantly put ashore 50 sacks of oats from his double barge, the *Smith & Evans*. After another grounding, Peters pulled his hair and angrily ordered another 51 sacks disposed of. Wasting no time with careful packing ashore, the oats were just dumped overboard into the river.

Captain Tracy, on the *Sir John Macdonald*, kept all of his load together until reaching the Moose Woods, where he was "forced to leave part of our cargo piled on the beach, and place some more in Captain Dillon's boat." The rowboats were put to good use for the *Nelles*, when the advance boat "found it would be impossible to take the barge through with its load."

The troops find "hard luck," shedding their unifoms and their modesty to push their beached barge back into the channel. The circle inset shows a stack of cargo jettisoned to lighten the boats. "AN ACCOUNT OF THE ADVANCES OF THE 7TH FUSILIERS OF LONDON," U. OF SASKATCHEWAN LIBRARY SPECIAL COLLECTIONS MSS 49 #17

Less impetuous than Peters, Smith had his crew gingerly place over a hundred sacks of horse feed on the bank.

Lieutenant George Reid, in command of the *Boyd & Crowe*, nonchalantly reported his boat to be taking things in stride after having jettisoned some of his cargo. "We found the barge floated all right, although it was repeatedly necessary for the men to get out and work the boat off sand bars." Lieutenant Horace Yeoman's *Hard Tack*, though having had to dump bags earlier, was able to pick up a hundred jettisoned sacks, and actually delivered more freight than it left with. Sometimes, jettisoning cargo was not enough. Even "after lighting up the barge," the 7th Fusiliers would have to haul out a rope for a tug of war wherein "we had to tow [the barge] up the river about 500 yards."

The whole journey was in fits and starts, "a succession of good runs and bad sticks on sunken sand bars." The Boyd company pilots had trouble with their sweep oars as well. The shallow water and the sand took their toll on the soft wood oars, and they had to be constantly repaired. Lieutenant N.R. Grieg, commanding the *Laurie*, finally threw the oars away and was forced to "construct new ones as best we could, lashing the several timbers together with ropes." Major Smith had to admit, "We had no one on board who had any experience in river navigation." When the men of the *Hard Tack* broke a sweep, they were forced to dismantle freight crates "and take nails out of boxes to fix it."

The crews of the *Leonard* and the *Sir John McDonald* struggled to make up lost time by getting up at 3:30 in the morning and travelling until dark. A further irritation was a northerly headwind that blew for three solid days, whipping up waves that overstrained the oars and countered the current. The *General Middleton* was

The pre-dawn reveille in the 7th Fusiliers camp, the beginning of a 16-hour day of travel and travail on the South Saskatchewan.

tossed into the shallows of a tributary, which cost its crew six hours of digging to get out of the creek's channel and back into the river. Then a dead-of-night thunderstorm buffeted the fleet and threatened to soak the contents of the uncovered barges.

The human toll was heavy on the Fusiliers, and the officers had high praise for their charges whose "day's work lasted from 4 a.m. to 8 p.m." Lieutenant Grieg of the *Laurie*, noted that the labours of the troops outweighed their modesty when they "had to undress and jump into the river in order to push the barge." Alexander Campbell's drawings reveal men working in icy waters, without pants and even fully naked. The dampness led to attacks of cramps and pneumonia as well, and many afflicted men suffered without medical attention. Cooks were kept busy boiling water to prevent the troops from drinking out of the river. Lieutenant Yeoman was grateful for his human resources: "Too much cannot be said in praise of the men who during the whole trip, were ready for anything. Some days the water would be very cold, but there was not a complaint from one."

Since the bulk of the food was carried on the lead barge, the men on stranded boats often went hungry. As medic, Campbell predicted starvation when "stock was taken of our provisions [and] found that we had but two days' rations." Dillon noted his shortfall jealously. "Rations were so limited that I had to limit my men to three, and afterwards two hard tacks per day, while I understand some of the flotilla had plenty and to spare." The only thing that seemed to save the boys from total starvation was when the river cooperated enough to enable barges to share supplies "to replenish our stock from time to time as we overtook other boats."

Diets might have been augmented from the abundance of geese, ducks and prairie chickens. But the 7th Riflemen were never able to do much with their Sniders than blow the birds to bits with their half-inch cartridge shot. The simple addition of a few shotguns would have avoided much of the hunger problem, and enabled the crews to live off the land, as "the outdoor life made it possible to eat anything and enjoy it."[30]

The funny thing about a sore back is how it sharpens the brain, and by the time the fleet reached the Elbow of the South Branch, the Fusiliers were beginning to figure out "on which side of the bar the best channel was to be found, and to manage the clumsy sweeps so as to steer clear of many difficulties."[31] The channel past the Elbow did get a little less treacherous for the amateur navigators, and groundings became less frequent.

As the flotilla neared the Moose Woods reserve of Whitecap, chambers were loaded, guns were kept at the ready, and the fleet was ordered to stay together. Breast works of cargo were set up on the boats to deflect hostile fire. Of course, Whitecap was in no position to threaten the Saskatchewan Brigade, though "there were two or three alarms through a sentry becoming too imaginative."[32]

Lieutenant John Weller's pioneer raft crew, the one that had liberated the barge from the *Minnow*, made it to Clarke's Crossing on May 16. Weller was confident of the Saskatchewan Brigade's chances, reporting "that with proper

(Right) The pre-dawn reveille in the 7th Fusiliers camp, the beginning of a 16-hour day of travel and travail on the South Saskatchewan.

(Below) The 7th Fusiliers near Saskatoon at sunset inspired Sgt. Campbell to break out his watercolours to document the scene.

Campbell's unit reaches the end of their voyage, at Clarke's Farm. *ALL ABOVE FROM* "AN ACCOUNT OF THE ADVANCES OF THE 7TH FUSILIERS OF LONDON," U. OF SASKATCHEWAN LIBRARY SPECIAL COLLECTIONS MSS 49 #17

appliances and trained men, no serious difficulty need be experienced." But Weller had come through on high water and did not experience the Saskatchewan Brigade's travails. Even so, he had taken 16 days, whereas even the slowest of the Fusiliers' craft had taken only 9.

The first Saskatchewan Brigade raft arrived at Clarke's on May 19, proud of the time they had made but keeping silent about the supplies so liberally thrown off. The other barges straggled in the next day. Major Kirwan noticed that parts of loads were missing, and communicated the shortfall to Laurie in Swift Current. Laurie, correctly surmising that cargo had been tossed overboard, demanded a full accounting, as Boyd & Crowe were to be paid based on tonnage delivered to Clarke's. Lieutenant Colonel Deacon was ordered to have each barge commander submit a report on the voyage, which of course gave 12 sides to the story.

The captains complied, reporting openly and honestly about where the supplies had disappeared. Bluntly they confirmed the losses and were only too glad to explain them. Captain Peters said "it would have been almost impossible to have taken the barges through with the heavy cargo on board." The captains made no excuses for their actions:

> "… the oats were not removed till every effort had been made to move the barges without doing so."
> "I was sorry to have to do this but as we were getting short of provisions it could not be avoided."
> "… we were under the necessity of dumping out sixty bags of oats."
> "we … piled 138 bags of oats on the left bank, say 35 miles from the Landing. After starting again we got badly stuck in the sand and got off with the greatest difficulty, even with the lightened barge … "

Campbell's unit reaches the end of their voyage, at Clarke's Farm. "AN ACCOUNT OF THE ADVANCES OF THE 7TH FUSILIERS OF LONDON," U. OF SASKATCHEWAN LIBRARY SPECIAL COLLECTIONS MSS 49 #17

"… after having all the men in the water for from five to six hours, I was compelled to throw from 40 to 50 bags of oats in the river, in order to float the barge."

"I ordered them to remove enough of the cargo to float the boat. There were about 75 bags taken off, all of which were piled on the shore."

The men of the 7th Fusiliers could not be taken to task, as their efforts brought as much of the supply base as the tiny fleet should have been expected to assume.

Lieutenant Grieg, on the *Laurie*, was luckier than most, and "succeeded in bringing our full cargo, with the exception of two bags of oats which burst in several places, owing to the inferior quality of the canvas." Lieutenant Harry Bapty, on the *Kerr*, lost no freight "with the exception of one bale of hay," which was lost overboard when his commander and ship's namesake, a red-faced Captain Kerr, "was endeavouring to move it to another part of the boat" and lost his grip on the bale. Lieutenant Bremner of the *Kelly* had meticulously logged the dispersal of food from his barge, and was only too pleased to report, "I threw none of my cargo overboard." But Bremner was fortunate in his barge's not having to carry heavy hay and oats, and thus being the only craft to have lost no freight.

The matter of the lost supplies never did get resolved. Middleton was so glad to see 400 fresh troops with supplies that he cheerfully gave Boyd a full receipt, which his firm could present to the government for payment. Boyd slyly made no mention of undelivered supplies, and was paid in full for the tonnage as loaded. Only Laurie seemed to be perturbed by the discrepancy, but since Middleton had authorized Boyd's voucher, the base commander threw up his hands.

With the Swift Current base nearly devoid of supplies, General Laurie's days as an "admiral" would soon be numbered. But as a stickler for logistics, and a military manager supreme, he was never satisfied with the explanations given him about the stores and supplies abandoned by both the Saskatchewan Brigade and the steamers. Irked that military provisions he was responsible for were going to waste, his suspicions were piqued when word came across his desk of local settlers covertly helping themselves to government supplies left on the riverbank.

Officers were sent to follow any suspicious-looking wagonwheel tracks near the "breaks" where the landscape gives way to the river valley, but nothing was found. When another Boyd & Crowe freighter left Saskatchewan Landing bound for Prince Albert, Laurie asked the civilian crew to keep an eye out for suspected caches, and if found, to cart the goods north. Laurie never received satisfaction on the matter, but, to his credit, he cast aspersions only on the Boyd & Crowe firm and not on the hard working Fusiliers, whose Herculean effort had brought the Saskatchewan Brigade to Clarke's Crossing against nearly insurmountable odds. Their journey is rarely spoken of in histories of the rebellion, but the barge flotilla was at least as important to the campaign as any fighting unit.

Surrender scene

Four days had passed since the *Northcote* opened the ball at Batoche. Having been turned back at Mission Ridge, Middleton went into camp mentality. As he fussed about the right time to strike, he angered his officers and the soldiers became trigger-happy.

On May 13, Colonel Williams of the Midland had had enough of the commanding officer's dormancy, and led his own charge. This time, the raid was successful and Williams was hailed as a hero of the ground battle.

A sad Métis folk song evokes the aura of the demoralized, defeated and deceased that lay strewn about the battlefield of Batoche:

Last Saturday night young William Tate,
Enrolled his scouts he would not wait,
But galloping up though he was late
Between the Forks and Carleton.

Tom Hourie too was in the crowd:
We heard the General praise him loud,
And for the French we've made a shroud
Between the Forks and Carleton.

Now Hudson's son and Tomkinson
They wrote and told us how 'twas done,
How Middleton had made them run
Between the Forks and Carleton.[33]

The mythical "William Tate" was not the only latecomer to the smoking ruin of Batoche. The *Northcote* and the crippled *Marquis* made good time on the return trip and put in at Batoche at 8 p.m. the evening of May 13, with the occasional gunshot still peppering in from rebel stragglers. "Every place there was a building, shots were popping at us."[34] Sergeant Braithwaite asserted that the ships "arrived just in time for the last half hour of the fighting."[35] The veterans of the ferry cable battle found the village in a far different state. The townsite was in ruins and those Métis who had not been killed, wounded or driven away were under arrest.

Many were carrying the white flag of surrender. Women and children wandered about from their hiding places in caves by the river, in shock from the devastation of their village and the death about. Middleton savoured the victory while quietly seething at officers like Arthur Williams and van Straubenzie, who had organized the final charge against orders. While the staff assessed the effects, they turned their backs on atrocities committed by their charges.

As the *Northcote* docked, there was shock and amazement: "All in the camp here thought the *Northcote* was lost and many of its passengers killed."[36] But little time was lost in greetings or blessings about their return from the dead, as infantrymen seemed too busy looting. Unchecked troops, their chests inflamed by victory, scampered about in search of souvenirs, and their commanders did little to discourage them. George Ham, despite having shouldered a rifle against Batoche, saw the victory orgy as a bitter pill to swallow. He was disgusted by the "distressing picture … offered by these Half-breed families; cruelly plundered and stripped by the volunteers." The soldiers shamed their battle honour by stealing anything that was not nailed down and destroying anything that was. Horrified at their behaviour, Ham called them "raving maniacs" who even destroyed bedding and persisted in "leaving the residents in the most destitute conditions."[37]

The infantry cadets disembarked from the *Northcote* and mindlessly joined in on the raid. George Ham decided he had better things to do. Among the captured Métis was the ferryman Alexander Fisher, who, styling himself as the "rebel lieutenant governor," affixed an official flag of faith and surrender to his damaged scow: "a picture of our Saviour painted on paper which was sewed on the cloth."[38]

As Fisher was taken into custody, curiosity led Ham, George Kerr and Shelton Andrews to take the battle-scarred ferry for a ride to the west bank, and Ham pronounced himself "the first man over on the other side of the river."[39] For all anyone knew, the other side was still armed and hostile, but as the trio stepped off of Fisher's scow, they approached the camp as if approaching an overcautious house cat, where

a Half-breed was seen crouching behind a high shelved bank on the side of the ferry trail. We hailed him, but he refused to come out. One of us then spoke in French to him, and a half-scared man walked out. He was Francis Boucher, and after a cordial shake of the hand he said he came from the Mackenzie River. He had been dragged into the trouble.

"Where was Riel?"

"Don't know."

"Which way did he go?"

"Don't know. He was on the other side of the river."

"When did you see him last?"

"Yesterday (Tuesday). Then he went away."

Leaving the old man, we climbed the steep, winding ascent, viewing the admirably constructed rifle pits which command the river, pits in the brush, pits on the stony lower bank of the river, where the water almost leaves them; stones piled up in semi-circular form, behind which they could crouch and deal out death and destruction. To the right is a hill, filled with the inevitable pits, and on the top is a white flag, emblem of the surrender. Over the ferryman's house and store to the left flies another white flag, but in the bushes there still float two red flags of the redskins.[40]

Ham found the Métis on the west bank "anxious to surrender," and he was the first to hear how Riel had used the ferry early on the morning of the last day of the battle, and used superstition to keep the men on side. "If the sky grew dark they would be defeated,"[41] Riel foretold. In fact the skies that morning were clear, but just before the charge, a gray thunder cloud moved in which only bolstered the rebels' confidence and made them more defiant. Ham found Boucher's 18-year-old son, also named François, cowering in a cave in the riverbank. Young Boucher's case was heart-wrenching, as his young, crippled wife had lain ailing in the cavern while" the bullets' ping and the shrapnel's whizz almost deafened her."[42]

Boucher the younger, with a good handle on the English tongue, struck a quick rapport with the reporter. Both were non-combatants, albeit on opposite sides. Boucher had witnessed the assault on the *Northcote* and gave Ham a Métis insight into the fight:

> I was hiding in the bush, and I was pretty scared. I don't like this fighting.
> When the ship came down the river one man shot hard at it. When it stuck
> on the ferry rope our men thought everything was smashed and the police
> all killed (they call the troops police). One man said that he had seen twenty
> police fall over board dead, and Riel was certain the boat would be his when he
> wanted it. He thought it was stuck on a sand bar down the river and you were
> all dead on it. On Sunday night he sent some men down to loot it, but when
> they got there the boat was gone. They came back and the Indians said that the
> devil had lifted the big iron (the anchor) up and the boat had gone away.[43]

As the soldiers plundered like bloodthirsty bargain shoppers, a more respectful Ham strolled about the landscape on his way back to the ferry and came upon a small clearing in the bush. The artifacts inside the grove moved him beyond words. A piece of thin board from a packing crate was nailed to a tree—no great find, except for its elaborate decorations. The board was draped about with a white, thinly woven cloth, and tacked to the placard with tin tags was a chromatic lithograph of the Sacred Heart of Jesus. The reporter realized then he had come upon the shrine where Boucher's crippled and terror-stricken wife had "knelt and prayed to God in the very midst of the swirl of life and death."[44]

Perhaps it was the days-old memory of the people who had defended their village so valiantly, and the sight of those same defenders strewn about as corpses. Maybe it was the indignity of the Canadian soldiers' looting. But Ham realized he was in the presence of a place of worship—the sad little, rain-soaked icon symbolic of God and the tragedy of Batoche. He backed out of the sacred site and left the shrine alone. Meanwhile, atop the hill, the Midlanders were stealing the bell from the church of St. Antoine.

Ferrying the wounded

The toll of casualties was high. The Métis were devastated, as their comrades lay dead throughout the fields and the village where, a few short months ago, they had been simple farmers eking a living from the brown soil now stained with the blood of their friends, relatives and neighbours. "Batoche is described as presenting a desolate appearance. Houses torn asunder with shells, with white flags surmounting the dismantled roofs, meet the eye everywhere. The enemy have surrendered, up to Saturday, 150 guns."[45]

The *Northcote*'s clerk, Rennie Talbot, a man in the business of numbers, wrote that "the latest count makes the rebel loss 51, that number of bodies having been found. General Middleton's loss was eight or ten, with about 35 wounded." Concerned as he was with affairs aboard his boat, Talbot also mentioned, with some satisfaction, the minimal harm his crew and passengers had suffered: "Strange to say, no one was killed on the boat, and but three men, one of whom was the carpenter, wounded—none fatally."[46]

The rebel leadership had crumbled. The prophet Louis Riel was in hiding, somewhere in the woods of the coulees and ravines nearby, which were being scoured relentlessly by the scouts. Gabriel Dumont, the legendary hunter who had marshalled the attack on the *Northcote* and the defence of Batoche, was on the run, too. Knowing a rope or prison awaited him, and only if he could survive the vindictiveness of the soldiers, Dumont, along with fellow hunter Michael Dumas, made a desperate and successful run for the Montana border, never expecting to see the South Saskatchewan again. His destination achieved, Dumont was sought out by a reporter from the *Fort Benton River Press* and revealed his regretful tale "of the attempt to capture the steamer *Northcote*, and remarked that if the ferry cable had been lowered six inches further they would have made the capture, which would have insured them supplies and ammunition."[47]

The battle-scarred *Northcote*, at right, returns to Batoche shortly after the town's fall. Its pilot house is barricaded with two-inch planks, and its smokestacks have been cut off by the ferry cable. The *Marquis* is at left, its pilot house also reinforced. GLENBOW ARCHIVES NA 363-51

The victor paid a price, too. Eight soldiers were dead, including Captain John French, the commander of his own Scouts regiment. With heavy hearts, the troops ended their looting frenzy to prepare their slain comrades' remains the best they knew how. Lewis Ord wrote in an uncharacteristically sombre tone of his fellow Surveyor Alexander Kippen, pierced cleanly through the brain by a skilled Métis sniper the day before. "In the afternoon we paid our last poor marks of respect to Lieutenant Kippen, whose body, placed in a rough coffin, we followed down to the steamboat that had arrived the evening before. It was to be sent to his father's home in Perth (Ontario) for burial."[48] Private Robert Allan's 90th Winnipeg were similarly experienced, with carrying the corpse of Private James Fraser as "C Company fell in and marched down to the river with [Fraser's] body,"[49] his brother, Private H.H. Fraser, tramping sorrowfully alongside. Amateur soldiering was no longer a game.

Ham tried to ascertain the whereabouts of other victims of the rebellion on his own. On the abortive Saturday morning raid, he'd noted an apparent lynching, and was determined to investigate. "I asked several who the man was that they had hanged on the Saturday previous. They all denied any knowledge of it. Some said the Indians had put up some feathers in the trees as a decoy for the shots of the police, but I told them feathers did not wear coat and pants. Still they vehemently averred that no one was hanged there. A dozen men in the steamer are prepared to swear that they saw a man dangling in the air. It is strange if so many could have been mistaken."[50] Nothing was ever determined about the hanging, and those same dozen sailors never knew whether they saw a death sentence or a hallucination.

The remains of French, Kippen and Fraser were loaded for their first and last steamboat ride of the war, with William Fitch of the 10th Royal Grenadiers. There was nothing to be done for the fallen, and Dr. Thomas Roddick was more concerned with the living as he "received orders from the General to prepare for the Batoche wounded."[51] Forty-six troops were in need of attention in the hospitals at either Saskatoon or Swift Current. These were destinations that, by jouncing wagon, for a man with an infected bullet wound, might as well be in Ottawa.

The *Northcote* itself was a casualty as well, what with its severed smokestacks and bullet-riddled hull. Middleton would still require the steamboat fleet to assist the Field Force in the campaign against Poundmaker and Big Bear. With the *Northcote* in a shambles, John Segers had to rule against joining any more such festivities. The general counted the bullet holes and agreed.

So the flagship was reassigned as a hospital ship to carry the many wounded back to Saskatoon.[52] Cavalry Scout Harold Rusden helped load the wounded on board. "It was a stroke of great luck to have this comfortable transport for the wounded. They were carried on board on stretchers and put in a large airy saloon. There is absolutely no motion on these boats, as there is no sea and the engines work noiselessly and without any trembling." Rusden's optimism was tempered by the relative comparison to wagon transport: "Had they been sent over rough roads in wagons without springs a distance of some sixty miles, many of them would have died on the road."[53]

As the smoke from battle was still clearing, Surgeon Major James Bell left the occupation of the town to other heads and "as fast as possible the wounded men were transferred in waggons to the ferry [landing]"[54] for loading aboard. Sergeant

The wounded of the North West Rebellion, from an instruction manual for army medics.
LIBRARY & ARCHIVES CANADA C 86543

Braithwaite was asked to "[superintend] the placing of all wounded men on the steamer to go to the base hospital [at] Saskatoon."[55] Assistant Surgeon H.A. Wright and Dresser Fred White attended to the 37 wounded men on the short voyage upstream.[56] Besides the troops, Bell also administered medical attention to a few of the rebels, but was unable to save three badly shot-up Métis. Two of the Exovedate council, Ambrose Jobin and Norbert Delorme, were taken on ship to the hospital. As Roddick later stated, his doctors were "to carry out the instructions of Her Royal Highness, to render assistance to foes and friends indiscriminately."[57]

As the *Northcote* docked, Saskatoon was being deluged with a violent spring rainstorm. The medics deemed the weather too inclement to move patients into town, and all spent the night aboard until the storm abated. Despite the precautions, Private Alexander Watson of the 90th Winnipeg succumbed to his wounds and died during the night watch at dockside.

Medical arrangements were problematic, for even if wounded or ailing soldiers survived the steamboat voyage or the bumpy 30-mile ride overland, they still had to survive the hospitals. The "hospital complex" at Saskatoon consisted of the schoolhouse, three settlers' houses and an assembly of tents. Sergeant William Wrighton made the place seem downright exotic: "We were all sent on board the *Northcote* on the 13th and brought up to a place on the Banks of the River called Saskatoon."[58] He and his fellow Midlanders had been shipped into a town so new that mapmakers couldn't find it.

Saskatoon was only intended as a field unit for primary care; the steamboat fleet was supposed to carry ailing soldiers to facilities on the railway to convalesce before shipment home. Proximity to Batoche made the field unit the busiest, tending to 80 patients, including Métis and Sioux Indians. But Saskatoon's facilities were antiseptic

Sketch by Dr. E. King of the jury-rigged hospital at Saskatoon. The three buildings in the foreground were used as hospitals. The bell tents were used by dressers and for the nurses' mess. Cottages in centre were occupied by Drs. Roddick and Bell and by the quartermaster. The ferry and the steamboat landing can be seen on the waterfront. *CANADIAN PICTORIAL & ILLUSTRATED WAR NEWS, 1885 SOUVENIR EDITION*

and modern compared to the disaster that passed as the Swift Current medical centre. A town with a rail link was preferred for a base hospital.

One of Middleton's early plans had been to build a proper wooden-frame hospital in Swift Current for use by the military. Justification for the building relied on conveying wounded back to Saskatchewan Landing by river. But with the *Northcote*'s difficulties, the general abandoned plans for a new building, and instead the CPR brought in three railway cars to double as a hospital at Swift Current.

Somehow, priority for even these rickety, makeshift medical facilities was skewed by military planners. Doctor Michael Sullivan described the situation: "The hospital car [was being] used as a dormitory by dressers, orderlies and surgeons, while the caboose was used as a dwelling by the Commandant General Laurie and the Surgeon in Command of the Hospital Corps. On further examination I found that an old, dirty, dilapidated car, deeply embedded in the mud, was used as the hospital. It was close to the railway latrines, the odor from which it could not escape."[59] Sullivan soon had the base hospital transferred to better facilities at Moose Jaw.

At 3:30 p.m. on May 14, on one of the mercy runs back to Saskatoon, Segers whistled a greeting to his old boss John Davis as the *Baroness* approached Clarke's Crossing. The coal boat's crew and the Midlanders aboard finally received the news about Batoche, as it "passed *Northcote*" with wounded and dead for Saskatoon."[60] Davis's vessel was followed by Josephus Todd's *Alberta* on May 17, having taken on the crew of the dormant *Minnow*, which tied up at Saskatoon.[61] The *Alberta* and *Baroness* spent the next two days unloading their cargo at the Clarke's base, and on May 17, Major Martin Kirwan ordered both boats to Batoche. The Galt boats were joining the hunt.

Prison boat

Besides use as freighters, battleships or hospitals, the riverboats were also prison transport. An anonymous writer to a Toronto paper asserted that "most of the prisoners have been allowed to return to their homes, but the ringleaders will be taken to Prince Albert to be tried."[62] But the informant was himself misinformed, for the prisoners were in fact taken upriver to Saskatoon, for transshipment to the Regina NWMP barracks. It fell to Rennie Talbot, as chief clerk of the *Northcote*, to keep track of those who were to ride to Saskatoon in chains. "All day to-day they have been coming in and giving themselves up and we have now eighteen of the ringleaders on board in prison."[63]

George Ham noted the tragic but necessary scene as the defenders of Batoche left their homes to become prisoners of the state that Riel urged them to spurn: "As the prisoners were brought up in a waggon, preparatory to being transferred to the steamer, a heart rending scene ensued. Imagining that they were to be hanged or sent away for ever, wives rushed up and fondly embraced their husbands, and then held up the prattling babes for the fathers to take a farewell kiss. The little ones laughed and crowed as babies will, but their childish glee was in strange contrast to the tear-stained faces of the women, whose anguish could not be concealed. One touch of nature makes the whole world kin; and those signs of grief from helpless women caused many a battle-stained soldier to turn aside and wipe away a tear. The women were comforted as well as words could comfort, and assurances were given that their husbands would not be harmed unless they were leaders. With grief partly assuaged, the women turned to their tents, their faces hid in their handkerchiefs. Let us leave them with their sorrow. The fortunes of war are to them a dreadful burden."[64]

Trooper Rusden "saw the rebel prisoners. They were packed tight in a sort of half-hold and amidships with a guard of Mounted Police over them and a more horrid, execrable-looking lot I think I never beheld." No chances were taken with the prisoners, who were sneered at with disdain by their army captors, though some did express a guarded pity. "I never saw a nearer resemblance to the brute beast. Some of the most notorious were chained together, others had a ball and chain attached to their leg. It was very mean-spirited, but I could not help throwing them a grin of satisfaction, at which they looked anything but pleasant."[65]

One of the wounded, who was neither rebel nor soldier, proved to be the most cantankerous. Father Moulin had been hurt in the first attack on St. Antoine's rectory, and was slated to be put on a steamer back to Saskatoon. But Moulin refused to accept charity

The captured Louis Riel on an exercise break near Middleton's headquarters tent.
LIBRARY & ARCHIVES CANADA C 003450

Captain George Holmes Young.
BRENDA BURNS, SASKATCHEWAN ARCHIVES BOARD

from his attackers, no matter how well intentioned. He insisted on being taken to Prince Albert, where he would only accept the care of the mission nun at St. Anne's Convent.[66]

On May 15, Louis Riel was found by three scouts and escorted before Middleton. After passing him off as "Riel's cook," the scouts snuck him past the vindictive camp guards and straight into Middleton's tent. Mentally and physically drained from days of hiding, Riel entered Middleton's presence a pitiable, defeated man. Even the arrogant Middleton sympathized with this one-time prophet, the seer who could seemingly hold a nation spellbound reduced to the mien of a shivering, timid rabbit. The general could take little glory in having vanquished this non-warrior. Showing more regard than possibly he had shown for many fellow officers, Middleton began the legal procedures against the chilled Métis leader Louis Riel by offering his greatcoat.

When the *Northcote* returned to Batoche for more patients, it was also boarded by a man in chains. Louis Riel was bound over to be shipped to the NWMP barracks at Regina, to be held for trial. Not wanting to spare any more troops than absolutely needed, Middleton charged a corps of lightly wounded soldiers and Chaplain Charles Pitblado to accompany the prisoner to Saskatoon and thence to his eventual final destination.

Commanding the 16-man prison detail was George Holmes Young, a captain of the Winnipeg Field Battery. The irony was exquisite: 15 years earlier, at Red River, Riel had imprisoned Young's father, the Reverend George Young. In spite of their mutual history, Young Jr. and Riel bore little animosity toward each other. When Young revealed his identity, Riel inquired about the elder. "And how is your father, the fine old gentleman?"[67] George Kerr, the Batoche storekeeper turned steamer scout, stayed with the *Northcote* and went on to Saskatoon with the boat and prison detail. Roderick Smith gave up his cabin for the captive and recalled that "Riel was the most inoffensive prisoner I ever saw. He was very quiet on the trip down on the boat."[68]

The defeated Riel was a hard man to hate, Young had to admit. Just the same, there were those who were determined to get at the prisoner. Frenzied soldiers, even the wounded aboard the *Northcote*, boasted of plans to kill Riel. Gabriel Dumont was still on the loose and presumed to be plotting the rescue of his comrade. Captain Young was determined to deliver his man safe, and shackled the prisoner to his own ankle. If anyone wanted Riel's head, they were going to have to kill a Canadian officer to get it. Fortunately the voyage south proved peaceful.

At Clarke's Crossing the *Northcote* put in and "halted … for about an hour to despatch telegrams." Telegrapher Stuart Macdonald's curiosity about the infamous visitor was sated when Young permitted him aboard to meet the man whose actions had animated Macdonald's keying hand so much over the past weeks. Macdonald's experience was like that of many who met Riel, hardly the idea of the revolutionary stereotype. "Riel … who was dressed quietly, and … in manner and appearance was as unlike a desperado or rebel chief as was possible to imagine." The telegrapher also couldn't believe the carefree atmosphere on the *Northcote* where Riel's "captors were treating him courteously and he appeared to have the liberty of the boat, though no doubt he was being closely watched."[69]

As the *Northcote* whistled greetings to the 7th Fusiliers barge brigade, Sergeant Campbell aboard the *Nelles* reported meeting the ship, but didn't realize the infamous passenger the steamer was carrying: "She had [Riel] aboard but we didn't know it till we reached Clark's."[70]

Riel and Young had much to discuss, and Reverend Pitblado joined in, debating military strategy and religious theology. Riel admitted to Young that he and Dumont had planned to capture the *Northcote* and hold the occupants as hostages to guarantee the army's compliance and buy time until Riel could inflame the Indians into uprising. As the craft that was his one-time target floated him to a trial and appeals that would culminate in a date with the gallows, Riel explained his evolved religious theory to Pitblado. Of the eight points dictated, the final one was the most prophetic for a man whose memory still haunts Canada: "We believe in the final salvation of all men."[71]

On May 20, the *Northcote* brought its captive passenger to Saskatoon, where Riel spent the night in a home along the waterfront. A "Riel slept here" mythology still exists as to just where Riel stayed or whether he was taken off the boat at all. Shelton Andrews, who occupied the cabin next to Riel's on the journey, seems to set it all straight when he reassures that the rebel chief was "kept in a big frame building the night they landed in Saskatoon."[72] Still, as myths usually go, old-timers have claimed no fewer than three residences in which he supposedly spent the night.

The officers and Louis Riel were anxious to present themselves with some form of civility. Dr. Roddick was one of these and requested a visit with Riel aboard the *Northcote*, in the hopes the revolutionary might grant him an autograph. Despite his anger at the government, Riel was by nature a somewhat gentle man, and scrawled Roddick a kind and respectful salute: "Sir, A man may be very able in taking care of the sick; he may understand his cases very well; and his medicines may be well chosen; but above all that the blessing of God is needed; and without it, there is no true success. Yours, L. 'D' Riel."[73]

Original orders had been for the prison detail to sail south with Riel on the steamer to the Elbow and convey him to Moose Jaw by cart. Captain Young thought better of the plan, for the river was still unguarded territory. Fearing another ambush on the *Northcote*, Young had George Kerr commission teamster William Henry Trounce to take his prisoner and the security detail by wagon train. "Whilst we were at supper George Kerr came in off the steamer *Northcote* just arrived and I engaged [him] to team out to Moosejaw."[74] Four more injured soldiers were assigned to increase the guard detail on the wagon train. Still shackled to the prophet, Young accompanied Riel overland from Saskatoon to Moose Jaw, and stayed with him on the train to Regina, where he was put into the custody of NWMP Superintendent Richard Burton Deane.

His duty as a prison ship master complete, John Segers presented a packet of orders from Middleton to Surgeon Major Bell, placing "the steamer at my disposal, for the transport of convalescent to the 'Elbow,' whence they were to take the trail to Moosejaw."[75] Bell was delighted with the prospect of having such an ambulance, and immediately made plans to transfer 28 wounded men to the new base hospital. Such a conveyance would save lives and time. To take charge of the patients on the voyage south, Bell assigned the river-bound Campbell Douglas. The war-wounded *Northcote*, itself still convalescing, was highly regarded by the doctors as "being a large and commodious steamer, [and] was well adapted for purposes of transport. The men were made very comfortable in the spacious staterooms and saloon."[76]

In the Aftermath of Batoche

Forks of ths Saskatchewan

Sturgeon River

Cole's Falls

Manitoba wrecked April 9
Marquis revived April 23

Arrivals to Battleford
North West May 24
Baroness May 25
Marquis May 27

Prince Albert
North West revived May 13

HBC Ferry

Battleford Fort Carlton

Gardepuy's Crossing /Lepine's Ferry

N. Saskatchewan River

Telegraph Coulee

Batoche
Marquis & Northcote return to Batoche May 13

Alberta & Baroness arrive May 17

Fusiliers arrive May 19
Clarke's Crossing Supply Base

Saskatoon Hospital

Northcote brings 37 patients to Saskatoon, May 14 delivers Riel May 20

Northcote delivers patents for Moose Jaw, April 23
The Elbow

River *Fusiliers leave May 11*

Sask. Landing Supply Base

Moose Jaw Hospital Regina

GORD TOLTON

On May 21, the *Northcote* sailed upriver with its convalescent cargo, wounded soldiers that had been deemed fit enough to make the trip to "the Moose Hotel" as the new hospital was called. The water had risen from late spring snowmelt, making for better navigation. Not having to travel to Saskatchewan Landing was also a preferential arrangement. It not only cut down the distance, but also meant the *Northcote* would not have to make the treacherous swing around the Elbow of the South Saskatchewan.

A dock was constructed at the Elbow, from which wagons could transfer patients to Moose Jaw.

Campbell Douglas was impressed with the ride as "most satisfactory." Douglas's patients were "well accommodated in cabins, state-rooms or mattresses on the cabin floor for the night." Douglas went so far as to describe the ship as antiseptic: "There were facilities for dressing those cases that required it in the wash-room."[77] He did not have quite the same praise for the overland trail from Elbow to Moose Jaw, however, and advised that no serious cases be sent on the *Northcote*, due to the trying circumstances of the overland trail. But then, Douglas hated horses anyway.

On May 23, the *Northcote* landed at the Elbow without incident, dropped its passengers and returned downriver the next day. The old flagship redeemed itself by saving lives in an era not noted for the survival of war wounded. But as with the *Northcote*'s typical luck, nobody noticed its accomplishment. Middleton had new priorities and a whole new fleet of steamers to play with. The tatterdemalion *Northcote* was left to the rapids of history.

A change in tactics: on to Prince Albert and Battleford

Having sent north everything that could float and a few things that couldn't, Laurie made a quick trip to Winnipeg on May 16, where he hoped to arrange for more supplies and teams for Battleford. A new ferry had been established, a modern 16 × 40-foot cable scow, built by Swift Current businessman F. Fraser Tims, that promised to regulate and modernize the crucial river-crossing portion of the Battleford Trail. But with the bulk of the river freighting craft now past Saskatchewan Landing and employed in the north, John Laurie saw little use in maintaining Swift Current as supply base.

The possibility of rebellion in the Alberta district had not come about. Two more steamers were in service, and there seemed little point in trains and ships carrying supplies further west than needed. Consulting by wire with Colonel Otter and Joseph Wrigley, Laurie decided to move the base to Moose Jaw, with its new base hospital and well-established trail to the Elbow.

Another factor in favour of Moose Jaw was the increased risk of attacks on wagon trains and messengers on the Swift Current/Battleford Trail, as more than 170 miles were left unprotected. The fears were not mere paranoia. On May 11, marauders had captured 31 wagons near Battleford. Two days later, NWMP Constable Frank Elliott was gunned down in the same vicinity.

On May 14, Middleton said goodbye to the Sisters at St. Antoine's, and offered to take them to safety in Prince Albert on the steamers. They refused, wishing to stay and help the Métis women and priests bury their own dead in the nearby cemetery. As one sympathetic soldier said to another, "Leave those Sisters alone; they won't come with us. They are brave and will remain faithful to their flag and their guns to the end."[78]

Unstirred, the column marched to Gardepuy's Crossing, 14 miles downstream from Batoche. Part of the brigade also accompanied the large number of transport wagons filled with supplies for the starving town of Prince Albert. On May 16, it was decided to cross the column to the west bank at Lepine's Ferry, to access the Prince Albert trail. Maxime Lepine, a hunter turned ferryman, had "a broad face, high forehead and [was] a very determined looking man."[79] He was also a Batoche defender only recently captured.

Journalist George Ham described Lepine's incarceration and interrogation this way: "Two hours after the capture of Riel his lieutenant, Maxime Lepine, delivered himself up. He is a big burly man, dressed in the ordinary clothes worn by half-breeds. He pretended to be disgusted with the entire movement, on his appearance, Gen. Middleton asked but two questions: 'Were you in the fight at Batoche's?' and 'Were you one of Riel's councillors?' To both of these Lepine simply answered, 'Yes.' Your correspondent interviewed him, but he professed not to be able to speak English, although he could understand the language. He denied all knowledge of the whereabouts of Dumont, but when asked if he had any statement to make shook his head and replied in French that he did not understand what we were saying to him. He was placed in the guard room and at dusk taken on board the steamer."[80]

Robert Allan said that the reach was "not a regular crossing, so we shall use the boat *Marquis*."[81] Lepine's ferry had earlier been discovered to be missing, either hauled away or perhaps destroyed by Lepine himself, so the *Marquis* was brought up for the operation. Private Allan said that, late in the day, even the *Northcote* was "engaged in getting the troops across."[82] Using the steamers should have sped up the process, relative to using a ferry scow, but Trooper Rusden still yawned as he complained of the "long and tedious business crossing a large transport over a broad and swift current with very bad banks for embarking and debarking."[83] The world now moved too slowly for hearts quickened by war.

The clerk of the *Baroness* reported that Colonel Bedson ordered the *Baroness* brought up, and presumably the *Alberta* also ferried the column.[84] Among the labourers assisting were some of the rebels turned prisoners. "Alexander Fisher … and Albert Monkman … were highly useful today as roustabouts, and carried goods from the boat to shore for hours."[85] Fisher the ferryman and Monkman the Riel councillor packed, toted and organized the ferrying as though nothing had happened. The military were finding the rank and file Métis were also hard to dislike, probably leading some to wonder why they had tried to kill each other a few days past. Such is the paradox of war.

The ferrying near complete, George Ham breathed the morning air, observed the fresh-faced troops buoyed by victory and the fine spring day, and fetched his pencil and pad to describe the routine scene with a lyrical lilt. "As I write, the last load of the baggage train is being ferried across the river, and in a few minutes the troops will be on their way to Prince Albert. The sun is shining brightly, the sky is unclouded, the birds are singing blithely, and the boys step out with firmer tread and lighter hearts than they have displayed for many a day."[86]

Middleton had one more bit of business to clean up back at Batoche. Riel had seen the ferry at the town as instrumental in the conduct of his war with the government, and had gone so far as to invoke his God to bless the rivercraft: "Guard for us our cable, O mother of the Son of God. O grant that our arms may annihilate the enemy at one blow, crushing them everywhere. We apply to you! The Church prays to you for it! Intercede for us! Save our ferry from every adverse thing."[87] Now, even with Batoche captured and Riel in chains, the general had communication that "Grant Vautour Indians were advancing from Battleford and … had to be stopped from crossing the river."[88] A detail was sent back with axes and bars to effect the destruction of Alex Fisher's ferry. "The cable has gone to the bottom of the river, the large post on which it strung is chopped down and there will be no destruction to passing steamboats at Batoche's again for some time to come."[89] One scow, possibly Lepine's displaced craft, had already been destroyed by cannon fire.

The building used as quartermaster's stores at Clarke's Crossing. "AN ACCOUNT OF THE ADVANCES OF THE 7TH FUSILIERS OF LONDON," U. OF SASKATCHEWAN LIBRARY SPECIAL COLLECTIONS MSS 49 #17

The sinking of the scow at Batoche put an end to the Carlton Trail, as Clarke's Crossing now became the main crossing for the region. Even the supply of flour was loaded aboard steamboats and taken away to Prince Albert. The town's importance in the North West began to wane. It struggled on as a farming centre, but by the early 1900s Batoche had been completely eclipsed by nearby railway towns such as Duck Lake, Rosthern and Wakaw.

The back of the rebellion broken, the government felt the effect of the war on its budget. It decreed that the number of intermediate posts be reduced, and that the supply at Clarke's Crossing be used to support both Middleton and Otter. Supplies destined for Battleford could be shipped by wagon the 30 miles to Telegraph Coulee on the North Saskatchewan. A relatively safe and previously underutilized trail also existed between Moose Jaw and Clarke's, via Saskatoon. So with the stroke of an executive pen on May 23,[90] boomtown Swift Current settled back into being a sleepy prairie village, and Saskatchewan Landing, the prairie port, was reduced to a mere ferry crossing.

As John Laurie wrapped up affairs at Swift Current and Saskatchewan Landing, he realized that some 500 tons of surplus stores sat by the river with no means of transport available. Knowing the resurrected *Northcote* would be returning upriver with wounded troops, he tried to arrange for the steamer to move the stockpile to Clarke's Crossing in two trips.[91]

At Clarke's, the 7th Fusiliers set up camp in a grove of poplars and soothed their sore muscles as they unloaded their dozen barges. The Fusiliers and the two Midland companies were to guard the supply base and await orders while their fellow soldiers sailed on. The normal ferry scow at Clarke's was missing, so the Saskatchewan Brigade barges were employed as temporary measures to transport goods back and forth as required. "Oats or supplies for Battleford had to be unloaded and taken by boat across the river."[92] With no cable, the ferrying was "no easy job as the current was very swift with no means of control but the clumsy sweeps."[93]

Alexander Campbell had a curious comment as to the loss of the regular ferry at Clarke's Crossing: "Here a Ferry was maintained until it was appropriated by the rebels for their use further down the river."[94] This was not the case, and Campbell was misinformed. In fact, the ferry had been appropriated by Middleton himself and poled downriver, where it was used during the Fish Creek scrap. The Métis had their own ferries. So it goes with wartime communication.

On May 18, the *Baroness* and the *Alberta* were ordered to the Hudson's Bay ferry, where the Midland troops joined the land-bound column, leaving the steamers to make the roundabout trip to the Forks and up the North Branch. The steamboat fleet—the *Baroness*, the *Alberta* and the *Marquis*—were ordered to assemble and join the *North West* at Prince Albert. Captain Davis was aware of Cole's Falls, the ship-breaking swifts between the Forks and Prince Albert. The *Baroness*'s clerk "sent [a] message to Mr. Markley, Pr. A., asking for help at the Forks to take steamer up Cole's Falls."[95] Arthur W.R. Markley was a Prince Albert storekeeper and insurance agent, a volunteer constable grazed at Duck Lake, who may have had something to do with either the HBC or the steamer *North West*, for the boat was tied up at town and may have been dispatched to assist the *Baroness*.

Intending to take command from Otter and Strange in their particular situations, Middleton's brigade marched into Prince Albert on May 19. Police Commissioner Acheson Irvine was on hand to greet the general, who received Irvine cordially in spite of his secret contempt for the police. Some of the resentment carried down into the rank and file, as Mounties found themselves defending the force's honour from some loose-lipped soldier.

The army set up camp on the river plateau. The scene described by Constable John Donkin was placid: "the broad river looked lovely in the evening light; the green islands with their rich foliage mirrored in its still bosom," while the camp was almost carnival-like: "What a luxury it was to us poor exiles to hear the bands discoursing the latest tunes at night … A small bear was tied in front of the General's tent. At the first signal of the drum this shaggy little ball of cinnamon-hued fur would dance wildly until the last note."[96] With spring greenery, band concerts, a dancing bear and socializing, an outsider could be forgiven for not believing this was a region under siege.

The North Saskatchewan River waterfront of Prince Albert. *CANADIAN PICTORIAL & ILLUSTRATED WAR NEWS, 1885 SOUVENIR EDITION*

The bulk of the brigade cooled their heels, feasting on the meats, jams and biscuits that town merchants such as the HBC foisted on them, at a healthy profit of course. While in Prince Albert, George Ham felt sanguine enough about the campaign to discuss the end of the rebellion and reveal mobilization plans he could only have gotten from Middleton—the plan of sending the *North West*, the *Alberta*, the *Marquis* and the *Baroness* to Grand Rapids, crossing Lake Winnipeg and taking the CPR and the Great Lakes home. He told his paper that "Toronto should get ready to welcome its gallant volunteers—if not all, at least a large proportion of them. When it does, your citizens will not see band-box soldiers, spick and span, but travel stained and bronzed veterans, with toggery the worse of wear."[97] But Ham was being a bit premature. Poundmaker had not surrendered and Strange's column wasn't even in communication. Perhaps Ham thought no news to be good news and had the impression the campaign was over. But full demobilization was still a month and half away.

With Prince Albert under control, Middleton prepared to depart for the troubled town of Battleford. For once, the fleet was ready, and May 21 was spent loading the boats with oats and beef. On the morning of May 22, with all the pomposity of a Gilbert & Sullivan officer, Middleton loaded his aides, Captain "Gat" Howard, the Midland Battalion and his half of A Battery onto the *North West* and steamed up the North Saskatchewan. Constable Donkin watched the scene from the shore as he and his besmirched fellow Mounties fiercely bit their stiff upper lips. "The craft were crowded, and gay with flags. Horses and guns occupied the lower decks, among which the Swampy Indians, who formed the crew, ran and climbed, and scrambled with the agility of monkeys. The balconies running around the many windowed saloons on board were filled with officers, in service forage caps and patrol jackets."[98]

Middleton, the "very model of a modern Major General," took the salute with the air of a retired officer on safari, "distinguished by a white helmet, with a grey tweed shooting suit on his portly form, and long boots and spurs."[99] Donkin related that "there was some delay in getting away from the moorings," as he documented an odd serenade provided by bandsmen and soldiers for the Prince Albert citizenry as they prepared for departure. "The strains of the *Girl I Left Behind Me* came from the band stationed on the poops. This was varied by the men singing *Sailing* in chorus. Then came a shriek from the whistles, the paddles splashed, and the expedition steamed away gaily to the stirring tune beloved of soldiers, and were soon lost to view among the lovely islands."[100]

Middleton had a few guests on board as well, including Charles Henty, a journalist of the *London Standard*, who had travelled across the seas and the North American continent to document this particular war of Empire. Henty went on to become a noted author of juvenile adventure novels, and this particular adventure was certainly novel. There was Assistant Indian Commissioner Hayter Reed, a Territorial bureaucrat with agendas and schemes of his own. Not aboard were any of Irvine's 175 Mounties, which was a shock to rank and file policeman John Donkin. "We volunteered en masse to accompany the General on his departure up the river, but our services were declined."[101] If there was going to be battle, Middleton made it plain the NWMP would have no part of it, a diplomatic snub illustrating his disapproval of the police.

Middleton took the unprecedented step of boarding his cavalry, Boulton's Scouts, horses and all. Subordinates scratched their heads in wonder at such a move. Was he, as surveyor Lewis Ord thought, going to use the mounts to "haul the vessel up the river by horse power if she stuck fast or if her machinery gave out"?[102] A possibility, for Middleton would not have had much patience for the warping process. No one could know for sure, though, for the general had not the tact to allow subordinates to know his mind. All Bowen van Straubenzie knew was that he had "orders to follow with remainder of force on steamers *Marquis*, *Baroness* & *Alberta* when they arrive."[103]

As for the *Marquis*, Captain Dougall had a problem trying to climb Cole's Rapids, for he'd hit a rock in the stream and gashed a hole in his hull. Eventually Dougall limped to Prince Albert, and on May 22, "Old Straw" loaded the 10th Grenadiers and the 90th Winnipeg aboard the *Marquis* and *Alberta* respectively, to follow his commander. With the delay for repairs, the remainder of the cavalry and the transport wagons took to the trail to supply Fort Carlton and march onward to Battleford on the shorter north-side trail. In preparation for the column's crossing, Irvine, still stinging, took a detail of 30 Mounties to Carlton, to reestablish and protect the ferry. Teamsters and soldiers were much relieved when the *Marquis* caught up at Carlton, and some troops "were relieved of the tedious march across the prairie."[104]

The *Baroness* did not reach Prince Albert until May 23, having had to be hauled across Cole's Falls by horsepower. When Davis's vessel did arrive at dockside, it "took on 38 tons supplies for troops, and 5 horses."[105] Davis also took on reporter William Laurie of Battleford's *Saskatchewan Herald*. Other passengers included the convalescent Major G.D. Dawson of the 10th Grenadiers, wounded at Batoche, and Jimmy Atkinson, a local courier. The next day, the *Baroness* took on more Winnipeg troops and arrived at Fort Carlton. Will Laurie delighted in the Winnipeggers' "who ... glory in the sobriquet of "The Little Black Devils."[106]

On the *Alberta*, Josephus Todd also had his problems getting to Fort Carlton. Carrying two companies of the 90th Winnipeg Rifles and towing two loaded scows, Todd had been the first out of port at Prince Albert. Soon they were passed by the bargeless *Baroness*, its crew eager to make up lost time. As the fleet passed the Sturgeon River, the passengers saw the carcass of the *Manitoba*, "sunken in a bay and a complete wreck."[107] But five miles before reaching Carlton, the *Alberta* nearly followed the *Manitoba* to the riverine equivalent of Davy Jones' locker. Todd snagged a submerged tree that gashed out "a hole three feet long and one foot wide."[108] Deckhands and soldiers alike rushed to the breach, buckets in hand, to bail river water from the hold. A carpenter soon found enough usable timber to patch up the gash. After nearly three hours, Todd had the boat underway, his crew having prevented the *Alberta* from becoming yet another casualty of Saskatchewan mud.

Sunday, May 24, the birthday of Queen Victoria, was celebrated by troops throughout the prairie theatre in the usual way "with games and races."[109] Aboard the *North West*, the strains of "God Save the Queen" rang through the valley of the North Branch as Middleton's officers performed an abbreviated church parade, a modest but sincere ceremony given the close quarters and the growing wear and tear on uniforms. "But in honour of her majesty the men tidy up a bit; officers, whose uniforms are travel stained and begrimed with powder, don their other clothes, the General setting the example." Even the lone Yank observed British tradition: "Capt. Howard appears in all the pomp and lustre that the regulation blue and gold of the Connecticut State Guard, with red plumed helmet, can shed."[110]

One such celebrant was James Austin, a private from H Company of the Midland Battalion whose bout with malaria prevented his boarding a Saskatchewan Brigade barge with his unit. Austin could have sat out the rebellion in Moose Jaw and returned home in comfort, but he was a God-fearing young infantryman destined to become a Presbyterian minister, and was made of sterner stuff. Anxious to rejoin his unit, Austin learned of a freight team leaving Moose Jaw to rendezvous with the *Northcote*, and broke the Sabbath to board the wagons bound for the supply base at the Elbow. Austin's memoirs would illustrate the new supply route, though unknown to him at the time, the intentions for use of the *Northcote* were sabotaged by the actions of Middleton. Austin recalled:

"Leaving Moose Jaw on Sunday we arrived at the Elbow on the Wednesday following [May 27] about 1:00 p.m., and here we pitched a tent and encamped to await the arrival of the steamboat *Northcote* … The teamsters unloaded their freight, and left it on the beach ready to be transferred to the steamboat, and departed on their homeward journey. Expecting to encamp at the Elbow for some indefinite time we took matters easily from the time of our arrival until after nine o'clock the next morning. While at breakfast we were surprised to learn that the teamsters had returned for their loads, and were to convey them overland to Clarke's Crossing for the *Northcote* was not coming to the Elbow."[111]

Communications were inadequate, and Austin's brigade could not know the *Northcote* had come and gone, and that the boat was no longer available for military service.

On May 26, a day before Austin's arrival at the Elbow, the *Northcote* returned to the south, bringing 29 wounded soldiers from Saskatoon. The grand old workhorse put in at the Elbow and off-loaded the invalided passengers for transport to Moose Jaw. But any plan Laurie may have had for a return freighting trip was thwarted by his commanding officer. On May 27, Middleton released the *Northcote* from military duty, returning it to civilian duty. Though it would do some freighting to Edmonton, most of the further military impressment on the river was left to the *Northcote*'s sister ships and the Galt steamers.

But no other rivercraft had seen the kind of excitement the HBC flagship had seen. The *Northcote*, its crew, the military collaborators, and even a wordy journalist had lived a great escapade aboard its decks. Never again would a vessel on the Saskatchewan River system know such adventure. Segers and crew spent their time repairing the battle damage, and company directors were glad to have them do so, especially since the government had agreed to pay for the restoration.

Middleton put the *Northcote*'s sister steamers into further war service for troop transport. Fully supplied at the front, the general instructed Laurie to send no further stores to Clarke's Crossing, and that any new casualties would be sent to Winnipeg via the Grand Rapids route when ships could be spared from war service. But Laurie still had his backlog of goods rotting at Saskatchewan Landing, and with no steamer available, he had to arrange a private contractor to forward the stores to Battleford. Food and forage would be welcome there in the anticipated campaign against Poundmaker.

To facilitate the overland, ferry and steamer supply system, the leftover brigade at Prince Albert was ordered to secure the ravaged Fort Carlton as a crossing and supply depot. The first to the scene was Shelton Andrews, who used his ferry expertise to reestablish the shuttle there as he had at Clarke's Crossing. After a terse conversation with some suspected rebels at Carlton, Andrews found the ferry "cut to pieces with ice"[112] as the Métis party rowed away in the only boat left. The ferry had to be completely rebuilt from scratch. To make matters worse, the cable Andrews' teams brought along to establish such a ferry was too short for the vast reach at Carlton.

Soon the police sentries arrived to ferry 170 teams and wagons across the North Saskatchewan and open a new trail to Battleford. With the ferry useless, Andrews waved down the first steamer, the *Alberta*, on May 25 to get the 10th Royal Grenadiers and their artillery across.

The layover would give the ship's carpenters a chance to do further repairs on the tree-damaged hull. With little to do, the 90th Winnipeg Riflemen wandered the ruins of the fort, and Private Robert Allan tried to catch some afternoon sleep in the engine room of the *Alberta*. Allan's slumber was rudely broken, though, when "I was roused at 3 and told to go on the *Baroness*,"[113] to relieve the *Alberta* of its cargo of troops before carrying on to Battleford.

The *Alberta* stayed behind to ferry the Mounties and cavalry across the river to patrol the north trail to Battleford. Rumours abounded about possible snipers from Poundmaker's band attacking the steamboats near the Eagle Hills. As some troops remained wired and wary on deck, a skeptical Private Allan was only worried about how to continue his siesta. He was not impressed with the new bunking arrangements on Captain Davis's crowded ship. "Will have to sleep in the hold. The place is crowded; there is water at the bottom and the air is foul."[114]

Allan was probably the only one who had it right. Not only was there no danger from Poundmaker, but in fact riders had come from the Cree/Stoney chief's camp with an important but polite message for the white war chief: "I send some of my men to you to learn the truth and terms of peace, and hope you will deal kindly with them. I and my people wish you to send us the terms of peace in writing, so that we may be under no misunderstanding, from which so much trouble arises."[115] Poundmaker, Pîhtokahânapiwiýin, had been the victim of enough rumours and propaganda; he was demanding the truth. Middleton replied, bluntly, in a letter written in his stateroom on the *North West*: "I have men enough to destroy you and your people or at least to drive you away to starve, and will do so unless you bring in the teams you took, and yourself and your councillors to meet me with your arms at Battleford on Tuesday, the 26th."[116]

Once past Fort Carlton, the river grew desolate again, and even George Ham, travelling on the *North West*, became overwhelmed by the landscape. Just a little bored, Ham let his pencil become lyrical again:

After Carlton is left not a solitary house on either bank is seen, not even an Indian tepee, not a vestige of life, except a few wild fowl, not a sign of civilization. We realize at last, to the full, that this is the Great Lone Land. All is eternal silence, broken only by the puffing and wheezing of the steamer. The steep heavily timbered banks, on which the dark emerald of the fir contrasts prettily with the lighter green tint of the poplar, become the barriers of a bare open rolling prairie, boundless as space itself; whose extent to the vision is only limited by the horizon. Again the timber appears on the banks, poplar only, small-sized, with budding leaves. The river is still torturous, the islands more numerous, the sand-bars more annoying. And so we creep on.[117]

Then, as if to answer Ham's placid thoughts or his boredom, nature proceeded to give him a show of weather to make his pencil dance even more stylishly:

A blinding rain storm sets in early in the morning, and skies only clear long enough to permit divine service being held in the sunshine; then the clouds gather again, and it seems as if Jupiter Pluvius had turned on the water and forgotten the combination. Later, a strong headwind, retarding our progress to about two miles an hour, drives away the clouds, the sun shines brightly again, and we go on poking our way cautiously past another sandbar and shoal.[118]

Affected by the steamers' war service, the Sisters of the Faithful Companions of Jesus, who had endured the battle and the horrors of Batoche, returned unscathed to their St. Laurent Mission. The nuns' superiors resolved to move the mission to Calgary, and on May 27 the Sisters were ordered "to take the first steamboat passing in front of our door on the South Saskatchewan and in this manner proceed to Medicine Hat from whence the railway would convey us to Calgary."[119] The nuns packed, but no boat came; all vessels were occupied in war work. The general's work took precedence over God's, an irony Middleton would have loved.

The fleet carried on to Battleford, and the *Baroness's* clerk was happy to report the run was uneventful. Roosters and watchmen had little to do but admire the scenery. "Water very smooth. Made good run."[120] But the purser failed to note the little river gift that Lieutenant Colonel Otter had dispatched to him. A trio of canoe-paddling Métis, led by a former Indian agent, Sam Ballendine, pulled alongside the steamer and presented an envelope. It contained the news Middleton wanted, news that would save him having to open another front: Poundmaker was coming in to lay down his arms.

Middleton aboard the *North West* landed on May 24, and on May 26 the *Baroness* "arr'd Battleford at 1 p.m. Troops disembarked. Telegraphed Galt arrival of steamer."[121] Private Allan lost yet more sleep while aboard. "Put in a bad night, being sick. Would not spend another like it for a good deal." On May 27, the *Marquis* brought up the rear. Troops at Battleford were surprised to find no one waiting for them at the gangplank. After all, this was supposed to be the staging point for the next punitive expedition against Poundmaker. But they knew not what Middleton and the Battleford folks knew, that war plans were on hold.

On May 26, a band of Cree rode in from the west to the police post of Fort Battleford. At the head of the band was the chief who had undeservedly gained the enmity of a nation. A ceremony was soon held culminating in the surrender of Poundmaker to General Middleton at Battleford. Another huge cog was removed from the gears of the rebellion. Part of the ceremony was the surrender of arms, as Poundmaker and company carried their weapons down to the river. Whether to get the guns away from Battleford where they could be recaptured, or to have them taken home as souvenirs, Middleton ordered the arms piled on the bow of the *North West* until "they made a great pile of junk—the old flintlocks red with rust and about six feet long."[122] Crewman Archie Ballantine was unimpressed with the captured arsenal cluttering up his decks: "Very few of the guns were of any value."[123]

On June 1, Private Austin arrived with a freight team to Clarke's Crossing, finally reunited with his battalion, one of the few of his unit that had not yet set foot on boat

Sketch of the militia using the Clarke's Crossing ferry by Captain H. de H. Haig. *ILLUSTRATED LONDON NEWS*

or barge. Those compatriots, the "men of G and H Companies had been acting as a transport force [the Saskatchewan Brigade] on the South Saskatchewan River with the 'navies' of the 7th Fusiliers"[124] and were on guard awaiting further orders.

The passage of May into June brought characteristically hot weather to the prairies, a signal that soon the river would swell with Rocky Mountain meltwater, and that brought a new challenge to the base at Clarke's Crossing. Telegrapher Stuart Macdonald was the first to hear the news of an advance flood from the operator at Swift Current. Concerned about the cache of provisions "within a few feet of the water on a flat shore," he took immediate action. "Knowing from experience how rapidly the river rose in those June floods, I hunted up the officer in charge and advised him to the conditions." The military mindset took charge again as the officer, probably Lieutenant Colonel Deacon, rebuked the telegrapher's warning, and "that he was quite capable of doing his duty without outside advice."[125]

Within 36 hours, the officer learned the folly of angering the river and ignoring local counsel. When the river began to rise, that same officer ordered "a great scurrying to secure men from the Midlands regiment across the river to salvage the supplies."[126] One of the Fusiliers' scows was put into action and weighed down with supplies and the men attempted to pole it over to higher ground on the other side. "But before reaching the further bank it sank, the men having a narrow escape for their lives, while the contents of the barge went to the bottom of the stream."[127] Soldiers scrambled furiously to get the goods off the sandy flood plain, but the river proved dominant. "Hundreds of cases, undermined by the water, toppled into the river and were carried away by the current."[128] Stuart Macdonald cryptically presented a scheme to some prospective river archaeologist. "At some future day, dredges deepening the river may come upon deposits of canned corned beef. So far as I know, the matter was never made a subject of investigation."[129]

The salvage and transfer of the provisions "across the river to the west bank" were coincidental with a change in tactics as the militia moved on to Battleford and Fort Pitt. "In the stores conveyed across the prairie were canned goods and clothing for the men … as well as for others further to the front."[130] James Austin's tale illustrates the two-day freighting operation, moving supplies between the North and South Branches across the neck of dryland between, saving the steamer fleet the circuitous trip around the two rivers' junction and avoiding further needless passage across Cole's Rapids.

The abandonment of Clarke's Crossing meant the 7th Fusiliers and the two Midland companies had to say goodbye to the love/hate relationship with the 12 scows they'd shipped north on. The last duty of the barges was to remove the bulk of the supplies and the troops to the west side of Clarke's. Little was ever said of what became of the dozen barges. One saw further service, but likely the rest were salvaged for lumber by local settlers. Private Austin described the 30-mile overland journey to the new base at Telegraph Coulee:

> On June 5 when reveille was sounded … tents were struck and we were
> on the march toward the North Saskatchewan River … we journeyed on our
> way, sometimes riding sometimes walking, according to the disposition of
> the teamsters. It rained all day, and we were not sorry to encamp about 5:00
> p.m., change our wet clothes and get between the blankets. After breakfast
> (7:00 a.m.) the next day we started afresh on our journey and at 2:00 p.m.
> we arrived at Telegraph Coulee.[131]

Alexander Campbell said it all: "Telegraph Coulee was only a name,"[132] an artificial construct on the map near the Elbow of the North Saskatchewan where a relay office linked the West's communication network. The Fusiliers unloaded their supplies and set up a base supply camp to facilitate the steamer fleet on the North Saskatchewan. "The location selected for the camp was a very desirable one, being high and dry, and not bad to look at."[133] But camping would be the extent of their involvement in the rest of their campaign. The efforts of the 7th Fusiliers were forgotten, and the Fusiliers were forced to watch as the Midlanders were shipped off to be reunited with their unit. Slowly all the scattered pieces of the command were coming together, assembling to converge on Big Bear, and by water they would go.

CHAPTER ELEVEN

The Chase

Boggy brigades and bored battalions

As Tom Strange entered the Fort Pitt country he had little reliable intelligence regarding a canny quarry. Knowing his colleague Colonel Otter was garrisoned downriver at Battleford, he chose two messengers to carry his request "acquainting him with the situation, so that, if necessary, a junction could be effected between his force and ours for the hemming in of the Indians and the disposal of the whole question."[1]

Strange's couriers were ex-Mountie Sergeant George B. Borradaile and Trooper William Scott, cavalrymen assigned to Steele's Scouts. But Borradaile and Scott would not carry the message by pony express; these particular post-men were to travel by river. Needless to say, the task was daunting, "an undertaking requiring both courage and resource, to go down by the river through the enemy's country."[2]

Armed with revolvers, Borradaile and Scott threw a clumsy old hulk of a canoe into the North Saskatchewan. The column was not yet at Fort Pitt, so the area was still questionable territory. As they neared the fort landing, the Scouts pulled ashore and hid until nightfall. After dark they launched again, using the inky blackness to slip quietly past Pitt, "which the Indians were even then setting on fire,"[3] according to a dramatic R.G. MacBeth. To make matters even worse on the nerves, Borradaile lost his revolver when the cowboy sailors

George B. Borradaile, Steele's Scout and river scout. GLENBOW ARCHIVES NA 2514-1

dunked themselves in the river. Landing at Battleford with the dispatch for Otter, they were surprised to see the great steamer *North West* in port, where their messages were delivered directly to the headquarters of General Middleton.

Without fanfare, Borradaile and Scott turned over the packets and were subsequently ordered to take two horses and return to their command posthaste. When Borradaile asked for a new revolver to replace the one he'd lost, Middleton snuffed and returned a brusque rebuke, stating "that he himself would go through that country with a stick,"[4] never mind a gun. The words were condescending, in a jealous tone intended for his rival Strange. As a further insult, incredibly, someone ordered Borradaile to carry a note pinned to his hat, a cryptic slap in the face bearing the words "I was not at Fish Creek—I was not at Batoche."[5] Middleton had allowed the unthinkable: he used subordinates to accuse a brother officer of shirking duty.

In the absence of Borradaile and Scott, Strange sent out three scouting parties on various trails. Two of these, Sam Steele's cavalry and a group of Métis scouts, reported back in due time, but the third, Mounties under Inspector A. Bowen Perry, took on an unauthorized reconnaissance of the entire trail between Fort Pitt and Battleford in an attempt to prevent any possible union between the forces of Poundmaker and Big Bear. All were oblivious that Poundmaker was on the verge of surrender. But to Strange, Perry seemed to have dropped off the face of the earth "without sending me any information and I neither saw nor heard anything of him for nine days."[6]

Unknown to Strange, Perry claimed to have found a trail leading south and east, and "took it upon himself" to ride all the way to Battleford. The ride was a frenetic one, and by the time Perry's group reached Battleford, they had covered 90 miles of hilly bush country in 36 hours.

Upon the return of Steele, an altercation with a party of Cree scouts was reported which had resulted in the fatal shooting of a chief wearing a huge Treaty medal. It was Mamonhook, who had led an outbreak at Saddle Lake.

But Steele also reported sighting 187 lodges, a large gathering that had to be their quarry. Strange sounded the alert and ordered a march to the lodges. Expecting battle, the column would travel light, leaving a detachment of Mount Royals behind to guard the camp at Fort Pitt. With what remained of the cavalry, and the Winnipeg Infantry riding in wagons, the force crossed the North Saskatchewan on the *Clover Bar*, hauling the police nine-pounder cannon from Fort Macleod. In the absence of Perry, whose men were the gun crew, Strange had one solution: bring the boats, which had yet to be unloaded. In the command of Lieutenant Colonel George Hughes, the 65th Mount Royal Rifles embarked "down the river in the boats, with orders to effect junction with me when within striking distance of the enemy."[7] Hughes was to "drift with the current with the speed of a marching column."[8] Orders were to disembark and follow the noise of any gunfire.

Coordinating the approaches by river and land was difficult, as the boats moved only as fast or as slow as the river. The best attempt was made, with the sweeps used only to avoid the sandbars. A few miles out of Pitt, the Alberta Force found their objective: Frenchman's Butte. This huge knoll, named for an anonymous trader slain there in the ancient past, rises out of the plain, and on the night of May 27, mounted warriors were spotted upon its bare ridge. Strange ordered his son, Harry, to bring up the nine-pounder, and some well-placed shells forced the warriors off the hill and into the thick brush on a ridge to the north.

With no word from Strange, Hughes's flotilla put in to shore to prepare dinner. But even as the boats were docking, "cooks were preparing the noon meal, when sharp ears heard the first sounds of Gen. Strange's attack. Everyone ceased all movement and listened. Rifle shots were to the left, from the north, and a deeper, muffled sound gave evidence that the nine pound cannon, brought from such a distance, was also in action."[9] The hollow boom of Harry Strange's artillery triggered the replacement of hunger pangs with blood lust. The riflemen grabbed their weapons and "advanced with alacrity on the first sound of the firing."[10]

Hughes barked orders to disembark and form up for advance. "Muscular arms manned the oars and in an instant the boats were nearing shore."[11] Few waited for the boats to near shore. "As soon as the oars touched gravel, a dozen men jumped from the boats into water, mud and reeds in order to tie up the boats."[12] In the rush, all attention was given to the coming battle. Greatcoats, luggage, provisions, even the fresh soup was left behind in the boats, in favour of rifles and heavy ammunition boxes. The Mount Royals would come to regret abandoning their supplies this way.

Quickly, to the sound of "Battalion, attention!" the riflemen fell in as their company commanders elaborated the skirmishing orders. But before departure, the Mount Royals kneeled for a brief but necessary ceremony. "Known for his happy heart, the French Canadian loves and venerates his religion"[13] and the mostly Catholic men of the 65th were no exception. Thus, on the banks of the North Saskatchewan, those who would soon be embroiled in battle solemnly bowed their heads as their brigade chaplain offered benediction and absolution. Their worship attended to, the infantrymen gathered up their weapons and charged up the riverbank.

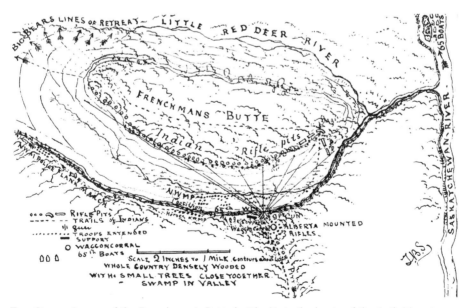

Tom Strange's map of the Frenchman's Butte battle. Note the boats of the 65th Mount Royals on the North Saskatchewan, at right. *GUNNER JINGO'S JUBILEE*

A little over a mile away was the riflemen's destination: another ridge, Red Deer Butte, not as high as Frenchman's but broader and more heavily wooded. At the bottom of the hill lay the Little Red Deer River, a marshy tributary draining into the North Saskatchewan. The sleepy Little Red Deer opened into a swampy expanse, providing the ridge with a protective moat, and offered a wide view of the woods and the low ground to the south. Here was the camp of Big Bear, a natural fortress where native strategists could easily see their enemy's approach and defend against it. Rifle pits had been dug into the top of the ridge, and trenches excavated to protect the warriors' families and the captives.

Just miles away, Strange halted his column with the advance of darkness and bivouacked for the night, posting a heavy guard and ordering cooking fires doused. The Mount Royals arrived with only the clothes on their back and the guns in their hands, having left everything else in the boats. They had no blankets, coats, bedrolls or even rations, their dinner left uneaten by the river. On the morning of May 28, Strange's force shambled through the keyhole-like passages to the open valley of the Little Red Deer. Once hostilities were initiated, the Field Force moved to the base of the hill. The field cannon was elevated to fire on the Cree positions, but had little effect. Steele's Scouts moved up the hill, but had to retreat to a brush patch near a creek. The other units flanked to either side along the creek. Infantry could not cross the swamps without being exposed, and when they tried, they "sank waist high in black mud."[14] Steele could not flank the encampments for the same reasons. It was as if the river watershed itself was commanded by Big Bear.

Another officer might have charged around the swamp. But Strange knew that dividing his forces to the sides would result in a massacre. He withdrew despite the risk of heavy gunfire as his force slowly came out from cover. Three men were wounded and one was pulled off an exposed area of the hill by the general himself. As the Field Force retreated, the Cree defenders did likewise and escaped to the north under the cover of fog. Mindful of the safety of the captives, Strange did not pursue. Expecting to hear at any time from Middleton, Strange ordered the Alberta Field Force to regroup at their camp at Fort Pitt.

Soon, Strange would realize he had lost his navy. While wagons took the bulk of the infantry back to Pitt, the 65th Mount Royals found their ride missing. The boats that had carried them to within marching distance of

Tom Strange's cavalrymen in action near Frencman's Butte as sketched by the general himself. *GUNNER JINGO'S JUBILEE*

the Little Red Deer had disappeared. A few token riflemen had been left behind to guard the boats, but once the main body departed, Sinclair and the HBC pilots were left to tend the barges by themselves. Ed Nagle and the other canoemen had paddled up and down the river's shoreline, ready to obey orders that never came. But when the voyageurs returned to the barges, their fleet was missing.

When the main battle had started and the distant thump of the nine-pounder was heard, J. Sinclair, the barge flotilla's captain, had sent a recon of riflemen up the riverbank. But the Cree had the riverbank covered better than anyone knew, and a single rifle shot over their heads sent the squad scurrying back to the river. Sinclair concluded that the fleet was exposed, so the boatmen decided to conceal the boats, which were still full of supplies for the entire brigade. They moved upriver in the fog and got in behind a large island to avoid a possible rebel raid on the provisions. But Sinclair's plan, though well-intentioned and effective, worked too well. The craft were designed to float with the current, not against it, and without the infantrymen to help man oars, the boats could not return even to their embarkation point, let alone Fort Pitt. Ed Nagle's canoes even lost communication with the barges, as they feared shouting through the fog could draw gunfire from either side.

Ultimately, Sinclair and the HBC pilots chose to let the craft drift downriver to Battleford, taking with them most of Strange's supplies, food stores and all. Jingo just shook his head as "the homeless 65th returned to me without food, blankets or even greatcoats."[15] With little else to do, the Mount Royals became landlubbers once more and rejoined their comrades at the Pitt camp. The floating "flourclads" were eventually found by the steamboat fleet advancing upstream and towed back to Fort Pitt, although some were rumoured to have gone directly on to Battleford.

The incident at Red Deer Butte became known, by mistake and repetition, as the Battle of Frenchman's Butte, a frustrating and indecisive stalemate for the

Strange's artillery fires on Big Bear's position near Frenchman's Butte.

The steamer *Marquis* intercepts a lost barge on the North Saskatchewan. The craft was one of the flotilla of General Strange that strayed during the Frenchman's Butte battle. Sketch by F.W. Curzon. *CANADIAN PICTORIAL & ILLUSTRATED WAR NEWS, 1885 SOUVENIR EDITION*

government. Like Duck Lake, Fish Creek and Cut Knife Hill, Frenchman's Butte became yet another colourful sobriquet for a battle of humiliation, though better understanding of native tactics had lessened the casualty rate for the force. Still, losing their provisions, not to raiders but to the vagaries of a river, only rubbed salt into the wound. Fortunately, a wagon train of supplies arrived the very next day from Edmonton to stave off starvation.

Fearful of the fate of the flotilla, Strange dispatched river scouts James Grant and Charles Rossiter in a pair of canoes to seek out the armada. The scouts had little more success looking for the barges or the steamers than when they had searched after the battle. Besides the provisions, communication with Middleton was critical, as Strange had gone into the Butte battle expecting his commander's ship to be whistling around the bend at any instant. Only a kernel of truth could be gleaned from the cacophony of crossed signals received from command. In one he'd been told a boat was on the way, brimming with troops to help in the chase. Another letter had said Poundmaker had surrendered and nothing at all would be sent. Strange wrote out a request for Middleton to send troops to the mouth of the English River, putting them behind where Big Bear was thought to be. But this was the third set of messengers he had lost touch with, and Gunner Jingo was beginning to feel like a landlocked Noah. "My couriers were like the ravens which were sent out from the Ark—they never came back."[16]

Swamp hunt

On May 29, with a ferry established at Carlton, the *Alberta* was able to get off crossing duty and sail on to Battleford. The fleet was finally assembled but the reunion was short-lived. The previous day, Inspector Perry's Mountie troop had ridden into Battleford to report on his commander's arrival at Fort Pitt. On consultation with Perry, Middleton ordered James Sheets to take the *North West* upriver to Pitt with a load of supplies, but Perry's intelligence was ignorant of the Frenchman's Butte fiasco. Steadfast in his belief that Strange was under no threat, Middleton sent few reinforcements, but allowed Perry's troops and horses to sail back to Pitt on the decks of the *North West*.

In Battleford, Middleton still had a column and a town to feed, both of them integral to the next phase of the campaign. Finding Battleford short on provisions, he sent the *Baroness* back to Prince Albert for supplies. A few passengers went along for the ride. British journalist Charles Henty made the trip, as did Andrew William McConnell, a dispatch rider, and his horse. Captain John Davis, tired of military freeloaders, charged one traveller a $5 deck fare. But Colonel Sam Bedson ordered Davis to take on humanitarian passengers: Hannah Dobbs, her 11-year-old daughter, Flora, and two small boys. Mrs. Dobbs's journey was a little sadder than most. Her husband, Arthur Dobbs, a cook and a former butler to the Lieutenant-Governor, had joined the Battleford Rifles and been killed at the battle of Cut Knife Hill. The rebellion had been a double tragedy for the Dobbses, as their home had been plundered of all their possessions as well. The journey on the *Baroness* was the first stage of the rest of the family's life as they went to stay with friends in Prince Albert.

On May 30, Davis made it to Prince Albert and "took on board 65 tons supplies for Battleford" and 13 sacks of welcome mail for the troops. The next day, he gave the order "to start and not wait for *Alberta*,"[17] not knowing that the ship had been ordered to Fort Pitt and was not coming to Prince Albert.

The *North West*, still oblivious to the new battle, had left Battleford on the 29th, and the next afternoon, 40 miles upriver, the ship found the canoe scouts Grant and Rossiter. To the river-weary messengers, the military seemed under the impression the war was over, for Middleton was not even aboard. Neither were there many troops

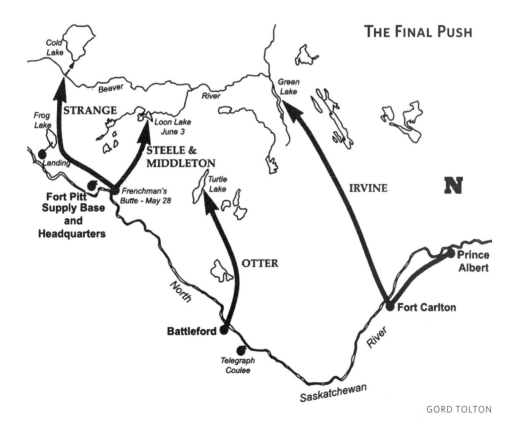

GORD TOLTON

aboard—only 25 infantrymen and a gaggle of newspaper reporters, and Perry and his Mounties. The ranking authority was Sam Bedson. When Grant and Rossiter came on board, the messengers gave word of Strange's encounter at Frenchman's Butte. "Big Bear was caught in a trap this time but he slipped out. They had battled for two days when General Strange gave us letters to give to Middleton. I believe he is short on provisions and bullets."[18] Bedson deduced that the tiny contingent aboard was not what Strange needed to chase the scattering bands. With a full army and a fleet to move it at Battleford, Bedson turned the ship around to pick up reinforcements.

Montreal reporter Ernest Chambers approached Grant and Rossiter, mindful that his readers would want to hear how the hometown boys, the 65th Mount Royals, had done in the latest battle. Rossiter did not disappoint. He told Chambers exactly what he wanted to hear: "You mean those happy little French devils from Montreal, all dressed in black and who are always singing? I am telling you that they are the smartest of Strange's entourage. They went to the battle as if it was a game and they did not want to retreat, wanting to charge with bayonets, even though they were up to their knees in mud."[19] The French "esprit de corps" was alive and well on the Saskatchewan.

Before the turnaround, Perry, exasperated that his cannon had gone into action without him, landed his policemen on the south bank to take an overland cutoff to the fort. Soon, Perry damned himself for his rashness. The horses and men were still tired, and a cold, heavy rain drenched the Mounties' woolen greatcoats. That was not the worst of it. The overland route to Pitt soon became waterlogged over "the passage of a swampy lake, over 200 yards wide, through which men had to wade waist deep, leading their horses."[20] Perry's horse marines rode through the boggy night and finally fell into camp at five o'clock the next morning.

After a well-deserved break at the fort site, Perry met Strange six miles downriver, where Strange was simmering over the indecisive battle and making plans to chase the combatants. He vented his outrage on Perry, and though diplomatic in his recollections, Strange likely gave the superintendent the chewing out of his life. He'd had no orders to ride to Battleford, and Perry's scouts had "become a nine days' wonder to me," his absence costing the force the use of trained artillerymen in the battle. Jingo saw Perry's actions as vainglorious and a challenge to his power: "Possibly he had some vision of Kudos for opening communication with General Middleton by his daring ride."[21] Strange saved his praise for the returned couriers Borradaile and Scott, who made it back from Battleford on May 29. When Borradaile told Strange of Middleton's crack about walking through the country with a stick, Jingo just filed it into the "pompous ass" category of personality.

When the *North West* returned to Battleford on May 30, Middleton crammed onto it—and onto the *Marquis* and *Alberta* as well—his favourite soldiers, the ones that were with him at Batoche: the 90th Winnipeg, the 10th Royal Grenadiers, the Midland Battalion and the Infantry School Corps. The cavalry units (the Dominion Land Surveyors, French's Scouts, Boulton's Scouts and William Herchmer's Calgary

Mounties) rode along on shore. In spite of the remark about walking through the country with a stick, Middleton didn't mind making sure he had the powerful Gatling along.

By the time the *Baroness* got back to Battleford, the story of Frenchman's Butte was beginning to break. Amid a flurry of orders, Davis spent June 2 ferrying 55 teams and wagons to the north side of the river. Just as he had snubbed the police, Middleton gave short shrift to Otter's brigade. None of the Battleford NWMP or local rifle companies,

The sternwheelers *Alberta* and *North West* taking troops up the North Saskatchewan to Fort Pitt. *THE GRAPHIC*

the Governor General's Guard or the Queen's Own Rifles were permitted to join the Big Bear hunt. The QOR were not happy about being left in Battleford, and demonstrated their discontent to the departing troops: "They would not give us a cheer, but remained in their tents while we marched." Two of the QOR would not be shut out, and snuck aboard one of the boats. But the stowaways were more than troublemakers, identifying one, Ambulance Private John Cameron, "as [having] a brother who is a prisoner of Big Bear."[22] The brother was William Cameron, the HBC clerk and survivor of Frog Lake. No one tried to stop Private Cameron on his family mission, for he was "bound to go." Sam Bedson could probably sympathize, for his own in-laws, the McLean family, were also in captivity.

Captain Sheets turned his fully brigaded ship back upstream on May 31. "We are on board and so are about thirty horses." On the trip, yet another unspecified scout signalled the *North West* "from the riverbank, perhaps to tell the General where Big Bear is."[23] Whoever and wherever the scout was and wherever he had come from, the news must have shaken Middleton, for he ordered the boat barricaded and soldiers braced, for an attack that never came.

The cramped quarters also took their toll. Some of the soldiers slept with the horses on board the *Marquis*. Robert Allan found a choice spot: "I made my bed under the cook's house which is raised two and a half feet above the floor."[24] That same cook had decided to start a little cottage industry, and was making and selling 25¢ pies to soldiers sick of their meagre rations. But the chef's enterprise could not contend with the knavery of the troops. He had about 40 pies and a bit of homemade bread cooling "when someone stole the whole lot of them."[25] The *Marquis*'s cook was just learning what many in the war zone were already learning: that the Canadian soldiers may have been heroes, but they often acted like pirates. As Allan had no sympathy for the cook, perhaps there was pie on his face, too.

As the fleet entered the Fort Pitt country they found a camp on an island with scows tied up on the shore. "I believe it is General Strange's boat with ammunition on board, as it was reported lost."[26] The boats were HBC boatman Sinclair's floundering flourclads.

The W&WTC steamer *Marquis* transporting the 10th Royal Grenadiers and the 90th Winnipeg Rifles up the North Saskatchewan, as sketched by Corporal E.C. Currie, published in the *Canadian Pictorial & Illustrated War News*, June 27, 1885.
GLENBOW ARCHIVES NA 1353-30

"The *North West* took the scow in tow and the people on board."[27] The provisions and baggage lost to Strange and the Mount Royal troops was returned, and the river armadas of Strange and Middleton were finally united.

Ninety miles upriver, the *North West* ran out of fuel stock and pulled into a wood camp on Pine Island to resupply. Wood on steamers was usually piled on the bow of the boat to keep it close to the boiler, but the *North West's* woodhawks had a storage problem. Poundmaker's stockpile of ancient weaponry lay piled on the bow, taking up premium space. Archie Ballantine reported Captain Sheets's remedy: "The old guns were in the way, so the whole bunch were dumped into the river."[28] Ballantine recognized the practicality of the captain's decision, but lamented the disposal. "We ought to have kept them for souvenirs to show what we were fighting against."[29] Middleton might have agreed, if only to illustrate the boast made to Strange's couriers. But when his commander did show up at Fort Pitt, Strange sarcastically noted the irony and reminded himself about the infamous "stick." "When he did come, he arrived with steamers carrying a Battalion of Infantry, Gatling guns, and Cavalry."[30]

Middleton arrived at Fort Pitt on June 2 and left naval matters and the *North West* to subordinates. Learning Strange had scouts in pursuit, Middleton followed the trail to the battle site at the Little Red Deer River. Weary of waiting for Middleton and knowing Middleton's jealousy would deprive him of making many more command decisions, Strange made a final decision and sent Sam Steele to pick up the trail. On arrival, Middleton took control from Strange, and with 150 infantrymen, a Gatling gun and five days' provisions, followed Steele.

The rest of the steamer fleet came behind and camped seven miles from Pitt on June 2. The troops were only too glad to sleep off the boats for a change, including Robert Allan, who seemed concerned chiefly with sleeping arrangements. "Pitched tents here. Beautiful scenery. We are near the banks of the river and there are trees all around us." One unspecified steamer went on ahead to camp that night with "mail, and six ill men … going aboard one of the boats."[31] The morning of June 3, when the infantry lined up for inspection, a rumour whispered through the ranks that the inspection was to ascertain the condition of the soldiers' boots. Those with poor boots could ride the steamers, while the rest would march. The result was comical if not predictable: "The boys put on the worst shoes that could be found, old rubbers, overshoes, moccasins etc."[32] Walking or sailing, the brigade gathered at Fort Pitt on June 4. The *North West* remained to await orders, while Julian Dougall took the *Marquis* upriver to Edmonton. Dougall's trip finally completed the connection between the settlements in the North West, and Edmonton residents cheered the reestablishment of supply and communication lines.

On June 2, the ridge where the battle had taken place was ascended without incident, and Strange was amazed by the fortifications that had been constructed there. Middleton was not impressed, but he was not one to give any quarter to a rival. Abandoned supplies including 65 carts and wagons were commandeered. Seven separate trails were found leading north from the battlefield, giving the impression that the bands had scattered. Hope for the captives returned when a scrap of paper was found, a hastily scrawled note from William McLean, on a page ripped from his edition of *Robinson Crusoe*, which attested to their good welfare. His daughters also managed to leave a trail of coloured pieces of ribbon on twigs.

With the Scouts and the full strength of the Canadian militia after him, Big Bear ordered the release of a few of the prisoners, and the seven paths converged into two. The pursuers followed both trails, leading to the safe recovery of Theresa Gowanlock and, soon after, Theresa Delaney. The ladies confirmed Sam Steele's direction of pursuit, and soon more prisoners were found, all in good shape. The prisoners were returned to Strange's camp at Frenchman's Butte, where the freed William Cameron was issued a horse and gun to turn the tables as a scout for the cavalry.

On June 3, after a two-day, 70-mile ride, Steele found a small Woods Cree camp in transition. "Two teepees standing and occupied, a few head of horse and oxen, the remainder moving towards and crossing a ford to [an] island or point, about 1,200 yards in advance."[33] The place was a marshy crossing of Loon Lake, known to the Cree as Makwa, where a narrow strip of boggy land bisected the lake, and should have acted as an insulator from any pursuers. Another few hours and the Cree would have been across and unpursuable. But in the daylight hours, Steele snuck to the top of a broad, steep hill that allowed his troops the same command of the battlefield that the Cree had enjoyed in the previous battle. This time, the rebels were caught in the mud. Rivers hadn't cooperated with the government troops, but maybe this northern lake would.

Before attempting a parley, a sentry noticed the Scouts on the ridge and raised the alarm. Steele ordered the horses into cover, and formed a skirmish line, as, at lake level, native gunmen found a position on the peninsula. A chief, Louison Mongrain, misjudged the situation and called to his men "to go at us, there were only six."[34] As Scouts ran down the hill, Cree scrambled up. Borradaile was able to avenge the insults he and his brigade had received from Middleton; he may have missed Frenchman's Butte, but now "certainly did his best to deliver the message—from his rifle—at Loon Lake."[35]

After a half-hour gun battle, Steele's men cleared the area, one arm of the Scouts charging through the brush to the ford. When a white flag was brought out to discuss surrender of prisoners, Mongrain ordered another fusillade from the peninsula. The Cree leader was determined to outlast Steele and cross the isthmus, threatening "to fight us and clear us out"[36] of the lake, which they finally did, though in a retreat. When Steele noticed one of the McLean girls fleeing across the land bridge, he halted fire and in the confusion the small band escaped. After three hours, six Cree were dead, including a well-loved chief, Cut Arm, while two Scouts were wounded. The land bridge where the battle took place has since been known as "Steele's Narrows."

As Middleton equipped to follow Steele, the *Baroness* brought up supplies and more troops to Fort Pitt. They had 13 sacks full of letters from home for the eastern troops, which the *Baroness*'s clerk handed over to Sergeant W.R. Nursey of the Winnipeg Field Battery. Profiled as a harried volunteer who might rather have been fighting, "Mr. Nursey, who is a bombardier when he is soldiering, and Provincial Auditor when he is not, was our obliging postmaster. The only thing that put him out was when every man in camp came to ask him each evening when the mail was going out or had it come in."[37] In addition to the mail, the crew had dispatches for Middleton, and passed them on to Bedson.

It would be a few days before Middleton received his messages, for he was on the warpath. Receiving word of the Loon Lake skirmish, Middleton raged over Steele's unauthorized pursuit. Composing himself, he decided to equip a brigade to go north himself as a backup for Steele. He ordered Tom Strange out of his sight, sending him to the Beaver River on a new mission to cut off a westward retreat. The assignment was also a means getting rid of Strange. In spite of his conduct as a military man, Middleton was emotionally incapable of dealing with equals.

After pilfering most of the cavalry, Middleton mounted up and headed north with 200 horsemen, determined not to let Sam Steele upstage him. But Middleton was showing signs of learning from the land. Advised that he was advancing into thick forests and muskeg bogs, the general put his men to work building several sets of travois, the style of transport that enabled the Indians to carry entire villages about the countryside, trailing their belongings on racks behind their mounts. But the travois were "needless, for waggons were taken right to the scene of the encounter."[38] The general lost a day or so waiting for the travois to be built, and took several transport wagons north with his camp supplies, the travois loaded on top, unused!

On June 7, Middleton arrived at the scene of Steele's fight. The six Cree bodies were discovered, five shot during the melee, and a woman, Sitting at the Door, who had committed suicide. But the general would not be stopped by the lake, and swam the horses and wagons through the shallow first ford. The second ford would not be so easy, but the troops noticed a crude pontoon bridge and a set of rafts left by the Cree. "Big Bear had crossed it in the same way, taking logs from old houses nearby; and his floating bridge was fixed and strengthened. Some of Big Bear's outfit had crossed the lake by rafts as well, for these were noticed on the opposite shore."[39]

The makeshift bridge and rafts were an indication the fugitives were nearby, and their failure to destroy the craft indicated their hasty desperation. Confident he was picking up the trail, Middleton left the wagons and made his crossing, swimming and rafting through the strong currents that separated the Upper and Lower Loon lakes, but soon was stalled. By June 9, the "island was traversed" and "a long muskeg was found, across which a large body of the fugitives had gone." Swatting black flies and mosquitoes, and the fords not far behind, Middleton smelled blood and the intelligence of his scouts was bearing fruit that the prey was at hand, as the accompanying journalist attested:

> During the day of waiting here a scout crossed, having three days' provisions on his horse, and reported finding rifle pits beyond the muskeg. The muskeg was about a mile and a half long and another scout who went part way across it saw bacon, flour, half-made moccasins, leggings and other articles dropped in the flight of the Indians. An ox had been mired and killed where he was, and what beef could be got at was taken away by the Indians. A large number of Steele's men also went across the muskeg: one of them did not dismount and lead his horse like the others, but rode all the way. There are plenty of marshes and sloughs where this would be impossible, and yet some can be crossed. To cross the waggons, the Intelligence Corps of surveyors offered to make a corduroy road of the spruce timber, which was continent, in less than a day.[40]

With the confidence of his troops and the knowledge that, as Sam Steele said, "delicate women and children had been able to traverse it a few days previously,"[41] the general decided to take the plunge. And plunge he did. At the head of his column, Middleton proceeded into the swamp "… to judge for myself."[42] With one soggy misstep, Middleton was mired literally up to his ass in ample evidence for his evaluation.

With canoes, shaky rafts and horses, the brigade tries to traverse the swampy second ford of Loon Lake in pursuit of the Cree. LIBRARY & ARCHIVES CANADA

Middleton and horse "sank to my saddle girths" in the sticky, wet northern gumbo. Soldiers on solid ground could not contain themselves and erupted in calamitous laughter, as horrified aides scampered to his aid in the quagmire, from which he was "extricated with great difficulty." Delivered back to shore, Middleton, red-faced and covered in organic matter, declared "the muskeg was impassable and ordered retreat."[43]

Though scarcely 20 miles from Big Bear, Middleton saw no way to follow. Obviously, the band had crossed the muskeg while it was still frozen. With his muck-encrusted tail between his legs, Middleton turned the column around, crossing the fords and destroying the pontoon bridge and rafts to prevent the Cree from following. Deciding the swamps were not conducive to one of his supply-laden marches, he abandoned the chase. The move was justified, for there was enough evidence that their quarry was splintered. Brushing the mud from his uniform and his ego, Middleton ordered his column to fall back to Fort Pitt.

If Big Bear were to be caught, perhaps the subordinates Irvine or Otter could catch him in the lake country to the east and cut the Plains Cree off before they could re-enter their more familiar parkland and river country. As the *Toronto Daily Mail's* war correspondent strategized,

> He knows of our arrival here. Green Lake is the most likely place for him to go to. In that case Colonel Irvine will be ready to receive him. He might not propose to go so far, and so make for Turtle Lake, where he can get plenty of fish, and near which are the plains—his own country, for only Woods Cree like the timber. There Colonel Otter will greet him. But he may simply camp where he is, beside some lake, and, until again disturbed, boast in the council how the Big Soldier Chief turned back at Loon Lake from a difficulty his women and children had surmounted.[44]

In years to come, prairie residents would be able to laugh at the exploits of Fred "Big Soldier Chief" Middleton at the Second Narrows. "Middleton's Muskeg," a popular cocktail would remind bar patrons throughout the North West of the day the British general discovered that even he could not walk on water.

Boat-building at Beaver River

Following Loon Lake, Big Bear's allies scattered, the Chipewyan returning to Cold Lake, and the Woods Cree headed out past Beaver River. With word of a raid on the HBC post at Beaver River, General Strange, now a subordinate in his own column, was to head off the last vestiges of resistance at Beaver River.

The forest country around Beaver River resembles a giant sponge, composed of the same black, gooey muskeg as had embarrassed Middleton at Loon Lake. As Strange recollected, the mud and the river's name are owed to "that emblem of Canadian industry" whose fur attracted the HBC to the area in the first place: "the beaver, which, cutting down trees with his teeth, causes them to fall across streams to make his dams and dwellings. The courses of innumerable streams are thus stopped, and they expand into swamps and numerous lakes."[45] The only animals that rivalled the beaver were the blackflies and the mosquitoes. The region was home to the Chipewyan, their own home reserve, from which they'd been absent since the start of the rebellion, after raiding the HBC post and taking the priest, Father Laurent Le Goff, captive.

Strange took the 92nd Winnipeg and the Mount Royals and returned to Frog Lake, where the men found long-forgotten caches of food to add to their provisions. The hike to the Beaver River was not like their other marches. His cavalries pirated by Middleton, Jingo Strange was left with only 35 Mounties. Uniforms were in tatters, and though the 30-mile march to the Beaver was entirely overland, someone forgot to tell the terrain, as they endured countless bogs and river crossings without benefit of ferries or corduroy road. Superintendent Perry noted conditions on the road to Beaver River and the performance of the Mount Royals: "The force moved to Beaver River, eighty miles distant, in three and a half days. The trail was most difficult, the gun sinking frequently to the axles, and only extracted by exhausting efforts on part of horses and men."[46]

Toronto Daily Mail reporter W.P. Mackenzie dubbed the Beaver River corps "the Alligators," and described their challenges:

Those swamps can be crossed by man. Horses which usually live in soft boggy terrain and which have large flat hooves, can also cross this type of terrain,

On the trail pursuing Big Bear: a transport wagon in a river crossing.

but other horses, particularly if they carry a rider, or if they are pulling a load, sink through the spongy crust formed by grasses and moss, into the muck underneath. In their efforts to get out, the horses break this soft crust and mix into the mud, thus becoming hopelessly bogged. there is only one thing to do to get them out: take the rider off or unhitch the horses. In several places, a deep swift-flowing waterway crossed their path, with its wet boggy banks, but the cannon was successfully dragged through all these obstacles.[47]

On June 7, Strange arrived at the Beaver River mission in advance of the column and found that the HBC storehouse was under threat of siege by the Chipewyan. Fugitives from Frenchman's Butte, the Chipewyan had arrived near the Beaver post intending to cross the river in their own canoes. The information was relayed to the main column, and the troops formed into advancing skirmish lines, marching in virtual silence for the remaining 12 miles. The advance scouts commandeered two boats near another HBC post and slept in the storehouse for the night. On arrival of the main contingent, pickets were set up all along the Beaver's bank.

When the local Indians arrived, Strange asked Father Le Goff to translate his promise to burn the whole village. The threat worked and convinced the Chipewyan to surrender. Nearly 50 warriors and their families laid down arms. Eventually charges were dropped against the Chipewyan, though the government withheld their annuities for years. In consultation with Le Goff, Strange enlisted some of the more trusted of the Chipewyan to travel downriver in canoes to locate the whereabouts of the still missing McLean family and about 20 other prisoners. Knowing that Big Bear had split a band off to the northeast of Loon Lake, the Chipewyan thought he might make for Lac des Iles, a lake abundant with fish, as starvation was taking hold of the fugitives. When his turnabout scouts found evidence that Big Bear had crossed the Beaver, Strange sought to build a fleet of canoes of his own to accompany the Chipewyan.

Assessing that the overland trails were impassable, Strange decided to pursue his quarry to Lac des Iles on the river. He proposed to row to the crossing found by the Chipewyan, while Colonel Osborne Smith, whose Winnipeggers had already crossed the Beaver and gone north, would lead another canoe brigade from Cold Lake and cross a series of interconnected lakes to Lac des Iles. Lieutenant Alexander and some troops of the Winnipeg Light Infantry had been repairing some of the boats found around the post, and Strange authorized him to prepare a large scow and four smaller boats. "The task was difficult without nails and proper tools, but wooden pins were used, and the omnipotent Canadian axe, wielded by the handy men of the Winnipeg Light Infantry, produced wonderful results."[48] Strange's marines might sail again.

The canoe activity made Strange melancholy. "The canoe is the true transport of the extreme North West Canadian wilderness, intersected as it is by water-ways and short portages." Boats seemed to pacify him and make him forget the transgressions of the besotted trail and his obstinate commander. But he was on a military campaign, and he recalled a recent, similar failure in a faraway land. "To go up the cataracts of the Nile with ... distant Canadian voyageurs was found to be a very different affair. The conditions were different; a fancied resemblance cost us Gordon."[49] Strange grieved for his fallen friend, and couldn't help but note the irony of Charles Gordon's fate and his own a world away from each other. Strange could reassure himself that though he was in unfamiliar territory, Big Bear was no Mahdi.

As the canoe-building continued, Strange and Osborne Smith took 100 men, provisions and canoes and marched to Cold Lake. Intelligence told them that Woods Cree were downstream and on the verge of surrendering themselves and the McLeans. The latter-day voyageurs were just getting set to embark when the word came. Sam Bedson had been scouring the woods, too, looking for his lost in-laws, and had found them en route to the Beaver River settlement.

With the hostages freed, Strange's Beaver River and Cold Lake fleets were cancelled, having never put a paddle in the water. On June 14, Middleton and Strange rendezvoused on the Beaver. Satisfied the prisoners had been freed, Strange and his men were ordered back to Frog Lake Landing, where the *North West* would return them to Fort Pitt. There, Strange's Field Force was to be broken up, and the cavalries and teamsters were ordered to retrace their steps back to Calgary.

While Middleton's and Strange's brigade marched and fought, in Battleford the men of Colonel Otter's command found their days to be "very uneventful ... just loafed around anyhow." Lieutenant Robinson Lyndhurst Wadmore of the Infantry School Corps, a veteran of Cut Knife Hill, was growing bored with garrison duty. Hearing Big Bear was being engaged, Wadmore and other Battleford troops were anxious to go join in. When that "evening, a steamer arrived ... nobody expected anyone by it."[50] When the boat docked the next morning, Wadmore was surprised and gladdened to see that the other half of his regiment was aboard: Major Henry Smith and the men who'd run the gauntlet on the *Northcote* at Batoche. Wadmore was "very glad to see them all."[51]

On June 5, Wadmore told his diary, the *Alberta* had arrived from Fort Pitt at 12:30.[52] It was then that Battleford received the news that Big Bear was on the run and had let several prisoners go. On June 7, the *Baroness* arrived at Battleford from Fort Pitt. On board were the released prisoners Theresa Gowanlock and Theresa Delaney. Also aboard were a couple of high-profile bureaucrats, James H.E. Secretan, a CPR executive volunteering to assist Bedson as assistant transport officer, and Hartley Gisborne, superintendent of the Dominion Telegraph Service, as well as 10 soldiers.

The two Theresas were somewhat confused as to what ship had brought them to Battleford, and told later in their ghost-written book, *Two Months in the Camp of Big Bear*, that they'd travelled from Fort Pitt to Battleford on the *Marquis*. But the *Baroness's* log bears out that they had taken the Galt ship. While at Battleford, Gowanlock and Delaney were given stateroom accommodations on the *North West* while awaiting their call to testify about their ordeal.

On June 8, Wadmore's corps struck camp and were ferried across the North Saskatchewan by a steamer. The *Baroness*'s clerk noted that the ship had "crossed 50 teams, 400 soldiers, 2 guns from south to north side at B'Ford."[53] The Battleford troops were at last on the chase through trail and marsh. Soon Wadmore's tension would be relieved. In the wake of Loon Lake, the commands of Otter and Irvine were ordered out of their river-bound garrisons and into the deep woods beyond the North Saskatchewan to cut off the line of escape of Big Bear's bands.

Otter's column was bound from Battleford to the offstream wilderness of Turtle Lake, accompanied by the Queen's Own Rifles. As the *Baroness* took the QOR across, a few of the bored brigadiers happened to notice some suspicious looking crates which most people knew to be packages sent from Toronto residents for the consumption of "the boys" to relieve the tedium of pork, beans and hardtack. Corporal George Henry Needler was one of those infantrymen nearby, and finally, despite orders not to touch the crates, curiosity got the better of them. A soldier, "an intelligent forager made a good guess at what they might contain. His sword bayonet was a handy tool that soon pried a couple of them open. Result—we had an unexpected and much appreciated snack then and there."[54]

Soon after greedily consuming a few of the delicacies, the soldiers came out of the trance of their feast and realized they were going to have to seal the crates back up. "To pry the boxes open was one thing, but to nail them up neatly again was another." Their resealing skills were not quite up to snuff, however, and the QOR officers were less than amused when they arrived at the waterfront. "When he saw what had been done, the Colonel lined us up and delivered a sermon which I wish could have [been] preserved in shorthand. For our O.C. was in command of a vocabulary that would meet the demands of any occasion." Needler and his fellow raiders were suitably impressed with the lecture. "It savoured of the best of the Old Testament."[55]

The QOR finished their crossing and were put on the trail to Turtle Lake. But before embarking, the red-handed troops paid a penance for their orgy of candy and canned fruits, from which the *Baroness* would benefit. "When the sermon was over, we rather took it for granted that he [the Colonel] would call it square. But no. That evening after crossing he set us to work loading the steamer up with cordwood."[56]

On June 10, Middleton received a telegram from his minister, Adolphe Caron, urging a quiet personal favour: "I would like you to bring back some souvenirs of your campaign for Sir John, Sir Hector Langevin and myself. Leave it to you to select what you consider of interest."[57] Middleton gladly replied: "Will do what I can to get you souvenirs but it is difficult to get anything as every one in camp is trying to get souvenirs also."[58] But before Middleton's Canadian career was over he would come to regret that "favour," as it would for all time stain his reputation.

Since the victory at Batoche, everyone in the force, from the highest echelons down to the lowliest buck private, was plundering the countryside for some tiny war trophy to call his own. A few days before, at Battleford on June 5, a police staff sergeant,

Sandy Warden, was ordered to prepare furs for transshipment east, furs confiscated from Charles Bremner, a Bresaylor Métis trader who was accused of complicity with Poundmaker. The order came from on high, from Hayter Reed, the martinet-like Indian superintendent, and Samuel Bedson, who, like Middleton and his government masters, saw little wrong with using their influence to get some memento. So, following orders, Warden's clerk, Constable Arthur Dorion, bundled the furs into several empty saddle boxes and hauled the concealed cargo to the steamboat landing, where it could be taken downriver after demobilization.

With Big Bear and confederates still free, the war was still officially on, however, and the focus had shifted to Fort Pitt as a base of operations and a destination for cargo-laden steamboats. Obviously the fleet could not follow the brigades in their movements in the northern woods, though given the swampy conditions faced by the troops, the pilots may have tried to follow had they been 20 years younger! Still, supplies were needed for the troops upriver, and the steamboat fleets were dispatched for the purpose. Archie Ballantine reported that the *North West* made daily trips from Fort Pitt to the Saddle Lake and Frog Lake Landings to bring up caches of provisions to sentries and convey any information that might arrive from Strange, Steele or Middleton in their muskeg marches, where "Scouts are coming and going all the time."[59]

With news of the Loon Lake affair, the *North West* and *Marquis* were also used as patrol boats, the *Marquis* chugging upriver with 50 troops of the 90th Winnipeg, and the *North West* watching the downstream shore with an equal strength of the 10th Royal Grenadiers, prepared to land troops at the first sign of any trouble. But the fugitives were smarter than to accidentally rendezvous with gunboats, and were never seen nor heard. To further facilitate communications, telegrapher Stuart Macdonald was ordered from his Clarke's Crossing office and went by steamer to establish a new telegraph station. With a lineman, a horse and buckboard, and small military escort, Macdonald cut into the line some 40 miles from Fort Pitt (near the modern town of Marshall, Saskatchewan). The new station was called "Straubenzie" in honour of Middleton's staff officer.

On June 9, the *Baroness* was ordered to Prince Albert for more supplies, and to resupply other bases along the way such as Carlton and Telegraph Coulee. Major Kirwan was instrumental in developing these river bases, and rode the *Baroness* to Telegraph Coulee. At the husk of Fort Carlton, Davis performed ferry duty again, conveying a troop of NWMP and 16 wagons across the river. At Prince Albert, Davis happily lugged 800 carcasses of fresh beef destined to sate the palates of troops sick of field rations. On June 11, the *Baroness* was back at Carlton and discharged a load of supplies for the NWMP.

In the late morning of June 12, young James Austin and his mates spotted the *Baroness* approaching the landing at Telegraph Coulee, and watched it steam right on by to Battleford. But two days later the *Baroness* was back, with a load of greatly

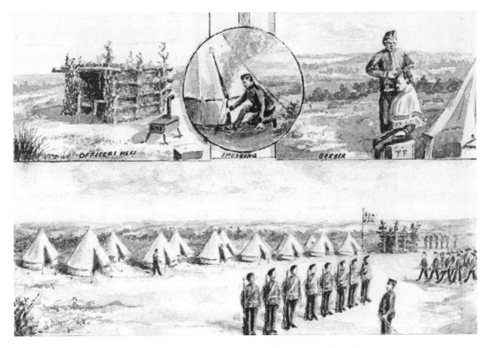

Alexander Campbell sketches the activity of the 7th Fusiliers during their lonely exile at Telegraph Coulee. "AN ACCOUNT OF THE ADVANCES OF THE 7TH FUSILIERS OF LONDON," U. OF SASKATCHEWAN LIBRARY SPECIAL COLLECTIONS MSS 49 #17

appreciated letters from the soldiers' families. For some unknown reason, the Midlanders' camp was transferred only three miles downstream to a new base known as Harrison's Landing, after the ranking officer of James Austin's H Troop.

After guarding the moored *Baroness*, the Midlanders were loaded for shipment to Fort Pitt. "About 1:00 p.m. we were aboard, and on our way to join the rest of the battalion. An officer, a Sergeant, and ten Pvts. were left as a guard until the arrival of men of the 7th Fusiliers. On board the *Baroness* we were somewhat cramped for sleeping quarters, but managed to lay blankets down on top of boxes or on the bare deck, while the mosquitoes made the night musical and attempted an unwelcome attack."[60] After a night of battling the legendary swarms of mosquitoes and blackflies that continually make northern Canadians grateful for winter, the *Baroness* reached Battleford and "took on 3 soldiers, and 2 pilots for N.W. Co."[61] One of the soldiers was Major C. Dugas, the paymaster of the 65th Mount Royal Rifles, one of the sentries on Strange's flourclads that had drifted off during the Frenchman's Butte battle. After a four-hour stop to unload stores, the steamer paddled upriver for Fort Pitt.

The *Baroness*'s passengers were disappointed that at Battleford they were denied the morbid treat of seeing the "rebels" that held a nation spellbound. "It had been our wish to visit the Police Barracks, where Poundmaker and other prisoners were lodged, but we were forbidden by the Maj. in command."[62] But those same commanders were no doubt willing for their charges to meet what would have been termed by political masters as "a good Indian." "A few miles beyond Battleford, we passed the reserve of

Moosomin, and had a sight of the teepees pitched in an opening amongst the trees. When the steamboat touched the shore the chief appeared in his regalia, and received much handshaking from our men as they gathered around him. The weather was splendid, and the voyage enjoyable."[63]

The *Baroness* made Fort Pitt on June 16, but the ship remained anchored in the current, a technique used to prevent a craft from beaching in shallows that are invisible in darkness. Pilots would bring their boats close to shore in the dawn hours, so the next morning Austin and his Midland troop went ashore, but immediately transferred themselves and their gear to the *North West* for passage to Frog Lake.

In that brief interlude, Austin and the Midlanders visited the camps of the campaign-weary veterans of the 90th Winnipeg Rifles, the 10th Grenadiers and the two artillery batteries. But Private Robert Allan saw the visit as less than social. The *Baroness* had brought mail, including parcels shipped from home for the troops of the 90th and the 10th. But the packages never made it off the *Baroness*, where the Midlanders had found them, "and they opened the boxes and stole the contents."[64] The pious future parson, Austin, never saw fit to mention that part of his comrades' hospitality. Nonetheless, the Midland "pirates" could at least toast their ill-gotten booty: "There was a good deal of whisky in the Private boxes."[65] When troops of the Queen's Own, the Midland battalion and the 65th Mount Royals converged on Pitt, boredom set in and "there was nothing much for them to do but beat the kettle drum and kick about the grub."[66]

That afternoon, the *North West* dispatched Austin's company at the Frog Lake landing. The stores were shifted into wagons for the 10-mile journey to the town that had been the site of the saddest and bloodiest altercation of the war. But Austin's comrades could bolster themselves with the thought that all eight companies of the Midland Battalion were reunited for the first time since crawling off the train at Swift Current. Few were gladder than the politician officer, Colonel Arthur Williams, who personally greeted the last of his scattered command.[67]

James Austin's curiosity about the war he'd all but missed came to a head when he reached Frog Lake village. "I had the opportunity to wander over the late settlement, visit the graveyard, and view the ruins caused by Big Bear. Until I realized the destruction of life and property I had little sentiment with regard to those whose rebellion we were endeavoring to quell, but the ruined houses, and the parts of a human body dug up amid the ruins made one's blood run cold and then heat up quickly."[68] The men in Austin's command could not know at the time the reality of Big Bear's involvement in the massacre and how he had tried to stop the murder. All they knew in the vacuum of military information were the names of his enemies and the grisliness before them. Any further enlightenment would be left to historians.

On June 17, the *Baroness* was ordered to Davis Landing to drop off supplies on the way back to Battleford. The ship left Fort Pitt, carrying another discharged prisoner, the Reverend Quinney, with Sergeant Grundy and three scouts also aboard. Upon arrival at Battleford, the clerk reported that the crew "returned wood to N.W.T. Co.," indicating that Captain Davis must have purchased some wood from town, fuel evidently not needed with the luxury of high water and plentiful timber along the river. With these conditions and seemingly unlimited army freighting on the North Saskatchewan, John Davis must have thought himself in steamboat heaven.

"June 20—The General arrived by boat"[69] to the base at Fort Pitt, with all of his mounted troops. On June 21, the Midland battalion was relieved of their uneventful guard duty at the abandoned town and steamboat landing. The *North West* had returned, and the Midlanders moved back to the base at Fort Pitt. On arrival, the Midlanders did not receive the customary cheer that soldiers' units give each other. The reason was simple: "on account of their opening the boxes"[70] of confections intended for other units, the Midland troop had violated a code of honour and few would trust them again.

Newly returned to Fort Pitt were the former captives. While in the camp, the frontier-bred McLean girls, in spite of their ordeal, showed their spirit and even took turns spelling off the soldiers to do sentry duty. "Mrs. McLean is reported to have said that she would consider it a favor if the government would let her shoot some of the Indians."[71] The McLeans surveyed the remains of their once-comfortable home, and then with the others boarded the *North West* for passage to Prince Albert, "steaming into the open water from the maze of islands to the west, and [coming] to her moorings opposite the centre of town." The hostages' safe return was the object of concern and curiosity of the town, as "they were the [most] observed of all observers." William McLean impressed Constable John Donkin. "In his white shirt and black clothes, with dark beard and portly form, he reminded me most forcibly of a merchant skipper in shore going togs."[72]

Donkin, as a red-blooded male trooper in an isolated town, was more impressed by McLean's daughters. "The girls were pretty and dressed in bright costumes, as though they were enjoying a yachting trip, or going to a fashionable watering-place."[73] No less impressive was the stern resilience of Mrs. McLean, "a thin woman with Indian blood in her veins, [who] carried an infant in her arms."[74]

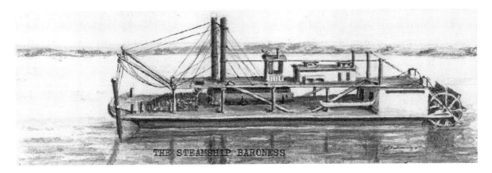

The *Baroness* at Telegraph Coulee. "AN ACCOUNT OF THE ADVANCES OF THE 7TH FUSILIERS OF LONDON," U. OF SASKATCHEWAN LIBRARY SPECIAL COLLECTIONS MSS 49 #17

The sad surrender of Big Bear

By June 9, Big Bear had reached the depths of his soul in leading his people to a peaceful resolution in the wake of the massacre at Frog Lake. After Loon Lake, the chief lost control of the unified Woods and Plains tribes he had held together over the past two months. He had ridden at the head of the Plains Cree as they made their way to Big Island Lake, but somewhere along the way the Woods Cree split off and headed for the Beaver River.

His meagre bands divided, Big Bear chose to head for Batoche, oblivious that the town had fallen a month before. Big Bear had received so little information about what Riel's forces were doing that he chose to dismiss any news as rumours or lies designed to confuse. As far as the old chief was concerned, his people's only hope at this late date lay in a true alliance with the Métis. Few shared his confidence. Those left in the band were hungry and tattered, many had lost their horses and were on foot, and those with mounts had to hang back in order to keep the column together.

One by one, they slipped away to surrender, believing their lot to be better with the soldiers than with their discredited leader. At least they would get something to eat. Big Bear knew he had little else to offer them, and did nothing to discourage anyone from leaving. Forty turned themselves in to Colonel Otter at Turtle Lake, and another group laid down their arms to Irvine at Green Lake.

Wandering Spirit surrendered, but others in his band were making for the U.S. border.
CANADIAN PICTORIAL & ILLUSTRATED WAR NEWS, 1885 SOUVENIR EDITION

By June 25, the moment of truth had come, as all their provisions had run out. Big Bear called a council to put the matter to a vote. Imasees, Big Bear's son, announced that he would not surrender and intended to lead the band to Montana to seek their fates. About 137 men, women and children were in his alliance, including Little Poplar, Lucky Man, Bull Boy, King Bird, Four Sky Thunder and Miserable Man. When the U.S.-bound party left, the once proud chief Big Bear was left with only his wife, a few women of the camp and his most trusted councillor, Two & Two.

Imasees was supposed to take his much younger brother, the youthful Horse Child. But Big Bear's younger offspring refused to abandon his father, and stowed away amidst the weaker band that followed the chief. Oblivious to his brother's actions, Imasees and his group left Big Bear and rode south past Birch Lake, hiding in the Thickwood Hills northwest of Battleford. When they emerged from the south end of the hills they were at the Elbow of the North Saskatchewan River.

Crossing the river, about 30 band members led by Wandering Spirit, Miserable Man and Four Sky Thunder decided to separate and go their own ways. The remaining hundred or so with Imasees reached the edge of the dry plain with over 400 miles of open prairie ahead to the 49th parallel. That open prairie in the month of July had little game to hunt and no settlements or trading posts until the South Saskatchewan.

Not far from where the Cree separated was Telegraph Coulee, the supply base and the camp of the 7th Fusiliers. One morning, the soldiers noticed a band near their camp carrying the white flag of surrender. The men of the 7th were ecstatic. "Not being willing to miss anything along the lines of rounding up the bad ones we promptly headed them into camp and put them under guard." Unknown to the officers, they had in their hands the ringleaders of the Frog Lake massacre. But Wandering Spirit and company were too cagey for the eastern boys, and identified themselves as a friendly band that had gone to Prince Albert for protection and were returning to their home reserve. Officers were skeptical. "This story sounded rather fishy," and opinion held that the band should be detained. But "the Commandant [probably Colonel W. De R. Williams of the 7th Fusiliers] believed their story and let them go."[75]

Their ruse successful, the band left, but not long after the officer who let them go had his heart jump into his throat when a Surveyor's Scout came to Telegraph Coulee and informed him of his error. The Scout had been trailing the group for some time, and identified them as fugitives. With no horse of his own, there was little the commandant could do but wire Fort Battleford, where Wandering Spirit's cadre eventually surrendered. The botched capture was the only excitement the 7th Fusiliers ever had during their month-long exile. But Sergeant Alexander Campbell took the time to make sketches of his regiment's experience, including one of the steamer *Baroness*.

Big Bear was reduced to a footsore fugitive chief with few followers, his command diminished by capture or desertion. On foot and left with only the most helpless of his tribe, including the boy Horse Child and the wizened councillor Two & Two, the deserted chief and his pitiable band shambled through the woods to attempt to reach the North Saskatchewan. They nearly walked directly into Otter's camp at Turtle Lake, but were able to slip away before being noticed. "They had no food and they were very hungry. When the soldiers were sighted again, the people had to scatter without their horses."[76] Passing into the Thickwood Hills, the band also had to be careful not to be noticed by Irvine's police, who knew the old chief was nearby. But Irvine couldn't close the loop, and Big Bear slipped through to the North Saskatchewan.

All this military activity must have made Big Bear realize that the back of the rebellion was broken. But he was a determined man with little faith in the Canadian government, its treaty agents, its military or its Mounted Police. Big Bear thought any surrender to these authorities could only end with him at the end of a rope. Only one white institution had ever dealt fairly and honestly with him. Big Bear had high regard for the Hudson's Bay Company, his people having known the men from the Bay for generations. He would surrender to the nearest HBC fort.

Fort Pitt was out of the question, for Big Bear himself had put it out of commission. The military now occupied Pitt, and besides, it was upstream. Downstream was Fort Carlton. That was where he would turn himself in to the Chief Factor. Big Bear had no way of knowing that Carlton was no longer in operation, but that was the only course he could take to stay out of the soldiers' hands. The old chief would, like his opponents, use the river to obtain his objective.

But in order to slip through, he would have to unencumber himself and get food for his followers. At the river and with no horses, he decided to take matters in hand and use a page from the white man's book. Big Bear set his people gathering timbers and fashioning a sturdy craft of their own: "The men quickly made a raft and loaded the women and children on it." As the children were boarding, the old chief was shocked to learn that his boy Horse Child was among them, having disobeyed the order to go south with his older brother Imasees.

Like Huckleberry Finn, they ran at night and concealed themselves in the bush during the day. On the first leg of their journey, the small party made their way to a small island, where they could hide until the next evening's journey. Young Horse Child was so exhausted from their days of desperate hiking through the woods that "his legs started to cramp and he fell in a heap beside the raft to sleep." Assuming they were safe on their island retreat, the band spread out and took refuge in the trees.

Horse Child, Big Bear's young son, stayed with his fugitive father to the end, even in his father's jail cell in Regina. GLENBOW ARCHIVES NA 635-3

But Horse Child's slumber was interrupted both by the throaty shouts of his father and by "an awful racket coming from the river." Big Bear was lying atop a small hill on sentry duty. "Together they watched a steamboat going by." As they scrambled for cover, the *Alberta* passed near the island on one of its many trips back and forth conveying supplies and troops. This particular trip was carrying a company of Midlanders to the Forks, bound for Saskatoon. "The soldiers on the boat were watching the island very closely but they did not see anyone." For sure they thought the steamer would continue churning on its eastbound journey.[77]

But soon, elation turned to terror for Big Bear's people when the boat came too close to the island, around a bend, and embedded itself in a sandbar. Big Bear knew enough about steamboats to know that if the boat were not soon freed, the island would soon be crowded with hordes of deckhands searching for just the right log with which to lever the boat off its high centre. Surely their position would soon be discovered. To make matters worse, the Midlanders decided to make camp and cook supper just yards from hidden people who were prostrate with hunger. "They made camp and the wind carried the smell of cooking food back to our people who had not eaten for 12 days; the smell of the frying meat was so good they were almost fainting."[78]

While the Midlanders ate and the *Alberta* crew worked, Big Bear quietly and quickly got his charges back on the raft and rowed to the south side, completely undetected. As they crept up the hill silently in the twilight shadows, the *Alberta*'s paddlewheel churned itself into the sand and boosted the ship's bulk back into open water, resuming its passage, totally oblivious to the unseen eyewitnesses.

Virtually without food or firepower, Big Bear decided to walk the women and children who remained with him to the Duck Lake Indian agency, where he knew they would be taken in and cared for. Eventually they made it to the "home of a half-breed Big Bear knew. The man's wife made them soup and fed them."[79]

As his people slept in anticipation for their surrender to the agency, Big Bear and Two & Two made arrangements for transport back to their own boat. Though an aunt tried to keep young Horse Child from leaving camp, the boy insisted on going with his father. "Horse Child raced over to the boat and climbed in beside his father. This is the first time Big Bear ever spoke sharply to his son." The old chief, worried that his youngest progeny might hang on a gallows beside him, cautioned: "'You think you are a man now, that is good. But being a man means that you must be prepared to die. Tonight we may all be killed.' Big Bear then allowed Horse Child to stay with the men."[80]

The Canadian media struggled to transform Big Bear into the Geronimo of the North, but the real "war chief" in shackles was a starving and sickly shadow of the leader he had been.
GLENBOW ARCHIVES NA 1010-24

Big Bear's raft resumed its voyage the next night and, by three o'clock in the morning of July 4, had made its way to a ferry crossing about five miles above the site of Fort Carlton. At the crossing, Big Bear was surprised to recognize a former trader from Carlton, James Garson, who had been living in a tent at the ferry since the post had burned. Big Bear approached the tent to ask Garson for food, but the startled purveyor only ran off to get the attention of the three Mounties camped on the north side of the ferry, guarding supplies.

"Mr. Garson shouted across that there were some Indians over on his side of the river. Cons. Warren Kerr of Battleford, A. Sullivan of Carlton detachment, and Nichols of B Troop went across to see, and found an Indian and a boy, whom they arrested. Continuing the search, Cons. Kerr found another Indian crouched in hiding behind a tent, and having seen Big Bear at Poundmaker's last summer, immediately recognized him as the much-wanted Indian and arrested him."[81]

The most wanted fugitive in Canada surrendered, as it was said, to the only troops in the West who were not looking for him. But even in his despair, Big Bear could be satisfied that he had achieved his objective of Fort Carlton and not been captured at any point before. It could only be a small comfort as he, his friend and his young son were carted away to Prince Albert.

Big Bear probably never realized the significance of the date of his capture, but may have been amused by its irony. As he was arrested, the U.S. crews of the steamboats, including those that had nearly stumbled upon him, were celebrating the 109th anniversary of the Declaration of Independence, the throwing off of British rule. Now Big Bear was a prisoner of that same rule, while his elder son and the last of his tribe sought and gained refuge under the Stars and Stripes. As the last "big gun" of the rebellion was placed in irons, the press declared the fighting over. But there were Cree rebels still at large, and their flight to the U.S. was far from uneventful.

A boatman in the wrong place at the right time

Three weeks after leaving the North Saskatchewan Elbow, Imasees's hundred-odd group of fugitive Cree reached the South Saskatchewan. The trip had been arduous: overland through open country, giving a wide berth to the well-trod Battleford Trail. But before they could make the break for the plains of Montana there would still be, as General Middleton's song said, "One More River to Cross."

Not that those conducting the campaign against the Cree were having any better luck with that tributary. Though spring had become early summer, the South Branch was high enough to cause problems for those who needed to cross it. Saskatchewan Landing was busy ferrying the wagons resupplying post-war Battleford. But the river crossing was far from a perfect procedure. On June 19, the hastily rigged ferry floundered as the steel cable snapped from the strain of heavy loads. Swift Current's ferry never had been much of a success, but fortunately for the citizens of the north, the steamer fleet had left a legacy: a flotilla of hundred-ton barges lying abandoned that could be commandeered to haul wagons across the reach.[82]

For Imasees and his band the swollen river posed greater concerns as they emerged at a wooded flat about 40 miles above Saskatchewan Landing. With women, children and belongings to look after, an unaided crossing would be problematic, even hazardous. Food was also an issue on their overland trek, as evidenced by the slaughter of an ill-fated ox that haplessly wandered away from some settler. The fugitive Cree still had nearly a hundred miles to the border and more meat would be needed to travel further. While the party encamped, Imasees sent out scouts to hunt game and perhaps find some way to ease the crossing. Just such a stroke of luck soon emerged in the form of one lone white traveller with a rowboat, whose lunchtime fish fry on an island near the flat became his last.

The occasion of the last violent death of the North West Rebellion was as odd as it was tragic. The whole war itself had been bizarre, but the circumstance that led to the death of George MacIvor is a little-known incident that occurred far from the battlefields, a fact that lay silent and distant from the main stream of history. In fact MacIvor was one of the few innocent bystanders, a man who only wanted to row his boat and stop to eat his lunch, and said he "was on his way to Prince Albert to join his two brothers."[83] George's brother Donald MacIvor was the fireman on the *Northcote*.

Family ties were enough to motivate George MacIvor to make a long, solo journey by rowboat from Calgary to Prince Albert. Having come to Calgary from British Columbia, MacIvor had dipped oars into Bow River water on July 8, 1885, beginning the first leg of his trip down the South Saskatchewan as it passed Medicine Hat. With family ties in Prince Albert, George thought it time for a brotherly reunion. Why he didn't take the train to Medicine Hat or Swift Current and sail from either of those points is a mystery. Nearly any change in time or circumstance would have saved his life, but MacIvor could not know that his journey would include a run-in with fugitive Cree warriors. After all, any glance at a newspaper would have assured him that General Middleton had crushed all vestiges of rebellion.

On a sultry Thursday noon, July 23, a hungry George MacIvor rowed ashore on a small gravel bar in the South Saskatchewan just south of the Great Sand Hills, still 43 nautical miles from Saskatchewan Landing. He lit a campfire and was just frying up a panful of freshly caught whitefish when his activity caught the notice of a Cree scouting expedition led by Bull Boy and Lucky Man. The expedition was the hunting party seeking food for their fleeing band, attracted by the tempting smells wafting from MacIvor's frypan. But George's rowboat also was an object of some attention.

Imasees, or Little Bear, led a party of women, children and warriors hundreds of miles across the prairie, hunted by the Canadian government. He made it to Montana, where his party's descendants still live today. But first they had to get past the South Saskatchewan River.
GLENBOW ARCHIVES NA 925-1

Though the South Saskatchewan in late July was subject to dropping water levels, it was still an obstacle for a migrating band evading capture and needing to get their families across as quickly as possible. Lucky Man eyed MacIvor's rowboat. After four months of his band's conflict with white authority, Lucky Man saw no reason to believe this lone boater would surrender his craft willingly.

George MacIvor was still oblivious to the party's presence, his attention firmly riveted on his lunch, when he leaned over the campfire and heard the whistle of a bullet pass between his arm and torso. The gunman's aim, though deadly, barely missed MacIvor, the round having passed through his shirt sleeve. The oarsman abandoned his fire and beat a hasty retreat to his rowboat. He shoved it into the water, but his escape was caught short when the boat ran aground on yet another South Saskatchewan sandbar.

As the Indian snipers on shore did their best to dispatch their quarry, MacIvor turned the boat over onto himself to shield his body from the seven or eight more rounds fired at him. One member of the hunting party, described by MacIvor as "one old buck," waded into the river toward him to seize the boat and personally eliminate its owner. So as not to hit their compatriot, the riflemen onshore ceased firing, causing MacIvor to peer out from his cover. But when he did, the approaching gunman levelled his old muzzle-loader rifle at MacIvor's body and fired point blank.

Though mortally wounded, MacIvor felt his adrenaline pumping overtime. Taking advantage of the fact that his attacker would have to reload, MacIvor jumped out of the boat and bolted back to his campfire. As the would-be assassin tamped in his powder to fire again, the boatman retrieved his embedded axe from a log near the fire. The gunman had not yet finished reloading when the hunter became the hunted, and George MacIvor planted the hatchet into the gunman's head, "knocking out his brains, I think."[84]

Whether MacIvor had actually killed his attacker was never certain to him, and isn't known to this day. George was unwilling to stay behind and risk further injury to find out. To make good his escape, he shoved off from the sandbar with the strength that comes from abject fear and the searing pain of his wound. Soon the craft was in the current, and Lucky Man did not pursue, as he tended to his own victim of the bizarre incident.

MacIvor let his boat drift downstream as he tried his best to stay alive and deal with his agonizing wound. By next morning, the rowboat had drifted into the ferry crossing at Saskatchewan Landing. Tied up at the Landing was the small Galt steamer *Minnow*. The hands jumped off their craft to pull the barely conscious man's boat into the Landing. MacIvor was immediately rushed to Swift Current and put on a train to Maple Creek, where he was treated at the NWMP barracks hospital. On July 25, Superintendent John Henry McIllree visited MacIvor's bedside and took his statement, resulting in the only details that are known of the incident.

The information was relayed to Constable Partridge, who led a patrol upstream on the north side of the South Saskatchewan in search of the attackers. Some distance upstream was found "the head and tail of a grey horse very recently killed; further on in the bush they found three brush teepees, and made a place where it seemed as if the skin had been tanned and a canoe made of it. A mile further on they came upon tracks of bare-footed Indians opposite a sand bar in the river. There were traces of a recent camp fire, and an axe hidden in the bush hard by. This was doubtless the spot."[85]

The patrol did not find Lucky Man or Imasees, and Constable Partridge's investigation turned up no trace of the attacker MacIvor thought he had killed in self defence. But the Cree had crossed the river without MacIvor's boat, having sacrificed one of their war ponies to build a watertight boat. The mystery remains as to whether George MacIvor actually killed his assailant or just gave him a splitting headache. What is known is that George MacIvor wouldn't live long enough to know, either, for he succumbed to his wound on July 29, 1885, in the Maple Creek barracks. He was buried at Maple Creek, in the police cemetery.

The Cree party—Imasees, Little Poplar, Lucky Man, Bull Boy and their women and children—made good their escape across the railway and into the Cypress Hills undetected. From there it was a cinch to cross into the relative safety of Montana, where all attempts to be extradited back to Canada would be resisted, until the U.S. government finally granted the fugitives the Rocky Boy Reservation.

CHAPTER TWELVE

The Voyage Home

Breaking camp for the last time

On June 18, the Sisters of the Faithful Companions of Jesus at Batoche realized that no steamers were coming to take them to Edmonton. The ships were occupied working for Middleton, so the nuns were told to go by wagon to Prince Albert, book passage to Edmonton, and take the trail to Calgary. They did get to Prince Albert overland, but still the boats were busy on their martial missions.

Only a reconditioned *Northcote* was available to return to commercial duties not exclusive to the military. On June 20 the flagship journeyed to Grand Rapids and returned with the 1885 season's first freight. Near Fort à la Corne, the pump that provided river water to the boilers burst due to an overlooked bullet hole. After repairs, the *Northcote* arrived at Prince Albert on June 30, the only steamer available for civilian passengers. There was such a demand for tickets and "such a large crowd on board" that even the Bishop, Vital Grandin, a man with no small influence, had "the utmost difficulty in obtaining passage on it."[1] The Sisters were unable to board, and had to take to the trail again, to Qu'Appelle, and reached their new mission at Calgary by rail. The Sisters' transportation problems only foreshadowed the steamboat industry's bleak future.

On June 23, from his camp tent at Fort Pitt, Colonel Arthur Williams wrote a letter to Duncan Chisholm, a friend in Port Hope. "I cannot tell you of our adventures in a few words, and the mail is just about closing. Our duties are incessant, and it is hard to find a few minutes to write consecutively. We have gone through much and have reason to be thankful for the prospect of a safe return homeward. The weather is unbearably hot to-day, but the nights are so cool that they pull us together again. I thank you so much, old fellow, for your kind words. Here is the postmaster saying that he wishes to close the mail bags, so goodbye at present."[2] The author's complaints about widely varying temperatures were more than just small talk about the weather: WIlliams didn't know it but he was in the first stages of typhoid fever.

On June 26, Williams sent A Company of his Midland Battalion on the *Alberta*, bound for Saskatoon to assist with transferring the wounded from the field hospital to the forks of the North and South Branches. The *Alberta* took civilians aboard as well— the hostage families: the McLeans and the Manns—to be transported to Battleford as the elder McLean told the press his tale.[3] The Midlanders were to set up camp for the injured and await the rest of the fleet. The *Alberta* descended Cole's Falls, dropped the Midlanders at the Forks, and made the bend to head up the South Branch to Saskatoon.

The *Alberta*'s mission to Saskatoon anticipated Middleton's plan for demobilization as reported with great accuracy by George Ham: "General Middleton's exact plan is not yet completed, but four steamers, *North West, Alberta, Marquis* and *Baroness*, will probably take the troops to the mouth of the Saskatchewan River, where, after crossing Lake Winnipeg in other steamers, they will take the C.P. Ry. to Port Arthur, and Toronto should feel ready to welcome its gallant troops within three weeks or a month."[4]

To demobilize, troops gathered at waterfront outposts along the river between Fort Pitt and Edmonton. The *Baroness* was dispatched upriver on June 27, timed so that "on her return in four or five days the whole brigade will go home. Boats are being provisioned for ten days' rations,"[5] but still "it will take every available transport vessel now in the service to move the troops in order to get the benefit of the present high water."[6] Still, the disgraced *Minnow* would be spared the demobilization trip to Grand Rapids, as would the *Northcote*.

Colonel Osborne Smith brought his Winnipeg unit in from Cold Lake, and some 70 wagon teams were engaged to bring the troops under General Strange's command from the Beaver River. The Mount Royals and the Winnipeg Light made a painful 54-mile march in two days. At Frog Lake Landing they were glad to take passage on the *Baroness* for themselves and the nine-pounder cannon. By June 27, Strange's command was all but returned, and Jingo put the respite time to good use, retiring to a stateroom on the *North West* to write his official report.

Sergeant William Parker told of a curious conversation with Strange while aboard: "While I was on the upper deck of the steamer *North West* chatting with Rev'd. George McKay and his brother Jimmy, General Strange was striding to and fro. Suddenly he stopped in front of me, called me by my name, and stated he was pleased to tell me that he had mentioned me in his reports."[7] Parker was puffed as a peacock, for a mention in dispatches was a formal recognition of exemplary conduct, the highest honour a rank and file non-com could hope for short of a Distinguished Conduct Medal. But Parker would be dejected to discover later that the mention never made it into publication. Strange himself would loudly decry that his report had been savagely edited.

On June 30, the *Baroness* returned upstream to Edmonton to return the garrisoned troops to their base. Those troops of the 65th Mount Royal that had occupied the makeshift Forts Normandeau, Ostell and Ethier marched north and assembled by the

North Saskatchewan for embarkment. A single company of the 92nd Winnipeg stayed behind to secure Edmonton against further unpleasantness.

The recommendation for moving the wounded by river came from the "Lone Canoeist," Dr. Campbell Douglas. His opinion of the river was positive, and his professional opinion was that they should not move by land at all if a water plan could be facilitated. "I would suggest that no serious cases of wounds should be sent [to Moose Jaw], the journey overland in unsuitable vehicles being too trying. Fortunately, there are only a few cases of this kind in Saskatoon; and when the Hospital is broken up, then they would be sent direct to Winnipeg by the Hudson Bay Co.'s boats as soon as the navigation of Lake Winnipeg can be performed by them."[8]

Douglas's counsel was heeded and no more patients were forced onto wagons. The doctor's superiors were excited at using the river to transport his charges home, and wired Winnipeg to authorize the necessary arrangements. "Having decided to utilize a barge for purpose of transportation, obtained permission … to take possession of the best among the number lying at Clarke's Crossing, and proceeded to get it fitted up."[9] An inspection was made of the motley dozen Saskatchewan Brigade scows, and the pick of the litter was chosen for refitting as a hospital barge.

Captain Thomas Tracy of the 7th Fusiliers was enlisted to perform the upgrade. An engineer by profession, Tracy had commanded the *Sir John A. Macdonald*, the scow chosen to be transformed into a hospital vessel. Tracy called the coincidence "an omen of success."[10] With the assistance of the Fusiliers, who were only too glad to do anything after a boring month guarding supplies, Tracy eagerly drew up blueprints, and began his refit.

The flexible 50-footer was made more rigid with four feet of extensions at either end, and the whole bulk decked over to reinforce the side walls. Rotten timbers were replaced and additional planking was added to the deck and sides to reduce the impact any rough water might have on patients. All due care was taken for the benefit of the wounded. All work was accompanied by rigorous scrubbing and the whitewashing of the entire craft to facilitate cleanliness and asepsis. For protection from the elements, an A-frame canopy of wood and white canvas covered the boat, and an interior curtain system helped with privacy and also baffled the noise from the steamer's engines.

Thomas Roddick was proud to report that "all is now in readiness for evacuating Saskatoon Field hospital, and we eagerly look for the arrival of the steamer."[11] As they waited, a few of the Fusiliers organized a Dominion Day fest of "games and amusements of all kinds for the benefit of the wounded."[12] On July 3, Josephus Todd's *Alberta* reported in at Clarke's Crossing and took the reborn *Sir John A.* scow in tow. The proud engineer, Tracy, and the Fusiliers' surgeon, J.M. Fraser, boarded the reborn medical ship to sail for the Field Hospital at Saskatoon, where 17 wounded soldiers, including John McDonald, the carpenter from the *Northcote*, would be loaded.

The little prairie war was the most excitement the residents of the tiny temperance colony of Saskatoon could have hoped to see, short of Riel's threat to burn their community to the ground. The war brought national attention to their town and provided employment for many settlers. With the military medics of the hospital set to leave and take their patients with them, townspeople threw a farewell soirée in their honour. "Tea was served from four to six and after that a short entertainment and after that was over dancing commenced which lasted till morning."[13] No word whether the good temperance folks allowed the soldiers anything stronger than tea after the program.

Doubtless one crewman in attendance found liquid refreshment. The *Minnow*'s Captain Maloney lent his questionable assistance to the crew of the *Alberta*. At nights, Maloney was sent to tend to the *Sir John A*. Thomas Tracy, unimpressed with the help, saw him as one of only two disturbing elements aboard: "the jar of the machinery during the day, and the never-to-be-forgotten snoring of Captain Maloney at night."[14]

While berthed at Saskatoon, the *Minnow* did provide a useful service to a man named Hunter, the town water hauler, in a story related by his daughter, Barbara Hunter Anderson. Hunter found himself somewhat over a barrel, so to speak, until he received assistance from one Red Jackson, a crewman who is named only in Miss Hunter's memoirs. "The June freshets came and the river became very muddy; Father got in deep water one day, the current caught the wagon and swept it out. Father jumped for the bank taking one barrel with him. The oxen swam back with the wagon without the planks and barrels. The steamboat *Minnow* lay anchored just below the shanty where Andy Plant, the first ferryman, lived, and Red Jackson, the man in charge of the boat, witnessed the accident and helped Father recover the barrel. I often took milk to the men on the *Minnow*."[15]

Sparing no expense for his patients, Dr. Douglas ordered chief nurse Miller and four other nurses to accompany the hospital barge, and quartered them in the state-rooms and cabin of the *Alberta*. "The wounded are doing well and the sick are comfortable."[16] Loaded with the convalescent, the *Alberta* turned around and headed downstream, stopping again at Clarke's for some sick Fusiliers. At Batoche, Todd stopped to wood up the ship, which provided time for some shore leave "allowing such of the wounded as could walk to revisit the scene of the fighting."[17]

After a night stop at the Hudson's Bay ferry, the *Alberta* and the *Sir John A*. reached the Forks of the North and South Branches at noon of July 5. It was fortunate that a camp was established, for doctors, patients and troops were to have a drizzly week's wait before they could continue. As Captain Tracy wrote, "The weather at the Forks was very disagreeable, being rainy most of the time."[18] The rain and the shakedown cruise from Saskatoon became something of a test of Tracy's backwoods shipwright skills. "A little water leaked in, the first day, through the upper joints from the wave in front,"[19] but a little oakum and a second tarpaulin of canvas kept the *Sir John A*. watertight.

The patients' comrades were still at Fort Pitt, spending a last week of leisure, reviews and sports. Horseracing, wrestling and tug-of-war occupied the days, as brigade commanders ran drill routines to polish rough discipline and keep the boys out of trouble. On June 25, the fleet brought the last unit in from Frog Lake Landing—the 92nd Winnipeg Light Infantry—who were somewhat the worse for wear. "One man had a pair of drawers on for pants."[20]

Few were happier to see the end of the fleet's military service than James Sheets. Released from the bureaucracy of the government and General Middleton, Sheets would soon be able to turn the Winnipeg & Western's attention back to freight service, and perhaps salvage the rest of the 1885 navigation season. With the first of July so near, the end of riverboat travel for another year was fast approaching, as the mountains and glaciers far to the west had all but released the last of the rivers' freshets. So, with one eye on the shipping and the other on the water level, Sheets insisted a start would have to be made damned soon if Middleton wanted to ship his troops home.

Before the removal, however, General Middleton allowed his assemblage to observe Dominion Day. No doubt the boys believed they had earned the glory of the day. Had they not fought and struggled to preserve Confederation? But in their righteousness, the thought probably never entered the soldiers' minds that their opponents too were Canadians, and that they had in fact fought their own version of a civil war. Nevertheless, a grand review of the regiments was held, followed in the evening by the talented singers and bandsmen of the 10th Grenadiers. Also that evening, the *Marquis* came up the river from Battleford with a few head of beef on the hoof. The cattle provided a welcome source of fresh food for soldiers and residents sick to death of canned beef and hardtack.

But it was back to business on July 2, as the mounted brigades and wagons were ferried across the North Saskatchewan for a march to Battleford, and home by way of Telegraph Coulee and Moose Jaw. Soldiers and sailors alike "had a busy time for a couple of days getting things in shape."[21]

When the soldiers finally got the order "that we go on the boats tomorrow," two days were spent staging the final evacuation. "Many fatigues to get the boats loaded,"[22] as the *North West*, *Marquis* and *Baroness* once again received all the camp appointments they were to carry. "Struck tents at 2 p.m. then packed up and the teams took them to the river." Breaking camp wasn't all drudgery. The 90th Winnipeg gave yet another band concert, while the less musically inclined provided a serenade of their own. "After the concert there was a cook's parade. Each battalion got all the pots and pans, bugles and anything that would make a noise."[23] The fun of the cook's parade caught on and became a focal point for a final hilarious break in the stress and strain. Boys will be boys, and despite the officers' best attempts to maintain decorum, the rank and file pounded on barrels and boxes and made flags out of trousers. Stiff upper lips quivered in amusement as the "mutiny" broke into an absurd cacophony.

Finally, on July 3, camp was struck and stores were loaded, the battalions stopping for an afternoon tea break before boarding. Then Fort Pitt was bade farewell with a bonfire, on top of which sat a crude effigy whose identity was not revealed by Private Robert Allan. Middleton and staff boarded the *Marquis* with the 10th Grenadiers. The rank and file of the Midland, the 65th Mount Royal and part of the 90th Winnipeg climbed onto the *North West*. The *Baroness* arrived from Edmonton in the morning and dropped its gangplank to load the rest of the human cargo. The clerk listed the officers that would ride on its once coal-stained decks: Major A. Bowen Perry, Captain Edward Palliser and two men of the cloth, Rev. W.A. McKenzie, a chaplain to the Alberta Field Force, and Rev. P. Prevost, the spiritual advisor of the 65th Mount Royal Rifles.[24] All would head to Lake Winnipeg, but some of the Winnipeg infantrymen were doomed to garrison Fort Pitt awhile longer.

The departure of the cavalries by land was good news to one infantryman, the bleary-eyed Robert Allan. For him, the highlight of the ride on the *Marquis* was that he was finally able to get some shuteye on a steamship without an equine bunk mate. "Slept comfortably—no horses on board this trip."[25]

Strange's Field Force, minus Tom Strange, marched home the same way they had come, via the Edmonton/Calgary Trail. The column arrived at Calgary on July 18, treading on much drier, firmer ground than when they had left the previous April. As they approached Calgary they still had one more river to cross before they could rest, but at least they didn't have to ford it. George Hamilton had his ferry in the water and was more than willing to take the business of ferrying Steele's Scouts into town.

Twelve-year-old George Henderson was one of a gang of youths who excitedly watched the activity of the Scouts waiting to take their turn on the ferry. Boys being boys, they all tried to get across the Bow to see the soldiers in all their glory, but gruff old George Hamilton kept chasing the young freeloaders off his raft. Still, Henderson conned his way on and made the trip. Young George knew many of the Scouts, three of whom—Joe Butlin, George Scott and Malcolm McKeller—ordered him to "go back on the ferry, George, and up to G.C. King's store and bring us our mail." Young Henderson gladly did the chore, bringing back two heavy bags of mail, though he had to hide in a wagon on the raft to avoid the wrath of the ferryman, who'd had enough of the boy who couldn't pay. On the way back, George could pay, as the cowboy soldiers tipped him with enough silver to amount to $11, an unheard-of fortune for a pre-teen.[26]

The sunset voyage

Prior to departure, Colonel Arthur Williams had taken sick. He did not particularly think himself terribly ill, believing it was merely a case of sunstroke. Nevertheless, the attending medic thought it serious enough to warrant attention, and arranged for him to lie down on the *North West* in Captain Sheets's personal stateroom. As the camp was struck, Williams gradually slipped into unconsciousness and by the time Captain Sheets guided the *North West* out of Pitt landing, the patient was comatose.

The steamers started early on July 4, but soon the *Marquis* struck a sandbar. The *North West* landed ashore to lighten its load in order to be better able to drag the *Marquis* off its silty perch. This process was routine to any of the soldiers, and the *Marquis* would soon be freed, but by that time a dark pall would be cast over the rest of the voyage to Battleford. James Austin was one of the troops lightening the *North West* for the tow job, when he cast a glance at the sternwheeler. "At 9:10 a.m., while we were on shore, the flag was at half-mast, and thus we learned that our gallant and beloved colonel had passed away."[27] Williams had succumbed to what was termed at the time as "sunstroke and anxiety [that] … brought on brain fever."[28] In fact, the "brain fever" was typhoid fever, brought on by exhaustion and the wet camp conditions.

Misery loves company, the sages often say, and it would seem that the lords of bad luck were doing double duty that morning. Just ten minutes after the colonel expired aboard the *North West*, a sergeant of the 65th Mount Royal, Prima Valiquette, succumbed to a similar affliction. Archie Ballantine, on watch at the time, thought Valiquette had appendicitis, probably from chill and severe exhaustion on the boggy march to Beaver River.[29]

For the remainder of the trip to Battleford, the Midlanders carried out the rituals of mourning. The carpenters of the *North West* sympathetically lent the soldiers some spare planking and tools to build a coffin for their leader. Nowhere in the brigade was a leader so beloved. He was not only their commander, but a civic leader, their Member of Parliament, and a colourful character in their home locality. He'd rallied their regiment to glory in the successful charge on Batoche, risking court martial and the wrath of Middleton. Now all that was left for his boys to do was lay his prostrate body in their homemade coffin lined with white cloth, pack the coffin in a huge ice chest, close the lid and lower him over the side of the *North West* for the rest of the voyage. Likely the Montreal riflemen of the 65th Mount Royal bestowed equivalent rites on their vanquished comrade Sergeant Valiquette.

Middleton was dumbfounded by Williams' passing, feeling "the irreparable and heavy loss that has befallen."[30] He praised the officer's dedication, acknowledging the pace and conditions that Williams had set in the campaign, "having succumbed after a short illness to a sickness doubtless brought on by the hard work of the late campaign. The gallantry and zeal of the late Colonel Williams in the field was as conspicuous as his kindness of heart and amenity of manners out of it, and his memory will receive all the honors from the country which he lived and died for."[31]

Williams' last voyage had to endure a last indignity when the *Marquis* ran aground again, not once but several times victim of the rapidly falling river. In the midst of a heavy rain and hailstorm,[32] the *North West*'s crews threw themselves into towing its beached sister ship, while the troops acquainted themselves with the inhabitants of a local Indian reserve, possibly Moosomin or Thunderchild. A curious "chief and three Indians came down to the boat," and as Private Allan told his diary, "I believe he is peaceful."[33] Allan and his compatriots showed no animosity toward the chief and shook hands with the native party before boarding the freed *Marquis* once again.

Upon arrival at Battleford the next morning, the Midlanders formed up into a funeral parade. A gun carriage was located, and Williams' makeshift coffin was loaded upon it and drawn by mounted artillerymen as the Midlanders marched behind with arms reversed and other regiments followed. After a funeral service in the police barracks, the casket was placed in a wagon bound for Swift Current. Sergeant Valiquette was similarly honoured, "being buried near the other victims of the trouble"[34] after prayers and mass in Battleford's Catholic church.

Arthur Williams' friend Chisholm in Port Hope didn't receive his letter until after hearing of the colonel's death. In tribute, he offered Williams' last written remains to the *Toronto Daily Mail*. Save for that short letter from beyond the grave, Williams' hoped-for record of the rebellion would go unwritten.

The funerals dealt with, command was determined to get as many volunteers home as fast as possible to get them off the payroll. As the top brass fussed and soldiers mourned, the crew of the *North West* were kept busy ferrying horses, teams and the Queen's Own Rifles from the north side of the river. Colonel Otter and his beloved QOR returned from their useless trek to Turtle Lake, which had kept them out of the chase and off the easy river transport. Undaunted, they loaded their camp stores and booked passage for the ride home.

The *North West* left Battleford on the morning of July 6, bearing a Queen's Own Rifles very disappointed with their billet. "We are disgusted that we are not going down with the 90th; the Midlanders are, from all accounts, anything but desirable companions."[35] In spite of the sympathy for the death of their commander, the Midlanders had worn out their welcome, their reputation as parcel pirates having preceded them.

Tom Strange was along for the ride, for financial reasons. His ranch and several of his troops had incurred out-of-pocket expenses in raising his Field Force, and Jingo saw only futility in trying to speak to Middleton about it. In the hope of dealing face to face with Colonel Jackson, the chief supply officer, Strange "was obliged to go to Winnipeg down the Saskatchewan in the long-unaccustomed luxury of a steamer, with the hopes of settling the claims for supply and transport service."[36]

The 10th Grenadiers and the 90th Winnipeg were to occupy the *Marquis* along with the Governor General's Foot Guards, while the 65th Mount Royal were transferred to the smaller *Baroness*. The fleet departed Battleford at the unholy hour of five in the morning to take advantage of the long prairie daylight. But two slumbering Midlanders were dumbfounded to realize they had missed reveille and their ride. Their troop captain evidently had glossed over the roll call, and didn't notice the slackers' absence until some way downriver.[37] No word on how or even whether they eventually got home.

The fleet made good time the first day out of Battleford, despite sandbars and high winds. In the midst of the gusts, Julian Dougall had to stop and tie up the *Marquis* or risk being tossed like a leaf. While waiting for the gale to falter, *Marquis* deckhands hit the shores with axes and saws to gather firewood. Troops of the 90th Winnipeg saw no need to assist. Starved for fresh fruit, they gathered wild strawberries on shore as the roosters chopped and packed timber. Dougall and crew had their revenge on the soldiers by signalling departure while the berry pickers scrambled across the shore to make the gangplank, "two men nearly getting left."[38]

In spite of the stops and overcrowded conditions, the campaign-weary troops on the *North West* were pleased just to not be marching or riding some backbreaking buckboard. The cuisine was also improved from the bully beef and campfire beans they usually consumed. "We fare very well today, our new cook, a Frenchman and formerly of 'B' Battery mess, proving an acquisition. This promises well for the trip. We have at dinner grace and bread, two luxuries unknown for months and either a great advance toward civilization."[39]

On the journey to Prince Albert, the steamboat pilots amused themselves by leap-frogging each other in a playful mock race that kept everyone entertained. Stopping en route at Telegraph Coulee, the *North West* met the two bored companies of the 7th Fusiliers that sat guarding supplies. Soon the 7th would not even have that to do, as the *Marquis* took on stores from the crossing: "provisions, lime juice and 300 pairs of pants." [40] The lime juice was to combat scurvy in men who had been so long on a diet of salted and dried meat. The pants would have been welcome, as many were in tatters from months of wear, though the boys were not allowed to have them until arrival at Winnipeg. The *Baroness* brought up the rear, but when the ships pulled out, the Fusiliers were left high and dry again without so much as an empty crate to guard. What's more, they were relegated to marching overland to the railway. Ironically, most of the units had come overland to the rebellion and were going home by water. The Fusiliers had come north on the river, but were now walking home, with the exception of Tracy and the few men assigned to the *Sir John A.*

The armies that cursed the steamers and the river for their tedious progress at the beginning of the campaign now sang the praises of the fleet. Casualties and deaths there had been, and much sadness. But in leaving the land they had cursed as they tramped its prairies and swamps, men like Richard Cassels wandered the decks growing sentimental about the river and the *North West*:

> We are so far enjoying our sail immensely; the scenery is not wonderful but there is always something pleasant to look at and the process of navigating the vessel affords ground for much amusement. The river itself is a most extraordinary one—a broad, shallow, muddy stream with tremendous currents and crosscurrents and full of innumerable shoals, islands and sandbars and with low-lying, thickly wooded banks of clay. The steamers are no less extraordinary than the river, and consist merely of a large flat-bottomed scowlike frame with gimcrack upper works and an immense stern wheel; our

boat, with six hundred men and heavy stores on board, draws little more than two feet of water. She is two hundred feet by thirty-six. Apparently there is nothing in the river that can hurt these boats; we run into the bank when and where we feel inclined and dash along in the most erratic manner.[41]

In describing the journey, Cassels felt compelled to mention the methods of the watchman checking for shallow water, just as Midlander Charles Clapp had done, but with a marked difference. Where Clapp's memories are almost always followed by a thud on a sandbar, Cassels's North Branch was a remarkably dissimilar stream.

Shoals are avoided if convenient but the old boat does not seem to put herself out on their account if they came in the way. Sometimes we get over them by sheer force, sometimes climb over them with our poles, and sometimes, but rarely, back off and try elsewhere. The system of sounding, too, is highly entertaining. An unfortunate hand plants himself in the bow armed with a long pole, which he monotonously and incessantly keeps poking into the unoffending waters, at each dig vociferating vigorously the depth of water that he finds. The changes are oftentimes most startling. 'Eight feet,' 'six feet,' 'five feet stout,' 'three feet and a half,', 'three feet'—is it to be crash? The poleman almost tumbles overboard as the pole fails to meet any resisting substance and all hands join vigorously in the welcome cry of "Noovvo bottom!..."[42]

The *North West* and the *Marquis* stopped to wood up and bide the night at the burnt-out remains of Fort Carlton. Robert Allan wasn't impressed: "All there is at

The *North West* at Prince Albert. GLENBOW ARCHIVES NA 1223-23

Bored Fusiliers attack the fish in the North Saskatchewan while relegated to their Telegraph Couleè camp, as sketched by Alexander Campbell.
"AN ACCOUNT OF THE ADVANCES OF THE 7TH FUSILIERS OF LONDON," U. OF SASKATCHEWAN LIBRARY SPECIAL COLLECTIONS MSS 49 #17

Carlton is a couple of tents."[43] James Austin again demonstrated his naïveté about native affairs when he wrote of the site: "We had another opportunity to view the destructive work of Indians in rebellion."[44] Austin and his buddies did not know that Carlton had actually been burnt by the NWMP, and nobody tried to correct their misconceptions. Mounties posted to the ferry were quick to regale their military rivals with thrilling tales of their "capture" of Big Bear.[45] One can imagine not only some embellishment of the tale but also some downplaying of the fact that the battered leader had intentionally walked right into their arms.

Sightseeing in Prince Albert ...

When the *North West* and the *Marquis* docked at Prince Albert early on July 8 to take on wood and water, their passengers were warned not to stray far from the docks, as the steamers were not expected to stay long. Despite the order, the troops were bound to check out the town, where the community cheered their arrival and enticed the troops to patronize their shops. "The men enjoyed a run around the town, and seemed in hilarious spirits, like schoolboys on the occasion of a 'breaking up.'"[46]

Cassels, starved for feminine charms, found other distractions when he was fortunate enough to meet the daughters of William McLean, rosy-cheeked young ladies he noted as "very good looking for the Northwest, rather taking, and full of interesting anecdote."[47] Spiritual needs were also attended to, by the Anglican Bishop John "Saskatchewan Jack" McLean.

The soldiers could not get enough of viewing native captivity, as they were "allowed to go around town and see Big Bear, his councillors and others who are confined in the police barracks,"[48] perhaps in a racially based gloating over a defeated enemy. But in the case of James Austin, it was more likely directed to satisfying the fresh-faced youth's callow curiosity about a world entirely alien to his own. "A visit to the Police Barracks enabled us to see in captivity the noted Cree chief Big Bear, one of his sons [Horse Child], and the fierce Wandering Spirit, besides a white prisoner, about whom I got no definite information."[49]

John Donkin further described the scene: "Our barracks were surrounded by a mob of excited soldiery. [Big Bear] was brought out for exercise, and seemed rather afraid at the unexpected amount of interest he was causing, as he shuffled along in his leg-irons, through the long lane of eager, sun-burnt faces."[50]

After spending a month in blackfly-infested muskeg bogs and soggy bedrolls in search of a fierce war chief, the soldiers had their jaws hit the floor when they finally laid eyes on him, seated on the floor of the barracks room of the Prince Albert NWMP post. "When he was captured he was literally dying of starvation and even now his bones are almost starting through his skin."[51] Hardly the model of a Sitting Bull or a Geronimo, the popular images of warlike Indians who could mesmerize a nation and occupy an army. Yet even in his desperation, mesmerize is exactly what Big Bear did. Donald MacIvor of the *Northcote* honoured him as "a king or prince in a white blanket."[52]

That blanket, now yellowing and tattered, was all that shielded Big Bear from embarrassment in the face of these crowds of uniformed gawkers. Charles Daoust of the 65th Mount Royals described a man "[t]out rapetissé sur lui-même, [qui] se sent humilié de sa défaite et de sa triste position. Avait-il donc tant combattu pour n'avoir après tout que l'avantage d'être examiné comme un animal rare d'une ménagerie quelconque?"[53] Could Daoust have known just then how fateful his turn of phrase would be? How ironic it would be that Big Bear would in fact spend his sentence in Stony Mountain Penitentiary tending the animals in warden Sam Bedson's private zoo?

Even the McLean daughters paid their respects, but unlike the soldiers, who could only gape, the girls felt the need to vent a little spleen upon their now caged former captor. "The young ladies could speak Cree like natives and were taken to see their former captors ... Here they gave the imprisoned aborigines a good telling off in their own tongue, and in fact, performed a sort of general commination service."[54]

... and marching to Moose Jaw

Meanwhile, the 7th Fusiliers, left off the final voyage, marched to Clarke's Crossing. By then the ferry had been replaced and the unit was able to cross in relative style, though the last load nearly resulted in disaster. The ferryman made a mistake in navigating the scow closer to the cable, for just as he did so, the cable in the winch slipped and unspooled. The boat drifted in the current, tautening the cable and shifting it sideways. The river was threatening to swamp the boat and submerge 30 troopers, when a quick-thinking horseman splashed out and got a second line onto the stern of the boat, holding it fast to allow the craft to right itself. "It was however touch and go as the boat was heavily loaded and the water was within inches of the gunwale."[55] After that, the Fusiliers marched overland to Moose Jaw, accompanied only by teamsters and Boulton's Scouts. Though the Fusiliers had been the unheralded sailors and workhorses of the war, they were not permitted to ride the water home with the veterans they had worked so hard to provision.

To the Big River and beyond

On July 9, General Middleton, enthroned on the *Marquis*, grumpily decreed that none of the steamboats should be allowed to precede his own and "he now orders us [the *North West*], although our boat is faster than his, to stay behind."[56] But Sheets, with a higher duty to the shipping business, ignored Middleton. He guided his *North West* out of Prince Albert even before the *Marquis* pulled in.

Prince Albert was the traditional dividing line between forest and prairie, and the assembled fleet sailed from the prairie parkland for the tree-laden, marshy reaches of the lower Saskatchewan. Nine miles further, the river too changed, narrowing from a lazy prairie meander to the rushing cascade of Cole's Falls. That was the first of many changes the wide-eyed homeward-bound would note on their voyage north.

One more stop was made, at the Forks, where the two branches of the river gather into a single forward rush toward Hudson's Bay. The *North West* was first to the Forks, where "a great surprise was awaiting us. The wounded had come down from Saskatoon and met us there."[57] The paddlewheeler *Alberta* would join the flotilla, with supply barges and the converted hospital scow. "It was a great scene to see the handshaking" as injured troops were reunited with their active compatriots. [58]

Arrangements for the Midlanders who were camped with the patients became a concern. The *North West* was overcrowded as it was, and initially Middleton accommodated the situation by inviting A Troop to ride on his boat, the *Marquis*. But no sooner had the soldiers shuffled their kit to the *Marquis*'s gangplank than the general "changes his mind once more"[59] and the already cramped passengers on the *North West* were sandwiched in with another 44 troopers. Despite the close quarters, Robert Allan felt that the provisions had gotten better, and couldn't contain his excitement that even fresh dairy was available: "We have milch cows on board."[60]

Patients put aboard the *Alberta*'s hospital barge included John Vinen, wounded on the *Northcote* at Batoche. As the fleet embarked, the *Alberta* proved to be the oddest sight as it pulled into the big river, encumbered by a cluster of barges around its own considerable bulk. On its port side was the refitted hospital barge, the *Sir John A.*, carrying 27 patients and their attendant dressers and nurses, while to starboard was a huge double barge carrying 200 Midlanders, to the relief of the other brigades, who detested them. At the bow of the *Alberta*, being pushed like a bumper car, was the provisions barge, loaded with firewood, meat, vegetables, barrels of fresh water and hay for the milk cows whose daily offerings for the benefit of the wounded were eyed greedily by the troops.

> Down the wild Saskatchewan in river boats we go;
> At last we reach Lake Winnipeg where a tug takes us in tow.
> On board a barge two regiments are shoved into the hold,
> Like sardines in a box we're packed, six hundred men all told.[61]

Once into the main stream, Middleton ordered the four pilots—James Sheets, Julian Dougall, John Davis and Josephus Todd—"to go on at full speed to Grand Rapids at the mouth of the river,"[62] as if the veteran rivermen might have had any other intention. The navigational term "warping" took on a whole new meaning, foreshadowing the meaning of the word as used in today's science fiction. Some soldiers previously believed the river steamers were little better than walking, but here they could be forgiven for seeming to experience the sensation of windburn.

An impatient Sheets set the pace as he "took the reins in his own hands" and led the vanguard and "left the rest waiting."[63] After the Forks, the military transport armada sailed to Fort à la Corne, where they gathered wood for the steamers' boilers. The winter supply depot sat silent, sealed and untended in the summer stillness, as the armies scurried about the banks for loose timber.

The *Alberta*, clumsily laden as it was, had great difficulty keeping up with the other ships. Each evening, Middleton would order Captain Dougall to halt the *Marquis* and wait so that the condition of the patients could be checked. Dense fog once forced the entire fleet to anchor early, but the pre-dawn light enabled an early start, "running at hours unheard of by the ordinary sober navigators of the river."[64] During the night, the fog had lifted but the humidity stayed, and night sentry Robert Allan again bemoaned his lack of rest. "No sleep for the mosquitoes and heat."[65]

Nearing the HBC's inland station on the river, Cumberland House, Sheets decided to save 16 miles by leading the fleet across Pine Island Lake (now called Cumberland Lake), entering and leaving the lake by way of two short drainage channels optimistically referred to as the Bigstone and Tearing Rivers. But any time savings proved unfounded, as the *North West* got halted by a sandbar, something Sheets thought he'd left behind. Over two hours were lost sparring the ship off the shoal and rectifying the damage.

Back in the main stream, the *Marquis* met a vision from the past, "a York boat with two half breeds in it."[66] Bishop Jack McLean was aboard the *Marquis* and elected to join the York boaters heading to Cumberland House. In spite of the Bigstone sandbar, when the fleet tied up at The Pas mission after midnight on July 10, they'd made incredible time since Prince Albert. Private Allan wasn't impressed with The Pas any more than he had been with Fort Carlton or Fort Pitt: "Come to a Hudson's Bay post with only two white men, all the rest are Indians,"[67] he yawned derisively. One of those Bay traders was equally indifferent to the soldiers that acted like pirates: "They were wusser than wild Indians, I never seed the like. They stole calves, an' dogs, and even babies' cradles!"[68]

The voyage afforded the troops a sort of decompression that enabled them to more readily adjust to their combat experiences. At The Pas, soldiers hit the water to let off a little steam in "a lot of bark canoes, and it wasn't long before the boys were out in them, with five getting upset." After all, as Robert Allan reported, you "could get a new canoe for $10."[69]

The officers aboard the *North West* hosted a social function to celebrate their service as lifelong yeomen of the British Empire adrift in yet another of Her Majesty's remote outposts. "Saskatchewan water, flavored with burnt brown sugar, or something that tastes like that, discussed amid the cheerful concomitants of song and speech, has the effect of suddenly developing between ourselves and our gallant comrades from the east the friendship that has been latent for the past three days."[70] For two officers in particular, who were from separate units, the camaraderie led to an incredible discovery: both had the same surname, and upon further discussion they realized with a start that they were twin brothers separated in childhood. The reunited twins, in a celebration of fate, climbed a stateroom table "and sang a rousing duet, which was received with great applause."[71]

A highlight of the festivity was a boisterous patriotic speech delivered by the eccentric but popular General Tom Strange, anxious to see the troops off and pay tribute to "the United Militia of Canada." This kind action, so uncharacteristic of British officers, may have endeared Strange to the junior ranks, but quite possibly irritated Middleton, who needed little provocation to inspire envy and spite.

At the time of their farewell tour, the militia were the heroes of the land. Officers were legends in their own minds, puffing their chests as they preened for one another. One who refused to revel in their light, however, was one Sergeant Davis. "When it was all over but the hangings, we were sent down the river on the boats; the biggest and best of the lot was the *Marquis* and of course most of the officers were on board."[72] Years later, the sergeant's comments emerged in a letter found in the papers of steamboat historian Molly McFadden, and so did the reason for his cynicism.

Sergeant Davis had a much larger concern. "At the stern of this big boat on the saloon deck was a row of latrines and one of them was padlocked. I was curious and asked the guard whose station was there. He lifted me up so I could look through the space over the door … the place was packed to the ceiling with bales, bales of fur belonging to General Middleton."[73] Davis and the guard said nothing of their discovery, but in time a Métis fur trader would come forward to reveal to the nation that their North West Rebellion heroes were common thieves, and that the culpability reached far into the high command.

From The Pas, the river turned into an inland sea as the fleet continued through the enormous expanse of Cedar Lake, 20 miles wide and 34 miles long. Before entering the lake, Josephus Todd stopped the *Alberta* and suggested the wounded be taken off the barges. The medics saw Todd's logic and the patients were transferred into the cabins of the *Marquis* and *Alberta*. Captain Tracy proved himself attached to his scow, the *Sir John A.*, lamenting its abandonment. "Our barge, which had served so well, was stripped of everything moveable; it was left at a little Indian village with a crowd of wondering Indians carefully examining it."[74]

The reason for the removal was safety. For a sternwheeler, crossing a large lake was very different from navigating a river. All rules changed on open water, as the driving wheel could at a moment's notice be rendered useless or the barges swamped. Any amount of wind on a seemingly glassy and placid lake could create waves that could batter the paddle wheels and cause a chain reaction with the frame that might dash the hull to kindling. The lake had to be crossed without delay, but with little current to push the craft along, the furnaces and the boilers had to be taxed to the maximum. Sheets shouted to his engineer to "make her bump for all she is worth and don't break anything."[75]

Furnaces boiling like hellfire created other problems as well. More steam meant a hazard of exploding boilers, and the increased stoking meant more hot cinders flying from the smokestacks and dropping onto the wooden decks. Cedar Lake was the making or breaking of the teamwork of a crew. Eventually, the lake was navigated without destruction by shipwreck, fire or explosion, as the professionalism of captain and crew shone through.

The flotilla then came to a clear, 33-mile reach of river free from sediments or gravel bars and flowing between heavily forested and rocky banks reminiscent of Great Lakes shores. Easing through a series of swifts, which were mild at that time in the season, rapids with names like Cross Lake, Roche Rouge and the treacherous Demi-Charge, brought the *North West* to the granddaddy of all the swifts, Grand Rapids, at five o'clock on Friday, July 10. Despite Middleton's orders, Sheets and his ship arrived two days ahead of the *Marquis* and the *Baroness*. The *Alberta* and its cluster brought up the rear a day later. For the *Baroness* and the *Alberta*, from landlocked Lethbridge on the faraway Belly River, this was their first visit to the northern port.

At the lakehead

At the foot of the rapids lay Lake Winnipeg, where shipping was ruled by William Robinson, commodore of the North West Navigation Co. and his fleet of sidewheelers plying the inland sea to the Red River. It was June 23 when Robinson first got the request from Middleton to be the force's ticket home. "I hope to be seen moving troops to Winnipeg by the Lake. Can you have steamers to meet them, say, in about ten or

The sidewheel laker *Princess* at Grand Rapids. At the end of the rebellion, William Robinson piloted this steamer, and towed its barge, the Red River, to transfer militia to Selkirk, Manitoba. C.R. TUTTLE, *OUR NORTH LAND*

twelve days from this: probable number of troops, roughly given, a thousand men and fifty horses. I suppose I must ration the men for the trip."[76]

Robinson's answer has been lost to time, but Middleton's next message from Fort Pitt indicates that Robinson and the general developed a rapport and were negotiating details for the soldiers, though catering for his own staff was heavier on the general's mind: "Can you not arrange to have steamer *Glendenin*, as well as your own two and the barges; all I want is that the men have arrangements for cooking, tea, etc. Can you arrange to have the cooking for the officers done; number of officers will be given you in a few days."[77] The *Glendenin* was actually the *Glendevon*, a vessel owned by Robinson's Dominion Fish Co., but Middleton would have to settle for the *Princess* and the *Colville*.

Surgeon Major James Bell had little trust in boat scheduling or the horse-drawn tram that connected the head and foot of Grand Rapids. Having heard the wild stories of the reckless pathway, Bell was horrified at the prospect of his fragile charges travelling upon it. With safety in mind, the surgeon telegraphed ahead asking Lieutenant-Colonel Edward Whitehead, the transport officer at Winnipeg, to coordinate the lakers' schedules with the riverboats' and to be sure to have the tram safely operating. Bell and staff did not want their patients to have to languish at the isolated Grand Rapids. "Please instruct North West Navigation Co. to facilitate movement of wounded over tramway at Grand Rapids and on steamer. Some of wounded too weak to leave their beds."[78] Bell wanted no misunderstandings, and emphasized "most important to have no accident."[79]

Whitehead agreed and set matters into motion with Robinson, and on June 25, the commodore left Selkirk, personally at the helm of the *Princess*, with the *Colville*,[80] accompanying. Both boats were loaded with the "fresh meat, eggs, compressed vegetables, comforts, etc."[81] ordered by Dr. Bell. Middleton's final telegram to Robinson was from Prince Albert, confirming time of rendezvous: "Leave this place at Noon. Hope to be at Grand Rapids in three days."[82] Robinson had already left Selkirk, but he knew his customers' needs and had his lake fleet ready with all concerns attended to by the time the armada made port.

When the troops saw the landing at the lake, they were surprised to find that some of the more spirited folks from Winnipeg had made the journey north to greet them. The landing had been decorated with streamers and bunting in honour of the hometown troops, the 90th Winnipeg Rifles. The Manitoba troops were touched, but their rival units were enraged by the selective salute. Archie Ballantine watched as the easterners reacted to the perceived insult: "There was quite a riot and they pulled down all the decorations and tramped them into the mud."[83] Obviously, professionalism was not a part of 19th-century Dominion service drill. Still, by the time the 90th actually arrived at Grand Rapids, enough of the accolades were evident to warm the Winnipeggers' hearts. "When we landed they had the badge of the 90th on the warehouse door, and underneath the word WELCOME."[84]

As the tramway moved the army's freight to the lake, soldiers made the march downstream, while a few adventuresome officers, fancying themselves latter-day voyageurs, shot the rapids in a York boat manned by some enterprising Swampy Cree. While the troops camped about the lake, awaiting Middleton's orders as to berth assignments, they caught fish. "Great fishing here, mostly pike. One man with a troll and boat caught ten."[85] George Needler was suitably impressed with the quantity and quality of the waters. "The pools along the stream were simply jammed with pike that tumbled over one another to get at the bait, which was just a bit of white rag on the hook. Some of them were so big that not skill but strength was needed to pull them out on land."[86]

The abundant fish, fried up over a roaring campfire, made a feast for the troops. There was plenty to go around, as some of the catch measured five feet in length. The northern pike even became currency, and officers looked the other way as "a ready exchange took place—fish for rum punch—and we were warmed up, even though clothes were not just dry."[87]

At the sleepy HBC store, the troops were shocked to find a trader so isolated that he had only recently heard anything about the rebellion, having no contact with the outside world until the sidewheelers brought in newspapers. The whole nation had known of most of the battles no more than a day afterward, and this gentleman knew nothing of the war fought on his own river! To add insult to the trader, some eager beaver still embroiled in the hunt for souvenirs shinnied up the flagpole and stole his company banner. Having had enough of plunderers, Middleton ordered that nobody would leave until the banner reappeared. Eventually the flag was found out in the bush, with no trace of the offender.

When Robert Allan and his fellow Winnipeggers arrived, they found that those accursed Midland pirates had been at it again. "The boat hands had a barge all fixed up for us, but the Midlands were here first and took possession."[88] Middleton's "restore the flag" order had meant another night spent at Grand Rapids, and Allan spent it in the well-ventilated hold of the *Princess*, yet another uncomfortable sleep in his never-ending search for blissful slumber. "Very crowded last night … Too crowded to undo our blankets … We are packed in like sardines."[89] Diary-wise this was the last time Robert Allan would mention any more problems with his bed rest.

By Monday, July 13, the sternwheelers, loaded with civilian and trade goods, were ready to return upriver to their normal affairs, bidding good riddance to military regimen, mercurial commanders and rowdy troopers. Middleton and staff and militia officers occupied quarters on the *Princess* and the *Colville*, while three barges towed behind—the *Red River*, the *Saskatchewan* and the *Nelson River*—carried the rank and file. In all, the abbreviated fleet carried nearly 1,100 men, destined for homes in Winnipeg, Ontario and Quebec.

The 300-mile trip across Lake Winnipeg was eventful weatherwise, with wind and summer rains exerting an influence on the landlubbers' stomachs. "A breeze sprang up and the old scow would get into the trough and wing around at a great rate."[90] George Needler was more descriptive in explaining his own predicament: "Lying crosswise in the rolling barges you were one moment upright and the next standing on your head."[91]

The swaying also brought to Needler's mind a concern about the possibility of shipwreck. "If the towing rope had snapped under the strain, things would have been nasty—there was a fair chance that we who were in the barges would have been blown ashore and drowned."[92] But the lakers' cables were made of sterner stuff than George Needler's stomach, and the barges remained steadfast. In spite of crowded conditions, the weather, the potential for disaster, and little to look at but open water, the brigades managed to stay entertained. "We sang songs accompanied by the cornet and violin until late."[93]

> Down the length of Winnipeg Lake we roll throughout the night,
> And on we're towed along the lake till Selkirk is in sight
> We disembark in double-quick time, we once more board a train;
> We're on our way for Winnipeg, we're getting near home again! [94]

In less than two days, the *Princess* and the *Colville* were in sight of home port, just above the mouth of the Red River, at Selkirk. Selkirk was a frontier boom town transformed from a trading post, a town that had its first frenzied growth when CPR engineers sought to take the railway across the Red River at the mouth. Predictably the bubble burst when the CPR went through Winnipeg instead. No matter, for the thrifty Scots still had the river and Lake Winnipeg to profit from, and did. The HBC's Saskatchewan River shipping network was a boon to Selkirk, and lake steamer business made it a centre of shipbuilding and commercial fishing. Eventually a feeder line from the CPR came to town, and the settlement prospered.

The Selkirk papers urged the town to turn out so "that the returning soldiers should be greeted in a manner expressive of the high appreciation of their deeds of valor entertained by our citizens."[95] No effort was to be spared and a general welcoming committee was struck. Carpenters, cooks and general volunteers scurried about, "determined to prove themselves equal to the occasion."[96]

A celebratory lunch was to be served, a menu "where hardtack had no place and corned beef did not appear."[97] A picnic area was set up on the town's parade grounds, with 3,000 feet of table space set up to accommodate the boys as the ladies of Selkirk pitched in to provide their welcome-home feast. The visit of the troops was to be the biggest thing ever to happen in town, and volunteers "all joined heartily in the cause"[98] with the precision of a military operation. After all, Selkirk was feeding an army.

With all the ducks in a row, "Wednesday morning dawned brightly, and people were early astir, members of the committee and the Mayor being especially busy in seeing after the arrangements."[99] Military men from Winnipeg had arrived and chartered the *Kathleen* to go to the mouth of the Red and accompany the sidewheelers in. Fortunately everyone was out of bed and ready, for the *Princess* was sighted at nine in the morning, four hours ahead of schedule. With sight came sound, as Selkirkers heard the *Princess*'s whistle, and soldiers hanging over the boards and shouting wildly from "decks crowded with scarlet-coated soldiers."[100] As Robinson navigated the last bend, the brass band of the 90th Winnipeg Rifles greeted their comrades and "struck up the strains of an inspiring tune, while cheer after cheer arose from the crowds on the banks and were answered back as lustily by those on the boats."[101]

The *Princess* docked first, then the *Colville*, and the troops streamed off, "their faces bronzed and showing the strain of the long journey,"[102] pumping hands and embracing people they did not even know. The subsequent luncheon could hardly have been more welcome, and town histories still speak of the day "the colourful uniforms seated at long tables on the flat east of the C.P. Hotel made an unforgettable sight."[103]

Amid the usual speeches by officials, members of the Queen's Own Rifles were annoyed by an overemphasis on Fish Creek and Batoche with little word of their own travails on the Battleford Trail and Cut Knife Hill. Selkirk's mayor, F.W. Colcleugh, gave a speech that inflated military chests and roused the jingoistic nature of Queen and country. "You deserve well of your country. You nobly supported the liberty and constitutional government by your valorous achievements in quelling the turbulence of discontented and traitorous subjects and have added a glorious page to our Country's story. You have shown what the children of young Canada, while yet in her teens, can dare and do in defence of law and order, and have given increased assurance of the stability of our institutions."[104]

Middleton, sick of delivering and hearing speeches, offered a brief reply of gratitude, and dismissed his troops to enjoy the day. Some walked about the town or napped beneath the many trees. Townspeople went on board the ships to visit and help feed the wounded. Somehow the Midlanders found a jug or two, and most of the other units were glad to be away from them. One of the Queen's Own was of a like mind, and dropped his $40 advance pay in a Selkirk bar. Fortunately, "his pals took charge of him till he sobered up."[105] In the afternoon, the order came to assemble at Bradbury Station to board the train for Winnipeg. The railway was on the west side of the Red, but the boys had landed and picnicked on the east, so it was time for one more short river trip, by ferry to Colville Landing, before marching up the hill to the station. As Selkirk waved goodbye to their short-lived company, they congratulated themselves on a job well done. "The day had been a great one for Selkirk and long to be remembered."[106]

The experiment in moving the wounded by river was so successful that an additional steamer was assigned to take 20 of the invalid patients from Selkirk to Winnipeg. Peter McArthur's *Marquette* pulled alongside and moored with the *Princess* for direct transfer of the wounded. On arrival, Surgeon Major Dr. James Kerr arranged for carriages and ambulances to move the injured from the riverfront through the streets of Winnipeg to the Headquarters Hospital. The convalescent could blame the enemy or the officers for their state, and say goodbye to river travel and questionable field hospitals, but had to nod a thank you to the medical staff and the steamboat and scow crews that had saved them from death's door. Thomas Tracy took pride in his accomplishment from the remarks of the patients who said "they suffered more in being carried by road from the river to the Hospital than in the other 1,100 miles by water."[107]

The rest of the soldiers were now on terra firma and could bid farewell to the Saskatchewan River system, its steamboats both side- and sternwheelers, and all its scows, ferries, barges, crossings and canoes, which formed a kind of bookend to the adventure of their lives. Still one more boat ride awaited, though, from Port Arthur to Owen Sound, for the railway tracks past the Great Lakes were still incomplete. The soldiers were treated to the relative comforts of the Great Lakes screw steamer the *Athabaska*.

Campbell Douglas's hospital ship plan was commended by the report of Dr. James Bell. "No one was the worse of the trip and many I believe were much better for it."[108] The river route saved lives among their bullet-battered bodies. As in the Bay of Bengal and the South Saskatchewan River, Dr. Douglas, the sailing surgeon and "lone canoeist," had once again fulfilled his Hippocratic oath.

Settling accounts

Before Frederick Middleton climbed aboard the *Marquis* at Fort Pitt he issued a set of congratulatory orders, "not forgetting the transportation service, which under its two able officers [General John Laurie and Colonel William Jackson] has so well aided us in our movements." He also gave a pat on the back to his soldiers and staff to "wish them all happiness and success in their several walks of life."[109] But the flowery dispatch belied the knife that Middleton was prepared to twist into the backs of Generals Laurie and Strange, two men who'd served him admirably, but whom he saw as challengers.

Middleton had already taken steps to eliminate irritants or rivals to his campaign authority. Chief among these was John Laurie, the officer who'd played the background logistics role while Middleton garnered the battle laurels. On June 24, Minister Caron was informed of the disposal of Laurie and the command and supplies under his responsibility. The base commander was ordered "on the 19th [June] to dismiss all his staff and to make up his accounts and proceed to Winnipeg where I should meet him in a few days. I also directed him to leave Captain [George R.] White in charge of the stores at Saskatchewan Landing until brought away by Steamer which would be sent up as soon as possible."[110]

On July 7, Laurie handed over his responsibilities in Moose Jaw to Lieutenant Colonel John Bremner of the Halifax Provisional Battalion, and took his leave of the prairie hamlets that had seen the nadir of his long military career. At Winnipeg he learned he would not see Middleton for another week. Laurie had little desire to see him anyway, and climbed back on the train for Nova Scotia, stopping only to report to the Minister of Defence, Adolphe Caron. Laurie's chief complaint did not come so much from any personal clash with Middleton. Time, work and distance took care of any professional jealousy, and it seems from the record that only Middleton bore that particular cross. Laurie's contention was that he had very few clear orders from his immediate superior, only to "go back to the line of railway and act for [Middleton]." Not one to bear a grudge, Laurie returned to his farm retirement.

General Tom Strange would be treated similarly to Laurie, but would not be as diplomatic about it. On his arrival in Winnipeg, he accepted an invitation to stay in the home of the HBC Commissioner, Joseph Wrigley.[111] One can only imagine the long evening spent by the two Englishmen in a parlour with brandy and cigars. Of particular interest may have been the common venting of spleen on the subjects of Middleton, Caron and the government in general, by a fighting man whose efforts had gone unnoticed by the press and by the impresario who'd managed the supply and transportation of the campaign from a remote desk in Winnipeg as his company's fortunes quivered because of the war.

Strange, who'd whipped his Alligators through the mud and built a fleet of flourclads to take on Big Bear, was snubbed professionally. Middleton's official report made only scant mention of the role played by the Alberta column in the pursuit of Big Bear, and Strange's own appendix to that report, as he claimed, was edited and rewritten without his knowledge. Middleton was awarded a knighthood and a $20,000 pension, while Strange and Otter received little beyond the wages of duty. Further, Strange's charges for expenses incurred in organizing the force fell on deaf ears at the War Claims Commission hearings: "I was obliged eventually to go on to Ottawa to see the Minister of Militia on that subject."[112] The British War Office also snubbed Strange, as his $200 monthly military pension, one that had built up for "thirty years service … in defence of Her Majesty's Government,"[113] was cut off abruptly, on the ground that he had returned to the service. Ironically, his stipend was restored at about the same time Big Bear was released from prison.

Dr. Thomas Roddick still had a little work to do after the *Alberta* evacuated his staff and patients from Saskatoon. As Middleton sailed off to the nation's accolades, Roddick spent a few days travelling the Métis camps at Fish Creek and Batoche, treating the wounds of Métis families devastated by the rebellion. He administered medicine to people who likely would have wished him dead a few weeks before, but true to his Hippocratic oath he could not refuse aid. With few resources left at his disposal, Roddick did what he could in the face of the Canadian government's ravages, leaving behind bandages, medicine, letters of introduction to the NWMP surgeons to guarantee further treatment, and even a little cash. Returning to Saskatoon, he settled accounts and arranged overland transport to Moose Jaw for the supplies that the *Northcote* was unable to haul south. When Roddick finally reached Winnipeg, he was happy to find his army patients intact, "all wounded looking better for the journey, and it is gratifying to be able to state that all the transshipments were made without the slightest accident."[114]

The soldiers gone, Sheets and company turned their attention back to shipping and swabbing, "hiring what men he could to load freight and clean out the boat." The HBC had a full year's supply to be transported. As Archie Ballantine put it, "When we arrived at Grand Rapids, both the warehouses were full to the top with goods to be taken up the river."[115] Ballantine carefully detailed the process of cargo-stowing.

> After we got the boat cleaned up we started to load the freight. The landing here was about fifteen feet above the deck of the boat and from there sliders, made of oak planks, hung at an angle of forty-five degrees. The bales slid down these. One of them was fitted with a block and line to let down the heavy bales. In a day or two, we were ready to pull out with two hundred and seventy-five tons of freight.[116]

As though he feared someone would change his mind at the last moment and draft the *North West* back into war duty, Captain Sheets rushed the crews in their loading. Sheets was ready to shove off in his beloved ship even before the troop-laden *Marquis*, *Baroness* and *Alberta* could arrive at Grand Rapids.

Joseph Wrigley had ministered to the affairs of his corporate empire from his Winnipeg office like a military leader himself. True, his position did not afford him an eyewitness view of the campaign, but Wrigley had worked coolly and professionally behind the scenes, toiling to organize supply lines, arrange transports and use the HBC infrastructure to assist the government armies. It probably would have been easy for a prima donna administrator to delegate many of these matters to subordinates. But Joe Wrigley was made of sterner stuff, as evidenced by the volume of telegrams he had sent and answered personally. The commissioner had recognized the seriousness of the situation and thrown himself with zeal into the attendant flurry of paperwork.

One could look at Wrigley's efforts cynically, of course. After all, he was essentially a chief executive officer, charged with maintaining his bottom line, including profits from contracts with the government. True enough, but in spite of consuming goods and keeping the fleet busy, the rebellion had been costly to the HBC as well as profitable for it. The violence had stalled many a settler from coming to the West, preventing the HBC and other merchants from fulfilling their mandate to foster agriculture. Trading posts had been raided of supplies. Expensive property such as steamships and Forts Carlton and Pitt had been damaged or destroyed. To say nothing of the human resource cost to the company.

Employees of the HBC had always had an unusual relationship with their corporate masters, their occupations less a job than a call to service. Many performed at the risk of the lives of themselves and their families, and this rebellion was just another example of those dangers, as evidenced by the captivity of the McLeans and William Cameron. In many cases, intervention by traders and factors such as Richard Hardisty had kept local natives out of the troubles. In many of their remote outposts, quick-thinking traders had averted tragedy at the modest cost of a sack of flour here or a side of bacon there.

By late July, Joseph Wrigley decided to unshackle himself from his ledgers and the telegraph. It was a time for this civilian general to tour his post-war realm. Was it a foreshadowing that he decided to visit Edmonton not by sail but by rail and trail? Whatever the reason, on July 23, Wrigley, with his son and his secretary, stepped off the train in Calgary, met by Chief Factor Hardisty. When their wagon arrived at Edmonton, they were met by a five-gun salute, a further indication that the HBC was more than just a business corporation. What CEO can say they have been greeted at a branch plant by a military salute?

Essentially, the Edmonton visit was a general meeting of the Chief Factors of the Saskatchewan, Peace River and Athabasca districts, a chance for them to plan strategy with their boss. There was even a wedding, as a trader married a factor's daughter. The HBC, after all, was a family. When the affairs of policy and accounts were over, Wrigley decided the company was owed a party and ordered one organized, not in the dank cabins of the fort, but in the tradition of the Mississippi River galas, aboard the decks of the *North West*.

The Wrigley dinner aboard the *North West*, as remembered by Archie Ballantine, was a gala affair.

A trestle table ran the length of the 120-foot saloon, with dinnerware of all sorts, including trays of birch bark. Gay Hudson's Bay blankets covered seats and benches. Bracket lamps hung from the centre of the cabin, casting a yellow glow over the scene. The guests, about eight o'clock, trooped down the hill from the fort and took their places. After dinner, each person in turn recited, sang, or told some tale of adventure … Meanwhile, down on the lower deck, the Company's servants sat in a large circle with plenty of food and kettles of steaming tea … At midnight, after singing Auld Lang Syne, the guests walked down the gang-plank and dispersed up the hill. The *North West* dropped down to the lower mill to load lumber and at 2:00 a.m. steamed off downriver.[117]

Whether it was nostalgia, romance or just a desire to see the river route that causes so many problems, Joseph Wrigley returned to his Winnipeg headquarters by sternwheeler. By July 30, his company was back to business.

But the final tale should be reserved for the sternwheeler that began the saga and saw the bulk of the action. Though it had officially returned to commercial duties and did not see service in the chase after Big Bear, the battle-scarred *Northcote* still had a bit of military business to finish up. One company of Winnipeg Light Infantry was still at Edmonton, and Captain Segers, after several days impatiently waiting at Fort Pitt for orders, sailed upstream to transfer the soldiers to Battleford.

Townspeople had heard the legends of Segers' run through the Batoche gauntlet, and all came down to the dock to gawk at the tattered spectacle of the *Northcote*. Among them were merchant John McDougall and his wife, Lovisa.[118] Captain Segers gave Lovisa a personal tour of the boat, and told the whole tale of the battle as he showed her each and every scar. "The bullet holes are all over—went right through into the inside stateroom doors." Lovisa had seen the boat for years as it brought goods for her husband's store to sell, and could not believe the damage. "The smoke stacks are all peppered as well."[119]

After a night's stay the *Northcote* was ready to be off.

At 11 a.m. the Co. was formed up in the fort in marching order, and presented a fine appearance as they came down the hill at a swing step to embark for home. As the boat turned out into the stream they were given cheer after cheer, hearty and heartfelt, from the large crowd on the bank which had assembled to see them off. The Edmonton Amateur Field Battery fired a salute of 5 guns from one of the Hudson's Bay Company's brass 4 pounders, and as the boat passed along, groups on the banks cheered themselves hoarse, to whom the red coats heartily replied.[120]

And so, as July became August, and with a bang and a roar, the *Northcote* ended the adventure it had begun barely three months before. With only the trials and sentencing of the rebellion's principals left to attend to, the West, as far as Edmonton and the steamships were concerned, could return to the business of growth and change.

CHAPTER THIRTEEN

Steaming into the Sunset

The evolving West

In November of 1885, two epic, parallel events signalled the end of old ways of life and the beginning of new ones. In a police barracks square in Regina, a rope was placed around a neck, a trap was dropped, and the man who had dedicated his life to the service of the children of the fur trade fell to his doom. Louis Riel paid the ultimate price for his part in the war on a river. Far from Regina, at Craigellachie, British Columbia, Sir Donald Smith, agent of change, hammered home the spike that completed a continent-spanning pair of steel ribbons. If anything, the Canadian Pacific Railway owed its fiscal life to Riel and his rebellion, for the government had provided the company with badly needed funds in exchange for services to the military. But the noose and the spike also changed the course of the West. The great plains were no longer the sole domain of Indians and traders. The prairies would now become the breadbasket of Canada and ultimately the world.

The dream of Sir Stafford Northcote had been to see the Hudson's Bay Company open up agriculture on the Canadian plains by way of the river. That dream was supplanted by the very railway with which the HBC had sought to ally itself. The steamboat experiment to support new settlement from Medicine Hat to Lake Winnipeg and back to Edmonton was doomed by that very river. The waterways were too unreliable—too shallow in places, too swift in others—and as operations during the rebellion had proved, the rivers were as unpredictable as the weather.

The arrival of the iron horse transformed the pattern of settlement. No longer would hamlets hug riverbanks. Now, boomers would rush to take up land alongside tracks, where shiny new towns would rise. And why depend on a huge, clumsy, old-world fur monopoly when a railway can come from virtually anywhere? Even the Galt family was putting plans in motion to supplant its coal fleet with a railway. Western Canada's version of the industrial revolution was on, a quiet upheaval that would seal the fate of the Saskatchewan riverboat.

In 1887, HBC Trade Commissioner Joseph Wrigley prepared his company for the eventual abandonment of its steamboat fleet, and unwittingly foretold the eventual demise of steam on the Saskatchewan.

> The loss on the operating account on the year's business is chiefly caused from only one half the usual amount of freight having been carried. This arises from the indisposition of shippers to send freight where there is great doubt as to the time of delivery caused by the uncertainty of the water in the river. Under present circumstances I fear this uncertainty of water may prove an insuperable obstacle to the success of the Company.[1]

Legendary river captains may have been able to sail up mountains or dry coulees on nothing more than heavy dew or beer suds, but few businessmen were willing to underwrite any more steamboat escapades merely on the basis of legend.

Old soldiers

Richard Cassels was a freshly minted lawyer when he answered the call of his militia, and when his service was finished he returned to build a successful firm, Cassels, Brock and Kelley. He became one of Canada's sharpest corporate lawyers and also represented important non-business clients such as the Presbyterian Church. He was named King's Counsel in 1910. His North West Field Force diary was published in 1983, along with those of Lewis Redman Ord and Harold Penryn Rusden, mentioned below, as *Reminiscences of a Bungle.*

Charles Salyer Clapp continued in a military career upon his return to Belleville, Ontario. He rose through the ranks in his original unit, the 15th Argyll Light Infantry, until 1890, when he was commissioned a lieutenant. Clapp served as an officer until retirement in 1902, after 22 years in the infantry. A manuscript of his 1885 experience still is in the family's possession, and has been published in *Saskatchewan History.*

With his experience in the Queen's Own Rifles behind him, G.H. Needler left the military for a life as a foreign-language educator. He continued studies at the University of Toronto, then left to study for four years in Europe, earning a PhD from Germany's prestigious University of Leipzig. Returning to Toronto, Professor Needler taught German at University College, University of Toronto, for 45 years. In 1914, an aging Needler again answered the bugle call, and took command of his school's COTC (Canadian Overseas Training Company) unit, drilling troops for the Great War. Retiring as professor emeritus in 1936, Needler published many works of literary criticism, and fortunately found time to set down his own prairie experience in *Louis Riel, The Rebellion of 1885*, published in 1957.

Lewis Redman Ord, the saucy government surveyor, quickly gathered his diaries and opinions into a contribution to a book that could only be called *Reminiscences of a Bungle, by One of the Bunglers*. It was published in 1886, and his wry humour was likely received coolly by the militia and government set. Ord could not have cared less about any reviews of his book, however, for he had a more tangible career to carry on with. Ord surveyed for the CPR until 1888, then disappeared into the jungles and pampas of Argentina. After 10 years he returned to Canada and worked on topographical surveys in the West until 1912. He returned to Ontario in 1921, where he lived until his death in 1942. His book was republished in 1983.

Harold Penryn Rusden left behind his diary as a cavalryman in French's Scouts, which was published in 1983 along with those of Cassels and Ord. But those words are all he left. We know not where he came from or where he went after the rebellion; pay lists and the diary are the only evidence that he ever existed.

Aylesworth Bowen Perry carried on with the Mounted Police. He rose through the ranks, eventually becoming commissioner of the force in 1900, truly one of the last of the "originals" left in the red serge uniform. In 1916, when Alberta and Saskatchewan enacted statutes prohibiting beverage alcohol, Perry, based on earlier experience he had had with the liquor trade, was outspoken in his belief that the laws were unenforceable. The following year, he cancelled the force's provincial policing contracts with the two provinces, and except for federal matters, the RNWMP was replaced by provincial police forces until 1928 in Saskatchewan and 1932 in Alberta. By the time Perry retired in 1923, Prohibition in Canada was already collapsing, enabling him to say "I told you so." He died in Ottawa in 1956.

Private James M. Austin returned with his Midland comrades, but laid down his rifle to pick up a Bible. He trained at Congregational College in Montreal and was ordained a Presbyterian minister in 1892. The Rev. Austin served a number of parishes in Ontario until, in 1907, the West called him back. Towns that didn't yet exist in 1885 now received their spiritual instruction from Austin. In 1915, he purchased a farm at Pathlow, Saskatchewan, and eventually spent his sunset years in Lashburn. In 1924, his memoirs of the rebellion were given to the United Church and eventually to the Saskatchewan Archives Board, which published them in *Saskatchewan History*. Austin died on June 4, 1949.

William Parker shook off his river chills, and the rebuff of being omitted from the final reports, to carry on to a life of distinction in the Mounted Police. He rode to Calgary with Steele's Scouts and that fall accepted transfer to Prince Albert, where he remained posted until 1903, with the exception of a leave of absence to join Lord Strathcona's Horse for service in the South African War. Parker's good service record led to fast promotions, to sergeant major in 1902, and to inspector a year later. He spent his sunset years in the force at Medicine Hat, where he commanded a large division. After nearly 40 years spent in a patrol saddle, Parker retired to civilian life as a realtor and insurance man, his large grin and ample mustache twinkling as he regaled the locals with boisterous tales of his adventures. Challenged to record those stories for posterity, Parker set about in his retirement to put pen to paper. Given the volume of his letters and diaries, it was one task he nearly failed to accomplish. The manuscript was still unpublished when Parker died in 1945. In 1970, his family donated his papers to the Glenbow Archives in Calgary. Historian Hugh Dempsey and publisher Mel Hurtig edited them into a book, *William Parker, Mounted Policeman*, 100 years after the title character took on that mantle.

Edward Braithwaite finished his service as a hospital sergeant with the NWMP in Lethbridge in 1892, to begin a private medical practice in Edmonton. In 1895 he became a coroner, and later chief coroner of Alberta and an inspector of hospitals. Before his death in 1949, he wrote an account of his time with the force for a colleague, who donated the reminiscences to the Glenbow Archives. They were subsequently published in *Alberta History*.

William Herchmer was cited by Colonel Otter as a "most valuable assistant." But when the superintendent returned to Calgary Barracks, he found his quarters in ruins, trashed not by rebels but by the very troops billeted there. He could gain little redress in accusing soldiers of the Queen in the destruction of his floors, carpets, piano, even his wife's dresses. Herchmer soldiered on, but in 1886 "Colonel Billy" lost the affection of his comrades when he jumped the queue and became assistant commissioner of the force. It was probably the circumstances of the promotion that annoyed senior officers more than anything. William's own brother, Lawrence Herchmer, with no police experience, had been named commissioner, and that was seen as a patronage appointment. The unpopular new commissioner immediately named William as his assistant even though others were in line for the job. The optics were bad, but the new commissioner needed someone he could trust at his side, and justified the nepotism. William died unexpectedly on New Year's Day in Calgary in 1892.

Private Robert Allan of the 90th finally got home to Winnipeg, and presumably to the decent sleep he could never seem to attain on a steamboat. He moved for a short period to Grafton, Minnesota, but eventually went west again, to operate a hardware store in Ponoka, Alberta. In 1920 he retired to Edmonton, where he lived until his death in 1942. His diary has been published in several journals and collections.

Sergeant George Borradaile just couldn't seem to get over the canoe experience. After 1885, he joined the Geological Survey of Canada and spent several years in the barrens and forests of the North, manning a paddle in the service of government scientists. Growing older, he returned to more civilized climes, as a commissioner assigned to resolve land issues for Scottish immigrants. Finally he settled down in Medicine Hat, working as a land agent for the HBC and as a Justice of the Peace. Medicine Hat was his choice for another reason as well: his years in canoes had given him tuberculosis and he needed the healing airs of the driest place in Canada. Borradaile died April 4, 1907, and was buried in Medicine Hat with full police honours.

Alexander Campbell, the hospital sergeant of the 7th Fusiliers, returned to his London home, but revisited the scene of his rebellion experience in 1913, when he joined the University of Saskatchewan at Saskatoon. By 1922, he was the university's first dean of pharmacy. He retired in 1928, and spent his days converting his sketches into watercolours to illustrate the memoirs he wrote. Campbell died in December of 1942, his book unpublished. But the manuscript—sketches and watercolours intact—made it down the hallways of the U of S to the possession of Jean Murray, a professor of history, and was left to the University Library in 1981. Campbell's "Account" was finally published, not on paper, but as a digital exhibit on the library's Internet site, at http://library2.usask.ca/northwest/campbell/campbell.html.

Dr. Thomas Roddick's amazing career in Canadian medicine continued. In an era that hardly knew of bacteria and their effects, Roddick as a field surgeon always fussed over sanitary conditions, even at the flung-together shacks and tents that passed for the Saskatoon military hospital. Medical colleagues marvelled at his results, and even Roddick couldn't believe his luck. "Hopeless cases recovered. Dead men were brought to life."[2] Such was not the case at Montreal General Hospital, where almost every amputation sent the patient to the grave. Studying the work of the British doctor Joseph Lister, Roddick introduced systematic programs of antisepsis to the hospital, and converted the rest of the nation to his thinking. He was also instrumental in establishing his alma mater, McGill Medical School, as one of the best schools of medicine in the world. He established the Medical Council of Canada in 1912, served in Parliament and was knighted for services to Canadian medicine. He died in 1923.

Dr. Campbell Mellis Douglas returned to Lakefield, Ontario, to devote the rest of his life not to healing, but to the invention he'd brought to the Northwest Rebellion: the folding canoe. In 1889, he grabbed the attention of the east-coast sailing elite when he rowed a 17-foot folding skiff 300 miles from New York to Boston, He capped that incredible voyage in 1893, paddling across the Great Lakes from Collingwood, Ontario, to the Columbian Exposition world's fair at Chicago, where he spent two months marketing his invention. When his wife, Eleanor, passed on, Douglas moved his family to England and rejoined the British Army. In 1894, he entered the boat he'd rowed on the South Saskatchewan, the *Saskatoon*, in a race across the English Channel, placing second. In 1900, he tried to sell his boats again at another world's fair, l'Exposition Universelle, in Paris. After that he gave up on hawking his boats and got back to enjoying them, even inventing another compact conveyance, a folding bicycle. In his sixties, Douglas was posted to Perth, Scotland, and spent much of his time pedalling throughout the Highlands, his boat folded behind him as he cycled, the bike folded in the canoe as he paddled. Dr. Campbell Mellis Douglas, VC, physician, soldier, sailor and inventor, passed away on December 31, 1909.

NWMP Inspector Francis Dickens never seemed to get over his role as the officer responsible for the surrender of Fort Pitt and its civilian occupants. His raft journey was his last act of note before an uneventful turn as the officer commanding Fort Battleford, where he seemed impotent as the police contingent came under the military command of the more dynamic Colonel Otter. One of Dickens' last acts in the police was accepting the surrender of Wandering Spirit, chief perpetrator of the Frog Lake killings, who was subsequently executed. Dickens soon resigned from the NWMP, and at least expected to be able to use his name and experience to make a living on the lecture circuit. But even that eluded him; just before his first speech, in Moline, Illinois, on June 11, 1886, his heart gave out at the age of 41. Dickens's death cheated historians out of true insight into him and his unhindered opinion of events in the rebellion.

Big Bear, the Cree leader whose only demand, for respect, led to his defeat, was tried and imprisoned for treason-felony along with his friend, Poundmaker. Their jailer in Manitoba's Stony Mountain Penitentiary was Sam Bedson. Both prisoners became ill in jail and were released, only to die soon after, their captivity having contributed to severe health problems. Big Bear's son, Horse Child, was young enough at the time, that in 1975 his wife, See-as-cum-ka-poo, was still around to relate the tale of Big Bear's starving flight from the military along the North Saskatchewan. Author Maria Campbell published the story in *Maclean*'s magazine in 1975. The remains of the rest of Big Bear's band made it to Montana, and escaped most attempts to extradite them. They lived as vagrants until the U.S. government finally relented and granted them their own reservation near the town of Box Elder, Montana.

Major General John Wimburn Laurie, the "prairie admiral," returned to his Nova Scotia farm. When the official reports regarding the conduct of the campaign against the rebellion were published in the Parliamentary Sessional Papers for 1886, General Laurie's report was noticeably absent, and with good reason. Shortly after his return home, he was stricken with an eye inflammation, making it impossible for him to read and write for over a year. By 1887, his sight returned enough for him to be able to make a late appendix to the official record. In his statement, Laurie makes probably the best of all accounts of the 1885 military commanders and, unlike his superior, Middleton, gave much credit where credit was due. Hudson's Bay Company Commissioner Joseph Wrigley received high praise for his cooperation and professionalism. Lieutenant John Weller, Laurie's adjutant at Swift Current, received an official pat on the back for his and his crew's Herculean effort in landing the *Minnow*'s barge of supplies at Clarke's Crossing. By request from Alexander Galt, Laurie praised the crews of the Galt fleet, and regretted that circumstances had prevented the *Alberta* and the *Baroness* from being able to live up to their full potential. Laurie considered the two sister ships as having been equal to the *Northcote* in service.

Lieutenant Colonel William Dillon Otter achieved the rank of major general, the first Canadian-born officer to command the nation's forces. In 1899, he took command of the 2nd Battalion of the Royal Canadian Regiment and travelled to South Africa for action in the Boer War. Though nearly retired by the time of the First World War, he was placed in charge of alien internment camps. Having been created a Knight Commander of the Bath, Sir William Otter died in Toronto in 1929.

Major General Thomas Bland Strange was also slighted by the commander, but then, Strange never cared much for Middleton anyway. It is said that Strange took command of the Alberta Field Force purely to irritate his old rival. After the campaign, he continued to run the Military Colonization Company ranch near Strathmore, in the locality known as Strangmuir, after the general's official residence. His son, Harry, left for the British Army soon after the rebellion. The absence of his son, together with Strange's own troubles with a broken leg and a devastating grass fire, made the rest of 1885 a trial for him. The killing blow came when his herds were obliterated in the deadly winter of 1886/87, and the ranch failed financially. Even a run for election as Member of Parliament fell flat when he could not even get his party's nomination. In ill health, Strange retired to England, where he quickly recovered. In 1894, he detailed his life and career in the British Army and the Canadian West in a quirky autobiography called *Gunner Jingo's Jubilee*. Strange's tome was a far cry from the usual stuffy memoir, and its narrative is as eccentric as the man whose name said it all. Thomas Strange died in England on July 9, 1925.

The triumphant victor of the rebellion became its most controversial figure after the trumpets and drums had finished their tributes. Major General Frederick Dobson Middleton's "Report on the Suppression of the North West Rebellion" earned him the enmity of many. His scathing attack on Commissioner Acheson Irvine and the NWMP was undeserved, but tarnished the image of the force in the Eastern press and caused a shakeup in the police's command structure. But the action that caused more harm to the general's reputation than anything else came from an unknown Métis trader.

During the rebellion, Charles Bremner, a Bresaylor Métis and captive of Pound-maker, had been found with a rifle that belonged to a slain policeman. After Bremner's arrest, Middleton seized the trader's property: his bundles of furs. But instead of holding the robes as seized property until the trial, the general gave the furs to his officers as souvenirs. Bundled robes were placed on the steamboats, to be given as gifts to Defence Minister Adolphe Caron, and presumably for the general himself. Middleton would live to regret his largesse. Not only were the furs stolen before the boats returned to Winnipeg, but the itinerant Charles Bremner proved capable of serving cold revenge.

After Bremner was found innocent of the flimsy charges and released, he swore out a complaint against Middleton. Middleton scoffed at the warrant, but Bremner was steadfast in his complaint and went to the media and the opposition Liberals with his story. By the time the case became public, Middleton had been knighted, awarded several honours and given a $20,000 bonus. The general looked forward to putting his feet up with a military pension and a cushy position as president of an insurance company. But when the scandal hit Parliament, it ended what was left of Middleton's military career and his new civilian prospects as well. In 1890, an investigation pronounced his actions in the confiscations illegal. He left Canada in disgrace and returned to England, where the scandal had not been heard of. In 1896, Queen Victoria named him official keeper of the Crown jewels in the Tower of London, where presumably his judgment was a little better. He died in London in 1898.

Back to business

George Ham carried on in Western journalistic circles, as a reporter with the *Winnipeg Free Press* until becoming managing editor of the *Nor'Wester* in 1887. He even found time to establish his own paper, the *Winnipeg Tribune*. But even the scribe of the River War yielded to the railway. After years of being one of Canada's most beloved humorists, Ham became advertising manager for the Canadian Pacific Railway in 1891, and held the post for 35 years. As an outgoing reporter with a talent for tickling funny bones, Ham made friends with many of the movers and shakers of history, and wrote about his experiences, including his gauntlet run on the *Northcote*, in a book called *Reminiscences of a Raconteur*. Published in 1921, the book is tragically long out of print, but it is well worth the effort to seek out this treasury of one of the era's finest writers.

George Henry Ham, journalist, humorist, raconteur and chronicler of the *Northcote*'s abortive raid on Batoche. PHOTO FROM HAM'S BOOK, *REMINISCENCES OF A RACONTEUR*

Owen Hughes celebrated the end of the rebellion by being named to the North West Council, the governing body of the territories that would one day become Saskatchewan and Alberta. The circumstances of his final years are uncertain.

Samuel Bedson, the Field Force's transport brigade commander, shook off accusations that he had a role in the Batoche looting and the scandal over the Bremner furs. Returning to his old job, as warden of Manitoba's Stony Mountain Penitentiary, Bedson soon became the jailer of his quarries, Poundmaker and Big Bear, a bizarre juxtaposition of roles as both enforcer and captor. The ironies only mounted with the jobs Bedson gave his prisoners: tending the buffalo herd the warden kept in his private zoo. There they were: the captive nomad princes, feeding and herding their ancestral legacy, which now existed only behind the same wire that held the chiefs themselves. Bedson's government favours continued in his being named aide de camp to the Governor General. He died in Ottawa in 1891.

One of the most efficient "admirals" of the rebellion fleet was HBC Commissioner Joseph Wrigley, On his August tour of Edmonton and posts in 1885, Wrigley rolled many heads and shuffled many managers as he struggled to keep from having to shut down company posts. The restructuring was an answer to conditions in the war's wake. The bookkeeping of the rebellion caused Wrigley an accounting nightmare as he tried to straighten out the receipts of a widely dispersed militia and submit them for payment by the federal government. A flurry of legal claims flew between Winnipeg, Ottawa and London. England, as the HBC tried to get payment for goods requisitioned by the army, for the exorbitant rates charged by teamster contractor William A. Bell, and for hard-to-prove losses of property and commodities at posts that were attacked. After the report of the War Claims Commission, the HBC had some of its claims redeemed, but the company remained out of pocket for some $45,000 in addition to the unaccountable damages.

None of the claims reflected the fact that, in the aftermath of 1885, the HBC's entire network was a mess. The northern posts were cut off from supplies by the shortened navigation season. Other circumstances combined to threaten the business itself: economic depression, a lack of capital, a 75 per cent drop in profits, and a 50 per cent drop in prices for fur, a still significant commodity in the company's ledgers.[3] From the troubled waters of the war, it would fall to Joseph Wrigley to get the HBC turned around and focused on its future. Though that future would no longer include steamboats on the Saskatchewan, the company did extend the sternwheeler era somewhat on more northern rivers.

Many of Wrigley's efforts to streamline the company were unsuccessful due to resistance and economics, but it was the Northern Stores that became his true legacy. He authorized construction of steamers like the *Grahame* and the *Athabasca* to ply

HBC Trade Commissioner Joseph Wrigley (seated at centre with legs crossed) with his post managers in 1887, the chief executive of a fur trade restructured from mercantilism into a modern corporation. ARCHIVES OF MANITOBA N 268

the Mackenzie and Athabasca Rivers, using Edmonton as a jumping-off point to the Arctic. In May of 1886, he would be honoured by the dedication of the *Wrigley*, a sternwheeler on the Mackenzie. Joseph Wrigley resigned from the HBC in 1891 and returned to England.

Banished from the *North West* and the *Marquis* that he built, Peter McArthur never had a role in the rebellion. Dejected, he withdrew to build his own boat, the *Saskatchewan*, on the Whitemud river off Lake Manitoba. In 1886, McArthur saw the *Marquis* again when he was hired to revive it from a wreck at Tobin's Rapids, and was only too happy to submit a whopping $20,000 bill for the job. His dismissal avenged, McArthur remained a mariner and lived the steamboat adventure on the Lake Winnipegosis tugboats that hauled logs on the long, inland sea. In 1899, he managed to get his hands on the steam whistle from the *North West* and installed it at one of his sawmills. The economics of the Great Depression finally put an end to McArthur's 60 years on the water, and 1936 saw the end of the skipper himself.

The Galt family's steamboat experiment ended with the rebellion, as the *Baroness*, *Alberta* and *Minnow* met various fates as business failures. But no tears were shed for the Galts, for it was onward and upward for every other facet of their enterprises. Their coal mines in the coulees made Lethbridge a household name and the slogan "Galt Coal Burns All Night" ensured customer loyalty far into the 1950s, until heating oil, natural gas and diesel fuel replaced King Coal as a fuel in homes and locomotives. The railway that replaced the steamboat line proved a success as well, as the company built lines extending to Montana and the mountain foothills. Huge land concessions negotiated with the Dominion, and a partnership with the Mormon Church in Utah, led to the start of the St. Mary's River irrigation projects, an idea that made a fortune for Galt shareholders and transformed the parched prairie of southern Alberta into an agricultural mecca that is the envy of the world.

The enterprising Sir Alexander Galt died in Montreal on September 19, 1893, but he lives on in history as one of Canada's fabled Fathers of Confederation and as the "ablest financier in the colonies."[4] The capital he raised brought the southern plains into the industrial age even before it entered the agricultural age.

Alexander's trusted son Elliott spent several years in Lethbridge building the coal, railway and land empire with his brother-in-law and close aide, Charles Magrath. He lived in Coaldale, a home in the river bottom that was "the most prestigious dwelling south of Calgary in its time."[5] The CPR eventually purchased the Galt railway interests, and in building its Crowsnest Pass section, it had to demolish Coaldale to make way for the new high level bridge. The Coaldale name carries on today as that of a town near Lethbridge. Elliott himself left Lethbridge in 1908, in failing health, to live alternately in Victoria, B.C., and Montreal. He died in New York on May 15, 1928. Today the Galt family is heralded as one of the main pioneer forces in southern Alberta. A mine hospital built in Lethbridge by the Northwest Coal Co. was named for Sir Alexander Galt, and both name and building stand today as an excellent museum and archives.

The Baroness Angela Burdett-Coutts died in 1906 and was buried in Westminster Abbey. Her title inspired the christening of the *Baroness*, and her legacy remains in two small southern Alberta communities. Burdett is a small grain town near Medicine Hat, on the railway line originally constructed with her money. The other town, Coutts, though also small, is notable as one of Canada's most important border crossings, the gateway to the Alberta plains opened by the foresight of investors such as the Baroness and the Galts.[6]

Sir Stafford Northcote, for whom Batoche's warship was named, was not idle during the North West Rebellion. The year 1885 was a vibrant one for Northcote, not on the battlefields or supply lines of Canada nor even in the HBC's corporate office, from which he had long since resigned. Rather, Sir Stafford's battle was in the British House of Commons, where he sat as leader of the Opposition. His machinations in June of 1885 brought down the government of Prime Minister William Gladstone just as Middleton's forces were quietly conquering the Saskatchewan woods. The fleet whose development he had overseen was serving Her Majesty's armies even as he himself was scheming to defeat Her prime minister. Ironically the issue that assisted Northcote in his attack was Gladstone's shoddy handling of the war in the Sudan, where HBC pilots had served. The year 1885 also saw Northcote receive a peerage, when he was made the First Earl of Iddesleigh.

Calculating the cost

The Winnipeg & Western Transportation Co. submitted a bill to the government for nearly $64,000, which included 201 days of service at $250 per day per boat, use of barges ($540), damage to the *Northcote* from Batoche ($950), demurrage charges for boats that waited empty at Fort Pitt ($1,000), and various sundry charges for materials, conveyances and freight transport, which the W&WTC believed were not included in the standard rate. Again the government greeted the river company with an army of accountants in the form of the War Claims Commission. The commission scrutinized the bill with a slide rule, taking into account everything from fuel economy, the cost of cordwood, and days lost due to low water. The government did not accept responsibility for the depth of river water and refused to pay for time lost when the boats could not run. Time was money and the W&WTC lost both. Even the depositions of Captain Sheets and clerk Rennie Talbot could not salvage the claims, and in fact their unwitting honesty may have cost their employer money. When the accounts were settled and various claims disallowed, the HBC subsidiary was paid only $53,634, for a loss of nearly $10,000 on its war service.[7] The claim for the *Northcote*'s battle damage was eventually appealed and allowed.

The friendly rival fleet, the Galt family's Northwest Coal & Navigation Co., suffered the same bean counters when they submitted nearly $79,000 worth of bills. Claims for lost barges, tarpaulins and lifeboats plus damage to the *Alberta*, *Baroness* and *Minnow* were disallowed, as the government felt the losses were part of the "natural obstacles of navigation" or "incurred by the dangers of navigation, or inefficiency of the pilots" and were not "a fair charge against the Department." To add insult to injury, tonnages and specifications were used to compare the coal boats with the W&WTC fleet, and by the time the accounting was done, $18,000 worth of claims were completely disallowed. But the NWC&NC had been fortunate enough, through Alexander Galt's high-level machinations, to carry many of their costs on the government hook. Galt had gotten a $20,000 cash advance from Defence Minister Caron before the boats had even dipped a paddle, and had charged more than $30,000 to the government during the course of the campaign. Taking advances and debits into account, the government figured it owed the Galts a little over $10,000.[8]

In the end, Middleton's steamboat experiment had cost the government less than $125,000 (not counting the cost of the barge brigades the 7th Fusiliers had taken to Clarke's Crossing), or less than 2 per cent of the $7-million it had cost to fight the war. Had the river cooperated, the tab would have been reduced by the cost for hired teams and by the amount of ordinary civilian freight shipped. Only acts of God and nature prevented the boats from being of more use, and not even Sir John A. Macdonald could command that.

Captains and crews sail on

The steamboat service on the Saskatchewan had a few more years of life in it, but it was a lingering death, just as it was for the mythic pilots and roosters who made the sternwheelers hum. The eventual fate of many steamboaters is a mystery. Presumably some moved back to the States. Some would have gone to work on the Manitoba lakers, some on other doomed steamboat experiments on the Canadian plains. Others would have moved on to the northern reaches of the Peace, Athabasca and Mackenzie, penetrating into the bush like restless frontiersmen, years ahead of the trains, highways and airplanes.

Those who'd lived through the *Northcote*'s nightmarish run past Batoche received a military award, the North West Medal. The medals also included scrip entitling the rivermen to an $80 bonus from the government or 320 acres of clear-title homestead land. There is little record as to who accepted which. Among collectors of militaria, however, the rarest 1885 awards are those inscribed to the *Northcote* crew, as there were relatively few of them and apparently most of the men sold their medals.

Captain John B. Davis always seemed to be a tenacious, though jinxed, navigator. Only inches of water had prevented his excursion over dry land from the Mississippi from giving him immortality as the first pilot on the Red. Instead, the usurper Anson Northrup's name appears in nearly every history book. Bankruptcy, tornadoes, boulders and fickle managers conspired to keep Davis unemployed, and even his rebellion assignment on the *Baroness* was carried out with broken bones. He finally returned to his home stream, the great Mississippi, where he commanded the *Sidney* in 1887. When the ship's owner decided to operate on the more profitable St. Louis/ New Orleans reach of the river, John Davis was again removed from command. He threw up his hands and withdrew into obscurity.

The snoring sot of the *Minnow*, Captain Maloney, is similarly lost to the mists of time. But judging from the fact that every one of the few sources that name him speak of him in a negative manner, and cannot even summon the will to give us his first name, he may be one character just as well forgotten. Maloney's tugboat received a scathing attack in the usually charitable General Laurie's lengthy report: "With a thoroughly incapable Captain she rendered no service whatever."[9]

Donald Macdonnell, the *Northcote's* assistant clerk, turned from the river to God. He was ordained an Anglican priest, and served on Indian reserves at Fort à la Corne, Red Pheasant, Thunderchild and Fort Hope. He died at Battleford on May 8, 1948.[10]

Macdonnell's supervisor, clerk Walter "Rennie" Talbot, was never heard from again, echoing one of his poetic entries from the ship's log of the *Northcote*: "Then may ye sae that all things must end, and so end I." [11]

Donald G. MacIvor, the fireman on the *Northcote*, seems to have continued his work as a blacksmith. He left the *Northcote* after the rebellion and worked as a farrier for the NWMP. Eventually, he retired to Edmonton. Of course, he was never reunited with his brother George, who unwittingly became the rebellion's last victim. In 1925, Donald MacIvor wrote a letter to his son, which gives us a time-tempered version of the *Northcote's* gauntlet run. His eight-page account is as reliable as any. As he told his boy, "This is the truth as far as I can remember at the time of writing and you know I am past my three score and ten now."[12]

Roderick Smith continued his life at Little Britain, a small town near Selkirk, Manitoba. In 1898, he accompanied other Selkirk fortune hunters to the Klondike gold fields. Upon his return, Smith engaged in business in Selkirk, operating a general store and a fishing business on Lake Winnipeg. His huge hands continued to build boats, including the steamer *Mikado* for a trawling venture. In 1900, he constructed the *Highlander*, a "fine boat [that] gracefully glided into the river as if eager to reach its natural element."[13] York boats still constructed for northern service also were built by Roderick Smith. For the HBC's 250th anniversary in 1920 he constructed a colossal commemorative vessel twice as big as the traditional York boat. Carpenter, merchant and steamboater Smith was well loved in Selkirk, where he was Grand Chief of the Scottish Society: high office in a community rife with Celtic expatriates. His funeral was one of the largest ever held in Selkirk.

Aaron Raymond Russell, a veteran captain whose record in the rebellion is hazy after his return from Sudan, completed the 1885 navigation season and moved on to warmer climes. With the future of river freighting in jeopardy, Russell proved unwilling to move into the sub-Arctic, where the future of steamboating lay. Instead he bought a fruit farm in sunny California, but forgot to leave a forwarding address. In 1915, a long-neglected life insurance policy with a St. Paul firm matured, but the beneficiary was missing. Aaron's former acquaintance, railway tycoon J.J. Hill, was stirred by the search and assisted with a widespread advertising campaign. Finally the long-retired pilot was found in a California seniors lodge, happy to receive the $300 in proceeds. The search also proved to be a boon for writer George Merrick, who published Russell's Nile diary in a Burlington, Iowa, newspaper.

William Robinson made his piloting career not on the rivers, but on the lakes. He had not participated in the Saskatchewan fleet, but did bring the troops to Selkirk. In the ensuing years, Robinson became prosperous developing sawmills on Lake Winnipeg and a lumber yard for the booming town of Selkirk, and in owning the steamboats that ferried the timber. By 1888, he had a fleet of five steamers on the lake. He also founded the Dominion Fish Co., which pioneered commercial fishing on the lake. In 1901, Robinson incorporated the Northern Crown Bank, an institution he later sold to the Royal Bank of Canada, and he remained a Royal Bank director until 1918.

Robinson was an energetic Selkirk builder and booster of his community, serving on hospital boards, the Winnipeg Board of Trade and several service and fraternal organizations. He even donated several hundred dollars to the construction of the first Selkirk General Hospital. He was said to have held a fund administered by the Selkirk Police for the needy, and also funded a lending library. William Robinson passed away in his Winnipeg home on August 20, 1936, at the age of 87.[14] Though he remains relatively forgotten by historians, Robinson was said to have employed more than 400 people in the first half-century of Manitoba's economic development. Both Robinson and his daughter, Idell, have streets named after them.

Captain James Sheets, the legendary swearing captain, commanded the *Marquis* for the 1886 season.[15] After that, however, he seems to have sailed off the face of the earth, though most historians agree he retired to a Dakota farm and was probably dead by 1888.

Captain Josephus Todd left the employ of the Galts after the rebellion and the abandonment of the Belly River fleet. Initially he wanted to retire to a Montana sheep ranch he had an interest in, where he hoped to "enjoy the upward tendency of the wool market." But the call of his natural environment, the Missouri River, beckoned and he eventually took command of the legendary *Rosebud* for the I.G. Baker Co. of Fort Benton, Montana. In 1887, Todd's crew of roustabouts protested for better wages and abandoned their stations near the Indian agency at Fort Berthold. The strikers felt Berthold was an appropriate place for a walkout, as they supposed Todd would not be able to find replacements. But Todd's time on the Saskatchewan, where so many Métis and Swampy Cree made fine deckhands, had taught him a lesson. Replacement workers were right at hand, hired right off the reservation, an amateur yet trainable crew of Gros Ventre, Ree and Mandan. Todd's old crew watched, first in derision, then in horror as Todd and his mate, leading by example, trained the new crew in the ways of lifting barges and toting bales, and steamed upstream to Fort Benton. The strikers' bluff was called as Captain Todd's novel crew "covered themselves with bacon, grease, dirt and glory on their trip [and] … worked remarkably well considering that this is their first experience." After making port at Fort Benton and starting the return trip to Bismarck, the native roosters "… poured out their souls in song to which five or six of them industriously kept time on old tin cans."[16] Josephus Todd died as he lived, a riverman, in St. Louis in 1899.

Captain E. Shelton Andrews, the Maritime pilot on the Saskatchewan, left his navigating days behind, as he stayed on in Saskatoon as a farmer and town father. His *May Queen* met the fate of a lot of steamers, robbed for engines and parts before being swept away in a flood. "The Captain," as he was known in the new town, even met his new bride shortly after the rebellion, when Mary Ellen Thomson came to town from Ontario to help settle her sister. Performing the evening milking chores for her sister's farm, she first met "the Captain" when "a man with a 'longhorn mustache' and a dashing manner," informed Miss Thomson, "Lady, that's not your cow." In less than a year, the misunderstanding turned to matrimony, as Mary Ellen Thomson and Shelton Andrews found their own mutual utopia. They left Saskatoon only once in their marriage, to try living on the West Coast. It didn't take, and soon the Andrewses were back in town and had built a red brick brownstone, where the captain and his bride lived, held dances, teas and the initial meetings of the Saskatoon Historical Association. Shelton Andrews died in 1935. Mary Ellen followed in 1956, a year after being named Saskatoon's Citizen of the Year.

Archie Ballantine worked steamboats again, but became better known in Prince Albert's burgeoning timber industry. He worked for the Sanderson Lumber Mill and in later years took a civil service job as the Dominion government timber inspector. Ballantine died in Prince Albert in 1942, but not before writing down his recollections of the 1885 navigation season, providing succeeding generations with a rare insight into an often forgotten aspect of history. His memoirs were published in *Saskatchewan History*.

Julian Dougall continued as the captain of the *Marquis* until 1888, when, according to Archie Ballantine, he became a "skipper on Mackenzie River vessels,"[17] possibly as captain of the *Wrigley*. Since little else has been found, we have to take Archie's word for it.

The last of the rebellion rivermen, John Scribner Segers, carried on as one of the great unsung characters of the history of the West. His career spanned four decades, and always he could be seen piloting steamboats on the edge of frontiers. Bruce Peel writes that he "indubitably sailed on more rivers than any other captain in history,"[18] no mean feat for a man identified by historians only as the "Captain on the *Northcote* at Batoche." He piloted on the mythic Mississippi, the Missouri, the border-bisecting

Red, the Minnesota, the Athabasca, the frigid waters of the Mackenzie, and the gold-laden Yukon. Our own story saw the remarkable Segers hauling British troops on the far-flung Nile in Africa, and of course, his service on both branches of the Saskatchewan in both war and peacetime.

After finishing up the 1885 shipping season on the *Northcote*, Segers left the Saskatchewan for good. In 1887, the *Edmonton Bulletin* reported the construction of a sternwheeler at Athabasca Landing under the supervision of Josie Smith. But when the *Athabasca* put into the river for service in 1888, the captain was John Segers. With ten crewmen, Segers ran the *Athabasca* on behalf of the Hudson's Bay Company, between Mirror Landing and the Athabasca River's own "Grand Rapids" as it supplied the far-flung Northlands. Besides Segers' vessel, Métis boatmen also shipped goods on the Athabasca, in scows. Ironically, many of these boatmen were refugees from the North West Rebellion, meaning crusty old Captain Segers found himself working side by side with men who just a few years earlier had tried to kill him at the Batoche ferry. John Segers spent 10 peaceful summers on the *Athabasca*, the longest commission of his career, but by 1897 he was ready for a change.

The lure of gold stirred John Segers' heart, and he traded in his steamboat captaincy for a pair of Yukon-bound York boats. Along with Frank Hardisty, son of the HBC factor William Hardisty, Segers was one of a party of 11 hardy frontier types who pushed out of Athabasca Landing for the goldfields, discarding the widely held notion that one had to enter the Yukon by way of the Alaskan panhandle. The Segers–Hardisty party left on August 18, 1897, and reached Fort Chipewyan a month later. Segers proved to be as steady a pilot on the rudder of the York boat as he was on the big wheel of the steamers, as his party called on the HBC posts of the northern frontier of the Athabasca, Slave and Mackenzie valleys until they reached the Mackenzie delta.

After the party split up, Segers and Hardisty spent the winter relaxing with their feet up before the fire at Fort McPherson, streamlining the York boat and waiting for spring breakup. When the ice went out, the two paddled furiously up the Rat River to McDougall's Pass. After a difficult crossing, pulling the boat over the Great Divide, the York boaters paddled down the Porcupine to the mouth of the Yukon River. Exhausted, Segers and company flagged down a ride to Dawson City on, of all things, a steamboat. The party paid for their passage and arrived at their destination on August 3, 1898, nearly a full year after departing.

John Segers never struck a claim or threw a pick into a gravel bar. By now he realized that boiling water coursed through his veins, and found another way to fortune by—what else—piloting a steamboat. Within days of arrival, Segers accepted the wheel of the SS *Sovereign*. On the Yukon, the captain made his own gold, and wrote to his daughter in Edmonton that he made more money in a day than he had in a month at Athabasca Landing for the HBC.[19]

In 1903, he invested his earnings in the SS *Quickstep*. His Yukon career ended when an earthquake and subsequent tidal wave landed his ship on top of a warehouse in

Nome, Alaska. A lawsuit was filed over the accident, giving the old pilot a hard lesson in liability procedure that finished his Yukon career, By 1903, Segers was once more back on the Athabasca River, working for the HBC's upstart competitor, the Northern Transportation Co., founded by the flamboyant "Peace River Jim" Cornwall. For the NTC, Segers skippered the *Midnight Sun*, and even worked on a rarity for western rivers, a sidewheeler, called the *Northern Light*. In his twilight years, Segers found himself prospecting in the mountains of Idaho, where a snow avalanche wiped out all in his travelling party. Segers survived the slide, but his health was never the same. He wound up in Rossland, B.C., where he died in 1909.

The river reclaims her fleet

It takes a chief trader of the Hudson's Bay Company itself to sum up the brief experiment of frontier steamboating: "These steamers gradually lost their usefulness. But they had served their day; and the enterprise, courage and foresight shown in building them at that period in such a remote and inaccessible part of the country, hundreds of miles from the source of material, were in themselves remarkable."[20] Slowly most of the riverboats used in the campaign against the rebellion faded into virtual nothingness, rotting on riverbanks as quaint memories or childhood playgrounds before finally catching fire or having parts cannibalized for machinery or building supplies. Eventually pioneer recyclers and nature left nothing but stories of sternwheelers on the riverbanks. Even the ice-tossed wreck of the *Manitoba* had a small bit of life left in it: its boilers were used in a succession of sawmills.[21]

The *Princess*, the sidewheel lake steamer that brought the troops to the rails at Selkirk, had a successful career as a lake freighter and passenger vessel on Lake Winnipeg. Eventually the *Princess*'s sidewheels were removed, and replaced by the more efficient twin-screw propeller system. The story of its end is one of the most tragic in inland navigation. On August 6, 1906, the ship had left Poplar Point on Lake Winnipeg with a load of fresh fish, nine passengers and seven crewmen, when a stiff wind shifted to the north. The gale whipped up 25-foot waves that swamped the craft. The engine room filled with six feet of water and doused the boilers, leaving the *Princess* powerless and at the mercy of the huge inland sea. As a lifeboat was loaded, the *Princess*'s hull split like a banana peel, throwing the remaining occupants into the bone-chilling waters. Captain John Hawes, characteristically, went to the bottom with his ship, as did three crew and two passengers.

The *North West* continued to be a force on the North Saskatchewan, where "the presiding genius in the pilothouse was Captain Josie Smith."[22] The old skipper of the *Lily* had been out of the country during the rebellion days, and came back in 1889 to "handle the mighty *North West* like a canoe." Smith "knew the river in the days when the canoe and the York boat were standard equipment," and "worked only from dawn to dusk." The ship was also the scene of another of Smith's talents: "At night, a fiddler swung out into the dance hall. And one of the best fiddlers on the river was … Josie Smith … handl[ing] a fiddle with the same ease as he could the *North West*."[23] But shipping times were lean, and with steamboat profits and wages spiraling downward, Smith had to rely on his own son to double as navigator and clerk.

The *North West* continued its service on the North Saskatchewan until 1897, even carrying picnic excursions to secluded spots upriver from Edmonton, but soon the railways closed in to install a bridge, blocking the *North West*'s route during construction. The ship's last season was marked by its delivery of nothing less than a key technology of the 20th century: an oil derrick and drilling equipment for a well being drilled by the Dominion government. For a couple years the vessel was beached at Edmonton, where it functioned as a warehouse. The ship was nearly destroyed on one of its picnic tours when a windstorm "spun the *North West* like a leaf"[24] and threatened to topple it onto shore. Its actual destruction would be no less dramatic.

The final fate of the *North West*, the last of the Prairie Warships, was, if nothing else, vivid and worthy of embellishment by local folklorists: "… if Edmonton were a seaport, and sea-minded poets were prowling the waterfront, looking for ideas, the final sailing of the *North West* would be the subject of many a sea-ballad."[25] In August of 1899, as the last crop of the 19th century was being harvested, Edmonton was struck by a torrential late summer rain, "nearly as persistent as a certain rain you'll find described in your family Bible."[26] The freak storm was enough to swell the river beyond its banks and cover Ross Flats, the *North West*'s usual resting spot. On the afternoon of August 17, the curious citizenry of Edmonton lined the banks of the North Saskatchewan when they heard the news that the *North West* was in trouble.

The torrent broke the boat free from its moorings and cast its mass violently downstream and toward the concrete piers of the low level railway bridge, still under construction. The crowd held its breath, as it looked like the river might allow the ship to pass safely between the piers. And gulped when it did not. With a crunching thud, the *North West* struck the pier, ripping out its engines on the concrete. For 10 thrilling minutes, the boat sat clinging to life on the pier, eventually breaking free and destroying the buildings of a coal mine on Grierson Hill. From there, Edmonton folk could only sigh as the ship left town for the last time, the pilothouse and upper deck all that was left above the water line. Two days later, the disintegrated wreck floated past Saddle Lake. "The *North West* had returned to the river,"[27] doomed by both the freak flood and that other engine of ruin, the railway bridge that blocked its path.

The *Alberta* was finally able to return to her home port on the Belly River on June 24, 1886, completing a circuit started nearly two years before. Her wartime tour had taken her into the war zone, to Edmonton, and to the far northern reaches of the Saskatchewan's mouth. The ship's engineer, Thomas McPherson, regaled the locals with stories of his rebellion service. Some of his tales, told to pharmacist John Higinbotham, stretched his wartime experience a bit. "He tells of picking up enlisted men along the route, and of their encounters with the rebels. In these skirmishes the boat was hotly peppered from the shores, but fortunately there were no casualties aboard."[28] Of course, investigation tells us that the *Alberta* had never been fired upon, causing one to believe Tom McPherson to be somewhat of a "folklorist," to put it nicely.

The Coal Banks the *Alberta* returned to in 1886 was a very different village from the one the ship had left. It was now a town with a new name, Lethbridge, and the community was building on top of the coulees to greet the railway. The first engineer on the first train into Lethbridge was that selfsame Tom McPherson, switching from gales to rails and leaving no doubt as to the fate of the Belly River coal fleet. Coal would now travel overland, and the grand experiment of the Belly River as a highway of commerce was finished.

The *Alberta*'s return was greeted not by brass bands but by workmen armed with bars, saws and hammers to gut the boat's innards. The engines ended up powering a new sawmill, utilized without even removing them from the boat. After beaching the craft, the paddle wheel was replaced with a rotating drum that operated the mill's machinery. Workmen at the saw yard used the vacant storerooms as a boarding house. In time the mill found other power sources, and the *Alberta* was left to the plunder of all. Jim Wallwork, a local raconteur, said the *Alberta*'s engines were shipped to St. Michael's, Alaska, and resurrected for use in a Yukon River steamboat.

The bell of the *Alberta* is all that remains of the Belly River coal fleet, in the collection of the Galt Museum in Lethbridge.
GALT MUSEUM & ARCHIVES
P199901031002-G

Its engine scavenged, the *Alberta*'s boilers were hauled over to the Galts' No. 1 drift mine, where the furnaces were fired for the benefit of an engine that pulled loaded coal cars by cable up the coulee bank on an inclined railway. When the mine was done with them, the same boilers were moved again, to the new powerhouse, where their steam generated energy for Lethbridge's first electric lights. Eventually, the boiler was recycled into recreational use, as ingenious miners turned it into a public bath, complete with hot running water, a luxury in the days before modern indoor plumbing. Local ranchers and townsmen came to the riverside and tore out doors, windows and planks from the scavenged ship, and it is said that two entire houses were built from the superstructure.

Finally, only the barest hull remained, used as a playground and diving platform by swimmers and by "kids who would play cops and robbers on the old *Alberta*."[29] Finally, the skeleton was cast to the troubled flood waters of 1902, crumbling in the torrent. As a CPR engineer, Jim Wallwork said that from his perch high atop Lethbridge's high level bridge, the boat's ribs could barely be made out as a shadowy image buried and rotting in the silt. For years, downstream ranchers would gather drifting planks for their own use. All that remained for posterity was the bell, saved for alarm use by the Lethbridge fire department. Firemen also rang the bell as a curfew to call off the streets the very youths who played about the *Alberta*'s remains. The bell survived time, and currently resides, fittingly, in the Galt Museum.

The *Alberta*'s sister ship, the *Baroness*, never returned to its birth port. It certainly tried, in 1886, with a cargo of farm implements destined for Fort Macleod. But near the eventual site of the town of Bow Island, the *Baroness* could not get past an obtrusive sandbar. The freight was unloaded for overland shipment, and the *Baroness* turned back to Medicine Hat. It would be its last voyage. The Galts seemed to want to erase the memory of their money-losing experiment by de-evolution, scrapping steamboat parts for whatever could be got for them. Again, only the engines remained valuable enough for the Galts, and in March of 1887, mining company mechanics removed the steam engines from the *Baroness* and shipped them to Lethbridge for use in their No. 3 mine. Mercilessly, its hulk too was parcelled out for ranch houses, culverts and souvenirs, and left to rot on the Medicine Hat riverbank near the CPR bridge until the hulk disintegrated in the same 1902 flood that claimed the *Alberta*.

The 1886 season saw the river's most luxurious ship, the *Marquis*, back on the Saskatchewan, with Jim Sheets in command. On July 26, the cruiser hit a boulder at the foot of Thorburn's (a.k.a. Tobin's) Rapids, and sank. There was some doubt as to the practicability of raising it, but Captain Sheets intervened on the *Marquis*'s behalf at a company inquest,[30] arguing that she was too integral a part of the steamer service to be left to the vagaries of the river. Sheets's advice was heeded and the *Marquis* was ordered raised and repaired. In charge of the operation was its builder, Peter McArthur, who finally got to be of some use to the river he was so mercilessly banished from by the company he'd helped to found.

In 1887, the *Marquis* was beached at Cumberland House. The ship was having extreme difficulty with upstream trips and proved to be no longer able to climb La Colle's Falls unassisted. In 1890, it was towed to Prince Albert by the *North West*, only to be inexplicably beached and abandoned by the company. Her saloon deck saw some local civic use as a dance hall. Salvage wood from her decks and hull were sold for house construction in Prince Albert. Some of the ship's fretworks were resurrected for marine use again, as they were still in serviceable shape for use in the construction of the riverboat *Saskatchewan*. The *Marquis* lay on the riverbank well into the 20th century, and photos show its remains as late as 1923. The boilers were unceremoniously used merely as deadweight filler to prevent hydroelectric poles from sinking into muskeg. The *Marquis*'s anchor is on exhibit in a museum at The Pas, Manitoba, while her bell and part of her flues are in the Prince Albert City Museum, where the local Historical Society meetings are kept orderly by the president's gavel, made from the wood of the *Marquis*.

The *Minnow* had little to do during the rebellion, thanks to the lackadaisical Captain Maloney. The Galts brought the *Minnow* home to Lethbridge, but in a couple of years they literally sold the little tug down the river. The Lamoureux brothers, lumber magnates based in Fort Saskatchewan, had a successful operation cutting timber high up on the North Saskatchewan. Timber was floated downstream to their mill on rafts, but a team of horses was needed to get the rafts back to their timber limit, a slow and costly arrangement.

In the summer of 1887, Joseph and Frank Lamoureux came to Lethbridge with $1,000 cash. They left town on the Oldman River with the *Minnow* while Elliott Galt pocketed their cash. The brothers sailed their tug to their town on the North Saskatchewan and used it to tow their rafts and gather log booms for their saw mill. Their French mother tongue rechristened the boat *Minou*, or Kitten, and it spent the next 11 years purring up and down the North Branch.

In September of 1887, the *Minou* delivered a boom of lumber and a barge of coal to Battleford. Judge Charles Rouleau once chartered it to supply his gold mine in 1895, but on the return trip it "got aground and partly filled with water. The town fire engine was taken down and pumped her out."[31] The Lamoureux brothers finally gave up on their *Minou* in 1898. As a relative, Hormisdas Lamoureux, who cut cordwood for the tug said, "They broke themselves with the boat. They put the profit in that." Paradoxically, Hormisdas thought, "If they had used horses they still would have been all right."[32]

The *Minou* was then sold to Cunliffe & Ball, a firm operated by Percy Cunliffe, a British remittance man who had a flourmill in Fort Saskatchewan. Cunliffe died soon after and the mill burned down. The *Minou* met the usual steamboat end when a flood broke it from its moorings and beached it up a creek off the river, leaving it to rot in the elements.

"The oldtimers speak of the steamer *Northcote* as the 'North Goat' and imagine she was named after some nanny-goat in the Arctic Circle."[33] Sir Stafford Northcote's namesake met her fate miserably and was in fact treated like some old goat. In the fall of 1886, Captain Jerry Webber was back in the country and in command of the

The *Northcote* stranded at Cumberland House, as photographed by Sir Edmund Walker of the Canadian Bank of Commerce during a tour of the Prairie provinces. GLENBOW ARCHIVES NA 303-237

Northcote when he struggled with low water on a cut-off on the upper reaches of The Pas River. He beached the ship on the shore of Cumberland Lake, an eternity away from the lower reaches it served so well. The *Northcote* never sailed again. At the ancient Hudson's Bay post of Cumberland House, the famous vessel was left forever on dry ground and abandoned unceremoniously by its mercantile masters.

Two of the first travellers to visit were members of an expedition sponsored by the Geological Survey of Canada in 1894. Canadian scientist Joseph Burr Tyrell and Scottish adventurer Robert Munro-Ferguson came through Cumberland on their way back from a canoe trip across the Barren Lands of the Far North, and were regaled by two Scottish factors, MacFarlane and MacDougall, in the lore of the *Northcote*. Munro-Ferguson sat transfixed as he was told the story of the running of the Batoche gauntlet. "The engineer and the captain were the chief objects of aim and had a lively time. The captain lay flat on the floor of the wheelhouse and steered so—looking through a crack! Several spokes were shot off his wheel and the cabin was honeycombed. The rebels lowered a steel cable and caught the *Northcote*'s after funnels at a narrow point of the river, but she pulled through."[34] For Tyrell, the stories were probably more relevant, for the activity of the North West Rebellion had delayed his geological work for weeks.

The Cumberland locals saw the *Northcote* as a landmark, especially for teenage couples who found the cabins excellent for moonlit rendezvous on long summer nights. In 1905, a priest, Father Bélanger, was horrified at the *Northcote*'s new-found reputation for premarital hospitality and asked the HBC to do something. Before long, a local Indian, Jimmy Greenleaf, was hired to douse the ship in coal oil and set it aflame in a pyre of piety. Religious fervour did to the grand old "North Goat" what armed rebellion and the treacherous Saskatchewan River could not. H.M.S. Cotter, an old HBC trader, said in 1931, "Fire, relic hunters and the elements have done their deadly work, and all that remains now are parts of her shattered floor timbers, the framework of the stern wheel, the massive cylinders, and the boilers."[35]

The *Northcote* did not have much more life left in her in 1886, so it was well that her passage through that bullet-riddled Batoche gauntlet was a history-making episode. In a barely accessible northern wilderness on the shore of Pine Lake, now rechristened the Cumberland, near the modern boundary of Saskatchewan and Manitoba, and a town colourfully known as Pemmican Portage, the remains of the once-mighty *Northcote* rest in abject obscurity. Her boilers are still visible, having been pulled from the river by a Caterpillar tractor and skids in 1971 and preserved on concrete

Even when nothing remains but its boilers, the *Northcote* provides shelter to a passing canoeist.
GEOLOGICAL SURVEY OF CANADA

blocks by the province as part of Cumberland House Provincial Park. A handful of tourists continue to make the journey, which until recently could be made only by boat or plane. In 1967, adventurer John van Tamelen and a party of canoeists decided to commemorate Canada's Centennial by paddling from Hudson's Hope, B.C., to the site of Expo 67 in Montreal. Along his route, van Tamelen stopped at Cumberland and picked up a rusty nail from the *Northcote* as a souvenir.[36]

While some remains of the historic *Northcote* still rest in remote obscurity, other pieces of the legendary boat are scattered about. The steam whistle is in the Fred Light Museum at Battleford, while three feet of deck planking are now a cribbage board owned by a Prince Albert resident. The bell is in the steeple of the Duck Lake Anglican Church. As well, a souvenir shop, antique store and artist's studio in Duck Lake has been refurbished to resemble the boat that lends its name to the shop, Northcote Art 'n' Antiques.

The antique ferries ...

The myriad non-powered rafts and scows that served as ferries for the forces of 1885 form a lasting legacy on the rivers they cross. The craft were replaced from time to time, as dictated by wear or increased traffic, but the locations of the crossings themselves remained. As settlers began to take up homesteads and build new communities, ferries were an important link in the transportation network of prairie Canada. Most ferries were eventually replaced by bridges as vehicular traffic grew, but many of them were still in operation far into the latter half of the 20th century. A fortunate few are in use still.

John Walter's familiarity with wood and the river netted him far greater yields than the annual $50 he made building York boats in the 1870s. For 20 years his *Belle of Edmonton* was an integral part of the incredible growth of Edmonton into a major city. The *Belle* was the prototype for all Western ferries to follow, which is hardly surprising, considering that Walter constructed virtually all of the early ferries used on the North Branch. His success from the ferries propelled him into prominence as the North Saskatchewan's principal timberman and builder of river vessels of all descriptions: ferries, steamboats, log booms, gold dredges and the flotilla of scows and odd craft that plunged into the Athabasca River carrying fur trade supplies and gold prospectors to the Arctic. It took the river itself to break John Walter. The flood of 1915 carried away all the symbols of his good fortune: his sawmill, the buildings on his flat, and hundreds of thousands of dollars worth of inventory lumber. Ironically, all that was left was a pair of steamboats, the *Scona* and the *City of Edmonton*, his least profitable ventures. After the flood, Walter couldn't even afford to operate them. He died on Christmas Day, 1920, a half-century to the day since he'd first seen Edmonton from a York boat.

Gabriel's Ferry, the farm and crossing once operated by the general of the Métis resistance, came into use again. Dumont himself was able to take advantage of a general amnesty to return to live and die in the area, but he had no interest in reviving the ferry. He was then an old man, but he would inspire another prairie "rebel," the young John Diefenbaker. Some years after Dumont's death, a ferry was revived as a connection between the villages of Wakaw and Rosthern, towns that didn't even exist in 1885. The ferry was eventually supplanted by a steel-span bridge, and a government sign commemorates the buffalo hunters' spiritual presence: "Gabriel's Bridge—South Saskatchewan River." Nearby, the old Clarke's Crossing, once crossroads of the North West, is now known as Clarksboro, site of a railway bridge on a Canadian National line. But there is still a modern, working ferry, which the history traveller can use between Saskatoon and the Fish Creek/Batoche battlefields.

Batoche's Ferry was never rebuilt after being destroyed by order of General Middleton. The townsite today is a National Historic Site, operated, ironically, by the very Canadian government that annihilated it in 1885. Time heals wounds, and here it becomes apparent that the true winners of the rebellion were the historians. The entire battlefield is represented, from Middleton's "zareba" camp, to the cemetery, to the rifle pits, to the still-standing St. Antoine's church and rectory, to the ruins and basements of Batoche village. The interpretive centre on site tells the whole story, including a scale model of the *Northcote* running the gauntlet of gunfire. Down by the actual river, however, a little more imagination is required. Happily, the terrain has changed little, with no signs of modern intrusion, but there are no signs of the ferry, the fateful cable or the *Northcote*. All that remains of the morning of May 9, 1885, is the river.

... and the modern river

River navigation on the Saskatchewan did not quite end with the rebellion. For a number of years steamers were able to operate where railways had not yet been built over the muskeg, mostly in the far reaches of the lower Saskatchewan. Steamboat service had a few more years of life, but it was a lingering death. Entrepreneurs came and went, but most found only heartbreak. The most ambitious one was the flamboyant Horatio Ross, whose early 20th century fleet was a spectacular failure, culminating in a catastrophic collision of his *City of Medicine Hat* with a Saskatoon bridge in 1908. Ross kicked around the river for years afterward, but from there it was a spotty history for steamers on the two branches, mostly as towboats for lumber or ore barges. The *Saskatchewan* served Cumberland House and The Pas for decades. Though some ships were seen into the 1950s, they remained only quaint reminders and operated mostly on the lowermost reaches of the Saskatchewan, in areas not yet serviced by railway or road. In effect, steamboats were a bridge between eras, a means for northern communities to survive until a set of tracks could get there. Eventually, the tracks themselves were supplanted by highways and bush planes.

All the soldiers, politicians and rebels are long dead today. The steamer captains and their crews are gone and their corporate masters are remembered only in print. The wooden boats have long since returned to the sod, and most people alive today hardly know they ever existed. Only one character from our story is still there to be seen: the Saskatchewan River and its tributaries, where the river improvements that could have made the steamers more viable never happened. There just was never enough political or economic support for the dredging that needed to be done. In reality, it probably would have been a fool's venture anyway. The river has a way of more or less doing what it wants, and it barely would have noticed anything 19th-century earth-moving technology would have been able to do to its channels.

It would take another era, a new century with bigger machines, more dollars and more know-how to challenge the river. As entrepreneurs and governments sought to tame and shape the streams to their will, governments demanded that the rivers be controlled, not for navigation, but for irrigation, hydroelectricity and municipal water supplies. The wars for the rivers are being fought not with rifles, carbines and steamboats anymore, but with writs and injunctions, shovels and earthmovers. The frontiersmen, soldiers and river pilots have been replaced by bureaucrats, irrigators, engineers and environmentalists.

As Captain Sheets could navigate his river using, as the observers said, "a big damn," modern society has taken a similar tack in that the cries are always to build a "a big dam." To this end, the Saskatchewan has been able to serve many functions. At Cole's Falls, the breakers that impeded progress to Prince Albert eventually came to be seen by town boosters as a means to produce electricity. But the project was fraught with disaster, and the river eventually won. Finally, in 1967, the Saskatchewan was tamed by the electricity merchants. Tobin's Rapids became Tobin Lake, the nerve centre of the E.B. Campbell hydroelectric station, as the river made possible the vast quantity of electrical energy that is consumed for comfort and industry. But the impact of the dam on the northern ecosystem was disastrous for those who lived off the river. The dam forever changed the water level of the Saskatchewan, and wildlife was banished from its own realm.

The Galt family traded steamboating for irrigation development, and what they started now makes the arid prairies bloom in southern Alberta and Saskatchewan by use of dams on the St. Mary's, the Oldman, the Bow and the massive Diefenbaker Dam at the Elbow of the South Saskatchewan. Large valleys have become reservoirs, supplies kept in stock to maintain what has become a billion-dollar agricultural industry, as possibilities unheard of in 1885 are realized today. The jury is till out on the environmental cost.

Despite the vaunted ingenuity of man, none of this development comes without a cost. The wild, flowing river is now in check. The floods that once sustained a wildlife environment are in danger. The very industry the river made possible now threatens it, as the growth of cities, larger industries and ever more intensive agriculture threaten the very quality of the water. The water we feed ourselves, our cattle, our grain, vegetables and hay, is being poisoned. By ourselves.

But in spite of all the engineering miracles, nature will find a way. In 1995, when research for this book began, June rains melted the Rocky Mountain snowpack and swelled the Oldman River reservoir until it could not be contained. The floodgates had to be opened, and the resulting tide filled the vast valley, damaging or obliterating everything in its path. The tributaries wreaked havoc on all communities and farms along the route, until uniting themselves into the South Saskatchewan for a massive frontal assault on the city of Medicine Hat. For a few days, the 'Hat became a "port town" once again, until the river flowed off to its destination in the forests of northern Manitoba.

Dams may come and dams may go, but the mighty Saskatchewan will always get the last laugh.

Epilogue

In the Wash of the Wheel

Historians usually refer to the steamers as having been of little consequence in the rebellion. But what those self-same academics fail to relate is that, after the campaign was finished, the fleet delivered the bulk of the fighting force to Winnipeg from Prince Albert in just two days, on a route that cannot even be driven today. The feat is indicative of what the Saskatchewan River fleet really could have done under better river conditions. After all, using the Mississippi as a warpath and steamboats as warships during the U.S. Civil War made an obscure, alcoholic general named Ulysses S. Grant a hero, eventually president of his country and an immortal legend. In Canada, using the same tactic on the Saskatchewan River during the North West Rebellion made a vain British general a laughingstock. But if the war had started a mere month later, would General Frederick Middleton have been regarded a military genius instead?

More than half a century after those days, with Canada embroiled in a much bigger, longer and more intense war overseas, a writer named A.J. Dalrymple visited the ribs and timbers of steamboat wrecks at The Pas. His solitary meditation there was interrupted: "There are whoops and yells from the dank interior of one of the old sternwheelers; and half a dozen youngsters armed with toy pistols and wooden swords leap out and dash up the slippery bank. They are playing 'soldiers and Indians.' From the Swampy Cree reserve across the river comes the dismal wail of a husky. It is taken up by another, and yet another. The eerie cry is passed from camp to camp. Then the town dogs join in the chorus, yelping defiance across the water. The howling ceases as suddenly as it started; and silence reigns in the Northland."[1]

Did the children playing amid the remains of the *Northcote* understand the significance of their brothers, fathers, cousins and uncles fighting in faraway places at just that moment? Prairie farm boys as U-boat fodder in the North Atlantic, the battle honours of their steamboat ancestors barely remembered. The successors to Middleton's cavalries were mechanized, amphibious, rolling through Sicily and Italy, Holland and France. At Dieppe, some of the young Canadians chewed up on waterlogged beaches were a proud unit called the South Saskatchewan Regiment.

The Cree boys playing among the *Northcote*'s bones had as large a stake in the Second War for the World as anyone. Among the million Canadians in uniform were the aboriginal descendants of the "rebels and resisters" of the North West Rebellion. Again they were laying down their lives, this time as brother Canadians. And though Canada's first peoples would still have much upriver paddling to go to reclaim and retain their ancestral societies, cultures and languages, for the course of the overseas campaign at least, Canadian soldiers of all origins were united shoulder to shoulder, never knowing whether they would ever again see their home and native prairie lands, or the majestic meanders of the great Saskatchewan River.

Two more decades would flow by when, in 1966, yet another writer would visit the rusty carcass of the grand old workhorse of the river shoals. With thoughts of the nearly forgotten war record of the SS *Northcote*, noted Saskatchewan historian Edward McCourt wrote the greatest of all epitaphs to the flagship, envisioning a greater glory of some imaginary alternative timeline:

> What a pity the Northcote couldn't have gone down opposite Batoche, her lone gun blazing away, flag flying, Captain Sheets, who hailed from Missouri, cursing his enemies and calling for more steam as the muddy waters closed over his head. At the very least, instead of being left to rot like unburied corpses in full public view, the steamboats might have had provided for them in some remote place, a final harbourage to which, when their time came, they might have gone off—like the elephants, whom in size and grace of movement they greatly resembled—to die in peace and privacy far from the sight of men.[2]

Appendices

I. CREW OF THE STEAMER *NORTHCOTE* – 1885

Captain & Superintendant: James Sheets
Pilot: John S. Segers, Aaron Russell (mentioned as being aboard, but not on North West Medal Rolls)
Engineer: Arthur L'Heureaux
Assistant Engineer: Daniel Hurst (Herce)
Clerk: Walter Rennie Talbot
Assistant Clerk: D. McDonald
Carpenter: John McDonnell, Roderick Smith
Fireman: J. Mc Andrews, Donald McIvor
Watchman: William Craiggie, Edward B. Haight
Steward: John Long
Cook: William McEwen
Waiter: Henry Elshan, Edwin James Hutchings
Mate: Angus McLeod
Deckhand: John Carson, Arthur Cave, John Chase, Xavier Gougeon, Richard Hughes, George A. Kerr, James John McLeod, William McLeod, Bernard McNeiel, William Minchington, Daniel Morgan, John Morgan, Francis Roland, Miner Simpson, John E. Sutcliffe, L.R. Unger

All above Received the North-West Medal, with the exception of Aaron Russell.

II. CREW OF THE STEAMER *BARONESS* – 1885

Captain: John B. Davis
Purser: Hugh McBeth (name unknown)

III. CREW OF THE STEAMER ALBERTA – 1885

(1 Captain, 2 engineers, 2 firemen, 2 pilots, 1 mate)–
Higinbotham, *When the West was Young*
Medicine Hat Times, June 24 1886
Captain: Josephus Todd
Pilot (name unknown): Bessel
Engineer: Thomas MacPherson
Clerk: T. Rooks
Nelson Todd, Wesley Todd are unaccounted for in 1885

IV. CREW OF THE STEAMER *MINNOW* – 1885

Captain: (name unknown) Maloney
Pilot (name unknown): Red Jackson

V. CREW OF THE STEAMER *NORTHWEST* – 1885

Captain (& Company Superintendant):
James Sheets
Cook: Dan Milligan
Watchman: Archie Ballantine

VI. CREW OF THE STEAMER MARQUIS – 1885

Captain: Julien Dougall

VII. BARGES & CREWS OF THE "SASKATCHEWAN BRIGADE"

George Gunn's Barge
Commanding Officer: Lieutenant John Laing Weller
Left Swift Current Creek May 1, 1885
Arrived Clarke's Crossing May 16, 1885

7th Fusilier contingent – Left Saskatchewan Landing May 11, 1885 (*Captain Leonard* left May 10)
Arrived Clarke's Crossing May 19–20, 1885

Commanding Officer: Lieutenant Colonel J. Deacon, Midland Battalion
Staff Adjutant: Captain W.M. Hudson
Brigade Orderly Officer: Captain Edward Harrison

Major Smith and *Captain Evans* (double barge)
Officer Commanding: Captain S. Frank Peters, #5 Company, 7th Fusiliers

Sir John Macdonald
Officer Commanding: Captain Thomas H. Tracy, C Company, 7th Fusiliers
Crew: A & C Companies

Captain Leonard
Officer Commanding: Captain Dillon, 7th Fusiliers
Crew: Captain Butler, 5 officers, 4 non-com. officers, 21 Troops – #2 & #4 Companies

General Middleton
Officer Commanding: Captain Edward McKenzie, 7th Fusiliers

Captain Kelly
Officer Commanding: Lieutenant Fred Bremner, 7th Fusiliers

Lieutenant Nelles
Officer Commanding: Major A.M. Smith, 7th Fusiliers
Crew: 4 officers, 28 non-coms & men of #4 Company
Major Gaitshore, Surgeon Fraser, Asst. Surgeon A. Campbell, Color Sergeant G. Jacobs

Boyd & Crowe
Officer Commanding: Lieutenant George M. Reid, 7th Fusiliers

General Laurie
Officer Commanding: 2nd Lieutenant N.R. Grieg, #2 Company, 7th Fusiliers
Crew: 32 men, parts of #1, # 3 & #4 Sections of # 2 Company

Hard Tack
Officer Commanding: Lieutenant Horace A. Yeoman,
Crew: 31 men – 2 officers, 29 non-coms & men

Captain Kerr
Officer Commanding: Lieutenant Harry Bapty, 7th Fusiliers
Crew: 35, Captain Kerr, Mr. Boyd

VIII. COMPENDIUM OF RIVER CRAFT INVOLVED IN THE NORTHWEST REBELLION – 1885

"Operations on Navigable Waters"
The undernamed craft were used for transport purposes on the Saskatchewan River : Steamers *Northcote, Northwest, Marquis, Baroness, Alberta, Minnow,* and 30 scows and barges.
During the operations the *Northcote* took part in the action of Batoche, and sustained considerable damage.
WILLIAM H. JACKSON, Lieutenant–Colonel, Deputy Adjutant General, Principal Supply, Pay, and Transport Officer To The North–West Forces.
Source: Jackson, W.H. , Sessional Papers of Canada, Dept. Of Militia & Defense, 9c, 1887

STEAMBOATS

Northcote – Built 1874 by Hudson's Bay Co.
Transferred 1883 to Winnipeg & Western
Transportation Co.;
Beached at Cumberland House, NWT, 1886;
burned c. 1903

Manitoba – Built 1875 by Merchants International
Steamboat Line; 1875 to Red River Transportation
Co.; c.1881 to Winnipeg & Western Transportation
Co.
Crushed by ice at Shell River, N.W.T., 1885

North West – Built 1881 by North West Navigation
Co.; 1884 to Winnipeg & Western Transportation
Co.;
Wrecked in flood at Edmonton, 1899

Marquis – Built 1882 by Winnipeg & Western
Transportation Co.
Beached at Prince Albert, 1890; burned c. 1909

Baroness – Built 1883 by North Western Coal &
Navigation Co.
Abandoned at Medicine Hat, 1886

Alberta – Built 1884 by North Western Coal &
Navigation Co.
Abandoned at Lethbridge, 1886

Minnow – Built 1884 by North Western Coal &
Navigation Co;
Transferred 1887 to Lamoureux Brothers;
Transferred 1898 to Percy B. Cunliffe
Abandoned on N. Saskatchewan, c. 1900

Source: Barris, Ted, *Fire Canoe* and Peel, Bruce,
Steamboats on the Saskatchewan

FERRIES	River	Owner or Operator
Calgary	Bow River	George Hamilton
Irish Washerwoman	Red Deer	Sage Bannerman
Belle of Edmonton	N. Sask.	John Walter
Clover Bar	N. Sask.	John Walter – Commandeered by Gen. Strange
Fort Pitt	N. Sask.	Military (*Clover Bar* raft)
Fort Carlton	N. Sask.	Hudson's Bay Company
HBC/Ft. Campbell	S. Sask.	Hudson's Bay Company/ NWMP
Lepine's	S. Sask.	Maxime Lepine; possibly destroyed at Batoche
Batoche	S. Sask.	Alex Fisher; formerly Xavier Létendre
Gabriel's Crossing	S. Sask.	Pierre Vandal; formerly Gabriel Dumont
Fish Creek	S. Sask.	Transport Service, temporarily operated by Captain E. Shelton Andrews
Clarke's Crossing	S. Sask.	Transport Service – formerly John Clarke
Saskatoon	S. Sask.	Andy Plant
Saskatchewan Landing	S. Sask	Sask. Coal Co.; Military; Fraser Tims

IX. NORTH SASKATCHEWAN FLOTILLA

*Big Bear, Hay Clad, Nancy, Bauset, Roy du Bord,
Clover Bar Ferry*

Notes

PROLOGUE

1 Ham, George Henry, *Reminiscences of a Raconteur*
2 Wishart, Bruce, "Paddlewheels on the Prairies," The Beaver, December/January 1989/90

CHAPTER ONE

1 Strange, Thomas Bland, *Gunner Jingo's Jubilee*
2 "History of Saskatchewan Waterways," Tourism Saskatchewan, Regina, http://canoesaskatchewan.rkc. ca/history.htm, accessed Oct 22, 2006.
3 Steele, Samuel, *Forty Years in Canada*
4 Peel, Bruce, *Steamboats on the Saskatchewan*
5 Ham, George, *Reminiscences of a Raconteur*
6 Merrick, George B., "Steamboats & Steamboating on the Upper Mississippi," *Saturday Evening Post of Burlington*, Iowa, May 8, 1915
7 Needler, George H., *Louis Riel, The Rebellion of 1885*
8 Unattributed, cited in O'Neil, Paul, & eds., *The Rivermen*
9 O-ge-mas-es, "Steamboating for the HBC on the Saskatchewan," *The Beaver*, April 1922
10 Goderidge, L.R., cited in Wickenden, Nick, "*Northwest* and *Minnow*," *Alberta Historical Review*, Summer 1957
11 MacKay, Elsie, "Captains All," in *Selkirk's 75th Anniversary*
12 O-ge-mas-es

CHAPTER TWO

1 Ship's history sheet, "Manitoba," Hudson's Bay Company Archives, in Archives of Manitoba, Winnipeg
2 Stardom, Eleanor, *A Stranger to the Fur Trade*
3 An unnamed HBC shareholder at the Annual General Court Meeting, London, England, June 28, 1871, quoted in Ray, Arthur, "Adventurers at the Crossroads," *The Beaver*, April–May 1986
4 *The Manitoban*, May 18, 1872
5 One source suggests that the unnamed boat may have been called "the *Saskatchewan*"; Ship's history sheet "*Northcote*," in Hudson's Bay Company Archives, Archives of Manitoba, Winnipeg
6 Northcote, Sir Stafford Henry, "Report of the Governor of the Hudson's Bay Company to Its Shareholders," London, England, Nov 1873
7 Cotter, H.M.S. "The Steamer Northcote," *The Beaver*, September, 1931
8 MacKay, Elsie, *Selkirk's 75th Anniversary*
9 Cotter
10 Ibid.
11 *Northcote* technical information cited in Peel, *Steamboats on the Saskatchewan*
12 Church Missionary Society Records & Correspondences, cited in Peel
13 *St. Paul Pioneer Press*, reprinted in *The Manitoban*, Oct 3, 1874
14 Hamilton, Robert, to McFarlane, Roderick, Aug 11, 1875, McFarlane correspondence
15 O-ge-mas-es
16 Marquis of Lorne, *Canadian Pictures*
17 *Saskatchewan Herald*, Oct 3, 1881
18 *Winnipeg Daily Times*, Sep 28, 1882
19 *Brandon Daily Sun*, Apr 24, 1881
20 *Manitoba Free Press*, June 1874
21 Ship's history sheet "*Marquis*," in Hudson's Bay Company Archives, Archives of Manitoba, Winnipeg

CHAPTER THREE

1 Ellis, L. Gregory, *The Stafford Family*
2 Higinbotham, John D., *When the West Was Young*
3 Lass, William, *A History of Steamboating on the Upper Missouri*
4 Ibid.
5 Greeley, Horace, quoted in Shepherd, George, "River Steamboats, Once Classic Mode of Transportation," *Scarlet & Gold*
6 Ibid.
7 Overholser, Joel, *Fort Benton, World's Innermost Port*
8 *Lethbridge News*, Railroad Edition, September 1890
9 Kelley, H.E., "Recalls First White Marriage in Southern Alberta," *Lethbridge Daily Herald*, Mar 29, 1924
10 Trew, Dora E., "Alberta's Prairie Steamer," *Canadian Cattleman*, Aug 1964; reprinted as "Lethbridge Had a Baroness" in Johnston, Alex, ed., *Boats and Barges on the Belly*
11 Ibid.
12 Clarke, Tom, "When Lethbridge Was a Port of Call for Steamers," *Lethbridge Herald*, Mar 5, 1927
13 *Macleod Gazette*, Mar 24, 1883
14 Ibid., Apr 14, 1883
15 Ibid., May 24, 1883
16 Ibid., June 4, 1883
17 Tom Clarke wrote that the planned length was 175 feet and wound up being actually 174 feet 6 inches. The Shipping Register from the port of Winnipeg lists 173 feet.
18 Letter, Stephens, Brit, to Wellington, Mr. & Mrs. Peter, Aug 19, 1883, printed in *Lethbridge Herald*, Golden Jubilee Edition, July 11, 1935, reprinted in Johnston, *Boats and Barges on the Belly*
19 Clarke
20 Ibid.
21 Ibid.
22 Dominion Day, now called Canada Day, is actually July 1, but in 1883 the date fell on a Sunday and celebrations likely were postponed to Monday in observance of the Christian Sabbath.
23 *Macleod Gazette*, July 14, 1883
24 Clarke
25 Ibid.
26 Higinbotham
27 Clarke
28 Marquis of Lorne, *Memories of Canada and Scotland*, cited in McDougall, D. Blake, *Princess Louise Caroline Alberta*
29 Higinbotham
30 Clarke
31 Galt, Sir Alexander, cited in Skelton, O.D., *Life and Times of Sir Alexander Tilloch Galt*
32 Barker, Ernest Neale, *Lethbridge Herald*, June 26, 1926
33 Liddell, Ken, *Calgary Herald*, July 30, 1956
34 Whitney, D.J., Sr., "Lethbridge Recollections," in Johnston, *Boats and Barges on the Belly*. Just such a seam can still be seen today, on the south bank of the Oldman River near Taber.
35 Ibid.

CHAPTER FOUR

1 Cowley, Rev. Abraham, Church Missionary Society, Records & Correspondence, cited in Peel, *Steamboating on the Saskatchewan*
2 "Report of the Board of Directors of the Winnipeg & Western Transportation Company Ltd.," Winnipeg, June 4 1883, Hudson's Bay Company Archives, F.41/1, Archives of Manitoba
3 *Yankton Press and Dakotan*, Mar 30, 1877; Letter, Davis, John B., to Davidson, William F., Mar 16, 1877, Davidson Papers, Minnesota Historical Society, St. Paul
4 Contract among Davis, John B., Davidson, Peyton S., and Card, B.C., Chief Quartermaster, Department of Dakota, Mar 20, 1877, Old Army Division, U.S. National Archives
5 Letter, Davis, John B., to Davidson, Capt. P.S., Apr 30, 1877, Davidson Papers
6 Letter, Flower, Mark, to Davidson, William F., June 30, 1877, Davidson Papers
7 *Prince Albert Times*, June 6, 1883, cited in Smith, T.R., "The Steamboat *Lily*," *Saskatchewan History* 17(2), 1964

8 *Prince Albert Times*, Oct 10, 1883
9 MacIvor, D.G., to son, 2 Feb 1925
10 Ibid.
11 Trow, James, Member of Parliament, quote cited in Woodcock, George, *Gabriel Dumont*
12 MacIvor
13 Wickenden, Nick, "North West and Minnow," *Alberta Historical Review*, Summer 1957
14 Stardom, Eleanor, *Stranger to the Fur Trade*
15 Russell, Aaron, in *Winnipeg Daily Sun*, Mar 25, 1885
16 Ibid.
17 Ibid.
18 Ibid.
19 Ibid.
20 Robinson, William, to Smith, William, Jan 10, 1885, from Stacey, C.P., *Records of the Nile Voyageurs*
21 Ibid.
22 Ibid.
23 Ibid.
24 Robinson
25 Russell
26 Ibid.
27 MacKay, Elsie, "Wm. Robinson, Captain of Industry," in *Selkirk's 75th Anniversary*
28 Ibid.
29 *Toronto Daily Mail*, Feb 6, 1885
30 Healey, Edna, *Lady Unknown: The Life of Angela Burdett-Coutts*
31 Russell
32 Robinson
33 Russell
34 *Winnipeg Daily Sun*, Mar 25, 1885
35 Kerr, John, as reported in *Winnipeg Daily Sun*, Apr 20, 1885
36 Ballantine, Archie, "Steamboating on the Saskatchewan," *Saskatchewan History*, Spring 1964.
37 Ibid.
38 Ham, George, *Toronto Daily Mail*, May 26, 1885 (story filed May 14, 1885)
39 St. Laurent Annals, 1885, Sisters, Faithful Companions of Jesus, *Journeying through a Century*
40 Ibid.
41 Ibid.

CHAPTER FIVE

1 Troy is now known as Qu'Appelle, but we will use Troy here to avoid conflation with Fort Qu'Appelle, an NWMP post some 18 miles north.
2 Telegram, Smith, D., to Caron, A., Mar 27, 1885, in Morton & Roy, eds., *Telegrams of the North-West Campaign*, hereinafter cited as *Telegrams*
3 Galt, A.T., to Macdonald, J.A., Mar 28, 1885, *Telegrams*
4 Caron to Wrigley, Mar 28, 1885, *Telegrams*
5 Wrigley to Caron, Mar 28, 1885, *Telegrams*
6 Tweed to Macdonald, Mar 30, 1885, *Telegrams*
7 Caron to Peeble, Mar 30, 1885, *Telegrams*
8 Wrigley to Caron, Mar 30, 1885, *Telegrams*
9 Caron to Wrigley, Mar 30, 1885, *Telegrams*
10 Ibid.
11 Wrigley to Caron, Mar 31, 1885, *Telegrams*
12 Ibid.
13 Ibid.
14 Caron to Wrigley, Mar 31, 1885, *Telegrams*
15 Wrigley to Middleton, Mar 31, 1885, *Telegrams*
16 Galt, A.T., to Caron, Mar 31, 1885, *Telegrams*
17 Middleton to Caron, Mar 31, 1885, *Telegrams*
18 Clarke, J.W., to Caron, Mar 31, 1885, *Telegrams*
19 Middleton to Caron, Apr 1, 1885, *Telegrams*
20 Clarke, J.W., to Caron, Mar 31, 1885, *Telegrams*
21 *Toronto Daily Mail*, Mar 30, 1885
22 Herchmer, William, Appendix B, Report of the Commissioner, NWMP, 1885
23 *Toronto Daily Mail*, Apr 11, 1885
24 Caron to Middleton, Apr 1, 1885, *Telegrams*
25 Van Horne to Caron, Apr 1, 1885, *Telegrams*
26 Ibid.
27 Caron to Van Horne, Apr 1, 1885, *Telegrams*
28 Van Horne to Caron, Apr 1, 1885, *Telegrams*
29 Caron to Van Horne, Apr 2, 1885, *Telegrams*
30 Middleton to Caron, Apr 2, 1885, *Telegrams*
31 Ibid.
32 Dewdney to White, F., Apr 2, 1885, *Telegrams*
33 Galt, E.T., to Caron, Apr 2, 1885, *Telegrams*
34 Van Horne to Caron, Apr 2, 1885, *Telegrams*
35 Molloy, R.J., to Caron, Apr 5, 1885, *Telegrams*
36 *Toronto Daily Mail*, Apr 8, 1885
37 Ham, George, *Toronto Daily Mail*, May 19, 1885
38 Letter, MacIvor, D., to his son
39 Galt, A.T., to Caron, Apr 6, 1885, *Telegrams*
40 Galt, E., to Caron, Apr 7, 1885; Caron to Van Horne, Apr 7, 1885; Van Horne to Caron, Apr 7, 1885, *Telegrams*
41 Galt, A.T., to Caron, Apr 7, 1885, *Telegrams*
42 *Toronto Daily Mail*, Apr 8, 1885
43 Middleton to Caron, Apr 9, 1885, *Telegrams*
44 Middleton to Caron, Apr 10, 1885, *Telegrams*
45 Galt, E.T., to Caron, Apr 11, 1885, *Telegrams*
46 *Toronto Daily Mail*, Apr 11, 1885

CHAPTER SIX

1 Imasees' name is also spelled "Ayimasis," also known to Americans as "Little Bear."
2 McLean, William, *Toronto Globe*, July 17, 1885
3 Ibid.
4 Big Bear to Martin, Sgt. John, from Cameron, W.B., *Blood Red the Sun*
5 Ibid.
6 Diary of Sleigh, Cpl. Ralph B., cited in Fryer, Harold, *The Frog Lake Massacre*
7 Ibid.
8 *Diary of Francis Dickens*, Lachance, Vernon, ed.
9 Sleigh
10 Ibid.
11 Ibid.
12 Ibid.
13 Ibid.
14 Ibid.
15 Parker, William C., from reminiscences published in *William Parker, Mounted Policeman*, Dempsey, Hugh, ed.
16 MacBeth, Rev. R.G., *The Making of the Canadian West*
17 MacBeth
18 Strange, Thomas Bland, *Gunner Jingo's Jubilee*
19 Ibid.
20 Ibid.
21 Ibid.
22 "Report of the Commissioner of the North-West Mounted Police, 1885," Report of Inspector Perry
23 MacBeth. Charles Constantine later joined the NWMP and became the first commander of the police in the Yukon district.
24 Ibid.
25 Strange
26 Ibid.
27 MacBeth
28 Ethier, In Chambers, History of the 65th Mount Royal Rifles
29 Ibid.
30 Strange
31 Ibid.
32 MacBeth
33 Strange
34 Ibid.
35 Ibid.
36 MacBeth
37 Strange
38 Ibid.

39 Ibid.
40 Ibid.
41 MacBeth
42 Strange
43 Ibid.
44 Ibid.
45 Ibid.
46 Ibid. The boats were named by Brown, Wayne F., in *Steele's Scouts.*
47 Perry
48 Strange
49 Zinovich, Jordan, *Battling the Bay*
50 Strange
51 MacBeth
52 Chambers
53 Strange
54 MacBeth
55 Strange
56 MacBeth
57 Strange
58 Ibid.
59 Ibid.
60 Orders issued at Vermillion Creek, May 20, 1885
61 Steele, *Forty Years in Canada*
62 Ibid.
63 Middleton to Strange, May 1, 1885, *Telegrams*

CHAPTER SEVEN

1 Dewdney to Caron, Apr 10, 1885. Morton, *Telegrams*
2 Special from Battleford, NWT, to *Toronto Daily Mail*, Apr 13, 1885
3 McKay, Ann Flora, *Prince Albert Daily Herald,* Apr 3, 1885. Subsequent Ann Flora Mackay quotes are from same.
4 Ibid., Mother Collings
5 Ibid.
6 Ibid.
7 Ibid.
8 Ibid., Mother Collings to Mother Superior Petit, Apr 20, 1885
9 Telegram, Middleton to Otter, Apr 9, 1885, from Otter papers in Library & Archives Canada, cited in Morton, Desmond, *The Canadian General*
10 Middleton to Caron, Apr 14, 1885, *Telegrams*
11 Macdonald, A. to Watson, R., Apr 2, 1885, *Telegrams*
12 Mother Collings to Mother Superior Petit, Apr 11, 1885
13 Middleton to Otter, Apr 11, 1885
14 Galt, A.T., to Caron, Apr 15, 1885, *Telegrams*
15 *Toronto Daily Mail*, Apr 13, 1885
16 Galt, A.T., to Caron, Apr 12, 1885, *Telegrams*
17 Ibid., Apr 13, 1885
18 Ibid.
19 Middleton to Caron, Apr 14, 1885, *Telegrams*
20 Quote cited in Stardom, Eleanor, *Stranger to the Fur Trade*
21 Caron to Middleton, Apr 14, 1885, *Telegrams*
22 Ibid., Apr 15, 1885
23 Galt, E.T., to Caron, Apr 16, 1885, *Telegrams*
24 Ibid., Apr 14, 1885
25 Galt, A.T., to Caron, Apr 14, 1885, *Telegrams*
26 Ibid., Apr 15, 1885
27 Ibid., Apr 16, 1885
28 Ibid.
29 Galt, E.T., to Caron, Apr 17, 1885, *Telegrams*
30 Caron to Galt, E.T., Apr 17, 1885, *Telegrams*
31 Middleton to Otter, Apr 13, 1885
32 Roddick, Thomas, "Report of Deputy Surgeon General," Sessional Papers 1886
33 Clapp, Charles Salyer, "With the Midland Battalion to Batoche," *Saskatchewan History*, Winter 1978
34 Middleton to Caron, Apr 14, 1885, *Telegrams*
35 Laurie, J.W., "Report of Major General Laurie," Sessional Papers
36 MacIvor, D.G., to son, Feb 2 1925
37 Laurie

38 Clapp
39 Ibid.
40 Diary of Stewart, Walter F., Staff Sergeant, Midland Battalion
41 Clapp
42 Kirwan, Miles W., May 3, 1885, "With the Midland," special correspondence to the *Toronto Daily Mail*, May 19, 1885
43 Ibid.
44 Ibid.
45 Talbot's Diary, via Ham, George, *Toronto Daily Mail*, May 19, 1885
46 Clapp
47 Talbot
48 Ibid.

CHAPTER EIGHT

1 Allan, Robert K., "A Riel Rebellion Diary," *Alberta Historical Review*, Summer 1964
2 Hughes, Owen, in *Prince Albert Daily Herald*, June 5, 1923, MSS C555/2/10.3h Morton Manuscripts Collection, University of Saskatchewan Library Special Collections
3 Telegram, Middleton to Caron, from 34 miles from Clark's Crossing, Apr 16, 1885, *Telegrams*
4 Ham, George, *Toronto Daily Mail*, Apr 28, 1885
5 Sources disagree on whether the correct spelling is "Clark" or "Clarke." Since most official telegrams read "Clarke," we will use that spelling here for the sake of consistency.
6 Ham
7 Campbell, Alexander, "An Account of the Advance of the 7th Fusiliers of London"
8 Andrews, Captain E. Shelton, paper given at proceedings of Saskatoon Historical Association, Apr 5, 1922
9 Allan
10 Middleton to Caron, Apr 18, 1885, *Telegrams*
11 Rusden, Harold Penryn, "Suppression of the Northwest Insurrection," in Macleod, *Reminiscences of a Bungle*
12 Andrews
13 Ham, George, in *Toronto Daily Mail*, Apr 27, 1885
14 Rusden
15 Andrews
16 Rusden
17 Ham, George, Apr 25, dispatch to *Toronto Daily Mail*, published Apr 27, 1885
18 Andrews
19 Rusden
20 Turner, John Peter, *The North-West Mounted Police*, vol. II
21 Johnston, E.R., *St. Paul Pioneer-Press*, May 8, 1885
22 Middleton to Johnston
23 Ibid.
24 Ibid.
25 Ham, George, *Toronto Daily Mail*, Apr 30 1885
26 Ibid.
27 Middleton, quoted by Johnston, E.R., in *St. Paul Pioneer Press*, May 8, 1885
28 Macdonald, J. Stuart, *The Dominion Telegraph*
29 McManus, Robert, *Toronto Daily Mail*, Apr 27 1885
30 Ham, George, *Toronto Daily Mail*, Apr 30 1885
31 Johnston
32 Ham
33 Kirwan
34 Ibid.
35 Ibid.
36 Ibid.
37 Williams, Lt.-Col. A.T.H., written orders to Midland Battalion aboard *Northcote*, relayed by Ponton, Capt. E.G., Adjutant, transcribed in Clapp, "With the Midland Battalion to Batoche," *Saskatchewan History*, Winter 1978
38 Kirwan
39 Stewart, Staff Sgt. Walter F., Midland Battalion, diary of; also cited in Granatstein & Hilmer, *Battle Lines*
40 *Northcote* log entry, Apr 24, 1885, Talbot, Walter R., in Ham, George, *Toronto Daily Mail*, May 19, 1885

41 Stewart
42 Letter of Wrighton, W.T., Apr 20, 1885, cited in Stanley, George F.G., "The Campaign of 1885," *Saskatchewan History*, Autumn 1960
43 Kirwan
44 Clapp
45 Ibid.
46 Kirwan
47 Ibid.
48 Clapp
49 Talbot
50 Ibid.
51 Stewart
52 Talbot
53 Ibid.
54 Clapp
55 Ibid.
56 Ibid.
57 Stewart
58 Ibid.
59 King, Dr. Edmond, *Canadian Illustrated War News*, July 11, 1885
60 Clapp
61 Talbot
62 Clapp
63 Ibid.
64 Ibid.
65 King
66 Kirwan
67 Ibid.
68 Stewart
69 Kirwan
70 Ibid.
71 Ibid.
72 Ibid.
73 Talbot
74 Ord, Lewis Redman, *Reminiscences of a Bungle*
75 Talbot
76 Ibid.
77 Ibid.
78 Kirwan
79 Clapp
80 Kirwan
81 Ibid.
82 Talbot
83 Kirwan
84 Talbot
85 Ibid.
86 Kirwan
87 Stewart
88 Clapp
89 Kirwan
90 Cited in Jack, Donald, *Rogues, Rebels and Geniuses*
91 Roddick, Thomas, "Report of the Deputy Surgeon-General"
92 All quotes from Campbell Douglas are from articles in *Forest & Stream,* July 9, 1885, and *Badminton Magazine,* Apr 21, 1897, which were condensed by Needler, G.H., in "The Lone Canoeist of 1885," *The Beaver*, June 1950, and in *Louis Riel, The Rebellion of 1885*
93 The name imparted to Dr. Douglas by Needler
94 Percival, John, *For Valour*
95 *Toronto Daily Mail*, Apr 28, 1885
96 Quoted in Mallory, Enid, "To the Rebellion in a Folding Canoe," *The Beaver*, Autumn 1985, and in Needler, G.H., "The Lone Canoeist of the Saskatchewan," *The Beaver*, June 1950
97 Mallory and Needler
98 Ibid.
99 Ibid. for all quotes in paragraph
100 Ibid.
101 Ibid. for all quotes in paragraph
102 Ibid. for all quotes in paragraph
103 Kirwan
104 Ibid.
105 Mallory and Needler
106 Ibid. for all quotes in paragraph
107 Ibid.
108 Wrigley to Caron, May 2, 1885, *Telegrams*
109 Roddick
110 Ibid.
111 Kirwan
112 Stewart
113 Kirwan
114 Ibid.
115 Ibid.
116 Roddick
117 Kirwan
118 Stewart
119 Ibid.
120 Talbot
121 Clapp
122 MacIvor, D.G., February 2, 1925
123 Talbot
124 Clapp
125 *St. Paul Pioneer-Press*, May 4, 1885
126 Macdonald, J. Stuart
127 Talbot
128 Ibid.
129 Ham, George, *Toronto Daily Mail*, May 16, 1885 (story filed May 3)
130 Ibid.
131 Boulton, Charles Arkoll, *Reminiscences of the Northwest Rebellion*
132 Ham, George, *Toronto Daily Mail*, May 7, 1885
133 Ham, George, *Toronto Daily Mail*, May 19, 1885 (from story filed May 6), all quotes in paragraph
134 Ibid.
135 Ham, *Toronto Daily Mail*, May 7, 1885
136 Kirwan
137 Laurie
138 Ibid.
139 Ibid.
140 Ibid.
141 Jackson, William H., "Report of Lt.-Col. Jackson, Principal Supply, Pay & Transport Officer, 1886"
142 No relation to Maj. Henry Smith of the Infantry School Corps, who figures in the text later
143 Summary of Journal of Steamer "Baroness" compiled by Peel, Bruce, in *Boats and Barges on the Belly*

CHAPTER NINE

1 Ham, George, *Toronto Daily Mail*, May 19, 1885 (from story filed May 8)
2 Middleton's order, via Talbot, Walter, *Winnipeg Daily Sun*, May 27, 1885; the text of the order is as written by Talbot
3 Talbot
4 Boulton
5 Ham
6 McCourt, Edward, *Revolt in the West*. The quote, while fictional, nonetheless fits the character of Captain James Sheets.
7 Riel, Louis, *The Diaries of Louis Riel*
8 Dumont, Gabriel, "Gabriel Dumont's Account of the North West Rebellion, 1885," *Canadian Historical Review*, September 1949
9 Ham, George, *Toronto Daily Mail*, May 19, 1885 (from story filed May 8)
10 Ibid.
11 Ibid.
12 Rusden, Harold, *Reminiscences of a Bungle*
13 MacIvor, D.G., to son, 2 Feb 1925
14 *Saskatchewan Herald*, May 11, 1885, "The Fight at Fish Creek"
15 Light, Douglas, *Footprints in the Dust*
16 Full listing of the *Northcote*'s crew appears in an appendix

NOTES   321

17 Allan, Robert K., "A Riel Rebellion Diary," *Alberta Historical Review*, Summer 1964

18 MacIvor

19 Ham, *Toronto Daily Mail*, May 20, 1885 (from story filed May 8)

20 Ibid.

21 Ham, George, *Toronto Daily Mail*, May 19, 1885 (from story filed May 8)

22 Ibid.

23 Dumont, Gabriel, 1903 dictated manuscript now held in Archives of Manitoba, published as *Gabriel Dumont Speaks*

24 Mulvaney, Charles Pelham, *The History of the North-West Rebellion*

25 Smith, Maj. Henry, App. C.1 to Middleton, "Report on the Suppression of the Rebellion"

26 Talbot, *Winnipeg Daily Sun*, May 27, 1885

27 Ibid.

28 Howard, Joseph Kinsey, *Strange Empire*. The only flaw in this otherwise excellent work, the erroneous placement of the Gatling on the *Northcote* has been repeated in several sources since, citing Howard.

29 Ham, *Toronto Daily Mail*, May 15, 1885

30 Ham, *Toronto Daily Mail*, May 20, 1885 (story filed May 8)

31 Ibid.

32 The name "George Macleod" was given by Ham, George, in *Reminiscences of a Raconteur*, but the *Northcote's* crew list as shown in Wilson, *Military General Service, North West Canada, 1885*, shows two Macleods, John and William. Likely either one, but probably John, is the man named by Ham.

33 Ham

34 MacIvor

35 Talbot

36 Clapp

37 Rusden

38 Andrews

39 Ham

40 Rusden

41 Dumont

42 St. Laurent Annals, 1885

43 Father Fourmond, "Journal de L'abbé Cloutier," Archives de l'archevêché de Saint-Boniface, St. Boniface, Man., cited in Hildebrandt, *The Battle of Batoche*

44 Ibid.

45 Telegram as transcribed in *Winnipeg Daily Sun*, May 9, 1885

46 Stonechild, Blair, and Waiser, Bill, expand on Indian involvement in the Rebellion in *Loyal till Death*

47 Garnot, Philippe, "Mémoire," Oblate Papers, Provincial Archives of Alberta

48 Talbot

49 Ham, *Reminiscences of a Raconteur*

50 MacIvor, Donald

51 Hughes, Owen, *Prince Albert Daily Herald,* June 5, 1923

52 Maj. Henry Smith

53 Hughes

54 Ham, *Reminiscences*

55 Ham, George, *Toronto Daily Mail,* May 15, 1885 (story filed May 9)

56 Ibid.

57 Hughes

58 Ham

59 Ibid.

60 Hughes

61 MacIvor

62 Fourmond

63 Ham

64 Dumont in *Canadian Historical Review*

65 Ham

66 Talbot

67 Ham, *Toronto Daily Mail*

68 Talbot

69 Anonymous, *Saskatchewan Herald*, May 18, 1885

70 Ham, *Toronto Daily Mail*

71 Ibid.

72 Letter from Garnot to Taché, "Métis Present at Batoche, May 9–12, 1885," Archives de l'archevêché de Saint-Boniface, Fonds Taché, cited in Hildebrandt, Walter, *The Battle of Batoche*

73 Dumont, *Canadian Historical Review*

74 Métis Memoirs, interview notes gathered by de Trémaudan, A.H., in Archives of Manitoba

75 Smith

76 Talbot

77 Ibid.

78 MacIvor

79 Ham

80 Dumont

81 Talbot

82 Smith

83 Talbot

84 Hughes, Owen, *Prince Albert Daily Herald,* June 5, 1923

85 Ham

86 Hughes

87 Talbot

88 Ibid.

89 Hughes

90 Dumont, *Canadian Historical Review*

91 Fourmond

92 Ham

93 Rusden

94 Middleton, *Report on the Suppression of the Rebellion*

95 Talbot

96 Ham

97 Ibid.

98 Andrews

99 Talbot

100 Andrews

101 Ham, *Toronto Daily Mail*

102 Ibid.

103 Cited in Ballantine, Archie, as reported by MacKay, Elsie, "Grand Rapids," in *Selkirk's 75th Anniversary*

104 Andrews

105 Talbot

106 Ham

107 Dumont, *Canadian Historical Review*

108 Ham

109 Talbot

110 Montizambert, Lt.-Col. Charles E., Report on A & B Batteries, from Strange, Thomas, *Gunner Jingo's Jubilee*

111 Ham

112 MacIvor

113 Ham

114 Andrews

115 Ham

116 Andrews

117 Ham

118 Ibid.

119 Wilson, Keith, *Hugh John Macdonald*

120 MacIvor

121 Ham

122 Hughes

123 Ham

124 Smith

125 Ham

126 Allan

127 Ham

128 Andrews

129 Hughes

130 Andrews

131 Ham

132 Ibid.

133 Smith, Maj. Henry

134 Ham

135 MacIvor

136 Mulvaney, Charles Pelham, *The History of the North-West*

Rebellion. Note: Mulvaney's book often uses other accounts without citing references or sources, including many found to be from George Ham.

[137] Newman, Peter C., *Merchant Princes*

[138] Tanner, Ogden, *The Canadians*

[139] Ham, George, *Reminiscences of a Raconteur*

CHAPTER TEN

[1] Hines, Rev. John, *Red Indians of the Plains*

[2] Ibid.

[3] Ibid.

[4] Ballantine, Archie, "Steamboating on the Saskatchewan," *Saskatchewan History*, Spring 1964

[5] Mother Collings to Mother Superior Petit, Apr 20, 1885, *Journeying through a Century*

[6] Allan, Robert K., "A Riel Rebellion Diary," *Alberta Historical Review*, Summer 1964

[7] Ibid.

[8] "Special to the *Mail*," *Toronto Daily Mail*, May 21, 1885, from anonymous letter written to correspondent at Winnipeg

[9] Mother Collings

[10] Ham, *Toronto Daily Mail*, for both quotes in paragraph

[11] Smith

[12] Ham

[13] Ibid.

[14] Braithwaite, Edward A., Reminiscences of a Hospital Sergeant, *Alberta History,* Winter 1991

[15] MacKay, Elsie, *Selkirk's 75th Anniversary*

[16] Allan

[17] MacIvor, D.G.

[18] Ibid.

[19] Ballantine

[20] Ibid.

[21] Campbell, Alexander, *Advance of the 7th Fusiliers of London*

[22] Campbell

[23] Ibid.

[24] Ibid.

[25] *Winnipeg Daily Sun*, May 10, 1885 (story filed at Saskatchewan Landing, May 9)

[26] Campbell

[27] All subsequent quotes of the Saskatchewan Brigade commanders (Lt. Yeoman, Cpt. Bremner, Maj. A.M. Smith, Cpt. Thomas Tracy, Cpt. R. Dillon, Cpt. S. Frank Peters, Lt. Reid, Lt. Greig, Cpt. McKenzie, Lt. Bapty) are from their reports in Appendix B to Laurie, J.W., Report of Maj.-Gen. Laurie, Sessional Papers of Canada, Dept. of Militia & Defence, No. 9d, 1887

[28] Report of Smith, Maj. A.M., Appendix B, Report of Laurie

[29] Campbell

[30] Ibid.

[31] Ibid.

[32] Ibid.

[33] From "Between the Forks and Carleton," folksong in Fowke, Edith, & Mills, Alan, *Singing Our History*, citing the *University of Toronto Song Book of 1887*

[34] Andrews

[35] Braithwaite

[36] Ham, *Toronto Daily Mail*, May 16, 1885

[37] Ham, George, *Toronto Daily Mail*, June 19, 1885

[38] Ham, George, *Toronto Daily Mail*, May 26, 1885 (story filed May 14, 1885)

[39] Ham, George, *Toronto Daily Mail*, June 16, 1885

[40] Ham, May 26

[41] Ham, June 16

[42] Ham, May 26

[43] Ibid.

[44] Ibid.

[45] Writer unknown, *Toronto Daily Mail*, May 19, 1885

[46] Talbot

[47] *Winnipeg Daily Sun*, June 12, 1885; from *Fort Benton River Press*, May 29, 1885

[48] Ord, *Reminiscences of a Bungle*

[49] Allan

[50] Ham, *Toronto Daily Mail*, May 26, 1885 (story filed May 14, 1885)

[51] Roddick, Sessional Papers 1886

[52] In his book *And Mighty Women, Too,* author Grant MacEwan writes that "the *May Queen*, with Captain Andrews in control, was briefly back in service, this time to move wounded men from the scenes of fighting to improvised hospital facilities at Saskatoon," but no primary evidence had been found that the *May Queen* was used at all in 1885.

[53] Rusden, from *Reminiscences of a Bungle*

[54] Bell, Sessional Papers, 1886, Surgeon-Major Bell's Report of Batoche

[55] Braithwaite

[56] Roddick, Sessional Paper

[57] Ibid.

[58] Wrighton, W.T., letter, cited in Stanley, George F.G., "The Campaign of 1885," *Saskatchewan History*, Autumn 1960

[59] Sullivan, Hon. Dr. M., Report of Purveyor General, Sessional Papers, 1886, No. 5

[60] "Summary of Journal of Steamer Baroness," from *Boats and Barges on the Belly*

[61] *Winnipeg Daily Sun*, May 16, 1885

[62] Anonymous, *Toronto Daily Mail*, May 19, 1885

[63] Talbot

[64] Ham, *Toronto Daily Mail*, May 26, 1885 (from story filed May 14, 1885)

[65] Rusden

[66] Collings

[67] Young, G.H., from trial transcript of *Queen v. Riel*

[68] Smith, Roderick; cited in MacKay, Elsie, *Selkirk's 75th Anniversary*

[69] Macdonald, J. Stuart, *The Dominion Telegraph*, for all three quotes in paragraph

[70] Campbell

[71] Riel, Louis, *Collected Writings*, Stanley, George F.G., ed., v. 3, no. 11

[72] University of Saskatchewan Library, Morton Collection Proceedings, cited in Kerr & Hanson, *Saskatoon: The First Half Century*

[73] MacDermot, H.E., *Sir Thomas Roddick*

[74] Letter, Trounce, William, to his mother, May 25, 1885, published as "From Saskatoon to Moose Jaw with the Prisoner Riel," *Saskatchewan History*, Spring 1981

[75] Bell, Sessional Papers, 1886, ". . . Bell's Report of Batoche"

[76] Ibid.

[77] Douglas, from letter in Bell, James, Sessional Papers, 1886

[78] St. Laurent Annals, 1885, Sisters, Faithful Companions of Jesus, *Journeying through a Century*

[79] Allan

[80] Ham, *Toronto Daily Mail*, May 20, 1885 (from story filed May 18)

[81] Allan

[82] Ibid.

[83] Rusden

[84] Journal of the *Baroness,* May 17, 1885

[85] Ham, *Toronto Daily Mail*, May 20, 1885

[86] Ham, George, *Toronto Daily Mail*, May 29, 1885

[87] Ham, George, *Toronto Daily Mail*, May 26, 1885

[88] St. Laurent Annals

[89] Ham

[90] Laurie

[91] Ibid.

[92] Campbell

[93] Ibid.

[94] Ibid.

[95] Journal of the *Baroness*, May 20, 1885

[96] Donkin

[97] Ham, George, *Toronto Daily Mail*, May 29, 1885 (filed May 19, 1885)

[98] Donkin, John, *Trooper & Redskin in the Far North-West*

[99] Donkin

[100] Ibid.
[101] Ibid.
[102] Ord
[103] Van Straubenzie to Caron, May 23, 1885, *Telegrams*
[104] *Saskatchewan Herald*, June 1, 1885
[105] Journal of the *Baroness*, May 23–24
[106] *Saskatchewan Herald*
[107] Allan
[108] Ibid.
[109] Ibid.
[110] Ham, George, *Winnipeg Daily Sun*, June 8, 1885 (filed on May 24)
[111] Austin, James M., Diary, *Saskatchewan History*, Winter 1985
[112] Andrews
[113] Allan
[114] Ibid.
[115] Text as interpreted to Robert Jefferson, Poundmaker to Middleton, and entered into Report of Middleton
[116] Middleton to Poundmaker, May 23, 1885
[117] Ham, George, *Winnipeg Daily Sun*, June 8, 1885 (filed on May 24)
[118] Ibid.
[119] St. Laurent Annals
[120] Journal of the *Baroness*
[121] Ibid.
[122] Ballantine
[123] Ibid.
[124] Austin
[125] Macdonald
[126] Ibid.
[127] Ibid.
[128] Ibid.
[129] Ibid.
[130] Austin
[131] Ibid.
[132] Campbell
[133] Ibid.

CHAPTER ELEVEN

[1] MacBeth, R.G., *Making of the Canadian West*
[2] Ibid.
[3] Ibid.
[4] Ibid.
[5] Strange, *Gunner Jingo's Jubilee*
[6] Ibid.
[7] Ibid.
[8] Chambers, *History of the 65th Mount-Royal Rifles*
[9] Ibid.
[10] Strange
[11] Chambers
[12] Ibid.
[13] Ibid.
[14] Strange
[15] Ibid.
[16] Ibid.
[17] Journal of the *Baroness*
[18] Chambers
[19] Ibid.
[20] Perry, A. Bowen, Report of, Appendix F, NWMP Commissioner's Report, 1885
[21] Strange
[22] Allan, Robert K., "A Riel Rebellion Diary," *Alberta Historical Review*, Summer 1964
[23] Allan
[24] Ibid.
[25] Ibid.
[26] Ibid.
[27] Ibid.
[28] Ballantine
[29] Ibid. Note: The author was once told a story of a Frog Lake area resident finding an old Hudson's Bay fuke, or trade gun, in the North Saskatchewan River in the 1980s. Would it be a stretch to think it was one of the Poundmaker weapons cast off the *North West* into the river?
[30] Strange, *Gunner Jingo's Jubilee*
[31] Allan
[32] Ibid.
[33] Steele, Sam, to Maj.-Gen. Strange, June 5, 1885, cited in *Gunner Jingo's Jubilee*
[34] Ibid.
[35] Strange
[36] Steele
[37] Boulton, C.A., *Reminiscences of the North-West Rebellion*
[38] *Toronto Daily Mail*, July 10, 1885
[39] Mackenzie, W.P., *Toronto Daily Mail*, July 10, 1885
[40] Mackenzie
[41] Steele, Sam, *Forty Years in Canada*
[42] Middleton, *Report on the Suppression of the Rebellion*
[43] Mackenzie
[44] Ibid.
[45] Strange, *Gunner Jingo's Jubilee*
[46] Perry
[47] Mackenzie, W.P., *Toronto Daily Mail*, reprinted in Chambers
[48] Strange
[49] Ibid.
[50] Wadmore, R. Lyndhurst, *Saskatchewan History*, Spring, 1989
[51] Ibid.
[52] Ibid.
[53] Journal of the *Baroness*
[54] Needler, George Henry, *Louis Riel, The Rebellion of 1885*
[55] Ibid. for all quotes in paragraph
[56] Ibid.
[57] Middleton to Caron, June 12, 1885, *Telegrams*
[58] Caron to Middleton, June 12, 1885, *Telegrams*
[59] Ballantine
[60] Austin, James, "Some Experience of the North West Field Force," *Saskatchewan History*, Winter 1985
[61] Journal of the *Baroness*
[62] Austin
[63] Ibid.
[64] Allan
[65] Ibid.
[66] Ballantine
[67] Austin
[68] Donkin
[69] Allan
[70] Ibid.
[71] Ibid.
[72] Donkin
[73] Ibid.
[74] Ibid.
[75] Campbell, all quotes in paragraph
[76] See-as-cum-ka-poo, *Maclean's*, September, 1975. All quotes in this account are attributed to this source.
[77] Ibid., for all three quotes in paragraph
[78] Ibid.
[79] Ibid.
[80] Ibid. for both quotes in paragraph
[81] *Saskatchewan Herald*, July 13, 1885
[82] *Winnipeg Daily Sun*, June 19, 1885
[83] "Report of the Commissioner of the North-West Mounted Police, 1885"
[84] Ibid.
[85] Ibid.

CHAPTER TWELVE

[1] St. Laurent Annals
[2] Letter, Williams, A.T.H., to Chisholm, Duncan, published in *Toronto Daily Mail*, July 10, 1885
[3] *Toronto Daily Mail*, June 29, 1885 (story filed at Winnipeg, June 27, 1885)
[4] Mulvaney, *North West Rebellion*, based on a press report
[5] "W.H.H.," *Toronto Daily Mail*, June 30, 1885 (story filed at

Fort Pitt, June 27)

6 *Toronto Daily Mail*, June 30, 1885 (story filed at Winnipeg, June 27, 1885)

7 Parker, from *William Parker*, Dempsey, ed.

8 Douglas to Roddick, "Report of the Deputy Surgeon-General," Sessional Papers 1886

9 Bell, Surgeon-Maj. James, "Report of the Deputy Surgeon-General," Sessional Papers 1886

10 Tracy, Thomas, "Report of the Deputy Surgeon-General," Sessional Papers 1886

11 Roddick, Thomas, "Report of the Deputy Surgeon-General," Sessional Papers 1886

12 Ibid.

13 Letter, Hamilton, Margaret, to Gibbon, Mrs. James, July 21, 1885, Saskatchewan Archives Board, cited in Kerr & Hanson, *Saskatoon: The First Half Century*

14 Tracy

15 Anderson, Barbara Hunter, *Two White Oxen*

16 Allan

17 Tracy

18 Ibid.

19 Ibid.

20 Allan, Robert K., "A Riel Rebellion Diary," *Alberta Historical Review*, Summer 1964

21 Ballantine, Archie, "Steamboating on the Saskatchewan," *Saskatchewan History*, Spring 1964

22 Allan

23 Ibid.

24 Summary of Journal of Steamer *Baroness* during the N.W. Rebellion, 1885, in Johnston, Alex, *Boats and Barges on the Belly*

25 Ibid.

26 McNeill, Leishman, *Tales of the Old Town*

27 Austin

28 Ibid.

29 Ballantine

30 Middleton, quoted in *Saskatchewan Herald*, July 6, 1885

31 Ibid.

32 "H.H.M.," in *Toronto Daily Mail*, July 8, 1885 (story filed at Battleford, July 4, 1885)

33 Allan

34 *Saskatchewan Herald*, July 6, 1885

35 Cassels, Richard Scougall, "The Diary of Lieutenant R.S. Cassels," in Macleod, R.C., ed., in *Reminiscences of a Bungle*

36 Strange, Thomas Bland, *Gunner Jingo's Jubilee*

37 Austin

38 Allan

39 Cassels

40 Allan

41 Cassels

42 Ibid.

43 Allan

44 Austin

45 Cassels

46 Donkin, John

47 Cassels

48 Allan

49 Austin

50 Donkin

51 Cassels

52 MacIvor, D.G., to son, 2 Feb 1925

53 Daoust, Charles, *Cent-vingt jours de service actif* (… a man "all shrunken in on himself [who] felt humiliated by his defeat and his sad situation. Had he fought so hard after all only to have the advantage of being examined like a rare animal in some zoo?" —translation Gord Tolton)

54 Donkin

55 Campbell, Alexander

56 Cassels

57 Allan

58 Ibid.

59 Cassels

60 Allan

61 Verse from "Pork, Beans and Hardtack," folksong found in

Fowke & Mills, *Singing Our History*, said to have appeared in the *University of Toronto Song Book of 1887*

62 Cassels

63 Ballantine

64 Cassels

65 Allan

66 Ibid.

67 Ibid.

68 Braithwaite, Edward A., "Reminiscences of a Hospital Sergeant," *Alberta History*, Winter 1991

69 Allan

70 Cassels

71 Preston, J.A.V., "The Diary of Lt. J.A.V. Preston," *Saskatchewan History*, Autumn 1955

72 Sgt Davis (full name & unit unknown), from Molly McFadden Papers in Archives of Manitoba, McArthur, D.C., to Medd, Agnes, Aug 14, 1949, cited in Barris, *Fire Canoe*

73 Ibid.

74 Tracy, Thomas, "Report of the Deputy Surgeon-General," Sessional Papers 1886

75 Cassels

76 Telegram, Middleton to Robinson, William, June 23, 1885, cited in MacKay, Elsie, "Wm. Robinson, Captain of Industry," in *Selkirk's 75th Anniversary*

77 Ibid., June 24, 1885

78 Bell, James, "Report of the Deputy Surgeon-General," Sessional Papers 1886

79 Ibid.

80 The name of the pilot of the *Colville* is not certain, but both Angus Morrison and Gilbert Spence Hackland are known to have helmed the vessel at various times; cited in MacKay, Elsie, "Captains All," in *Selkirk's 75th Anniversary*.

81 Bell

82 Telegram, Middleton to Robinson, William, July 8, 1885: MacKay

83 Ballantine

84 Allan

85 Ibid.

86 Needler, George, *Louis Riel, The Rebellion of 1885*

87 Ibid.

88 Allan

89 Ibid.

90 Ibid.

91 Needler

92 Ibid.

93 Allan

94 Fowke & Mills

95 *Selkirk Herald*, July 18, 1885

96 Ibid.

97 MacKay, Elsie, "The Troops Return," from *Selkirk's 75th Anniversary*

98 *Selkirk Herald*, July 18, 1885

99 MacKay

100 Ibid.

101 *Selkirk Herald*

102 MacKay

103 Ibid.

104 Colcleugh, F.W., *Selkirk Herald*, July 18, 1885

105 Needler

106 *Selkirk Herald*, July 18, 1885

107 Tracy

108 Bell, Dr. James, cited in Mallory, Enid, "To the Rebellion in a Folding Canoe," *The Beaver*, Autumn 1985

109 General Orders, quoted in *Saskatchewan Herald*, July 6, 1885

110 Telegram, Middleton to Caron, June 24, 1885, *Telegrams*

111 *Toronto Daily Mail*, July 17, 1885

112 Strange

113 Ibid.

114 Roddick

115 Ballantine, both quotes in paragraph

116 Ibid.

117 Peel, Bruce, *Steamboats on the Saskatchewan*, from

remembrances of Archie Ballantine in Peel's possession
[118] No relation to the Macdougall missionary family
[119] Letter from McDougall, Lovisa, cited in MacGregor, J.G., *Edmonton Trader*, for both quotes in paragraph
[120] *Edmonton Bulletin*, Aug 1, 1885

CHAPTER TEN

[1] Letter, Wrigley, Joseph, Mar 26, 1885, cited in Peel, *Steamboats on the Saskatchewan*
[2] Roddick, cited in Jack, Donald, *Rogues, Rebels and Geniuses*
[3] Stardom, Eleanor, *Stranger to the Fur Trade*
[4] *Lethbridge News*, Sep 21, 1893
[5] Johnston, Alex, et al., *Lethbridge, Its Coal Industry*
[6] Coutts also has special meaning for the author: it was his childhood home, and his father was on the first Town Council.
[7] War Claims Commission Report No. 3 and Supplementary Reports 20 & 62 re War Claim 24
[8] War Claims Commission Report No 23 re War Claim 201
[9] "Report of Major-General Laurie"
[10] Light, Douglas, *Footprints in the Dust*
[11] *Northcote* log entry, May 5, 1885, Talbot, Walter R., cited in Ham, George, *Toronto Daily Mail*, May 19, 1885
[12] MacIvor, D.G., to son, Feb 2, 1925
[13] *Selkirk Record*, Apr 20, 1900
[14] MacKay, Elsie, "Wm. Robinson, Captain of Industry," in *Selkirk's 75th Anniversary*
[15] Ship's history sheet, "Marquis," Hudson's Bay Company Archives, in Archives of Manitoba, Winnipeg
[16] Overholser, Joel, *Fort Benton, World's Innermost Port*
[17] Cited in Ballantine, Archie, as reported by MacKay, Elsie, "Grand Rapids," in *Selkirk's 75th Anniversary*
[18] Peel, Bruce, *Steamboats on the Saskatchewan*
[19] MacGregor cites the letter in his *The Klondike Rush through Edmonton*, but does not list a source

[20] Cotter, H.M.S., "The Steamer Northcote," *The Beaver*, September 1931
[21] McCarthy, Martha, "Steamboats on the Rivers and Lakes of Manitoba, 1859–96"
[22] Cashman, A.W. "Tony," radio broadcast on CJCA, Edmonton, Oct 26, 1952, from file "FB Wickenden" in Glenbow Archives, republished in Cashman, A.W. "Tony," *The Edmonton Story*
[23] Ibid.
[24] Ibid.
[25] Ibid.
[26] Ibid.
[27] Ibid.
[28] Higinbotham, John, *When the West Was Young*
[29] McKenzie, Wilbur, in Johnston, *Boats and Barges on the Belly*
[30] Sheets, Capt. James, "Declaration on the practicability of raising the Steamer *Marquis*, dated Thorburn Rapids, 17 Aug, 1886"
[31] *Edmonton Bulletin*, Aug 30, 1895
[32] Interview with Hormisdas Lamoureux, cited in Wickenden, Nick, "*North West* and *Minnow*," *Alberta Historical Review*, Winter 1957
[33] Cotter
[34] Diary of Robert Munro-Ferguson, Thomas Fisher Rare Books Library, University of Toronto, cited in Inglis, Alex, *Northern Vagabond*
[35] Cotter
[36] van Tamelen, John, *Canada by Canoe*

EPILOGUE

[1] Dalrymple, A.J., "Old Saskatchewan Steamboats," *The Beaver*, June 1943
[2] McCourt, Edward, *Saskatchewan*

Bibliography

A note on sources

One should be up front: unless a historical writer is researching an extremely localized subject, such as from an oral or family source, there really is not a lot of "new" history to be brought to light. There are only new ways to present it, and newer insights to be gained by going after a particular aspect of history that may not have been fully explored before, such as the role of riverboats in the Northwest Rebellion. These tales have been seen before, but never in quite this manner. The idea first occurred to me as I was writing my first book, *Rocky Mountain Rangers*, in 1994. Working with the Lethbridge Historical Society, I became familiar with one of their earlier publications, *Boats and Barges on the Belly*, a compilation of articles about steamboats on the Oldman River, a stream I have never strayed far from in my life.

Paragraphs originally written utilizing that particular source were excised from my *Rangers* manuscript, and through the magic of computers, stuffed into a file, with the thought that it might make a nice article someday. The paragraph turned into an article that never ended, until it finally landed up as the book you are reading today. I used many sources, both archival and published, but in my acknowledgments I must single out three in particular that were never far from my desk during this writing, three writers whose shoulders I have been both proud and humbled to have stood upon.

The first is the aforementioned Alex Johnston, Lethbridge's pre-eminent and benevolent historian, a man I had the privilege of meeting only once and the misfortune of never being able to get to know very well. *Boats and Barges on the Belly* was the book that piqued my interest in this subject, and the link that led from the notion of boats hauling coal from Lethbridge to Medicine Hat, to my own interest in the Northwest Rebellion. *Boats & Barges* was a collection of sources which, knowing Alex's reputation, I could be confident would be accurate and well founded.

In that collection were articles by Bruce Peel, who expanded that interest into a rare, authoritative classic, *Steamboats on the Saskatchewan*. Peel had a way of turning the cold facts and data of the brief career of sternwheelers on the West's Big River into a book that could not be put down, and demanded to be reread often for fear a researcher might miss some portion of the lore that could give his own writing credibility.

Peel's book enthused another writer before me, a journalist named Ted Barris, who wrote *Fire Canoe* in the 1970s. Barris wrote popularly and turned the data from Johnston, Peel and others into a remarkably well-written and fast-paced book that only the dullest of readers could possibly not be enthused by. The recollections of river travel obviously stirred the poetry in Barris's soul, while also adding to the research the others before him had assembled.

There are many others as well whose writings have inspired me in this work: Eleanor Stardom, Edward McCourt, Grant MacEwan, Hugh Dempsey, Desmond

Morton, Rod Macleod, Rudy Wiebe, J.G. MacGregor, Douglas Light, Peter Charlebois, Tony Cashman, Walter Hildebrandt, Andy den Otter, Jordan Zinovich, Victor Carl Friesen and Jack Lepley, among many others whose works I have cited. And of course I must thank in whatever way I can the many, many primary sources of the era, whose own "I was there" quotations really took me back to the year 1885. Without their foresight in writing of their experiences in the rebellion and leaving it around where I could find it, this script would just be colder.

Books

Anderson, Barbara Hunter, *Two White Oxen: A Perspective of Early Saskatoon, 1874–1905*, memoirs of Barbara (Hunter) Anderson (1874–1951) compiled & edited by Anderson, George W., & Anderson, Robert N., rev. ed., [R.N. Anderson, Lethbridge], 1983

Anderson, Bern, *By Sea and By River*, The Naval History of the Civil War. Greenwood Press, Westport, Conn., 1962

Barris, Theodore, *Fire Canoe: Prairie Steamboat Days Revisited*, McClelland & Stewart Ltd., Toronto, 1977

Barron, F. Laurie, & Waldram, James B., eds., *1885 and After: Native Society in Transition*, Canadian Plains Research Center, Regina, 1985

Baum, Daniel Jay, & Mallette, Penelope, *Times Past: 1885*, IPI Publishing Ltd., Toronto, 1885

Beal, Bob, & Macleod, R.C., *Prairie Fire: The 1885 North-West Rebellion*, Hurtig Publishers, Edmonton, 1984

Blevins, Winfred, *Dictionary of the American West*, Facts on File, New York, 1993

Boulton, Charles Arkoll, *Reminiscences of the North-West Rebellion*, Grip Printing & Publishing, Toronto, 1886 (republished as *I Fought Riel*, Robertson, Heather, ed., 1985)

Brown, Wayne F., *Steele's Scouts: Samuel Benfield Steele and the North-West Rebellion*, Heritage House, Surrey, BC, 2001

Cameron, W.B., *Blood Red the Sun*, Kenway Publishing Co., Calgary, 1950

Cashman, A. W. (Tony), *Edmonton Exhibition: The First Hundred Years*, Edmonton Exhibition Association, Edmonton, 1979

Cashman, A. W. (Tony), *The Edmonton Story: The Life and Times of Edmonton, Alberta*, Institute of Applied Art, Edmonton, 1956. See also, under Journals etc., Steam Navigation Research Project, 1955–1956.

Cashman, A. W. (Tony), *The Best Edmonton Stories*, Hurtig Publishers, Edmonton, 1976

Cassels, Richard Scougall, "The Diary of Lieutenant R.S. Cassels." See Macleod, R.C., ed., *Reminiscences of a Bungle*.

Chambers, Ernest (English trans. Fleshman, Dave), *History of the 65th Mount Royal Rifles in Western Canada*, Montreal, 1906, [Dave Fleshman], Calgary, 1992

Charlebois, Dr. Peter, *Sternwheelers and Sidewheelers: The Romance of Steamdriven Paddleboats in Canada*, NC Press Ltd., Toronto, 1978

Clay, Charles, *Swampy Cree Legends: Twenty Folk Tales as told to Charles Clay by Kuskapathcees, the Smoky One*, Macmillan, Toronto, 1938

Clink, William L., ed., *Battleford Beleaguered, 1885: The Story of the Riel Uprising from the Columns of the Saskatchewan Herald*, [William L. Clink] Willowdale, Ont., 1985

Daoust, Charles, *Cent-vingt jours de service actif: récit historique très complet de la campagne du 65ième au Nord-Ouest*, Eusèbe Senecal & fils, Montréal, 1886, accessed November 29, 2006, at Peel's Prairie Provinces, http://peel.library.ualberta.ca/bibliography/1423.html

Davis, William C. and eds., *First Blood: Fort Sumter to Bull Run*, "The Civil War" series, Time-Life Books, Alexandria, Va., 1983

Dempsey, Hugh A., *Big Bear: The End of Freedom*, Douglas & McIntyre, Vancouver, 1984

Den Otter, Andy A., *Civilizing the West: The Galts and the Development of Western Canada*. University of Alberta Press, Edmonton, 1982

Dickens, Francis (Lachance, Vernon, ed.), *Diary of Francis Dickens*, Jackson Press, Kingston, Ont., 1930

Dodds, Gordon, Hall, Roger, & Triggs, Stanley, *The World of William Notman: The Nineteenth Century through a Master's Lens*, David R. Godine Publishing, Boston, Mass., 1993

Donkin, John George, *Trooper and Redskin in the Far North-West*, S. Low, Marston, Searle & Rivington, London, 1889

Dumont, Gabriel (English trans. Barnholden, Michael), *Gabriel Dumont Speaks*, Talon Books, Vancouver, 1993

Ellis, L. Gregory, *The Stafford Family, Pioneer Community Builders*, City of Lethbridge Archives, Alta., 1992

Flexner, James Thomas, *Steamboats Come True: American Inventors in Action*, Little, Brown & Co., Boston, Mass., 1944, rev. ed. 1978

Fowke, Edith, & Mills, Alan, *Singing Our History: Canada's Story in Song*, Doubleday Canada Ltd., Toronto, 1984

Friesen, Victor Carl, *Where the River Runs*, Fifth House Ltd., Calgary, 2001

Fryer, Harold, *The Frog Lake Massacre*, Frontier Publishing, Calgary, 1975

Gould, Ed, *All Hell for A Basement: Medicine Hat 1883–1983*, City of Medicine Hat, Alta., 1981

Granatstein, J.L., and Hillmer, Norman, *Battle Lines: Eyewitness Accounts from Canada's Military History*, Thomas Allen Publishers, Toronto, 2004

Gregory, David, et al., *Athabasca Landing: An Illustrated History*, Athabasca Historical Society/Athabasca University, 1986

Haestie, Elizabeth, *Ferries and Ferrymen in Alberta*, Glenbow-Alberta Institute, 1986

Ham, George Henry, *Reminiscences of a Raconteur: Between the '40s and the '20s*, Musson Book Co., Toronto, 1921

Hardy, W.G., ed., *Alberta Golden Jubilee Anthology*, McClelland & Stewart, Toronto, 1955

Healey, Edna, *Lady Unknown: The Life of Angela Burdett-Coutts*, Coward, McCann & Geoghegan Inc., New York, 1978

Higinbotham, John D., *When the West Was Young: Historical Reminiscences of the Early Canadian West*, 2nd ed., Herald Printers, Lethbridge, 1978; first published by Ryerson, Toronto, 1933

Hildebrandt, Walter, *The Battle of Batoche: British Small Warfare and the Entrenched Métis*, National Historic Parks & Sites, Canadian Parks Service, Environment Canada, Hull, Que., 1985

Historical Association of Saskatoon, *Narratives of Saskatoon, 1882–1912*, Saskatoon, 1927

Howard, Joseph Kinsey, *Strange Empire: A Narrative of the North West*, J.W. Morrow & Co., New York, 1952

Inglis, Alex, *Northern Vagabond: The Life and Career of J.B. Tyrrell, the Man Who Conquered the Canadian North*, McClelland & Stewart, Toronto, 1978

Jack, Donald, *Rogues, Rebels and Geniuses: The Story of*

Canadian Medicine, Doubleday Canada, Toronto, 1981

Johnston, Alex, *Boats and Barges on the Belly*, City of Lethbridge & Lethbridge Historical Society, Alta., 1965

Johnston, Alex, & Den Otter, Andy A., *Lethbridge, a Centennial History*, City of Lethbridge & Lethbridge Historical Society, Alta., 1985

Johnston, Alex, Gladwyn, Keith G., & Ellis, L. Gregory, *Lethbridge, Its Coal Industry*, Lethbridge Historical Society, Lethbridge, Alta., 1989

Jones, David Laurence, *Tales of the CPR*, Fifth House Ltd., Calgary, 2002

Kerr, D.G.G., *Historical Atlas of Canada*, Thomas Nelson & Sons, Toronto, 1975

Kerr, Don, & Hanson, Stan, *Saskatoon: The First Half Century*, NeWest Press, Edmonton, 1982

Lass, William, *A History of Steamboating on the Upper Missouri*, University of Nebraska Press, Lincoln, Neb., 1962

Lepley, John G., *Packets to Paradise: Steamboating to Fort Benton*, Pictorial Histories Publishing Co., Missoula, Mont., 2002

Light, Douglas W., *Footprints in the Dust*, Turner-Warwick Publications, North Battleford, Sask., 1987

MacBeth, Rev. R.G., *The Making of the Canadian West: Being the Reminiscences of an Eye-Witness*, William Briggs & Co., Toronto, 1898

Macdonald, J. Stuart, *The Dominion Telegraph*, Canadian North-West Historical Society, Battleford, Sask., 1930

MacGregor, James G., *Blankets and Beads: A History of the Saskatchewan River*, Institute of Applied Art, Edmonton, 1949

MacGregor, James G., *Edmonton Trader: The Story of John A. McDougall*, McClelland & Stewart Ltd., Toronto, 1963

MacGregor, James G., *The Klondike Rush through Edmonton, 1897-1898*, McClelland & Stewart, Toronto, 1970

MacGregor, James G., *Senator Hardisty's Prairies, 1840/1889*, Western Producer Prairie Books, Saskatoon, 1978

MacIntosh, Robert, *Boilermakers on the Prairies*, Lodges 146 & 555, International Brotherhood of Boilermakers, Iron Ship Builders, Blacksmiths, Forgers & Helpers, Winnipeg, 1979

MackKay, Elsie, *Selkirk's 75th Anniversary*, Selkirk 75th Anniversary Committee/*Selkirk Enterprise*, Selkirk, Man., 1957

MacLennan, Hugh, *Seven Rivers of Canada*, Macmillan of Canada, Toronto, 1961

Macleod, R.C., ed., *Reminiscences of a Bungle, by One of the Bunglers, and Two Other Northwest Rebellion Diaries*, University of Alberta Press, Edmonton, 1983

Marquis of Lorne, *Canadian Pictures*, Religious Tract Society, London, 1885 (republished as *Canada One Hundred Years Ago: The Beauty of Old Canada Illustrated*, Bracken Books, London, UK, 1985)

Marquis of Lorne, *Memories of Canada and Scotland*, Sampson Low, Marston, Searle & Rivington, London, 1883. See also McDougall, D. Blake, *Princess Louise Caroline Alberta*

McCourt, Edward, *Revolt In The West*, Macmillan of Canada, Toronto, 1966

McCourt, Edward, *Saskatchewan*, Macmillan of Canada, Toronto, 1968

McDougall, D. Blake, *Princess Louise Caroline Alberta*, Legislature Library of Alberta, Edmonton, 1988

McNeill, Leishman, *Tales of the Old Town: Calgary 1875-1950*, Calgary Herald Publications, Calgary, 1950, republished 1967

Milligan, John D., *Gunboats Down the Mississippi*, Arno Press, New York, 1980

Milligan, John D., ed., *From the Fresh-Water Navy: 1861-64: The Letters of Acting Master's Mate Henry R. Browne and Acting Ensign Symmes E. Browne*, United States Naval Institute, Annapolis, Md., 1970.

Morton, Desmond, *The Canadian General: Sir William Otter*, Hakkert, Toronto, 1974; also in series Canadian War Museum Historical Publication no. 9

Morton, Desmond, *The Last War Drum: The North west Campaign of 1885*, Hakkert Ltd., Toronto, 1972

Morton, Desmond, & Roy, Reginald Herbert, eds., *Telegrams of the North-West Campaign, 1885*, Champlain Society, Toronto, 1972

Mulvaney, Charles Pelham, *The History of the North-west Rebellion of 1885*, A.H. Hovey & Co., Toronto, 1885

Needler, George H., *Louis Riel: The Rebellion of 1885*, Burns & MacEachern, Toronto, 1957

Newman, Peter C., *Merchant Princes*, v. 3 of *Company of Adventurers*, Viking Canada, Markham, Ont., 1985-91

O'Neil, Paul, & eds., *The Rivermen*, "Old West" series, Time-Life Books, New York, 1975

Ord, Lewis Redman. See Macleod, R.C., ed., *Reminiscences of a Bungle*

Overvold (Burger), Joanne, & Clovis, Allan, eds., *A Portrayal of Our Métis Heritage*, Métis Association of the Northwest Territories,1976

Overholser, Joel, *Fort Benton, World's Innermost Port* [Joel Overholser], Fort Benton, Mont., c1987

Parker, Georgean C., *Proud Beginnings: A Pictorial History of Red Deer*, Red Deer & District Museum Society, Red Deer, Alberta, 1981

Parker, William C., *William Parker, Mounted Policeman*, Dempsey, Hugh A., ed., Glenbow-Alberta Institute, Calgary, Hurtig Publishers, Edmonton, 1973

Peel, Bruce, *Steamboats on the Saskatchewan*, Western Producer Prairie Books, Saskatoon, 1972

Percival, John, *For Valour: The Victoria Cross—Courage in Action*, Methuen, London, UK, 1985

Potyondi, Barry, *Selkirk: The First Hundred Years, 1882-1982*, National School Services, Winnipeg, 1982

Red Deer East Historical Society, *Mingling Memories*, Red Deer East Historical Soc., Red Deer, Alta., 1979

Riel, Louis (Stanley, George F.G., ed.), *Collected Writings of Louis Riel*, 5 vols., University of Alberta Press, Edmonton, 1985

Riel, Louis (Flanagan, Thomas, ed.), *The Diaries of Louis Riel*, Hurtig Publishers, Edmonton, 1976

Rusden, Harold Penryn, "Suppression of the Northwest Insurrection." See Macleod, R.C., ed., *Reminiscences of a Bungle*.

Russell, E.T., *What's in a Name: The Story behind Saskatchewan Place Names*, Western Producer Prairie Books, Saskatoon, 1973

St. Laurent Annals, 1885. See Sisters, Faithful Companions of Jesus, *Journeying Through a Century*

Saskatchewan Archives Board, w/illustrations by Brenda Burns, *The Nor'Westers*, Saskatchewan Archives Board et al., Regina, 1985

Sisters, Faithful Companions of Jesus, *Journeying through a Century: Sister Pioneers 1883-1983*, Sisters, FCJ, Edmonton, 1983

Skelton, O.D., *Life and Times of Sir Alexander Tilloch Galt*, Oxford University Press, Toronto, 1920

Stacey, C.P., *Records of the Nile Voyageurs, 1884-1885: The Canadian Voyageur Contingent in the Gordon Relief Expedition*, Champlain Society, Toronto, 1959

Stardom, Eleanor, *A Stranger to the Fur Trade: Joseph Wrigley and the Transformation of the Hudson's Bay Company, 1884-1891*, Rupert's Land Research Centre, University of Winnipeg, Man., 1995

Steele, Col. Samuel B., *Forty Years In Canada: Reminiscences of the Great North-West*, Dodd, Mead & Co., New York, 1915

Stonechild, Blair, & Waiser, Bill, *Loyal till Death: Indians and the North-West Rebellion*, Fifth House Ltd., Calgary, 1997

Strange, Thomas Bland, *Gunner Jingo's Jubilee*, Remington Co., London, 1893, republished by University of Alberta Press, Edmonton, 1988

Tanner, Ogden, & eds., *The Canadians*, "Old West" series, Time-Life Books, Alexandria, Va., 1977

Trémaudan, A.-H. de (English trans. Maguet, Elizabeth), *Hold*

High Your Heads: History of the Métis Nation in Western Canada, Pemmican Publications, Winnipeg, 1982

Turner, John Peter, *The North-West Mounted Police 1873–1893,* 2 vols., King's Printer, Ottawa, 1950

van Tamelen, John, *Canada by Canoe,* [John van Tamelen], Hudson's Hope, BC, 1972

Western Writers of America, Duke, Donald, ed., *Water Trails West,* Doubleday & Co., Garden City, NY, 1978

Wiebe, Rudy, & Beal, Bob, eds., *War in the West: Voices of the 1885 Rebellion,* McClelland & Stewart, Toronto, 1985

Wilson, Barbara M., ed., *Military General Service 1793–1814/ Egypt Medal 1882–1889/North West Canada 1885: Index to the Medal Rolls,* Spink & Son Ltd., London, UK, 1974

Wilson, Keith, *Hugh John Macdonald: Manitobans In Profile,* Peguis Publishers, Ltd., Winnipeg, 1980

Woodcock, George, *Gabriel Dumont,* Fitzhenry & Whiteside, Don Mills, Ont. , 1978

Zinovich, Jordan, *Battling the Bay: The Turn of the Century Adventures of Fur Trader Ed Nagle,* Lone Pine Publishing, Edmonton, 1992

Archival sources

Andrews, Captain E. Shelton, "Proceedings of fifth meeting of Saskatoon Historical Association held at the home of Captain Andrews 5 April 1922," MSS C555/2/4.1c V, Morton Manuscript Collection, University of Saskatchewan Library Special Collections, Saskatoon

Bell, Surgeon-Major James, at pp. 366–67 of "Report of the Deputy Surgeon-General," App. 5G to "Report upon the suppression of the rebellion in the North-West Territories and matters in connection therewith, in 1885," Department of Militia & Defence, Sessional Papers of Canada No. 6a, 49 Vict., 1886, accessed November 29, 2006, at Peel's Prairie Provinces, http://peel.library.ualberta.ca/bibliography/1396/414.html

Bergin, Darby, "Report of the Surgeon-General," App. 5 to "Report upon the suppression of the rebellion in the North-West Territories and matters in connection therewith, in 1885," Department of Militia & Defence, Sessional Papers of Canada No. 6a, 49 Vict., 1886, University of Lethbridge Library, Government Documents Section, Lethbridge, Alta.; also accessed November 29, 2006, at Peel's Prairie Provinces, http://peel.library.ualberta.ca/bibliography/1396/375.html

Campbell, Alexander, "An Account of the Advance of the 7th Fusiliers of London," MSS 49 #17, University of Saskatchewan Library Special Collections, Saskatoon

Davidson, Peyton S., Papers, Minnesota Historical Society, St. Paul

Davis, John B., Davidson, Peyton S., & Card, B.C., Chief Quartermaster, Department of Dakota, contract among, March 20, 1877, Old Army Division, U.S. National Archives

Garnot, Philippe, "Mémoire," Oblate Papers, Provincial Archives of Alberta, Edmonton

Hughes, Owen, in *Prince Albert Daily Herald,* June 5, 1923, MSS C555/2/10.3h Morton Manuscripts Collection, University of Saskatchewan Library Special Collections, Saskatoon

Jackson, Lt.-Col. William H., "Report of Deputy Adjutant-General, Principal Supply, Pay & Transport Officer and Chairman of War Claims Commission, on matters in connection with the suppression of the rebellion in the North-WestTerritories, in 1885," Department of Militia & Defence, Sessional Papers of Canada No. 9c, 50 Vict., 1887, University of Lethbridge Library, Government Documents Section, Lethbridge, Alta.; also accessed November 29, 2006, at Peel's Prairie Provinces, http://peel.library.ualberta.ca/bibliography/1470/2.html

Laurie, Maj.-Gen. J.W., "Report of Officer Commanding, Base and Lines of Communication, upon matters in connection

with the suppression of the rebellion in the North-West Territories in 1885," Department of Militia & Defence, Sessional Papers of Canada No. 9d, 50 Vict., 1887, University of Lethbridge Library, Government Documents Section, Lethbridge, Alta.; also accessed November 29, 2006, at Peel's Prairie Provinces, http://peel.library.ualberta.ca/bibliography/1479.html

MacIvor, D.G., to son, 2 February 1925, MSS-C550/2/3.3, Morton Manuscript Collection, University of Saskatchewan Library Special Collections, Saskatoon

McFarlane correspondence, Library & Archives Canada; also published openly in *Winnipeg Standard,* Aug 28, 1875, and cited in Peel, *Steamboats on the Saskatchewan*

Middleton, Maj.-Gen. Sir Frederick D., "Special Report," App. 1 to "Report upon the suppression of the rebellion in the North-West Territories and matters in connection therewith, in 1885," Department of Militia & Defence, Sessional Papers of Canada No. 6a, 49 Vict., 1886, Needler, G.H., ed., University of Lethbridge Library, Government Documents Section, Lethbridge, Alta.

Nimmons, Dora Trew, "Reminiscences of Baroness River Boat," Papers GM964.7231 and GM969.4701-41, City of Lethbridge Archives, Alta.

Northcote, Sir Stafford Henry, "Report of the Governor of the Hudson's Bay Company to Its Shareholders," Hudson's Bay Company Archives, Archives of Manitoba, Winnipeg

"Report of the Board of Directors of the Winnipeg & Western Transportation Company Ltd.," Winnipeg, June 4 1883, F.41/1, Hudson's Bay Company Archives, Archives of Manitoba

"Report of the Commissioner of the North-West Mounted Police, 1885," Ottawa, 1886. (Reprinted as *Settlers and Rebels, 1882–1885,* Coles Publishing, Toronto, 1973)

Roddick, Thomas, "Report of the Deputy Surgeon-General," App. 5G to "Report upon the suppression of the rebellion in the North-West Territories and matters in connection therewith, in 1885," Department of Militia & Defence, Sessional Papers of Canada No. 6a, 49 Vict., 1886, University of Lethbridge Library, Government Documents Section, Lethbridge, Alta.; also accessed November 29, 2006, at Peel's Prairie Provinces, http://peel.library.ualberta.ca/bibliography/1396/407.html

Sheets, Capt. James, "Declaration on the practicability of raising the Steamer *Marquis,* dated Thorburn Rapids, 17 August 1886," Hudson's Bay Company Archives, C.7/91, Archives of Manitoba

Ship's history sheets "Manitoba," "Marquis," "Northcote," Hudson's Bay Company Archives, Archives of Manitoba, Winnipeg

Smith, Maj. Henry, App. 1C.1 to "Report upon the suppression of the rebellion in the North-West Territories and matters in connection therewith, in 1885," Department of Militia & Defence, Sessional Papers of Canada No. 6a, 49 Vict., 1886, accessed November 29, 2006, at Peel's Prairie Provinces, http://peel.library.ualberta.ca/bibliography/1396/87.html

Stewart, Staff Sgt. Walter F., Midland Battalion, Diary of, online version prepared with assistance of Ernest Neufeld of Weyburn [Sask.] *Review* retrieved November 12, 2006, from http://web.mala.bc.ca/davies/letters.images/W.F.Stewart/diary.4.htm

Summary of Journal of Steamer *Baroness* during the N.W. Rebellion, 1885. See, under Books, Johnston, Alex, *Boats and Barges on the Belly.*

Tracy, Thomas. See Roddick, Thomas, "Report of the Deputy Surgeon-General"

War Claims Commission, Report Nos. 3, 20 & 62 regarding War Claim 24, and Report No. 23 regarding War Claim 201, all in App. 4 to "Report upon the suppression of the rebellion in the North-West Territories and matters in connection therewith, in 1885," Department of Militia & Defence, Sessional Papers of Canada No. 6a, 49 Vict., 1886, all four reports accessed November 29, 2006, successively in the order cited above, at Peel's Prairie Provinces, http://peel.library.ualberta.ca/bibliography/1396/121.html; */1396/149.html; */1396/204.html; and */1396/151.html

Journals, Magazines, Websites, Manuscripts

Allan, Robert K. (Allan, Iris, ed.) "A Riel Rebellion Diary," *Alberta Historical Review,* Summer 1964

Austin, James, "Some Experience of the North West Field Force etc.," *Saskatchewan History,* Winter 1985

Ballantine, Archie, "Steamboating on the Saskatchewan," *Saskatchewan History,* Spring 1964

Braithwaite, Edward A., "Reminiscences of a Hospital Sergeant," *Alberta History,* Winter 1991

Clapp, Charles Salyer (Roy, R.H., ed.), "With the Midland Battalion to Batoche," *Saskatchewan History,* Winter 1978

Cotter, H.M.S., "The Steamer *Northcote,*" *The Beaver,* September 1931

Cowley, Rev. Abraham, Church Missionary Society, Records & Correspondence. See, under Books, Peel, Bruce, *Steamboats on the Saskatchewan*

Dalrymple, A.J., "Old Saskatchewan Steamboats," *The Beaver,* June 1943

Dumont, Gabriel, "Gabriel Dumont's Account of the North West Rebellion, 1885," *Canadian Historical Review,* September 1949

History of Saskatchewan Waterways, http:// canoesaskatchewan.rkc.ca/history.htm, accessed October 22, 2006, Tourism Saskatchewan, Regina

Lachance, Vernon, ed., "Diary of Francis Dickens," *Bulletin of the Department of History and Political and Economic Science in Queen's University, 59,* May 1930. See also, under Books, Dickens, Francis (Lachance, Vernon, ed.), *Diary of Francis Dickens*

Mallory, Enid, "To the Rebellion in a Folding Canoe," *The Beaver,* Autumn 1985

McCarthy, Martha, "Steamboats on the Rivers and Lakes of Manitoba 1859-96," unpublished MS, Manitoba Culture, Heritage & Recreation, Historic Resources Branch, Winnipeg, 1987

Merrick, George B., "Steamboats & Steamboating on the Upper Mississippi," *Saturday Evening Post of Burlington,* Iowa, May 8, 1915

Needler, G.H., "The Lone Canoeist of the Saskatchewan," *The Beaver,* June 1950

O-ge-mas-es, "Steamboating for the HBC on the Saskatchewan," *The Beaver,* April 1922

Preston, J.A.V., "The Diary of Lieut. J.A.V. Preston," *Saskatchewan History,* Autumn 1955

Ray, Arthur, "Adventurers at the Crossroads," *The Beaver,* April–May 1986

See-as-cum-ka-poo (Mary PeeMee) as told to Campbell, Maria, "She Who Knows the Truth of Big Bear," *Maclean's,* September 1975

Shepherd, George, "River Steamboats, Once Classic Mode of Transportation," *Scarlet & Gold,* 19th ed., 1938

Smith, T.R., "The Steamboat *Lily,*" *Saskatchewan History* 17(2), 1964

Stanley, George F.G., "The Campaign of 1885: A Contemporary Account" (Letter of Wrighton, W.T., Midland Battalion), *Saskatchewan History,* Autumn 1960

Steam Navigation Research Project, 1955–1956, collection compiled by Wickenden, Nick, file "FB Wickenden," Glenbow-Alberta Institute, Calgary

Trew, Dora E., "Alberta's Prairie Steamer," *Canadian Cattleman,* August 1964. See also, under Books, reprinted as "Lethbridge Had a Baroness," in Johnston, Alex, ed., *Boats and Barges on the Belly*

Trounce, William Henry, "From Saskatoon to Moose Jaw with the Prisoner Riel," *Saskatchewan History,* Spring 1981

Wadmore, R. Lyndhurst (Ross, David, ed.), "The 1885 North-West Campaign Diary of R. Lyndhurst Wadmore, Infantry School Corps," *Saskatchewan History,* Spring 1989

Whitney, D.J., Sr., "Lethbridge Recollections." See, under Books, Johnston, Alex, *Boats and Barges on the Belly*

Wickenden, Nick, file "FB Wickenden." See Steam Navigation Research Project, 1955–1956

Wickenden, Nick, "*North West* and *Minnow*: Two Saskatchewan River Steamers," *Alberta Historical Review,* Summer 1957

Wishart, Bruce, "Paddlewheels on the Prairies," *The Beaver,* December/January 1989/90

Newspapers (cites are in notes)

Brandon Daily Sun

Calgary Herald

Canadian Illustrated War News

Edmonton Bulletin

Lethbridge Daily Herald

Lethbridge News

Macleod Gazette

Manitoba Free Press

The Manitoban

Medicine Hat Times

Prince Albert Daily Herald

Prince Albert Times

Selkirk Record

St. Paul Pioneer Press

Saskatchewan Herald

Toronto Daily Mail

Toronto Globe

Winnipeg Daily Sun

Winnipeg Daily Times

Winnipeg Free Press

Winnipeg Standard

Yankton Press and Dakotan

Index

GORDON E. TOLTON was born and raised in southern Alberta on a mixed farm and ranch. A self-taught historian, he has worked with the Fort Whoop-Up Interpretive Centre in Lethbridge, the Riders of the Plains Commemorative Troop in Fort Macleod, the Great Canadian Plains Railway Society in Stirling, the Lethbridge Historical Society, the Historical Society of Alberta and the United Farmers of Alberta. He is the author of *Rocky Mountain Rangers* and *The Buffalo Legacy*.